When you get home:

  * Take Week 2 Quiz or
    print quiz

- Ch 3 read
- watch week 3 video
- Answer questions
- take quiz & print when done

Theories and Strategies of Family Therapy

Theories and Strategies of Family Therapy

Jon Carlson

Governors State University

Diane Kjos

Governors State University

Allyn and Bacon

Boston ▪ London ▪ Toronto ▪ Sydney ▪ Tokyo ▪ Singapore

Editor in Chief: *Karen Hanson*
Series Editor: *Patricia Quinlin*
Editorial Assistant: *Annemarie Kennedy*
Senior Marketing Manager: *Brad Parkins*
Editorial-Production Administrator: *Michael Granger*
Editorial-Production Service: *Chestnut Hill Enterprises*
Composition and Prepress Buyer: *Linda Cox*
Manufacturing Buyer: *Suzanne Lareau*
Cover Administrator: *Linda Knowles*
Electronic Composition: *Omegatype Typography, Inc.*

Copyright © 2002 by Allyn & Bacon
A Pearson Education Company
75 Arlington Street
Boston, MA 02116

Internet: www.ablongman.com

Between the time Website information is gathered and published, it is not unusual for some sites to have closed. Also, the transcription of URLs can result in unintended typographical errors. The publisher would appreciate notification where these occur so that they may be corrected in subsequent editions.

Library of Congress Cataloging-in-Publication Data

Carlson, Jon.
    Theories and strategies of family therapy / Jon Carlson, Diane Kjos.
        p.   cm.
    Includes bibliographical references and index.
    ISBN 0-205-27403-X
    1. Family psychotherapy.   I. Kjos, Diane.   II. Title.

RC488.5 .C3635 2002
616.89'156—dc21
                                                                2001046131

Printed in the United States of America

10   9   8   7   6   5   4   3   2   1   06   05   04   03   02

CONTENTS

PREFACE

We have had the opportunity to train professional counselors and therapists for several years. The field of therapy is relatively new and family therapy one of the most recent disciplines. Writers have attempted to capture what family therapy is about in numerous books and articles. However, we have never felt that the written word alone can accurately describe what occurs in family therapy. Since 1995 we have been videotaping the master therapists and family therapists working with real clients in order to more accurately capture this process (Carlson & Kjos, 1998, 1999, 2000). Our students have discovered that seeing is believing (and also learning!). This book brings together the master family therapists and connects them to the videos related to the theory and techniques being described. We believe that students can deepen their understandings with words and actual therapy sessions. It is recommended that students read the book and then watch the corresponding video in its entirety.

Each chapter of *Theories and Strategies of Family Therapy* follows a similar outline. This allows the reader to compare and contrast the fifteen different approaches. We believe that this will allow the student (and practitioner) to develop their personal approach by integrating the approaches in a way that works for them. We do not advocate any one approach but rather believe that each approach has validity dependent on the family and situation. We believe that students (and practitioners) need to be familiar with the various approaches and strategies in order to effectively tailor interventions to the myriad of problems and families challenged by today's world.

The chapter format calls for a brief description of the theory and what makes it significant. The philosophical and historical facts are also presented. The authors then delineate the clinical perspective and how their approach deals with today's diverse family forms. The authors provide detail about how their theory is practiced and then reference sections in the corresponding video that shows the theory in practice. Each also provides references for further learning and study.

We hope that you and your students find this book useful. We believe that there are no other textbooks in the area of family therapy that allow for such complete learning of these important theories and strategies.

We wish to thank the couples and families that allowed us into their personal lives so that we can learn how to help others.

Jon Carlson
Diane Kjos

CONTRIBUTING AUTHORS

Harry J. Aponte, MSW, LCSW, currently directs the Family Training Program of Philadelphia and trains therapists in a variety of locations within and outside of the United States. He has an appointment as clinical associate professor Hahnemann University in Philadelphia. He is advisory editor on a variety of professional journals in this country and abroad, including *Family Process.* Mr. Aponte was a teacher of family therapy at the Menninger Clinic and director of the Philadelphia Child Guidance Clinic. He has published *Bread & Spirit* through Norton, a book that speaks to therapy with today's poor in the context of ethnicity, culture, and spirituality.

Mary Smith Arnold, Ph.D., is a University Professor at Governors State University in the Division of Psychology and Counseling. She also conducts workshops on diversity issues using her own model, Unlearning Oppression.

James Robert Bitter is professor of Counseling at East Tennessee State University. He is the former editor of the *Journal of Individual Psychology.* He is a member and former delegate of the North American Society of Adlerian Psychology. Together with three other colleagues, he is a founding member of the Adlerian Training Institute in Boca Raton, Florida. He is currently developing with Bill Nicoll various models and interventions for Adlerian Brief Therapy.

Donald L. Bubenzer is a professor in the Counseling and Human Development Services Program at Kent State University. Along with John West and Jim Bitter, Don edited *Social Construction in Couple and Family Counseling.* His interests include the use of social constructionist and narrative approaches to leadership, administration, and counseling and the measurement of the subjective.

Jon Carlson, Psy.D., Ed.D., is a professor of psychology and counseling at Governors State University, University Park, Illinois and psychologist at the Lake Geneva Wellness Clinic in Lake Geneva, Wisconsin. He is past president of the International Association of Marriage and Family Counselors and founding editor of *The Family Journal: Counseling and Therapy for Couples and Families.* He holds a diplomate in Family Psychology, ABPP, and Marital and Family Therapy, ABFamP. He has authored twenty-five books, one hundred and twenty articles, and produced over one hundred professional videotapes.

Bill Davis, LCSW, CSAC, is in private practice in the Norfolk–Virginia Beach, Virginia area. He specializes in working with adolescents and adults with substance abuse and chemical dependence issues, as well as the usual psychotherapy concerns. Additionally, he has specialized in experiential work in individual, family, and group settings. He is also a contractor with ETP, Inc., providing clinical preceptorship for Navy alcohol counselors. He is on the faculties of the Satir System and the Satir Institute of the Southeast.

Edward J. DiCesare, Ph.D., is in the private practice of psychology and has specialized in the area of Marriage and Family for the last eighteen years. He is a consulting psychologist to the counseling department of Harcom College. He was formerly the director of Psychology, codirector of the hospice and founder and director of the Family Illness and Loss Program at Bryn Mawr Hospital. He was previously the director of Family Therapy and Training of Presbyterian Village, Bryn Mawr, Pennsylvania.

William J. Doherty, Ph.D., is professor of Family Social Science and director of the Marriage and Family Therapy Program at the University of Minnesota. In 1992, he received the Significant Contribution to the Field of Marriage and Family Therapy Award from the American Association for Marriage and Family Therapy. He is past president of the National Council on Family Relations. Among his eleven books, he is author of *Soul Searching: Why Psychotherapy Must Promote Moral Consultation* (Basic Books), *Take Back Your Kids: Confident Parenting in Turbulent Times* (Sorin Books), and *Take Back Your Marriage: Sticking Together in a World That Pulls Us Apart* (Guilford).

Katherine B. Guerin, Ph.D., is a teacher of family systems theory and clinical practitioner of family therapy, and a charter member of the American Family Therapy Academy, a fellow of the American Orthopsychiatric Association, as well as the author of several book chapters and journal articles. Among her research interests is the goodness-of-fit of the individual child's temperament in the family system.

Philip J. Guerin, M.D., is a clinical practitioner, lecturer, and author of three major textbooks, *Family Therapy: Theory and Practice* (1976), *Evaluation and Treatment of Marital Conflict* (1987), *Working with Relationship Triangles* (1996), as well as numerous book chapters and journal articles. He has served on editorial board of *Family Process, the Family and Readings.*

Bill O'Hanlon, MS, LMFT, has authored or coauthored eighteen books and has taught more than 850 seminars around the world. He has published thirty-eight articles or book chapters. His books have been translated into French, Spanish, Portuguese, Swedish, Finnish, German, Chinese, Bulgarian, Turkish, and Japanese.

Steffanie O'Hanlon, MSW, LISW, is the coauthor of two books, *Brief Couples Therapy Homework Planner* and *Evolving Possibilities,* as well as articles on family therapy. She completed advanced training in family therapy at the Cambridge Family Institute.

Diane Kjos, Ph.D., is a Professor of psychology and counseling at Governors State University, University Park, Illinois. She also maintains a private practice, offers private supervision, and supervises interns through the university. Dr. Kjos is President of the National Career Development Association. She has coproduced three video series in the areas of brief therapy, psychotherapy, and family therapy.

Jean A. McLendon, LCSW, has a multiservice private practice of psychotherapy and organizational consulting in Chapel Hill, North Carolina. She directs Satir System's nationally recognized personal and professional development training program. She has taught the Satir approach to change and growth in Europe, the Middle East, the South Pacific, Canada, and across the United States. She is an AAMFT (American Association of Marriage and Family Therapy) supervisor and has served on the faculties of the University of North Carolina, the National Institute of Mental Health Staff College, and Union Institute. She is currently on the faculties of Avanta, the Virginia Satir Network, the Satir Institute of the Southeast, and the Whole Systems Organizational Design graduate programs at Antioch University in Seattle and Chicago.

Domeena Renshaw, M.D., was born, raised, and went to medical school in Capetown, South Africa. After general medical and surgical work in Mission Hospitals there, she has been at Loyola Medical School since 1965. She founded the Loyola University Sex Clinic in 1972 in the Department of Psychiatry and is a full time professor of Psychiatry.

Angela Roberts is a counselor in general and private practice in Wales. She is a registered nurse and health visitor in the United Kingdom with advanced degrees in nursing, education, and counseling. She is currently using narrative therapy as a means of coconstructing new lifestyle stories in everyday living. She is a member of the faculty at the Adlerian Summer School in Green Park.

Michi Rose, Ph.D., holds a MAT in Education from the University of Chicago, a MSW from Western Michigan University, a Ph.D. in Bio-Social Behavior from the University of Pennsylvania, and has done postdoctoral work in London in the area of Behavior and Communication. She maintains a private practice as well as making herself available to therapists across the nation who choose to do their own inner IFS (Internal Family Systems) work. She has led IFS trainings from Hartford to Seattle, and also teaches the Advanced IFS Training Course.

David E. Scharff, M.D., is codirector of the International Institute of Object Relations Therapy, Clinical Professor of Psychiatry at the Uniformed Services University of the Health Sciences and Georgetown University. He is a teaching analyst at the Washington Psychoanalytic Institute, former president of the American Association of Sex Educators, Counselors and Therapists (1988–1989), and former director of the Washington School of Psychiatry (1987–1994). Dr. Scharff has authored and coauthored several books with Jill Savege Scharff in object relations theory concerning individual, family and couple therapy, including *Object Relations Family Therapy* (1987) and *The Primer of Object Relations Therapy* (1992). He maintains a private practice in psychoanalysis and psychotherapy in Chevy Chase, Maryland.

Jill Savege Scharff, M.D., is a teaching analyst and associate supervising child analyst at the Washington Psychoanalytic Institute, codirector of the International Institute of Object Relations Therapy, clinical professor of Psychiatry at Georgetown University, and a psychoanalyst in private practice in Chevy Chase, Maryland. Her books include *Foundations of Object Relations Family Therapy* (1989), *The Autonomous Self: The Work of John D. Sutherland* (1994), *Projective and Introjective Identification: The Therapist's Use of Self* (1992), *Object Relations Family Therapy* (1987), *Object Relations Couple Therapy* (1991), *Scharff Notes: A Primer of Object Relations Therapy* (1992), and *Object Relations Therapy of Physical and Sexual Trauma* (1994), *Object Relations Individual Therapy* (1998), and *Tuning the Therapeutic Instrument: The Affective Learning of Psychotherapy* (2000). She is series coeditor of the Library of Object Relations at Jason Aronson, Inc.

Richard C. Schwartz, Ph.D., is the director of the Center for Self Leadership as well as adjunct associate professor, Department of Education and Social Policy, Northwestern University. He is known as the developer of the *Internal Family Systems Therapy* (New York: Guilford). Dr. Schwartz is a popular workshop presenter and author of many other books and articles as well as the new video series *Couples Counseling* (Boston: Allyn & Bacon).

Kim Snow obtained her master's degree in counseling from Governors State University, Illinois. She currently works at Oak Lawn Family Services part-time and remains actively involved at Governors State University working with Dr. Jon Carlson on several projects. When she is not working, Kim enjoys spending time with her husband and their eight children.

Manford A. Sonstegard is Professor Emeritus at the Marshall University College of Graduate Studies in Charleston, West Virginia. An international consultant on Adlerian Psychology, he currently resides in England where he offers training and engages in private practice. He is a past president of the North American Society of Adlerian Psychology and the British Society of Individual Psychology. In the United States, he edited and cofounded the journal *Individual Psychologist*.

After completing his doctoral studies at Columbia University, **Richard B. Stuart** moved to the University of Michigan where he directed studies evaluating family-based services to delinquents, behavioral techniques for managing overeating, and multiple strategies for improving couple's interaction. These studies were continued through his subsequent tenure at the Universities of British Columbia, Utah, and Washington. He is the author of more than one hundred articles and several books that have been translated into Spanish, German, Portuguese, French, and Mandarin Chinese. He is a fellow in two divisions of the American Psychological Association and a diplomate in Family Psychology on the American Board of Professional Psychology.

John D. West is a professor in the Counseling and Human Development Services Program and coordinator of these master's and doctoral programs in counseling at Kent State University. Along with Don Bubenzer, John served as interview editor for *The Family Journal: Counseling and Therapy for Couples and Families*. His interests include the study of social construction as well as the study of narrative perspectives in education and counseling.

Theories and Strategies
of Family Therapy

1 Structural Family Therapy

HARRY J. APONTE AND EDWARD J. DICESARE

Harry Aponte

Brief Description of Theory

Structural family therapy (SFT) addresses the individual or family's concerns in the context of how those involved currently organize their relationships around the issue to be resolved. Change unfolds from family members reorienting their thinking and restructuring their relationships so as to change the dynamics that generated the pathology. Structural therapists actively engage in the present with family members as they enact their struggle in the session. The therapist *joins* (Minuchin, 1974, pp. 133–137) the family interaction at strategic junctures in ways that impede old patterns of thinking and relating and build on their strengths to generate new patterns leading to immediate, palpable results.

1

However, while the therapy tends to be focused and brief (Aponte, 1992b; Aponte, 1998a), its goal is deep and lasting change. Special attention is paid to the enduring structures that undergird relationships, that is, the positive and negative *alignments* among members, the *boundaries* that define their roles and participation in family subsystems, and the *power* that determines who influences the outcomes of their interactions (Aponte & VanDeusen, 1981, pp. 312–313). Traditionally, SFT has emphasized and worked through the dynamic structures of the family system. Today, from the current authors' perspective on SFT, the model also pays special attention to therapists' use of self (Aponte, 1992a; Aponte, 1994a) and clients' moral ability to freely choose a direction in life, and the resources of their spirituality (Aponte 1994b). The model is active, strength-based, and outcome-oriented.

Significant Characteristics of the Theory

Evolution of the Theory: How the Theory Came to Be and Its Antecedents

Structural family therapy (SFT) was developed to meet the needs of poor inner city youth and their families (Minuchin, Montalvo, Guerney, Rosman, & Schumer, 1967). It had the good fortune of developing theoretically at the beginnings of psychotherapy's discovery of systems theory and family-oriented technique. It grew at the interface of abstract systems theory and the pragmatics of working with poor families.

SFT is a systems-based theory. One of its primary organizing principles is that "changes in a family structure contribute to changes in the behavior and the inner psychic processes of the members of that system" (Minuchin, 1974, p. 9). The core social context of the therapeutic model is the family, where the actions of individuals are strongly influenced by the dynamics of the family system to which they belong.

The practicality of the structural approach was the result of the model's pioneers' early experiences at the Wiltwyck School for Boys, a residential treatment facility populated mostly by troubled, poor African American and Puerto Rican youngsters in New York state. An action-oriented approach was necessary, one that could readily expand the therapeutic field from the individual to the family and larger social context. Communication was extended from the purely verbal medium of traditional therapy to the nonverbal and spatial. The priority of the therapy shifted from the traditional emphasis on insight to outcomes that would be experiential and palpable from the outset of treatment.

What Makes This Theory Different or Unique?

There is probably nothing in the structural model that is exclusive to it today. So much mixing and integration has taken place among the original family therapy models, along with new developments in therapy, that today we reflect more on emphasis than exclusivity. Still, there are certain original concepts of the structural approach that remain characteristic of the model today. In its original conception, the focus of treatment moved from the individually oriented, historical, disease model then prevalent in psychoanalytic thinking to a family-oriented, current experience, outcome approach.

The approach attempts to create the family's reality within the current session through enactment. The structural model views the past as "manifest in the present and . . . available to change by interventions that change the present" (Minuchin, 1974, p. 14). The past is active in the present through its influences on personal life outlooks, coping styles, and relationships. In structural family therapy, the enactment of a family's problem (Aponte & VanDeusen, 1981, p. 329; Minuchin & Fishman, 1981, pp. 78–97) is the signal intervention that best characterizes the model. It is the display in session of a characteristic way in which the family organizes itself to deal with a family issue. The structural therapist creates an environment in the session that invites and may even instigate the family to relive *now* its domestic ordeal. The immediacy of the experience allows the therapist to observe, join, and intervene in the actual struggle with all of its native intensity.

Another property of SFT is its centering of the therapeutic process on the abilities and power of the family, underscoring the notion of therapy as a "search for strength" (Minuchin & Colapinto, 1980). The structural therapist actively engages with the family to impede old, pathological transactional patterns (Aponte & VanDeusen, pp. 335–336) while working with the family's strengths to build new patterns. This momentum toward change is embodied in a session's new problem-solving experiences.

To accomplish all this, the structural therapist engages with the family "in an active and personal manner" (Aponte & VanDeusen, 1981, p. 325). In fact "change [occurs] through the process of the therapist's affiliation with the family" in order to position him- or herself to restructure "the family in a carefully planned way" (Minuchin, 1974, p. 91). From the beginning of SFT, the therapist was active and integral to the happenings in the session. The therapist's real-time personal engagement with the family was the corollary to the immediacy of the family's enactment of its struggle in the session The personal energy of the therapist was added to the motivation and strength of the family, blocking the pathological, and creating the momentum for positive change.

How Is the Theory Like Others?

The postmodern world is critical of traditional therapy's notions of the "expert" therapist who can "understand" and has the "power" to "fix" (O'Hanlon, 1994; Reichelt & Christiensen, 1990; Wylie, 1994). There is a postmodern reaction in the world of therapy against hierarchy, power, and the assumption of the ability to know reality. Structural theory's emphasis on structure, concrete issues, and an active, interventionist therapist, all seem to buck the modern trend. However, while the differences in philosophy are quite real, today's SFT speaks amicably to the spirit of modern society's concerns through its deepening and developing of the human and spiritual dimensions of structural family.

While postmodern theory speaks of "social construction" (Hoffman, 1990, p. 3), today's structural theory will talk of a therapist and client constructing a shared perspective that begins with an agreement on the values platform of the therapy (Aponte, 1998b, pp. 44–45). While the postmodern world speaks of the "socially constructed world in which both therapist and client live and work" (Goolishian & Anderson, 1992, p. 14), today's structural therapist may refer to personally colored values and the worldviews of client and therapist that meet in therapy (Aponte, 1994b, pp. 168–185). While constructivist theory will speak of enlarging the "sense of choice" by sacrificing "moral and scientific absolutes" (Hoffman, 1990, p. 4), today's structural theory will hold to a moral and scientific reality but, at the same time, recognize the essential freedom of the human will and base its approach to change on that ability to make a free moral choice (Aponte, 1999).

While a second-order view expects "therapists [to] include themselves as part of what must change" (Hoffman, 1990, p. 5), today's structural outlook speaks of the "intimacy" of the therapist's relationship with the client (Aponte, 1998a). Today's structural viewpoint also shares something of the interpretation of Volosinov's "determinism 'from within' " that links narrative's construction of reality to the "material activities of addressing and responding to each other" (Lannamann, 1998, p. 396). This notion resonates with SFT's *enactment,* in which the client's spin on reality takes form in the actuality of the interaction.

Today's structural therapy acknowledges a soul to the therapeutic process that lies in the human bond between therapist and client. It recognizes the ultimate mystery of the human spirit, and bases its work on the free will of the human being that can, must, and will choose its own path. The therapist's power is powerless in the face of the client's free will. The therapist's knowledge meets the unknowable of the human soul. The therapist who is expert in the professional sphere is quite humbly nonexpert in the human dimension of the therapeutic encounter.

The theoretical foundation of the structural model also makes it a genial theory with which to combine and integrate other therapeutic theories about human functioning (Aponte & DiCesare, 2000; Lebow, 1997). Its basic principles address the dynamic interaction between the structure of human systems and the functioning of the individual. In the conceptualization of structure, the model offers a lens through which to understand and articulate that interaction. In the techniques of enactment and the active, strategic use of self within that family enactment, SFT offers tools with which to relate to and influence the underlying organizational patterns of any systemic interaction. These contributions of structural theory can be integrated into any model of therapy that deals with people in a social context.

Philosophical and Historical Background

Individuals Associated with the Theory

Structural family therapy is most closely identified with Salvador Minuchin. His close colleague, Braulio Montalvo, was one of the significant contributors to the early development of the model. The contribution of Minuchin, his collaborators, and others can be illustrated by publications that emphasized the origins and notable developments of the model. Among the original writings that set the foundation of SFT are:

> Minuchin, S., Montalvo, B., Guerney, B., Jr., Rosman, B., & Schumer, F. (1967). *Families of the slums.* New York: Basic Books.
>
> Minuchin, S. (1974). *Families and family therapy.* Cambridge, MA: Harvard University Press.
>
> Minuchin, S., Rosman, B., & Baker, L. (1978). *Psychosomatic families.* Cambridge, MA: Harvard University Press.
>
> Minuchin, S. & Fishman, H. C. (1981). *Family therapy techniques.* Cambridge, MA: Harvard University Press.
>
> Aponte, H. J. & VanDeusen, J. M. (1981). Structural family therapy. In A. S. Gurman & D. P. Kniskern (Eds.), *Handbook of family therapy* (pp. 310–360). New York: Brunner/Mazel.

More recent publications that expand on some of the developments about the person of the therapist and spirituality in therapy are:

> Aponte, H. J. (1992a). Training the person of the therapist in structural family therapy. *Journal of Marital and Family Therapy, 18*(3), 269–281.
>
> Aponte, H. J. (1994b). *Bread & spirit: Therapy with the new poor.* New York: W. W. Norton.

Changes and Stages of Theory Development

Today, SFT continues to be broadly applicable with the universal relevance of the theory's explication of structure, and the technique's real-world, problem-solving focus. The model has been applied not only to family, but also to other systems in which people organize to carry out life's functions (Aponte, 1976; Aponte, 1991; Aponte, 1994b; Deacon, 1996). We perceive SFT's boundaries as broadened to include not only practical family activities, but also the philosophical and transcendental of the human experience (Aponte, 1994b). The role of today's active therapist has deepened to contain a use of the therapist's self not only in a technical, but also in an intimately personal and value-valenced interaction with clients (Aponte, 1992a; Aponte, 1998a; Aponte, 1999).

Over time, structural family therapy has been more generally integrated into the broader world of family therapy. Concepts from the model, such as *enactment* (Gerson, 1996, p. 208) and *ecostructure* (Bibb & Casimir, 1996, p. 105), have been adopted into other therapeutic orientations. Structural family therapy has also evolved from its earlier technical roots. For example, early texts used the vocabulary of *boundaries* and *subsystems* (Minuchin, 1974, pp. 53–54). Later, the vocabulary shifted to *alignment, boundaries,* and *power* (Aponte & Van-Deusen, 1981). The past as active in the present is expanded now into the past also informing us about the "whys" of the present. The genogram, a standard in family therapy (McGoldrick & Gerson, 1985), has enriched today's concept of structure by becoming integral to SFT's "historical hypotheses" (Aponte, 1994b, p. 37). History as "why" adds a depth of meaning to structure so that current behavior is viewed not only as manifest patterns, but also at the deeper levels of personal meaning and motivation.

The *enactment,* a critical technical component of SFT, is also looked at today from more complex perspectives. Traditionally, the therapist in the enactment remained outside the interaction (Minuchin, 1974, pp. 140–142). However, today's structural therapist may pursue similar goals even when central to the family's enactment. The therapist may actively pilot the interaction of family members by determining the therapeutic goal of the interaction and selectively eliciting reactions directly to him- or herself. The centralized therapist exercises greater control in family interactions. The family members interact through the therapist. What is essential to the enactment is that the communication not be a disembodied intellectual debate, but a fully engaged transactional experience, in this instance with the therapist mediating the interaction. Therapists may choose that centrality when they need to manage family interactions that may be getting out of hand. They may also play a central role when using the enactment not just as an assessment tool but also as a purposefully directed effort to convert new thinking into new behavior.

As noted earlier, what began as conceiving the therapist as part of the therapeutic system with the family evolved into a more detailed treatment of the personal role of the therapist in that process. The original axiom of SFT stated that "when a therapist works with a patient or a patient family, his behavior becomes part of the context" (Minuchin, 1974, p. 9). This axiom presaged the emphasis in structural family therapy on "the person of the therapist" in the eighties and nineties (Aponte, 1982; Aponte, 1992a). Structural family therapists do not only train to be clinicians who strategically join with families to block destructive transactions and create new boundaries. They have evolved into clinicians who use their personal life experience to understand and relate to clients more deeply, as well as to enrich clients' therapeutic experience with emotion and perspectives from their own lives (Aponte, 1992a; Aponte, 1994a).

Furthermore, structural therapists are taking more deliberate responsibility for articulating to themselves their personal values and spirituality, and determining how to use both in their clinical thinking. What originally aspired "not to educate or socialize it, rather to repair or modify the family's own functioning so that it can better perform [its] tasks" (Minuchin, 1974, p. 14) has evolved into today's accent on therapists' purposeful work with values that give a spiritual dimension to the process of change in therapy (Aponte, 1985; Aponte, 1995).

The original systems foundation of structural family therapy was based on the idea that "the whole and the parts can be properly explained only in terms of the relations that exist between the parts" (Lane, 1970). Today's philosophy stresses the moral responsibility and personal freedom of the individual within the family system. The therapist bases the process of change on clients' free will choices.

> They must experience therapy as a place where they discover their inner potential to determine their lives' direction . . . They can achieve the freedom to exercise fully their ability to make attitudinal and spiritual choices . . . (Aponte, 1994b, p. 9).

Clients are not chess pieces for a strategizing therapist, but human persons morally responsible and personally empowered to choose the course of their lives. The therapist helps identify the decisions key to movement toward change and the values that support those choices. The therapist lends personal encouragement to clients' efforts, and puts into play technical strategies that facilitate clients' decision making and the actualization of new approaches to life.

Relevant Research Related to the Theory

As noted earlier, structural family therapy grew out of the federally funded research done on the treatment of the poor minority residents of the Wyltwick School for boys. This research established the basic concepts of family structure and a model specifically crafted to work with structure. Follow-up research focused on the relationship between specific symptomatology and family structure. The research included, among other things, investigation of families with members suffering from psychosomatic symptoms (Minuchin, Rosman, & Baker, 1978), alcoholism (Davis, Stern, & VanDeusen, 1977), and drug addiction (Stanton, Todd, & Associates, 1982).

Much research in the family therapy field on families of patients with psychosomatic symptoms, as well as with drug problems, has been influenced by the earlier structural investigations. Some of the earlier hypotheses about how family structure links to these symptoms have been supported and some not. Similarly, some of the conclusions about the usefulness of structural interventions have been validated and some not. Nevertheless, it is evident that the concept of family structure has served as a valuable construct for studying and understanding psychosomatic illness (Kog, Vertommen, & Vandereycken, 1987; Northey, Griffin, & Krainz, 1998; Onnis, Tortolani, & Cancrini, 1986; Wood, Watkins, Boyle, Noguera, Zimand, & Carroll, 1989). Structural research has also made its contribution about family roles, loss in families, recruiting family members, and structural interventions to other studies in addictions (Cancrini, Cingolani, Compagnoni, Costantini, & Mazzoni, 1988; Cleveland, 1988; Coleman, Kaplan, & Downing, 1986; Wermuth & Scheidt, 1986).

The core concepts of SFT continue to influence research in the general area of family therapy with children (Abelsohn & Saayman, 1991; Kerig, 1995). Structural concepts have been recently applied to questions of family and culture (Fisek, 1991; Jung, 1984; Santisteban, Coatsworth, Perez-Vidal, Mitrani, Jean-Gilles, & Szapocznik, 1997). The model has also been been applied to the business and industrial world (Deacon, 1996). Structural family theory and therapy has made contributions to research in the family therapy field and related areas of social services, medicine, education, and business.

Clinical Perspective

View of Human Functioning

Structural family therapy views people's current experience as the context in which they struggle with life's challenges and from which they grow and define themselves. Altering the personal, family, and social structures underlying people's efforts in these personal challenges is meant to free them to make healthier life choices. The structural therapist looks to identify the particular issue and circumstances in which people face these challenges.

> In the videotape, the therapist immediately reaches for a specific area of concern for the family (2–2). The parents identify how Pam, their daughter, becomes angry, particularly with her mother. The therapist reaches further for specific instances and they settle on mealtime, a basic family function (2–5). The therapist proceeds under the assumption that this ordinary family activity contains dynamics critical to this family's distress. Indeed, the family's discussion of breakfast leads to the unveiling of Pam's dependency and her rivalry with her mother for father with father's collusion. There would need to be some shift in the structure of the parents' relationship with Pam for her to experience the freedom to relate differently to them.

How the Theory Sees Mental Illness

Mental illness is complex and mysterious beyond our capacity to fully explain it and, therefore, to cure it. The myriad approaches to the understanding and treatment of mental illness all have something to offer about the nature of mental illness and its treatment. SFT's focus is on the social context in which people's functioning becomes stuck in self-defeating and hurtful patterns of thinking and behaving. It is to these tangled knots of human reaction and interaction that the structural model seeks to bring some order so that people can gain the mobility and power to overcome the stuckness and to be free to change.

> In the videotape, Pam, a mentally handicapped young woman, was adopted into a household where the natural daughter suicided. She fearfully resists growing up. Her retired father spoils her and fosters her dependency on him. Her working mother is in conflict with her about her lack of personal responsibility for herself at home. The question is, how can Pam grow up under the current circumstances? How she and her parents

meet today's particular challenge to her emotional development affects the course of their respective personal lives and relationships.

How Change Occurs

Change takes place through the choices people make in circumstances that allow and support change to take root. No matter how difficult a situation, if there is a potential for change, there will exist the possibility for people to choose to be and act differently from their accustomed stuck patterns of the past. Therapists have the task of helping identify the stuck place, accessing the specific context of potential change, and mobilizing the positive forces in people to support beneficial choices. The final act of choosing and implementing the suitable steps belongs to the client, not the therapist.

> Pam faces the question of whether to choose greater personal independence or cling to her childish dependency at home (2–35). Her chance to grow rests on whether her father can loosen his hold on her and her mother can become more affectionately connected to her while disengaging from Pam's battle for control. If mother and father can also look more to each other for understanding and support, they will be able to give Pam the room to manage her own life without losing either of them. The structural therapist's task is to foster in the moment a specific experience in which the family can engage this new paradigm.
>
> If the therapist can promote an emotional environment in the session in which all three family members feel safely and caringly connected to each other, they will have less need to maneuver for control. Judy must feel her mothering is important to Pam. Adrian must see that his opinions are taken seriously by mother and the therapist, and that Pam's being close to her mother will not cut her off from him. Pam needs to know that if she grows up more she can still have a relationship with each parent and the parents will stay together. Experiencing a gradual shift in these directions relaxed the family environment and made it safer for them to admit their respective roles in the problem and look at their options. Pam was able to speak of herself as a "spoiled brat" because this admission came in a loving environment of both safety and potential for change. She was free to choose greater maturity, and her parents a more shared parenting. They could all freely choose to heal together.

Range of Application

So long as therapy is in any degree dependent on people's choices in a facilitating relationship, there are no limits to where SFT can contribute to change. Obviously, resolving people's issues more or less depends on change in the family and/or other social contexts. The more the resolution of an issue depends on change in personal relationships, the more SFT will have to offer. Structural therapy can be the exclusive approach, or the complement to medication, insight, learning, strategic, or conditioning therapies.

Application to Various Diagnoses or Problems

Diagnoses define the field in which the work of therapy will be done. The structural model does not pretend to be a cure-all. It offers a way of pursuing change through a therapy that engages actively and in real time with people's struggles, mobilizing their potential to change with and through their interactions with family and other social environments. It is most effective where there are available family or others connected to the struggle who can participate in and contribute to the new experience. Problems that are essentially based on family relationships are directly appropriate to SFT. Individual issues, whether biological, as in bipolar disorders, or characterological, as in borderline personality, can use structural interventions in the family as a context that facilitates change. The family becomes the context in which they can engage their struggle in new ways with the help of others.

> In Pam's situation, a diagnosis of developmental disability would not obviate the necessity for family work to support her emotional development. Could one not imagine Pam receiving individual help to manage life in a living arrangement outside the family? Perhaps the parents could do this for her, but given the degree of family enmeshment it would probably be wiser to provide them with help to nourish their own marital relationship while Pam receives help from someone else to forge her own relative independence. Concurrent whole family work could facilitate Pam's efforts to grow up, jointly supported by her parents.

Application to Diverse Family Forms

Consideration for Current Constraints

"Current constraints" refer to present realities. The family form defines the limits and potential of those realities. The single mother raises her children, male and female, without a father, and possibly with a grandmother. The poor underorganized family, likely with tenuously involved father or fathers, confronts both an internal weakness of organization and a want of social supports. Today's divorced and blended families face extraordinary and sometimes daunting complexity. SFT can help bring organization to these difficult family situations. More challenging for the model is society's isolated individual, which we find more of today than ever. Even then, SFT will be thinking of how to build human connections into the person's life, even if not family. SFT has something to offer wherever we are considering human relationships. Other limitations to applicability are those that arise from therapists' values about what constitutes a fitting family. Those values delimit means and goals in any model of therapy.

Relationship to the Past

The structural approach developed at a time of innovation and creativity in the field of family therapy revolving around founders of schools of therapy. That historical context tended to isolate the models from one another. The structural model leaned more toward the end of the spectrum that is strategic and away from the psychoanalytic, historical, and more growth-oriented models.

Therapist's Stance and Style

Nature of the Family–Counselor Relationship

The structural family therapist is active and involved. Within the boundaries of a professional role, the therapist joins with the family at a personal level. The therapist assumes one of two technical stances, promoting change in the family either from outside their interactions or from direct participation within their interactions. In both cases, structural therapists reach inside themselves to reflect on their personal emotional reactions, their histories, and their values to understand and empathize with the clients with whom they are now engaged. They select as best they can from what is accessible to them of their emotional and spiritual life and personal experiences in order to connect with their clients in ways that strategically are in line with their therapeutic plan. What and how they put of themselves into the therapeutic relationship is an essential part of the structural clinician's intervention in the therapy.

> The therapist first made room for Pam's family to interact spontaneously around their respective interpretations of what their difficulties were. They pulled hard in different directions. The therapist felt powerless in the face of an initially inarticulate young lady, a defeated mother, and a defensive and aloof father. His only recourse was to attempt to connect and care about them and their plight. As the family became less defensive, he was able to be more active with them. At a personal level he attempted to elicit from each their stories in a genuinely caring, albeit direct, engaging manner. The connection he achieved cultivated a safe ambience for the family to do its work. They began to share more of their distress with him, and what they needed to do became clearer. In the safer environment engendered by the personal trust in the therapist, they could consider risking change.

Counselor Self-Talk

Therapists' mindsets are all-important when they intend to actively connect with a family. In SFT, engagement with the family is very personal. Whether dealing with mindsets, emotions, or values, therapists are looking within to their own past personal experience as a lens through which to see the family now. They are similarly looking at what they are personally experiencing in the circumstance of their current interactions with the family. From what they can connect to in themselves plus their sense of the family's therapeutic needs, they forge some notion about how to relate to the family to be most helpful. There is a strategic component to SFT that calls for therapists to consciously choose which parts of their current experience and past history to utilize in their interactions with the family.

> When the therapist with Pam's family found himself attending more to the articulate adults than to the inarticulate daughter, he learned something about the daughter's self negation. He then noted his own need for affirmation, which the mother's ready feedback provided, and resolved to reach out to Pam by inviting the mother and her to interact around Pam's breakfast (2–5). As Pam became involved with her mother, she reacted emotionally, which opened up her pain (2–6 and 2–7). The therapist stayed connected with Pam about her conflict with her parents around the preparation of food, a strong symbol of her emotional dependence on them, and encouraged more intense interaction with them (2–8 to 2–19). The therapist reached the parents through Pam, and drew them into wanting to help her be less protected and spoiled (2–20 to 2–30). Inwardly connected to his own family life, he spoke to the parents' love for their daughter and they came together for her (2–31 to 2–42). He needed to relate to his own family experience to touch theirs.

Specific Interventions Related to Theory

Intervention Strategies Associated with the Theory

1. The structural family therapist identifies an actual situation that represents a family's theme, and brings it into the session with all the intensity of home life—an enactment.

   > With Pam's family, the therapist asked Judy, the mother, to give an example of when Pam gets angry with her (2–5). As she offered one, Pam began to cry. Instead of inquiring into history or requesting detailed explanations of the example, the therapist asked Judy to turn to her daughter right there, and talk with her about her tears and about the issue (2–7).

2. The structural therapist identifies where the potential is for positive choices for change. The therapist looks for where the clients can choose a new path, and works with choice potential.

With Pam the therapist highlights the choice to grow up and not be a "spoiled brat." The choice becomes specific about how she would cooperate with her parents about breakfast (2–20).

3. The therapist builds on the positive to foster change in the session and at home. The strengths of the family and its members are the building blocks of the therapy.

    Toward the end of the session, the therapist highlights Judy's love for Pam (2–31). He works from the assumption that Pam wants her mother's love (2–33). He invites Judy to give Pam a chance to choose her mother's attention (2–34). He speaks to Adrian, the father, as the family expert, asking his assessment of Pam's behavior with Judy, affirming that what he has tried was right and that he has just to persevere (2–36 to 2–40). Finally, the therapist validates the positive experience they have had as a family in the session (2–42).

4. The structural therapist strengthens, where possible, the new behavior of the parties in some basic structural reorganization of the family that will support the change.

    In Pam's situation, he sought to have the father not compete with the mother for Pam's affection. On the contrary, it would help Pam if he supported her closeness to Judy (2–37). The mother's and father's joining to give Pam the security of connected, cooperating parents freed her from the dependency on her father and permitted her to choose both to be closer to her mother and assume greater responsibility for her life.

5. The therapist encourages an experience in and outside the session that will embody that change.

    The therapist ended the session by inviting Pam to reach out to both her parents' hands, symbolizing her connection to both of them rather than to one against the other (2–43). Had he continued working with the family, he would have looked for specific opportunities to encourage these new attitudes and behaviors at home.

When and How Interventions Are Best Applied

In SFT the interventions are best applied when family members are emotionally engaged in what is taking place in the session. The experience needs to feel "lived" and not like something merely being talked about. When people are fully present with each other and with the therapist, more of them is accessible to the experience of change.

The session began with an enactment (2–7) and ended with an enactment (2–43). It was full of emotion and personal interaction. There was anger and there were tears. At the end, there was even some understated rejoicing (2–44). The therapist sought to engage personally with them encouraging their connecting more deeply with each other.

Give Specific Instructions for Implementing One or More Interventions

For implementing the *enactment*, the heart of the structural approach to therapy, the therapist either allows a spontaneous interaction or fosters one. Early in therapy, the therapist usually learns about the family by observing, without pursuing change, either by staying in the background as they spontaneously interact or by sparking an interaction about their issue. The therapist may also invite reactions directed to him- or herself, thereby exploring their interactions through him or her. These enactments are explored in relation to a specific issue because structure is so complex that it can be quite different from one concern to another. The therapist looks not only for pathological patterns, but also for the potential of constructive change. As the therapist identifies pathology and potential, he or she strategically but genuinely engages with the family in ways that impede the negative and promote positive interactions. The therapist can explicitly request a family member to relate to another in a new manner. Preferably, however, the therapist joins with the family in a personally invested, natural manner that draws them into the more constructive interaction. The therapeutic intent is strategic, but the experience feels natural. At first the therapist observes, but as the issue is better understood and the family becomes more amenable to change, the therapist helps create momentum for the new vision through new experience. However, the final choice for the new life paradigm belongs exclusively to the family and its members.

Case Example

There have been a number examples cited, including an exploratory enactment early on and a prescriptive enactment that ended the session.

> Early in the session (2–7) the therapist was watching how the mother and daughter interacted. As he asked Judy for specific examples of when Pam became angry with her, Pam looked upset. The therapist pointed this out to Judy, who responded that "Pam cries a lot." He then asked Judy to find out from Pam "what is going on right now." When the mother did, Pam said, "nuttin." Judy confirmed that this was Pam's usual response to that question. The therapist followed up by inviting mother and daughter to talk concretely about pancakes and French toast, which opened up the family's struggle around Pam's dependency.
>
> At the end of the session (2–43), at the point that it appeared that the parents were together and Pam had just declared she wanted *both* her

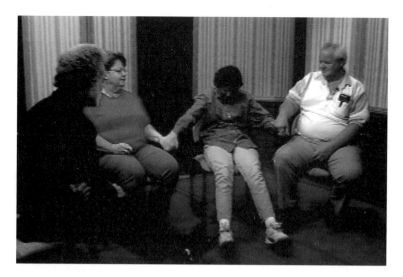

Aponte w/ client

parents to love her, the therapist asked Pam to reach out her hands to both parents simultaneously. He prescribed an action that was likely to give life and validity to their achievement in the session. Pam did reach out and all held hands. This was a prescriptively requested enactment. However, in a spontaneous enactment, Adrian, the father, gestured to Judy to embrace Pam, which she did and Pam fell into her arms. He reacted triumphantly as they held each other. This spontaneous exchange between the parents, which was consummated by mother and daughter's hug, capped and confirmed the goal of the session. Pam could safely let go and reach for an emotional connection with her mother without fearing the loss of her father or contention between her parents. She and her parents experienced in session what they had been working for. The change was real and rewarding.

Summary

Strengths and Limitations of Theory

A strength of SFT is that it is a clearly articulated model for working in a practical goal-oriented manner with current issues in the context of the family. The theory, technique, and underlying philosophy are readily grasped and implemented.

The limitations of the model, if they are to be called that, are that, like other models of therapy, it cannot embody nor does it pretend to contain all that is necessary to understand and facilitate healthy change in human behavior. The structural model is but a contributor to the various therapies that are evolving for the benefit of people in distress.

Implications for Further Research

The current stage of the development of the structural model has taken a variety of paths, including what is represented here. These developments call for investigation of current thinking, particularly the effort to incorporate into this technically and strategically oriented approach to therapy more personal and spiritual dimensions.

Also, of special interest would be investigations that would test the viability of the integration of the theory and technique with other approaches to therapy. This is clearly where the field is headed. There are obviously some therapeutic models that blend more easily than others. Some criteria need to be identified to understand the bases for good and bad fits between models of therapy. Integration of therapeutic approaches should be an occasion for more, not less, disciplined thinking about what we are doing as therapists.

Questions to Consider

Within the model itself, what still needs further development is the question of values, worldviews, and spirituality, and their relationship to theory and technical approaches. The philosophical and spiritual base of the therapy has a profound impact on matters of determining standards for pathology, desirable goals, and appropriate means to solutions. Therapists are still relative novices at making the connections between spirituality and treatment methods. For a practical, outcome-oriented approach like SFT, it becomes terribly important that this connection be made in ways that are understandable and accessible to the average clinician.

Sources for Training

Specialized Training Opportunities and Certification:

Minuchin Therapy Center for the family: 212-481-3144

Philadelphia Child and Family Therapy Training Center: 215-242-0949

Resources for Further Study

The following are videotapes of clinical sessions by Harry Aponte that can serve as training tools for SFT:

A house divided: Structural family therapy with a black family. Golden Triad Films, 1990, Kansas City, MO.

Tres madres: Structural family therapy with an Anglo/Hispanic family. Golden Triad Films, 1990, Kansas City, MO.

A daughter who needs a mother. Washington, DC. AAMFT Master Series, 1992.

Williams family: Strength and vulnerability. Research and Education Foundation, Washington, DC. AAMFT, 1995.

Clinical Application of Forgiveness. National Conference on Forgiveness, University of Maryland, 1996.

Family therapy with the experts: Structural therapy with Harry Aponte. Boston, MA: Allyn & Bacon, 1998.

REFERENCES

Abelshon, D., & Saayman, G. (1991). Adolescent adjustment to parental divorce: An investigation from the perspective of basic dimensions of structural family therapy theory. *Family Process, 30*(2), 177–191.

Aponte, H. J. (1976b). The family–school interview: An eco-structural approach. *Family Process, 15*(3), 303–311.

Aponte, H. J. (1982). The cornerstone of therapy. The person of the therapist. *Family Therapy Networker, 6*(2), 19–21.

Aponte, H. J. (1985). The negotiation of values in therapy. *Family Process, 24*(3), 323–338.

Aponte, H. J. (1991, July). Home/community-based services: A two tier approach. *American Journal of Orthopsychiatry, 6*(13), 403–408.

Aponte, H. J. (1992a). Training the person of the therapist in structural family therapy. *Journal of Marital and Family Therapy, 18*(3), 269–281.

Aponte, H. J. (1992b). The black sheep of the family: A structural approach to brief therapy. In S. Budman, M. Hoyt, & S. Friedman (Eds.), *The first session of brief therapy: A book of cases* (pp. 324–342), New York: Guilford.

Aponte, H. J. (1994a). How personal can training get? *Journal of Marital and Family Therapy, 20*(1), 3–15.

Aponte, H. J. (1994b). *Bread & spirit: Therapy with the new poor.* New York: W. W. Norton.

Aponte, H. J. (1995, Fall). Political bias, moral values, and spirituality in the training of psychotherapists. *Bulletin of the Menninger Clinic, 60*(4), 488–502.

Aponte, H. J. (1998a). Intimacy in the therapist–client relationship. In W. J. Matthews & J. H. Edgette (Eds.), *Current thinking and research in brief therapy: Solutions, strategies, narratives* (Vol. 2, pp. 3–27), Philadelphia: Taylor & Francis.

Aponte, H. J. (1998b). Love, the spiritual wellspring of forgiveness: An example of spirituality in therapy. *Journal of Family Therapy, 20*(1), 37–58.

Aponte, H. J. (1999). The stresses of poverty and the comfort of spirituality. In F. Walsh. (Ed.), *Spiritual resources in family therapy* (pp. 76–89), New York: Guilford.

Aponte, H. J., & DiCesare, E. J. (2000). Structural theory. In F. M. Dattilio & L. Bevilacqua (Eds.), *Comparative treatment of couples problems* (pp. 45–57), New York: Springer.

Aponte, H. J., & VanDeusen, J. M. (1981). Structural family therapy. In A. S. Gurman & D. P. Kniskern (Eds.), *Handbook of family therapy* (pp. 310–360), New York: Brunner/Mazel.

Bibb, A., & Casimir, G. J. (1996). Haitian families. In M. McGoldrick, J. Giordano, & J. K. Pearce (Eds.), *Ethnicity and family therapy* (2nd ed., pp. 97–111), New York: Guilford.

Cancrini, L., Cingolani, S., Compagnoni, F., Costantini, D., & Mazzoni, S. (1988, September). Juvenile drug addiction: A typology of heroin addicts and their families. *Family Process, 27*(3), 261–271.

Cleveland, M. (1988, September). Families and adolescent drug abuse: Structural analysis of children's roles. *Family Process, 20*(3), 295–304.

Coleman, S. G., Kaplan, J. D., & Downing, R. W. (1986, March). Life cycle and loss: The spiritual vacuum of heroin addiction. *Family Process, 25*(1), 5–23.

Davis, P., Stern, D., & VanDeusen, J. (1977). Enmeshment–disengagement in the alcoholic family. In F. Seixas (Ed.), *Alcoholism: Clinical & experimental research,* New York: Grune and Straton.

Deacon, S. (1996). Utilizing structural family therapy and systems theory in the business world. *Contemporary Family Therapy, 18*(4), 549–565.

Gerson, M-J. (1996). *The embedded self: A psychoanalytic guide to family therapy.* Hillside, NJ: Analytic.

Goolishian, H. A., & Anderson, H. (January, 1992). Strategy and intervention versus nonintervention: A matter of theory. *Journal of Marital and Family Therapy, 18*(1), 5–15.

Hoffman, L. (1990, March). Constructing realities: An art of lenses. *Family Process, 29*(1), 1–12.

Jung, M. (1984). Structural family therapy: Its application to Chinese families. *Family Process, 23*(3), 365–374.

Kerig, P. K. (1995). Triangles in the family circle: Effects of family structure on marriage, parenting, and child adjustment. *Journal of Family Psychology, 9*(1), 28–43.

Kog, E., Vertommen, H., & Vandereycken, W. (1987, June). Minuchin's psychosomatic family model revisited: A concept-validation study using a multitrait-multimethod approach. *Family Process, 26*(2), 235–253.

Lannamann, J. W. (1998, Winter). Social construction and materiality: The limits of indeterminancy in therapeutic settings. *Family Process, 37*(4), 393–413.

Lebow, J. (1997, March). The integrative revolution in couple and family therapy. *Family Process, 36*(1), 1–17.

McGoldrick, M., & Gerson, R. (1985). *Genograms in family assessment.* New York: Norton.

Minuchin, S., Montalvo, B., Guerney, B., Jr., Rosman, B., & Schumer, F. (1967). *Families of the slums.* New York: Basic Books.

Minuchin, S. (1970). The use of an ecological framework in the treatment of a child. In E. J. Anthony & C. Koupernick (Eds.), *The international yearbook of child psychiatry: The child in his family* (pp. 41–57). New York: Wiley.

Minuchin, S. (1974). *Families and family therapy.* Cambridge, MA: Harvard University Press.

Minuchin, S., & Colapinto, J. (Eds.). (1980). *Taming monsters* (videotape). Philadelphia Child Guidance Clinic.

Minuchin, S., & Fishman, H. C. (1981). *Family therapy techniques.* Cambridge, MA: Harvard University Press.

Minuchin, S., Rosman, B., & Baker, L. (1978). *Psychosomatic families.* Cambridge, MA: Harvard University Press.

Northey, S., Griffin, W. A., & Krainz, S. (1998). A partial test of the psychosomatic family model: Marital interaction patterns in asthma and non-asthma families. *Journal of Family Psychology, 12*(2), 220–233.

O'Hanlon, B. (1994, November/December). The third wave. *The Family Therapy Networker, 18*(6), 18–29.

Onnis, L., Tortolani, D., & Cancrini, L. (1986). Systemic research on chronicity factors in infantile asthma. *Family Process, 14*(2), 107–121.

Reischelt, S., & Christiensen, B. (1990, September). Reflections during a study on family therapy with drug addicts. *Family Process, 29*(3), 273–287.

Santisteban, D., Coatswroth, J. D., Perez-Vidal, A., Mitrani, V., Jean-Gilles, M., & Szapocznik, J. (1997). Brief, structural/strategic family therapy with African American and Hispanic high-risk youth. *Journal of Community Psychology, 25*, 453–471.

Stanton, M. D., Todd, T. C., & Associates. (1982). *The family therapy of drug abuse and addiction.* New York: Guilford.

Wermuth, L., & Scheidt, S. (1986, March). Enlisting family support in drug treatment. *Family Process, 25*(1), 25–33.

Wood, B., Watkins, J. B., Boyle, J. T., Nogueira, J., Zimand, E., & Carroll, L. (1989). The psychosomatic family model: An empirical and theoretical analysis. *Family Process, 28*(4), 399–417.

Wylie, M. S. (1994, November/December). Panning for gold. *The Family Therapy Networker, 18*(6), 40–48.

2 Culture-Sensitive Family Therapy

MARY SMITH ARNOLD

Mary Smith Arnold

The field of family therapy holds that, to fully understand the individual, one must view the individual within the context of the family. However, the field has been slow to accept *culture* as a significant context that would aid our understanding of the family. Most approaches and models within the field have been centered on dynamics within nuclear, white, middle-class, heterosexual families. Furthermore, even within this narrow focus, family therapists also ignored within-group differences such as ethnicity, religion, sexual orientation, class, and region. This narrow focus allowed the field to simultaneously avoid, suppress, and dismiss cultural differences and social inequalities based on gender, race, class, and sexual orientation within families (McGoldrick, 1998). Family therapy homogenized families and adopted a cookie-cutter attitude toward families and the application of family therapy models to families and their problems.

Over the last two decades, culture has become central to our understanding of families. Many practitioners and scholars are calling for the centralizing of culture in our practice, research, and training programs (Arnold, 1994; Falicov, 1983; Green, 1998b; Hardy & Laszloffy, 1992; Ho, 1987; McGoldrick, 1998; McGoldrick, Pearce, & Giordano, 1982). Increasingly, the point of view that treated certain families as cultural anomalies, such as African American, Asian American, or Latino families, and Caucasian families as the norm is being replaced by an understanding that *all* families are cultural models. All families are shaped by their daily rituals, traditions, historical experiences, and sociopolitical circumstances. This broader view of culture has also opened the way for Caucasian as well as family counselors of color to see themselves as cultural beings.

The purpose of this chapter is to present Culture-Sensitive Therapy (CST) and the basic techniques for engaging clients in a cultural dialogue throughout the therapeutic process. This chapter reflects my point of view as a counselor educator who supervises marriage and family counselors.

A Brief Description of CST

CST is a commitment to move culture and its many implications for social life from the margins to the center (Hooks, 1984) of the healing process. It is an effort to appreciate the worldview, experiences, and values of clients. It also incorporates the social context of the family, which includes their "network of social supports, and the large public sectors such as education, business, and social services, as well as the broader sociopolitical . . . climates of our communities and countries" (Hair, Fine, & Ryan, 1996, p. 291). Particular attention is given to social identities that influence and shape family form and dynamics, such as those based on sexual orientation, race, or disabilities. The goal of CST is to shift our viewing stance from looking through the lens at a particular family to moving within the family's viewing frame of reference. It is an attempt to peer through the family's lens rather than the wholesale application of theoretical concepts to families and their problems.

CST assumes that culture influences how problems develop and are defined by families and counselors. It assumes that solutions and strategies for solving problems are embedded within the multifaceted and dynamic cultural experiences of families. CST also holds that moving into the family's frame of reference(s) requires an understanding of oneself as a cultural being. CST assumes that, the more open the therapist is to learning from the family about their cultural and social context, the more likely effective and appropriate change will occur within the family or the social context of the family.

Significant Characteristics of the Theory

Evolution

CST grew out of a response to changing social forces that critiqued and impacted family therapy as a treatment process. The challenges posed by feminists, postmodernists, and the development of the "fourth force" (Pedersen, 1991) in individual psychotherapy that calls for attention to racial and cultural differences have provided a platform for family therapists to incorporate culture into their work.

The second wave of feminist struggle in the United States set off a profound and widespread critique of societal institutions centered on gender inequalities. Family therapy did not escape scrutiny. Hare-Mustin (1978), in an earthshaking article, challenged family therapy as an instrument of the status quo that kept women disempowered within patriarchal family systems. Controversial, hotly contested, and often polarized discussions burst onto the family therapy scene generating new ways to think about problems within families as well as the very idea and function of the family in society. Feminist family therapists sought to revise traditional models of family therapy to incorporate analysis of gender inequalities, developed models of feminist family therapy, and moved women's issues to the forefront in training programs. In 1977, Betty Carter, Peggy Papp, Olga Silverstein, and Marianne Walters cofounded the Women's Project in Family Therapy. They conducted training workshops across the country and in Europe in order to help family therapists understand the impact of gender in families. Their twenty-year collaboration has enhanced training, advanced theory, and provided new techniques for identifying and addressing gender issues in families.

Another broad societal trend that influenced family therapy in the late 1980s and into the 1990s was postmodernism. The perspective that there can be no single truth or absolute reality also shook the foundations of family therapy. Cookie-cutter approaches to families and their problems had to give way to the view that the therapist is not the expert. Therapists are beginning to acknowledge that families come into therapy with their "own stories, which may be more or less useful than ours, but no more or less true" (Nichols & Schwartz, 1995, p. 120).

Unlike the feminist critique, postmodernist ideas were more widely embraced by the Caucasian male family therapy establishment. With postmodernism, the ideas of pluralism and diversity among families were adopted into the field (Nichols & Schwartz, 1995). Conceptions of "the family" as nuclear, male-headed, and middle-class were reexamined and the focus on family structure as the primary indicator of health or dysfunction shifted to understanding families through the stories that family members construct. However, one aspect of the postmodern infusion into family therapy was to accept that truth is relative and, with this, comes a tendency to dismiss the social construction of privilege based on race, gender, class, and sexual orientation.

A third trend that influenced family therapy, and the one that most directly links to CST, was the rise of the multicultural movement in society and its affect on the broader mental health professions (Gushue & Sciarra, 1995). The persistent demands of some scholars that the field of psychology acknowledge the impact of racism on clients of color and the potential for harm due to ethnocentrism within the profession led to a groundswell of interest in cultural differences. The original work of Grier and Cobbs (1968) in psychology, Thomas and Sillen (1972) in psychiatry, and Wrenn (1962) in counseling paved the way for an implosion of literature examining the ethnocentric bias within psychotherapy (Sue & Sue, 1999) and cultural differences between other racial groups and the Caucasian middle classes (Atkinson, Morten, & Sue, 1979). This massive reevaluation affected practice, research, and theoretical formulations.

Feminism, postmodernism, and multiculturalism are forces that have reshaped all of society over the last thirty years and they have also reconfigured family therapy (Nichols & Schwartz, 1995). The reconceptualization of family therapy is in the early stages of development, altering theory and practice by degrees rather than causing a total revolution in all quarters of the family therapy field. Still, it is unlikely that the field will return to the days when a small number of Caucasian men dominated every aspect of it.

Within the most progressive quarters of the family therapy field, an appreciation for culture, gender, race, and class emerged as the raw material with which to recast family therapy. CST grew from the efforts of many second-generation therapists to address the inequalities posed by a field dominated by the values of Caucasian middle-class men who failed to account for the effects of racism, sexism, classism, and cultural diversity.

What Makes the Theory Different?

A major difference in CST from other approaches is its commitment to understanding families and their problems by fully engaging the complexities posed by the social context in which the family is embedded. Therefore, the larger social systems that intersect with family life and serve as conduits of racism, sexism, classism, heterosexism, and other forms of oppression are addressed. So if a family presents with the commonly labeled problem of "an overinvolved mother and a distant father" this patent way of describing what is presented would be assessed in light of cultural factors: racism, sexism, and power discrepancies rooted in gender. Gender is shaped within a cultural context. Ideas and behaviors associated with gender vary across cultures. Therefore, what the family brings to therapy—differences and similarities that represent an intricate web of culturally based socialization experiences of individual family members, serves to guide the therapeutic process. External and internal differences within families, whether they grow out of varying generational experiences, levels of acculturation, English language fluency, or class differences, are considered as contributing to the family's interactional expanse and framing of the problem(s).

The CST approach is also different from traditional models of family therapy because it seeks to enter the frame of reference of the family rather than uniformly applying a set of theoretical concepts to every family seeking counseling. Some might confuse entering the family's frame of reference or viewing life through their lens with the technique of "joining" the family (Minuchin, 1974). However, this requires a deeper understanding of the impact of sociopolitical forces on the family and its worldview (Sue & Sue, 1999). Peering out from the family's frame of reference requires a knowledge of the historical, political, economic, and social realities of specific cultural group(s) and a recognition that families and their individual members are variously and differentially affected by these larger contextual circumstances. Minuchin (1974) describes joining as "accept[ing] the family's organization and style and blend[ing] with them" (p. 123). Viewing through the family's lens goes beyond this to figuring out *how* the family's structure and transactional patterns have been shaped and formed in response to larger sociopolitical forces. Viewing through the lens of the family allows the therapist to change her relationship to the family's social context from distant observer to that of ally to the family.

Another difference, closely related to viewing through the family's frame of reference, is seeing the links between the family's problem or concerns and the experiences of oppression that the family's cultural group experienced over time. Issues of oppression are brought into the counseling process by seeking family histories through their stories. Constructing a family genogram is a useful strategy for gathering such information. In many other approaches, issues related to oppression are completely ignored. In other instances, the counselor attempts to alter the family's perspective of the oppression to aid the family in forming more effective coping responses to the oppression. Often the latter approach has the effect of denying the family's real circumstances. In CST, oppression is recognized as a powerful determinant of family life. Questions of power and privilege are brought into the therapy process for examination. Families are encouraged to examine their relationship to the dominant culture relative to their "minority" status as members of a disadvantaged group(s), migration patterns, varying levels of fluency with the English language, degrees of acculturation, and any other sociopolitical factor that might impact their group('s) experiences with oppression and relative power within society.

Families are not homogeneous. In any given family, several members may be part of a socially identified group(s) that is targeted for oppression. For instance, any family can have gay or bisexual members, biracial members, disabled members, or members who practice a different religion or come from a different racial or cultural group. In addition to being targeted for oppression by the dominant culture, families of color can also act out internalized oppression or attitudes of the dominant culture against themselves (Arnold, 1997). Ferreting out the many implications that oppression has for life within the family is an important part of mobilizing the family to work for change.

Another difference in CST from other approaches is the valuing of the experiences and cultural perspectives of the family over that of the traditional family systems models. Blind adherence to a particular theoretical stance is dismissed, set aside, or totally abandoned in favor of the cultural perspective of the family, privileging the specific family's frame of reference over theoretical constructions about "the family."

It is important to note that privileging the family's frame of reference does not mean that therapists condone or support aberrant or oppressive social behavior just because it is a cultural practice. The culture-sensitive therapist realizes that such practices are often the result of a useful cultural practice gone awry due to oppression. Very often it represents the installation of a practice from the dominant culture that is out of sync with the family's culture of origin. A good example of the latter is the use of alcohol by many cultural groups. In Europe, the landed gentry or nobility often paid their peasant workers with vodka instead of wages. Of course, this practice took a special twist in the Americas when traders and the government "paid" Native Americans in "fire water" instead of promised goods. Centuries later we see high rates of alcohol use and abuse among groups that were exploited and targeted for alcohol consumption by the oppressor group. It is important for counselors to have knowledge of the historical conditions and to remain nonjudgmental as they work with families to find alternatives to destructive behaviors.

How Is the Theory Like Others?

CST is not a set of formulations comprising a model developed by any one theorist. CST was developed and advanced by theorists and practitioners from a variety of theoretical perspectives. It represents a corrective response to family therapy methods that had essentially ignored the shaping influence of culture and societal oppression on families (Green, 1998a). Therefore, CST is a basic attitude that underlies all effective therapy. Therapists who take a cultural-sensitive approach to their work believe in the significance of culture and incorporating culture and sociopolitical knowledge into every aspect of the therapeutic process, from the initial stages of assessment through termination and follow-up procedures.

There are no founding mothers or fathers of CST. There is no *one* model or representation of CST. This may be due to the relatively short period of time that family practitioners and theorists have been focused on culture. It may also be due to the complexities related to the dynamics of culture. Another reason may be that theorists and practitioners alike have remained connected to the model that they were trained in or adopted early in their work with families. They have expanded or modified their model(s)-of-origin (MOO) to include culture and the sociopolitical context of the family into their work. Therefore, those who take a CST approach may use many of the theoretical constructs and techniques of their MOO. Still others may pick and choose aspects from a number of theoretical models, taking an eclectic or integrative approach to theoretical applications. Regardless of the theoretical model(s) employed by the counselor who is culture-sensitive, she takes a critical stance toward theoretical constructs and is willing to subordinate theory to the specific sociopolitical and cultural experiences of the family. Such counselors become interrogators of theory posing questions related to the cultural efficacy of the model(s).

CST, along with other approaches in family therapy, considers the family the most useful level of involvement for addressing the problems of individuals.

Most recently, family therapy has begun to view "the self-in-the-system" and to view social behavior in relation to the inner experience of the individual as well as the interaction between family members (Nichols, 1987). Engaging families at the level of the system or "organic whole" (Nichols, 1987, p. 8) and the individual's intrapersonal conflicts and challenges has become more common among family therapists. Yet, as Nichols points out:

> Clearly, the family is one of the most useful contexts within which to understand and influence behavior. But it is not the only one. Looking *outward we may discover economic and social forces that must be reckoned with;* looking inward we often find personal rigidities which will not readily yield to interactional influences (Emphasis added, p. 8).

In CST counselors work on three levels of analyses: (1) the "social forces that must be reckoned with," (2) the family as an organic whole pressed and pressing against these social forces, and (3) the individual's intrapersonal conflicts, especially those that grow from the internalization of oppressive societal messages. The acknowledgment and emphasis placed on the emotional and psychological impact of oppression on the family and its members are also an important aspects of CST.

Several clinicians have presented cultural-specific models for working with particular cultural groups. Still, to date, there is no one model that delineates how culture should be incorporated into the counseling process. Certainly, it would be a contradiction for those who purport to value cultural diversity to assert that there is only *one* way to approach cultural issues in therapy. Therefore, not advancing a singular model seems consistent with the multicultural perspective. It also seems to fit with a vein of interest that has run throughout psychotherapy literature for the last thirty years: the idea of "tailoring" therapy to the specific needs of a particular family in therapy. Every family would be treated as unique and every stage of therapy would be geared toward providing the specific therapeutic response to the specific problem and style of the family (Carlson, Sperry, & Lewis, 1997). Family therapy is not a precise science; we are a long way from the precision suggested by the idea of tailoring therapy, but CST moves us closer to that ideal.

Philosophical and Historical Background

Individuals Associated with the Theory

During the 1970s, therapists and scholars, primarily people of color, suggested the value of incorporating cultural factors into the therapeutic process. Their work was considered tangential and only applicable to the specific cultural group. These scholars consistently implored the field to acknowledge the ethnocentric nature of family therapy and pointed out the potential harm to clients resulting from the ethnocentric bias within the field. It took the urgings of

Caucasian therapists and scholars to move the profession to examine the significance of culture in all families.

Although there is no one creator of a cultural therapy model, there are people who can be credited with advancing and legitimizing cultural perspectives in family therapy. The first among these is Monica McGoldrick, a third-generation Irish American woman, and her colleagues (McGoldrick, Pearce, & Giordano, 1982). McGoldrick was the first to address ethnic and racial differences by presenting cultural templates that therapists could use as a frame of reference to peer into families that were different culturally from themselves. In an edited volume, McGoldrick and colleagues presented nineteen "cultural paradigms," highlighting cultural themes and points of continuity within specific ethnic groups. What was heartening about the book was that it included Caucasian or European ethnic heritage groups. The mere inclusion of European heritage groups such as Anglo-American and German American families jolted our thinking and helped many to see "that ethnicity pertains to everyone and influences everyone's values, not just those that are marginalized by the dominant society" (McGoldrick, Giordano, & Pearce, 1996, p. ix). The 1982 first edition, and this expanded second edition, was the single most important tool in helping educators and practitioners understand and address the range of cultural diversity among families.

McGoldrick is the director of the Family Institute of New Jersey in Metuchen, New Jersey, as well as an associate professor at the Robert Wood Johnson Medical School. She has authored or coedited seven books, including her latest work, *Re-Visioning Family Therapy* (1998). She was trained by Murray Bowen, and considers Virginia Satir and Lyman Wynne influential figures in her work. In her work as a clinician, the influence of these early pioneers is visible. Although her clinical work continues to have a transgenerational focus, she has incorporated feminist values as well as the importance of the sociopolitical context into work with families (Arnold, Parmer, & Sanders, 1995).

Another significant figure in the push to get family counselors to understand the difference that culture makes within the dynamics of families is Celia Falicov. She is an Argentinean-born, Jewish, working-class woman who immigrated to the United States in 1961. Falicov's contribution has been her consistent emphasis on the multiple sociopolitical events that impact and define family identities. She helped to broaden our view of culture to include overlapping and interlocking social contexts such as language, age, a rural, urban, or suburban setting, occupation, education, political ideology, and level of acculturation in addition to race, ethnicity, and gender. Trained as a psychologist at the University of Chicago, her interest in culture and the sociopolitical circumstances began in her youth and were honed as a helping professional. In 1998, Falicov wrote:

> From a young age, I was aware that history and sociopolitical events shape a family's destiny. Growing up in a country where families' lives are profoundly altered by political ideologies and economic instability, I knew that to understand family distress, one must always include events that occur outside the boundaries, control, and wishes of the family (p. vii).

Falicov is an associate professor of clinical psychiatry at the University of California, San Diego. She also maintains a private practice in that city. She was the president of the American Family Therapy Academy (AFTA) for the year 2000–01, and has also many publications to her credit.

Another influential figure in the effort to promulgate a cultural perspective in family therapy is Kenneth Hardy. He is an African American, working-class male who was trained as a marriage and family therapist. Hardy is a professor in the Marriage and Family Therapy Program, Department of Child and Family Studies in the College for Human Development at Syracuse University.

Hardy and his colleague Tracy Larzloffy have authored several important articles on the significance of culture. He has spoken to large audiences of family practitioners, urging them to view the historical and societal wounds inflicted on oppressed families as a central theme in family life. Hardy has urged counselors to examine the "residual effects of slavery" on African American families, in particular, but also on the general consciousness of all Americans. He holds that counselors must explore their own racial identity and challenge the tenets of the dominant "pro-racist ideology" that exists in the United States if we are to be effective family counselors (Hardy & Laszloffy, 1998). Hardy has been the strongest voice within the profession calling for an acknowledgment of racism within the field of family therapy and, thereby, pointing to the need for racially sensitive training of marriage and family counselors.

The number of family counselors who view culture as a major organizing principle in family life has increased dramatically during the decade of the 1990s. This is evidenced by the attention given to cultural issues at major professional meetings such as the International Association of Marriage and Family Counselors (IAMFC) Distinguished Presenter Series held at the annual American Counseling Association Convention. IAMFC has sponsored programs featuring noted theorists on valuing a cultural perspective such as Monica McGoldrick (1993), Kenneth Hardy (1995), Mary Arnold and Jon Carlson (1996), Harry Aponte (1998), Marianne Walters (1998), and Laura Brown (1999). McGoldrick (1998) adeptly chronicled this phenomenon within the field when she wrote:

> Beginning in the 1990s, cultural diversity workshops became more common at major family therapy meetings . . . there was some acknowledgment of how researchers had ignored the experience of families of color. Accepted definitions in the field were also now open to question: It was being recognized that these definitions had labeled both people of color and women as deficient—'undifferentiated,' 'emmeshed,' or being 'highly emotional' (p. 16).

The changes that McGoldrick describes above are in large measure the work of countless therapists, especially people of color, who called attention to racism during the 1960s, 1970s, and 1980s, and to the alliances created by the leading figures discussed above, led by McGoldrick herself.

Stages of Theory Development

During the earliest period of development, or stage one, of family therapy there was an emphasis placed on understanding the key processes that govern the behavior of all families. Efforts were concentrated on discovering the "properties that governed families as a 'system' " (Hoffman, 1981, p. 17). The common thinking was that all families were alike in their basic needs and functioning. This period is marked by a lack of awareness of gender, class, and cultural dynamics within families. Ethnocentrism dominated the field, a belief that all families were like middle-class, Caucasian families in the United States, the largest group of clients. Additionally, most therapists were Caucasian, middle-class, and male. This notion was more implicit than explicit in the work and conceptual models that emerged within the field during this period.

Minuchin and his colleagues (Minuchin, Montalvo, Guerney, Rosman, & Schumer, 1967) were notable exceptions to the standard ethnocentric practices of early models that saw Caucasian middle-class families as the exemplar for all families. They were the first among the family therapists to speak of class and race. Their work with poor families helped therapists to see that "a life of poverty profoundly affected the family system" (Gushue & Sciarra, 1995, p. 587). The notion that all families looked and acted the same had to give way, minimally at least, to the realization that economics affected family structure and interactions. Later, during the 1970s and 1980s, Minuchin was criticized by feminists for characterizing poor families as "underorganized" and lacking in structure without articulating the effects of sexism and the lack of power, in private and public spheres, on single-parent and poor families. Still, the work of Minuchin and his colleagues was one of the few originating models of family therapy to have evolved its ideas through working with disadvantaged families.

Stage two of the development of a cultural perspective in family therapy was characterized by an effort to explain or interpret "minority families" to primarily Caucasian middle-class therapists. This period occurred during the 1970s. Clinicians, often "minorities" themselves, suggested treatment models and strategies for working with specific cultural groups such as Asian (Tinloy, 1978), African Americans (Harper & Stone, 1974) and Latinos/as (Cromwell & Ruiz, 1979). The development of culturally sensitive treatment approaches to particular groups often called for modifying a traditional model to incorporate the unique cultural heritage of the minority group. The focus was on the special features of the minority group. Although such models were and are still needed, at the time they did little to challenge the dominant paradigm within the field. Caucasian middle-class families were still viewed as the norm. All other families were seen as deviant from the norm, requiring the counselor to obtain additional information or modify techniques rather than change the way she perceived families.

The third stage of development of a cultural perspective in family therapy was marked by a throwing off of the status quo's point of view that only families of color were exotic or strange. Counselors began to see the diversity among

Caucasian families and explain the differences as rooted in ethnic and cultural experiences. A larger number of counselors began to speak of culture as defining and significant for all families. It seemed as if the simple declaration that Caucasian families were also cultural models set the scene for an open and wide-ranging debate on the value of attending to culture when working with families. Resistance sprang up, especially among the leaders in the field who held that their treatment approach worked across all cultures. A debate occurred between McGoldrick and her colleagues and those who opposed them. The question of whether or not the therapist should approach culture from an *etic* or *emic* perspective was debated back and forth. The etic (or universal) perspective holds that all human beings are fundamentally the same, therefore the rules that govern families apply across cultures. Greater emphasis is placed on similarities across groups rather than group differences. The emic (or cultural-specific) perspective holds that culture shapes human identity and that it defines and limits human possibilities. This view acknowledges variations within cultural groups. However, culture is viewed as the overarching influence on values, norms, and behavior.

The cultural perspective in family therapy is gaining ground and a new phase, stage four, is currently developing. There is greater convergence in the thinking of those who advance the importance of culture. The view of culture has expanded to take salient social identities as significant in the complex interactions within families and between the larger social context in which they are embedded. The complexities presented by the ever evolving, fluid, pervasive, yet elusive nature of the implications of culture has caused practitioners to continue to expand their field of vision to effectively serve families. Stage four is marked by the recognition of this complexity and by the willingness of the counselor to place herself in the role of learner with the family serving as teacher.

Another important feature of this stage, closely related to the idea of counselor as learner, is the notion that the counselor must understand herself as a cultural being and as a product of a particular social context. The distant posture of the expert clinician is abandoned for a more authentic exchange between counselor and client families. The willingness to face one's own prejudices and privileges has led to a greater awareness of the role oppression plays in the circumstances that create the problems that families bring to counseling. Counselors are becoming more aware of the need for social advocacy to help alter the larger social context that is so adverse to families.

In the United States, many people think of culture as a set of aesthetic expressions related to such things as food, clothing, and music; they do not recognize that the social, political, historical, economic, and spiritual aspects of family and community life are also characteristics of one's culture. Culture is intricate, multifaceted, and multilayered. Culture is shaped by society yet it also transforms that which presses against it, creating variations and new conditions. Laird (1998) asserts that our fixed, narrow ideas of culture "prevent us from recognizing the dynamic complexity and continuous changing nature of ethnic, racial, gender, social class, or sexual identity and experience" (p. 23).

Relevant Research Related to the Theory

A body of research on the effectiveness of CST has not yet developed. CST is still in its infancy. The accumulation of clinical observations and the integration of knowledge from cross-cultural psychology and multicultural counseling, combined with sociological and clinical perspectives of the family, are fertile ground for creating a research agenda. Most often clinical practice precedes parsimonious theoretical formulations and empirical research. Certainly, this has been true for the field of family therapy.

Gushue and Sciarra (1995) suggest four conceptual paradigms that they consider useful for understanding families in the context of culture: intercultural differences, acculturation, racial/cultural identity, and bilingual theory. Each one of these conceptual models has generated an impressive body of research although it is primarily related to individual functioning. However, the implications of results from the innumerable studies growing out of these models point the way to confirming the power of culture within families as well as the relevancy of CST as a therapeutic approach.

Clinical Perspective

View of Human Functioning

CST recognizes that human nature is expressed through cultural patterns that are rooted in varying worldviews. A worldview is a particular way of seeing and relating to the universe and human experiences. Many cultures have a worldview based on collaborative and communal values, unlike most European and European American groups, whose worldviews are expressed through competitive and individualist values. The imposition of one set of values over others leads to domination and oppression. European values have dominated the world's stage for centuries.

CST views problems as arising out of social interactions, particularly interaction originating from clashes in cultural values and sociopolitical domination or oppression. CST also believes solutions and strategies for solving problems and promoting healing are embedded in the historical and contemporary cultural experiences of families. Clinicians look for explanations of the problem in the cultural and sociopolitical experiences of the family. This means that a nonblaming stance is taken within therapy, while, at the same time, taking responsibility for harmful behavior is emphasized. If the source of the problem is rooted in oppression, such as sexism or racism, it is identified as such.

Although a nonblaming stance or seeing the circularity of human interactions is a hallmark in family therapy in CST, similar to feminist family therapy, circumstances such as domestic violence and child sexual assault are viewed as behaviors that must be stopped and squarely placed on the shoulders of the perpetrator. Lewis (1993) raises important questions about the dilemmas that therapists face when they are unwilling to subvert theory to advocate or support clients who are in such abusive situations. Incidents such as incest should not be misread as a cultural practice but seen for what they are—the result of sexist oppression. Working with families in a cross-cultural context around these issues requires the greatest patience and sensitivity to differences between the clients and the therapists.

Therapist's Stance

The therapist enters the counseling relationship as a collaborator and learner. Delineating one particular style or stance for every therapist that uses a culture-sensitive approach would be impossible because many have retained their MOO. However, therapists who embrace the approach of placing culture at the center of the therapeutic process act more as cultural bridges than "experts." Such therapists are willing to learn from the family about its history, culture, and current context.

In my own work with families, I have retained many ideas from my earliest training in marriage and family therapy. I take an ecological perspective (Arnold, 1994), and integrate ideas from Family-of-Origin (Bowen, 1978), Structural (Minuchin, 1974), and Conjoint Family Therapy (Satir, 1967). However, all of these ideas are viewed through the prism of cultural knowledge gained from the family as well as a general understanding of how culture shapes family dynamics. Sensitivity to culture adds to the search for origins of problems and the spectrum of solutions.

In addition to these considerations, I integrate into my work an understanding of the forces of oppression as determining and destructive forces in cultural and family life. I place an emphasis on the emotional and psychological effects of oppression on the family because oppression influences family structure, shapes family history, and mediates family dynamics. It would be difficult for me to work with any family without noticing the impact of sexism on the dynamics within the family. Often families are faced with multiple forms of oppression that generate a complex set of circumstances. Racism, sexism, and classism are powerful proscriptions consigning families to a constant barrage of social and personal trauma. Such families are often referred to as "chaotic" or "problem saturated." I call these families "oppression saturated."

It is important to note here that all families experience the effects of one or more forms of oppression. Sexism is the most commonly acknowledged form of oppression that families must wrestle with. Families are shaped by the sexist roles that are evident in a patriarchal society. Families are often driven into therapy in an attempt to negotiate constraining sex roles that disadvantage women and girls and privilege men and boys. Racism is often ignored in counseling, as is the impact of poor or working-class status and sexual orientation. Families may also be oppressed due to religion, physical disabilities, language fluency, and immigrant status.

Interventions Related to Theory

The goal of CST is to assist families with gaining an understanding of their social context and to use that understanding to mobilize their resources to resolve problems and improve family functioning. I often refer to culture and social context as being like water to fish or air to human beings, essential but not part of our conscious awareness until there is a threat of losing it. Families most often know their social and cultural context but still have little awareness of how the pieces fit together to detract from or enhance family functioning. A set of strategies for encouraging such awareness has emerged from clinicians that take a CST approach. Key elements in the CST approach include:

- Initial phase—listening for the spoken and unspoken elements of the family's story(s); noticing the family presentation. In the telephone interview you might get one impression of a family, but when you meet them they are entirely different. For example, a Caucasian woman might call about her acting-out adolescent daughters, but when they arrive for the first session you see the obvious: her children are biracial/bicultural, Iranian and Polish. The elements of difference within a family are often apparent yet never spoken about among family members.

- The cultural context—posing the question, "What is your ethnicity?" or "How do you think racism affects your family?" This question is often hard for therapists to broach but it is the most helpful thing you can do early in the session or counseling process because you start the collaborative relationship at this point. The client becomes the teacher and you become the learner. This question changes the dynamics in the relationship by bringing into the room the expert knowledge of the clients. An example of this occurred in the videotape when I asked John and Martha about their ethnicity. Their responses were quick, clear, and instructive.

TH2 (23):   I'm curious about something, Martha and John. I'm really curious about your families . . . like what your ethnicity might be . . . If you go back in your family tree, where do people come from?

M (32):   Ah, I'm 100 percent Polish, if that means anything.

F (37):   Irish . . .

F (38):   English, Swedish, German.

TH2 (26):   Let me ask you something. Do you think the Irish is dominant?

F (39):   Oh, definitely. Definitely . . .

F (40):   Stubborn, hardheaded, stand my ground. No, you are not going to walk over me anymore.

- Probing for more cultural knowledge—filling in the gaps in the therapist's knowledge regarding the cultural group(s); searching for a deeper understanding of the particular family's cultural context (intercultural and biracial issues, levels of acculturation, immigration patterns, language fluency, sexual orientation, religious, gender, and class differences): listening for variations, similarities, and points of conflict. The following sequence regarding religion is an example of probing for cultural knowledge. We learned that Martha's ethnic and religious background is mixed. In future sessions, it would be necessary to probe deeper to find out how Martha came to identify herself so strongly with her Irish ethnicity rather than the other parts of her ethnic and cultural heritage.

TH1 (69):   I want to ask one more question. Just to get information. Is religion important to you guys?

M (56):   It is to me.

TH2 (60):   What is your faith?

M (57):   Catholic.

F (62):   I am a converted Catholic.

TH2 (61):   So religion wasn't part of your upbringing?

F (61):   It was, but I was raised Southern Baptist, and it was . . .

TH2 (62):   How does that happen to a good Irish girl like you?

F (62):   Well, see, my mother is not the one that's Irish. My father was Irish. My mother's the English, German, American Indian in there . . .

■ Cultural links to the problem—posing tentative cultural explanations for the existence of the problem(s). This involves selecting a theme or behavior(s) commonly shared within a particular cultural group; conveying to the family the possibility that the problem(s) grow from their cultural or social context. The themes of strong Irish women and immovable Polish men in the videotape are examples of linking cultural explanations to the problem.

TH1 (25):   . . . The Polish are well known for being stubborn, too.

TH2 (30):   . . . They are like rocks . . .

F (41):   Like that ___ down on his backside.

TH1 (28):   And the more you push . . .

THE2 (31):   The more they get close to the earth like rocks. It's an embeddedness.

TH1 (29):   Do you think that makes any sense to you guys?

M (33):   Oh, definitely.

TH2 (32):   . . . Irish women are really strong.

F (42):   Behind every great man there is a woman.

M (34):   An Irish woman?

F (43):   Pushing, pushing.

■ Elicit family's feedback—posing the questions "Does any of this make sense to you" or "What part of this makes sense to you?" At this point, the therapist is listening for areas of confirmation and rejection of the tentative cultural explanations of the problem(s). Family members are asked to generalize to other areas of their lives if they confirm the explanations and to discuss differences within the family. If the family or specific members of the family reject the cultural explanations, they are asked to offer their thinking on the problem(s). John and Martha were asked if the cultural themes we were pursuing in the session made "any sense" to them (Th1 [29], p. 000). There was a response of firm agreement from Martha and more tentative agreement from John (M [33], p. 000).

- Links to oppression—teasing out what is cultural from what are adaptive behaviors or responses to oppression. The counselor takes a teacher stance and places the concerns of the family in a larger social, historical, and political context. Sometimes this is totally new information for the family other times it is an "ah ha" experience, "We knew that but never thought of it in that way before!"
- Cultural explanations elaborated or revised—involving an ongoing process throughout counseling in which the therapist and the family continue to expand, revise, and alter their perceptions of the family's ability to thrive, survive, and cope with challenges. Examples or stories from the historical and extended family's experiences are used to frame the current issues.
- Affirming strengths—continuing throughout the process the therapist identifies and affirms the strengths within the family and their cultural group(s). If the family is intercultural or interracial their courage and fortitude in coming together and staying together against the odds is affirmed.

Techniques

- Establishment of a climate of acceptance and appreciation—embracing the family and their differences. Flexibility, creativity, humor and a willingness to expose a little of oneself is useful in the initial stage of counseling.
- Genogram—an essential assessment tool and ongoing aid to the counseling process (McGoldrick, Gerson, & Shellenberger, 1999). I often start the genogram, and then ask families to take it home, think about it, add to it, and create categories such as household pets or no pets, who sang or danced in the family. This adds to the number of specific family themes and gives the family more control over the process.
- Family-of-origin scripts—ask clients to tell what their lives would have looked like if they had fulfilled the expectations associated with their cultural group, for instance, "What would your life look like if you had lived your life according to your family's expectations" or "like a good _____ man (or woman)?" The follow-up questions explore how family members stuck to the script or improvised on it. Pointing out the gendered nature of family scripts is important to helping family members see the disappointment or frustration they may feel with their role in the family or the role of other members in the family.
- Search for group identification issues—teasing out internalized oppression (Arnold, 1997) issues among family members. Strong identification with one's group(s) does not automatically indicate a positive view of one group(s) or oneself. Asking each family member "What do you like best about your ethnicity (or group), and "What do you like least about your

group?" can help family members articulate how they feel about their ethnic identification. The internalized negative messages can burden clients with feelings on a continuum from self-doubt to self-hatred.

- Depathologizing—empowering clients, eliminating the climate of blame and hopelessness within the family, and identifying the cultural factors and sociopolitical circumstances that generate the problem(s). The counselor's comments can affirm seemingly odd behaviors, such as not trusting persons outside of one's group, avoiding the police, flashes of anger, or draw a wide circle around an abusive partner with statements such as "That seems like a reasonable response to oppression." The follow-up discussions are geared toward empowering family members to change the larger circumstances, to resist oppression.

- Victory stories—collecting a set of positive stories from the historical and extended family's experiences. Family members can develop a family history project or seek accurate information about a family myth or incomplete story. Stories of flight toward freedom, migration struggles, and survival against the odds provide families with a more accurate picture of their history and intergenerational struggles. This process is one of reclaiming and recovering identities if they have been hidden or suppressed, as in the case of Jews, European ethnic origins, gay people, or mixed racial identities.

Video Case Example

The first strategy in CST is fundamental to all approaches: listen well to each member of the family. To listen to the family's story, while staying alert to the diversity within the family and the varying perspectives of individual members on their common story, is the first task of the culturally sensitive counselor. The therapist is listening for the cultural messages that underlie the story. She is listening for the *unspoken* as well as the spoken. Additionally, because the therapist does not know every nuance of the cultural life of the family, she must listen for the blank spaces in her own knowledge. Ferreting out the ethnic identification issues, especially the negative internalized aspects, of individual family members is also an important part of the process. The therapist must bring the cultural knowledge she has about the family's cultural group(s) and ask the family for help with filling in the blanks and sorting out what may or may not be true for their family.

I listened carefully to the story that John and Martha told about their family. It seemed to me that they had very different styles in dealing with life's daily ups and downs. John presented as more accepting of things he feels are beyond his control. On the other hand, Martha presented as tenacious and less accepting of things beyond her control.

TH2 (3):   But are you really struggling with being a stepparent?

M (11):   Being a parent in general. Not necessarily being a stepparent. Just being, you know. Plus the kids are at that age, you know, early teens, they are, drive you nuts.

TH2 (4):   So, Martha, what do you think keeps you together and what pulls you apart?

F (4):   . . . I get monosyllable answers to anything I ask his son when he is there. Most of the time he won't even say 'hello' or 'goodbye' unless he's told to say 'hello' or 'goodbye.' I've gone rounds on this where I just try, and try, and try. I get so perturbed and upset with it that, I just throw my hands up and say 'I don't care if he ever speaks to me again.'

My thinking at that point was that the difference in styles might be related to different ethnic origins. I wanted to hear more about how they relate to one another and their children. The question that was forming in my mind was a simple one: "What is your ethnic background?" When I ask this question, clients are often confused by it and need a little time to process the question. John did not need a period of reflection. His response was: "I am 100 percent Polish. *If that means anything*" (M [32]).

I found his response interesting. The second part of his response, "if that means anything," might suggest that he has internalized a negative image of his ethnic group, and, therefore, himself as powerless. He is a member of one of the most commonly maligned ethnic groups in the United States; Polish jokes can be told in almost any setting. Of course, I would have pursued and confirmed this in later sessions.

Martha stated that her ethnicity is Irish but quickly added other components of her identity: English, Swedish, and German. When I asked Martha if she thought the Irish was dominant her response was:

F (39):   Oh, definitely. Definitely.

TH2 (27):   So the Irish is really . . .

F (40):   Stubborn, hardheaded, stand my ground. No, you are not going to walk over me anymore.

She embraced her Irish identity with pride and passion. I asked myself, what might cause her to distance herself from the English, Swedish, and German parts of her cultural heritage? Again, in later sessions I would want to tease out what her fervor for the Irish identity means to her sense of self. However, in the first session (in this case the only session with John and me), it was too early in the process to unravel her complete cultural history. But the reactions of Martha and John indicated that their ethnicity has been an important component of their personal identities.

The immediate identification they have with their ethnicity suggested to me that ethnicity might provide an effective, believable, and nonpathologizing explanation for their family conflict that each would accept. I searched for cultural messages. I wanted to know what each thought about general cultural themes such as "strong Irish women" (McGoldrick, 1996) and distance as a response to conflict in Polish families (Folwarski & Marganoff, 1996). Martha and John resonated to these themes. Of course, over time each theme would be more fully developed and articulated. But, even in this brief encounter, John and Martha glimpsed that their behavior might have something to do with their ethnic roots.

It is important to note here that ethnic and gender identities are intricately tied together. In fact, I believe there is no stand-alone ethnic identity that can be separated from being male or female. For instance, the identity of an African American woman is similar yet different from that of an African American male and vice versa. The same would be true for any other cultural group such as the Polish and Irish.

John's desire for closeness with Martha certainly has cultural implications. The distant, nonresponsive behavior associated with Polish men does not promote intimacy. The tendency to avoid conflict and to distance by way of alcohol is a strong cultural pattern among Polish families. Additionally, the gendered societal pattern that tells men that they should be autonomous and self-reliant converges with, strengthens, and legitimizes the ethnic pattern. MohdZain (2001) states that: "[C]ounselors need to encourage men to get in touch with their deep sense of longing for relational connectedness . . . (p. 59).

On the other hand, the strong, self-asserting, sometimes antagonistic, approach associated with Irish women does not always create a warm intimate space for the men in their lives, either. The braiding of the Irish cultural message "men are dogs" and need "pushing" with the societal message that women are responsible for the emotional well-being of men keeps Martha locked in an unproductive pattern of frustration and disappointment. I would challenge the gendered pattern of Martha's feeling that she must take care to promote the emotional relationship between John and his son. I would also encourage Martha to see men as capable and possessing emotions, albeit with different forms of expression.

Their learned cultural styles will have to change if they are to each get what they want from the relationship. In my summary comments to them, I suggested that they must learn to turn off the cultural tapes that keep them apart.

> **TH2 (90):** . . . You two are really working against some real heavy, I think, cultural messages. I think the cultural message that women aren't responsive is a very clear Polish cultural message for men . . . And I think that the message that men are irresponsible and have to be pushed is a very strong Irish message for women. And finding out how to work with those messages, how to turn off some of those culture tapes; that will allow you to be together . . .

If I were to continue with this family in counseling I would seek to learn more about each of their cultural identities, migration, extended family, and social support issues. I would search for and highlight family strengths. I would attempt to change their patterns by encouraging them to resist cultural prescriptions that are no longer useful for their family. Because I am African American, I would open a space to give them an opportunity to explore race and racism with me. I would include the children in future sessions. I would point out for the benefit of all family members that the children have a wider range of cultural behaviors and beliefs from which to select.

Summary

Underlying Culture-Sensitive Therapy is the fundamental belief that culture and social context are powerful shaping forces in the lives of families and their communities. Every family is unique, yet every family is nested within a cultural and sociopolitical context. Clinicians and educators who place culture at the center of their work are more likely to get closer to the ideal of tailoring (Carlson, Sperry, & Lewis, 1997) their treatment and training to the specific needs of the clients. Accessing the family context can serve to depathologize family problems, and reveal family strengths and strategies to solve those problems. A CST focus raises the expert status of the family and actively involves family members in the search for solutions. Because CST uses the language and experiences of the family, there is nothing new to learn, only something to do differently. The number of clinicians who view culture as a major organizing principle in their work with families is increasing across all theoretical orientations.

Training Opportunities

The Family Institute of New Jersey
Monica McGoldrick, Director
312 Amboy Avenue
Metuchen, NJ 08840

They offer workshops, an annual conference, and a three-year training program. Scholarships are available. The FINJ is committed to cultural diversity and the empowerment of the disenfranchised in society.

The Family Institute of Westchester
Betty Carter, Director
147 Archer Avenue
Mount Vernon, NY 10550

Training is focused on gender issues. Specializing in gay and lesbian couples and families. They offer a three-year training program and a two-year externship.

In addition to the above formal training centers, there are numerous conferences and workshop offerings. Listings in professional news outlets such as *Counseling Today*, published by the American Counseling Association, and *The Monitor*, published by the American Psychological Association, are resources.

Additionally, all Council for Accreditation of Counseling and Related Educational Programs (CACREP)-approved counseling programs include multicultural curriculum materials.

REFERENCES

Arnold, M. S. (1994). Ethnicity and training marital and family therapists. *Counselor Education and Supervision, 33*(2), 139–147.

Arnold, M. S. (1997, May). The connection between multiculturalism and oppression. *Counseling Today, 39*, 42.

Arnold, M. S., Parmer, T., & Sanders, J. L. (1995). Interview with Monica McGoldrick: On the significance of cultural factors and gender in family therapy. *The Family Journal: Counseling and Therapy for Couples and Families, 3*(3), 265–273.

Atkinson, D. R., Morten, G., & Sue, D. W. (1979). *Counseling American minorities: A cross-cultural perspective.* Dubuque, IA: W. C. Brown.

Bowen, M. (1978). *Family therapy in clinical practice.* New York: Jason Aronson.

Carlson, J., Sperry, L., & Lewis, J. A. (1997). *Family therapy: Ensuring treatment efficacy.* Pacific Grove, CA: Brooks/Cole.

Cromwell, R. E., & Ruiz, R. A. (1979). The myth of macho dominance in decision making within Mexican and Chicano families. *Hispanic Journal of Behavioral Sciences, 1*, 355–373.

Falicov, C. J. (Ed.). (1983). *Cultural perspectives in family therapy.* Rockville, MD: Aspen Systems.

Falicov, C., (1998). *Latino families: A guide to multicultural practice in therapy.* New York: Guilford.

Folwarski, J., & Marganoff, P. P. (1996). Polish families. In M. McGoldrick, J. Giordano, & J. Pearce (Eds.), *Ethnicity and family therapy* (2nd ed., pp. 658–672). New York: Guilford.

Green, R. (1998a). Race and the field of family therapy. In M. McGoldrick (Ed.), *Re-visioning family therapy: Race, culture, and gender in clinical practice.* New York: Guilford.

Green, R. (1998b). Training programs. In M. McGoldrick (Ed.), *Re-visioning family therapy: Race, culture, and gender in clinical practice* (pp. 111–117), New York: Guilford.

Grier, W., & Cobbs, P. (1968). *Black rage.* New York, NY: Basic Books.

Gushue, G. V. & Sciarra, D. T. (1995). Culture and families: A multidimensional approach. In J. G. Ponterotto, J. M. Casas, L. A. Suzuki, & C. M. Alexander (Eds.), *Handbook of multicultural counseling* (pp. 586–606). Thousand Oaks, CA: Sage.

Hair, H., Fine, M., & Ryan, B. (1996). Expanding the context of family therapy. *American Journal of Family Therapy, 24*(4), 291–304.

Hardy, K. V., & Laszloffy, T. A. (1992). Training racially sensitive family therapists: Context, content, and contact, *Families in Society: The Journal of Contemporary Human Services, 364–370.*

Hardy, K. V., & Laszloffy, T. A. (1998). The dynamics of a pro-racist ideology: Implications for family therapists. In M. McGoldrick (Ed.), *Re-visioning family therapy: Race, culture, and gender in clinical practice* (pp. 118–128), New York: Guilford.

Hare-Mustin, R. T. (1978). A feminist approach to family therapy. *Family Process, 17*, 181–194.

Harper, F. D., & Stone, W. O. (1974). Toward a theory of transcendent counseling with Blacks. *Journal of Non-White Concerns in Personnel and Guidance, 2,* 1991–1996.

Ho, M. K. (1987). *Family therapy with ethnic minorities.* Newbury Park, CA: Sage.

Hoffman, L. (1981). *Foundations of family therapy: A conceptual framework for systems change.* New York: Basic Books.

Hooks, B. (1984). *Feminist theory: From margin to center.* Boston: South End Press.

Laird, J. (1998). Theorizing culture: Narrative ideas and practice principles. In M. McGoldrick (Ed.), *Re-visioning family therapy: Race, culture, and gender in clinical practice* (pp. 20–36). New York: Guilford.

Lewis, J. A., (1993). Family therapy and intrafamilial child sexual abuse: Theoretical Dilemmas. *The Family Journal: Counseling and Therapy for Couples and Families, 1*(3), 237–239.

Lewis, J. A., & Arnold, M. S. (1998). From multiculturalism to social action. In C. C. Lee & G. R. Walz (Eds.), *Social Action: A mandate for counselors* (pp. 51–65). Alexandria, VA: American Counseling Association and ERIC Counseling and Student Services Clearinghouse.

McGoldrick, M. (1996). Irish families. In M. McGoldrick, J. Giordano, & J. Pearce (Eds.), *Ethnicity and family therapy* (2nd ed., pp. 544–566). New York: Guilford.

McGoldrick, M. (1998). *Re-visioning family therapy: Race, culture, and gender in clinical practice.* New York: Guilford.

McGoldrick, M., Gerson, R., & Shellenberger, S. (1999). *Genograms: Assessments and interventions.* (2nd ed.). New York: W. W. Norton.

McGoldrick, M., Giordano, J., & Pearce, J. K. (Ed.). (1996). *Ethnicity and family therapy* (2nd ed.). New York: Guilford.

McGoldrick, M., Pearce, J. K., & Giordano, J. (1982). (Eds.). *Ethnicity and family therapy.* New York: Guilford.

Minuchin, S. (1974). *Families and family therapy.* Cambridge, MA: Harvard University Press.

Minuchin, S., Montalvo, B., Guerney, B. G., Jr., Rosman, B. L., and Schumer, F. (1967). *Families of the slums.* New York: Basic Books.

MohdZain, A. Z. (2001). Feminist family therapy and the male perspective. In J. Carlson (Series Ed.) & K. M. May (Vol. Ed.), *Feminist family therapy: The family psychology and counseling series* (pp. 53–63). Alexandria, VA: American Counseling Association.

Nichols, M. P., & Schwartz, R. C. (1995). *Family therapy concepts and methods* (3rd ed.). Boston, MA: Allyn & Bacon.

Nichols, M. P. (1987). *The self in the system: Expanding the limits of family therapy,* New York: Brunner/Mazel.

Pedersen, P. (1991). Multiculturalism as a generic approach to counseling. *Journal of Counseling and Development, 70*(1), 6–13.

Satir, V. (1967). *Conjoint family therapy* (rev. ed.). Palo Alto, CA: Science and Behavior Books.

Sue, D. W., & Sue, D. (1999). *Counseling the culturally different: Theory and practice* (3rd ed.). New York: John Wiley and Sons.

Thomas, A., & Sillen, S. (1972). *Racism and psychiatry.* New York: Brunner/Mazel.

Tinloy, M. Y. (1978). Counseling Asian-Americans: A contrast in values. *Journal of Non White Concerns, 6,* 70–76.

Wrenn, C. G. (1962). The culturally encapsulated counselor. *Harvard Educational Review, 32,* 444–449.

3 Adlerian Family Therapy

JAMES ROBERT BITTER
East Tennessee State University

ANGELA ROBERTS
Oswald Center, Wales, United Kingdom

MANFORD A. SONSTEGARD
Private Practice, England

James Robert Bitter

Alfred Adler (1870–1937) was a contemporary of Sigmund Freud. For about nine years, Adler participated in the early meetings of the Vienna Psychoanalytic Society, presenting clinical papers and case studies that were often at odds with Freud's position. By 1911, the differences between Freud and Adler were so great that the two men and their respective followers split forever.

Adler eventually called his approach *Individual Psychology*, but, far from a singular focus on individual clients, Adler used the term to denote *holism*. Unlike Freud's reductionism, Adler posited an indivisible human organism that could only be understood systemically. Unified by a self-created *goal of completion, perfection, or significance*, Adler believed that each person functioned *purposefully* within *an interactive social context* that both influenced that person's development and was, in turn, transformed by the presence of that person (Ansbacher & Ansbacher, 1956).

The first social system that humans experience is most often the family. It is within this context that children first seek ways to belong and develop patterns of behavior and interaction that they hope will bring them significance and value. While family structure and parental processes have an influence, children are always active agents within the family. They impact the development of others in the family as much as others influence them. They test the uses and limits of power, strive for success, discover connections and boundaries, enact roles, find their place among siblings, form coalitions, follow or challenge rules, and note similarities and differences. All of these activities are expressed in purposive behaviors and patterns of communication (Walsh & McGraw, 1996).

The family system always changes and adapts with the birth of each child. Each child's effort to find a place with the family system is enacted between birth and school when mistakes in assessment, understanding, and implementation are easily made. In addition, parenting is still the only *adult* activity for which neither license nor *effectiveness* training is required; indeed, one is not even required to be an adult to start a family. Families without problems, therefore, are mythical. Adlerians believe family problems—and even dysfunctions—are the result of discouragement: discouraged and discouraging children usually interact with equally discouraged and discouraging parents in patterns that are often generations old and culturally or community supported.

Between the end of World War I and the early 1930s, Adler and his colleagues persuaded the Viennese school system to establish thirty-two child guidance centers (Mosak, 1995). Adler would use these centers to consult with families in an open forum, helping parents, teachers, and interested community members to understand family interactions, family–school relations, and a "problem child's" view of life and life's demands. Adler's early work with families is the basis for what is now called *Adlerian Brief Therapy with Families* (Bitter, Christensen, Hawes, & Nicoll, 1998).

Modern Adlerians still use open forums when they can be established, because the community support for change in an open setting has much more impact on the family than anything a therapist can initiate alone. Further, the confidentiality that is lost in an open forum is supplanted by an augmented degree of accountability. Interventions with the parents and the children must make "common" sense as well as psychological sense within the family's community (Christensen, 1993). Whether applied in an open forum or a private session, however, Adlerian family therapy is a "treatment process [that] stresses education to promote growth and change. The therapist addresses the interactions within the family system and changes the interpersonal system" (Carlson, Sperry, & Lewis, 1997, p. 42).

A Brief Description of Theory

Adler designed a psychology and therapeutic approach that were both comprehensive and widely applied (Ansbacher & Ansbacher, 1956). Individual Psychology addressed personality development, child development, education, psychopathology and criminal behavior; religion, spirituality, and values; gender issues; and parent–teacher education as well as therapeutic interventions with individuals (children and adults), groups, couples, and families (Sweeney, 1998). As with all dynamic approaches, *Adlerian family therapy* has developed and changed over the six decades since Adler's death. It is now both a self-contained model of therapy and a reflection of the theoretical foundations presented in Individual Psychology.

Theoretical Foundations

Adler (1931, 1927/1969) described the basic movement of children as *striving*. Adler suggested that children first experienced *inferiority feelings* that motivated their initial striving for success. When we watch children today, we often see striving without any sense of inferiority initially until their striving falls short of an intended outcome. Whether *inferiority feelings* precede *striving* or vice versa, it is clear within the first six months of life that they are "two phases of the same psychological phenomenon" (Adler, 1930, p. 36). The overall movement of children, when it is not thwarted, is toward growth: toward becoming more capable, being able to do more, and achieving success.

As children grow older, their striving starts to reflect the *goals* (both immediate and long-term) that their *patterns of behavior* intend. Here, Adler was influenced by the philosophy of Hans Vaihinger (1965). Vaihinger believed that humans were less concerned with *truth* than they were with *use*. He had noted that humans often act on ideas and ideals or goals that are purely *fictional*. These fictions sometimes serve as behavioral guides ("honesty is the best policy"), idealistic positivism ("all people are created equal"), or interactional rules ("treat others well, and they will treat you well"). It does not matter that fictions cannot be scientifically proven. Their value is in their *usefulness;* that is, whether they help most people to live a better life. Adler (1927/1969) adapted Vaihinger's concepts into a *teleological* model of human personality. Adler posited that young children eventually, perhaps by the age of five or six, create a *fictional life-goal* that is their picture of themselves as *perfect, complete* or *"self-actualized,"* to use Maslow's (1970) term.

Adler believed that once the life-goal was formed, it acted as a fictional endpoint, a *fictional finalism*. The life-goal *unified the personality* such that every thought, memory, feeling, action, interaction, immediate goal, value, belief, and conviction could be seen as a *movement* toward and a reflection of that goal. This unified movement was expressed over time in *patterns of behavior* and *characteristic approaches to coping and living* that Adler called the person's *style of living* (or lifestyle). Understanding a person's goals, purposes, or intentions accounts for what people do, makes sense out of their repetitive patterns, and tells us much about who they are and who they intend to be.

The context in which children first exercise their striving and develop a style of living is most often the family. It is the family system that will have the greatest influence on the development of individuals. Adler (1929, 1927/1969) delineated three approaches to parenting that were more likely to rob children of their courage and to exaggerate normal feelings of inadequacy into a dysfunctional *inferiority complex*. The three approaches were *feeling sorry for the child* (which was very common when children were born with or developed early organ inferiorities); *pampering, over-protecting, or spoiling* the child; and *hating, neglecting, rejecting, or abusing* the child. Of these approaches, pampering, doing for the children what they can do for themselves, and spoiling, giving in to children's unreasonable demands, are the most common today, while hated, neglected, and abused children constitute one of society's most serious social problems. Rudolf Dreikurs, Adler's most important student and colleague, also noted the importance of considering *family atmosphere, family values,* and children's *goals of misbehavior* (Grunwald & McAbee, 1985), concepts we will define. The single most important Adlerian contributions to family therapy are based on Adler's (1929, 1931, 1927/1969) original formulations of *family constellation* and *birth order*.

The family constellation is a human system that includes "parents, siblings, and others living in (or impacting) the family of origin" (Griffith & Powers, 1984, p. 41). As a system, it includes the people involved, their developmental processes, and their actions and interactions. In this sense, the family is an organismic system rather than a mechanistic one: It will develop and change over time; it may reach a similar endpoint from multiple directions; it will strive to become more ordered and complex rather than chaotic and disordered; it will occasionally produce unpredictable, spontaneous, and perhaps even creative activities or movements; and, always, it generates *meaning* that emanates from and governs the system (von Bertalanffy, 1968).

Adler (1930, 1931, 1938) generally gave only passing consideration to parents and other adults in the family constellation before he would fully develop the influence of birth order on children. Adlerians believe that birth order is a *vantage point* from which one views life. There are many possible ways to view life from a fixed vantage point; The only thing that a person cannot do is change the vantage point itself. An oldest child, therefore, may interpret being "first" in any of many possible ways and adopt behaviors to maintain that position, but she or he will not all of a sudden see and approach life as, say, a youngest child. Adler assigned descriptions to five birth positions that served as probabilities or working hypotheses until confirmed or modified by a given family; these five psychological positions were the experience of being an *only* child, an *oldest* child, the *second of only two*, a *middle* child, or a *youngest* child of three or more.

Only children and oldest children share in common a high *drive* for achievement, a drive that may or may not ultimately be fulfilled (Falbo, 1977). Both have mom and dad all to themselves for at least a short period of time, and the parents seem to have a strong influence on initial development. The only child, however, will never be dethroned. She or he will most likely develop adult language systems sooner and orient personal striving in relation to parental values. "Only children may be conservative, but they also may become rebels. They either take on all the parents' values or rebel against them. They seldom take a middle course in life" (Grunwald & McAbee, 1985, p. 72). Only children are often used to being the center of attention; they can be pampered, overprotected, and spoiled; they may also receive the care, affection, and resources that contribute to a high degree of success.

Oldest children almost always become impressed with their position of being "first," and they will do almost anything to maintain that position. Oldest children can be timid, extremely sensitive, or easily hurt, especially when their position in life is threatened. Many oldest children are serious, dependable, responsible individuals who seek adult approval. They may also have a tendency toward perfectionism. Oldest children often accept the parental mandate that they "be a good model" for their siblings. They may be experienced by the younger children as "bossy," but oldest children believe that they are simply giving guidance.

The second-of-only-two child maintains a very strong focus on the oldest child, most often becoming the opposite of what they believe the first to be. He or she may feel very competitive with the first child, always trying to catch up, and can appear to always be in a race. In whatever the first born excels, the second will avoid and vice-versa. Second-born children will never have their parents' undivided attention. They seek parental attention by being different.

The birth of a third child turns second-borns into middle children. Middle children often describe their position as "squeezed-out," and they see life as unfair, with neither the advantages of being first nor the service associated with being youngest. They sense that the oldest and the youngest align against them, and that they take the fall. They, too, are sensitive to criticism, feeling that they are being bossed. They develop a life stance of comparing themselves to others, often rebelling against both expectations and traditions. They often seek a peer group to whom they give more allegiance than the family.

Youngest children will never be dethroned. They are usually good at putting others, especially their parents, in their service. They may act helpless and dependent, but they are, in fact, the strongest of all the children, for they get the most with the least effort. Youngest children can be good entertainers. They often are good observers, and they use their observations to develop in areas and ways that none of the older children have attempted. Because they are the "babies" of the family, they may experience themselves as special or, conversely, as unwanted. The special ones often get pampered, overprotected, or even spoiled. The unwanted may sense that they do not have a place, are hated or neglected.

Adler's (1931) emphasis on the child subsystem was evident even when he discussed parents in an unhappy marriage. While he acknowledged the dangers for children raised in a disruptive marriage, he immediately suggested that they would be skilled at reading dissension and playing one against the other. His emphasis on children as active agents in the family is important to remember.

Children do not merely react: they interact, often having more success at changing their parents than the other way around.

Adlerians consider a number of additional variables in describing a family constellation: how many years there are between siblings; the effects of disabilities, illnesses, death, trauma, and so on; the effects of parental favoritism or childhood talent or beauty; whether a child is the only boy or girl in the family; the effect of being a twin; what happens when families are blended; and the effects of special attention from grandparents, to name a few. Each of these considerations taken together helps to form a picture of how each person fits into the system and how each is likely to act and interact. It is the actions and interactions within the family and the interpretations that each person assigns to these that give initial meaning to children's lives and to the family as a whole.

Adler believed that no person or system could be understood outside of the social context. Further, no part would determine the whole. The person was more than the sum of individual parts, because each person will *use* his or her parts to achieve *goals* and *purposes* created in and for specific contexts. The family, being one of the most influential contexts, both impacts individuals within it and is changed by them. Today, Adlerians note that the family is also part of a larger community and culture, each of which have values and rules of interaction about how men and women should be, about raising and educating children, about getting along with self and others, and so forth. Just as no person can be understood outside of his or her social embeddedness, neither can a family be understood divorced from the social contexts of its existence. In this sense, Adler and his followers, like many of the Gestalt therapists, have been significantly influenced by Jan Smuts' (1926/1996) beliefs about *holism*.

An Adlerian Value System

Following his return from World War I, where he served as an Army Physician in Krakow, Adler introduced the concept of *Gemeinschaftsgefühl* ('community feeling') into his psychology (Hoffman, 1994). He had noted that the survival of the human psyche—the human soul—even in the most devastating of circumstances, depended on this community feeling, this feeling that one was connected to humanity and that one's well-being was related to his or her connection with others. In everyday life, community feeling had an action line that Adlerians call *social interest* (Ansbacher, 1992). People with social interest are interested in the welfare of others and are seldom self-absorbed. They function cooperatively and live interdependently. They develop a sense of courage, have self-confidence, and greet life with a sense of humor. They are not lost in their private logic and sense of things, but share a "common sense" with others in the human community. Adler felt that *Gemeinschaftsgefühl* and social interest were the antithesis to pathology in individuals and to dysfunction in families and other human systems.

Adler (1938) believed that social interest existed in children as an innate potential that required development through its exercise in everyday life. In this sense, breast-feeding is an example of an early cooperative experience between mothers and babies. Even such early nurturing, however significant, is not enough. Adler felt the mother would need to redirect the child, first toward the father and then toward others. Coupled with parental *encouragement*, social interest stands in opposition to exaggerated feelings of inferiority and discouragement.

The development of community feeling and social interest acts as a guide for the Adlerian therapist. It says that some ways of living are better than others, that not all ways of coping and living are of equal value. The community feeling and its social interest serve as a foundation for moral action, and, in its largest implementation, is at the heart of living both a healthy and even a spiritual life. Some thirty years after Adler's death, the eminent researcher of stress, Hans Selye (1974), would sum up a healthy and productive life in a similar manner: Humans ought to live in such a way as to "earn thy neighbor's love" (p. 126).

Rudolf Dreikurs's Contributions

During the years from 1920–1934, Rudolf Dreikurs worked with Adler and other Adlerians in the Viennese Child Guidance Clinics (Terner & Pew, 1978). Dreikurs moved to the United States before World War II. Over his distinguished career, he would organize, systematize, and extend the use of Adlerian psychology in psychiatry, counseling, music and art therapy, family and group psychotherapy, and education. Dreikurs introduced open-forum family counseling to the United States by integrating an understanding of the family's constellation with a unique approach to discovering and disclosing the goals of children's misbehavior.

Dreikurs (1940) first formulated the four goals of children's misbehavior to delineate the purposive etiology of disturbing behaviors in children (see Figure 3.1). Dreikurs's four goals, *attention-getting, power struggle, revenge,* and *demonstration of inadequacy* (or *assumed disability*), are typological descriptions/explanations for consistent patterns of misbehavior in children. Dreikurs (1957) declared that all misbehavior in children could be understood from the perspective of one of these four goals. These goals were immediate (as opposed to life-goals) and were largely unconscious or out of the child's awareness. Indeed, a lack of awareness facilitates a certain fluidity of action and safeguards the child from having to consciously confront the uselessness of misbehaviors.

Adlerians use three levels of investigation to determine the child's mistaken goal. The first is to obtain a description of the child's behavior from the parents in specific detail (often asking for the last time the problem occurred). The second is to discover what the parent and child do interactively around the problem behavior, with the child's response indicating which goal is intended. The third is to ask the parent(s) to disclose what feeling is present when the misbehavior is in full exhibit. Dreikurs believed that parents would feel exactly the way that the child wanted them to feel. By aligning this data, it is possible to ascertain the goal(s) toward which the child is striving (see Table 3.1).

Further, Dreikurs (1950) believed that goals could be disclosed to children in a tentative manner, and that a correct disclosure would lead to what he called a

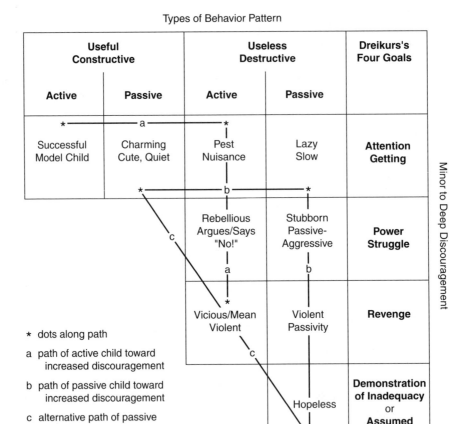

FIGURE 3.1   Dreikurs's Four Goals of Children's Misbehavior

recognition reflex, a little smile and a twinkling of the eyes that a child might give when "caught." Dreikurs's remarkable system raised unconscious goal processes in children to consciousness and gave them an opportunity to consider other approaches to their *need to belong*. By adding goal recognition and disclosure to an understanding of the family constellation, Dreikurs was able to structure and systematize the family therapy interview for generations of Adlerian counselors (Bitter et al., 1998; Christensen, 1993; Dreikurs, Corsini, Lowe, & Sonstegard, 1959; Grunwald & McAbee, 1985; Lowe, 1971, 1982; Sherman & Dinkmeyer, 1987; Sweeney, 1998).

Dreikurs (1948) was one of the first to assert that family atmosphere had an enormous impact on the development of children. Initially, he differentiated the effects of autocratic/authoritarian parenting and permissive parenting from what he called *democratic* parenting. The latter, today, would be called authoritative–responsive parenting. Parents who function in an autocratic or

TABLE 3.1   Identifying the Mistaken Goals of Children's Misbehavior

Mistaken Goals	Observed Behavior	What the Child Does When Corrected	Adult Response	The Change Process
Attention Getting	Model Child Charming Pest Nuisance Lazy	Stops for a short period even just a few minutes	Perhaps initially pleased with "good" behavior; Then irritated annoyed or frustrated	Do the unexpected; Avoid undue attention; Take time for training; Change the situation
Power Struggle	Rebellious Argues Fights Stubborn Passive-Aggressive	Keeps going with the misbehavior May intensify misbehavior	Angry Challenged Defeated	Sidestep all power struggles; Act, don't talk; Set limits & stick to them
Revenge	Viciousness Violence Vandalism Meanness Violent Passivity	Intensifies misbehavior Misbehavior becomes mean	Hurt	Stop training & focus on relationship; Encourage strengths; Return friendship for hurt
Demonstration of Inadequacy or Assumed Disability	Acts Hopeless Gives Up	Limited or no interaction	Despair Helplessness	Encourage any positive behavior or movement; Change the atmosphere & enjoy the child as she or he is

authoritarian manner are oriented toward control; they seek obedience. Initially, children may try to meet their parents' demands (out of fear more than desire), but they almost always rebel, either overtly or covertly, as they get older.

Such children grow up without confidence in their own judgment. They always need someone to tell them what to do and how to do it. This lack of confidence in their ability to make intelligent decisions prevents them from achievement based on decision making. Often they know the answer, yet leave the question unanswered out of fear of making a mistake (Grunwald & McAbee, 1985, pp. 18–19).

Permissive parenting, on the other hand, robs children of the courage and stamina needed to confront difficulties in life and to adequately resolve the basic tasks of life. Children in a permissive atmosphere are pampered and often indulged or spoiled because parents give into the children's demands in order to keep the peace. They may be overprotected when parents feel that life is overly dangerous: They want to protect their children, but they really communicate a sense of fear about just living everyday.

Dreikurs's approach to child-rearing expected parents to be leaders in the family system, leaders who would prepare children to live in a democratic society where they would have to think and act for themselves but also in cooperation with others (Dreikurs, 1948; Dreikurs & Soltz, 1964). Dreikurs (1957) saw teachers and parents as sharing in the responsibility of raising the next generation and extended his approach to the classroom (Dreikurs, Grunwald, & Pepper, 1982). In both settings, he posited a basic *social equality* between adults and children; not that adults and children were the same, but that they had the same right to respect, dignity, and value, regardless of any personal quality or deficiency (Dreikurs, 1971). Dreikurs taught parents to use *encouragement* and *natural* or *logical consequences* to effect the kind of democratic leadership that he felt children needed in order to be prepared for society and for life (Dreikurs & Grey, 1968).

In the little over a quarter century since Dreikurs's death, the concept of family atmosphere has grown as a therapeutic assessment. We now recognize that there are hundreds of atmospheres that more specifically describe family processes. For example, families can be oriented toward fun (play), athletics, or activities in general. Families can be socially committed or, on the other hand, withdrawn and protective. Families may be child-centered, or, conversely, children may be considered a bother and constantly dismissed. Families may be rule-, routine-, ritual-, or culture-bound. And families can be a jungle, dangerous, explosive, or unpredictable when parents are abusive. Family atmospheres set the tone of daily living and act as the contextual background for personal and systemic development.

When both parents agree on a belief, value, or conviction, Adlerians call it a *family value.* Family values have the effect of placing an unavoidable demand on the members of the system. Each child must decide whether he or she will accept the required value or rebel against it, but can seldom simply ignore it. When both parents support a given religion, believe in the importance of education, or expect everyone to contribute to the welfare of others, they are promoting their family values. It is possible that *all* of the children will accept and implement the value in their lives. It is just as possible that only a few of the children will adopt the family value. Sometimes birth order predicts who will follow the value and who will not, but all children will address a true family value in some manner. Adlerian family therapists believe that children are most likely to misbehave in relation to perceived family values.

Dreikurs also introduced an assessment process by asking an individual parent or the family as a whole to present a *typical day.* By exploring who does what with whom at each point during the process of the day, Adlerians are able to identify mistaken goals, ineffective communication and interaction, the family atmosphere, and family values as well as pressure or conflict points in daily living and coping strategies. The typical day will reveal family structure and boundaries, roles, routines, rules, and levels of cooperation or competition (Sherman & Dinkmeyer, 1987).

Conscious Motivations

In an attempt to bridge the work of Adler and Dreikurs, Ansbacher (1988) suggested that there might be three types that could subsume Dreikurs's four goals. Bitter (1991) later reformulated these types into three new goals for children's misbehavior that he believed were more conscious than the goals in Dreikurs's typology. These goals, *getting, self-elevation,* and *avoidance,* also seemed to occur less frequently in comparison to Dreikurs's goals.

Conscious motivations are more common in very young children than older ones even though they require a certain level of conscious decision making. Very young children, for example, sometimes operate on the assumption that they should *get* whatever they want, no matter what it is or to whom it belongs. The motivation of *getting* can be completely conscious, because the child has no social prohibition against taking what is wanted. Adults may think of taking something as "stealing," but the child is simply getting what she or he wants. In fact, until children develop a concept of "misbehavior," much of early childhood behavior will be consciously motivated.

We can use lying as an example of the conscious motivations of both *self-elevation* and *avoidance.* In order to lie, even a young child must know what "the truth" is and consciously say something false. Otherwise the child may be mistaken, but she or he is not lying. Let us say, for example, that a boy tells his first-grade teacher that he met Michael Jordan during the summer, and Michael liked him so much that he took him to meet his family and then to a basketball game. Assuming this story is a lie, what is the motivation? In a general sense, it might be to gain attention, but the more likely hope is that he will gain in importance (*self-elevation*). Let us also consider a more expedient lie: A parent returns home to find a broken mirror, and asks the son who broke it; the boy denies with intensity that he broke the mirror—even though his culpability is later established. What is his motivation for lying? Clearly, the most probable goal is to *avoid* punishment.

Other examples of these goals easily come to mind. Trying to buy or bribe another child to be a friend happens with young children who want a specific friend, but feel they can't *get* or have that child's friendship. Some temper tantrums also serve the goal of *getting* just what the child wants. Tattling can be for the purpose of gaining attention, to be sure, but it also may be to make oneself look good (*self-elevation*) at the expense of another. When one child in a family is the best at being "bad," there is almost always a "saint" who gains in *self-elevation* by comparison. Procrastination is a common example of *avoidance* of failure that even preschoolers will employ.

The relationship between conscious and unconscious goals can be represented as a pie chart (see Figure 3.2). It should be noted that Dreikurs's more unconscious goals will account for far more misbehavior in children than Bitter's conscious motivations, and that Adlerian family therapists will almost always

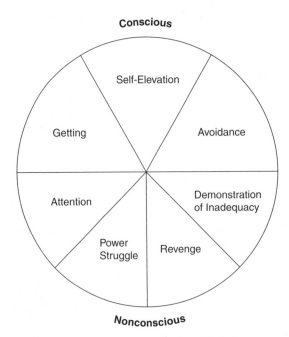

**FIGURE 3.2   Conscious and Nonconscious
Motivations of Children's Behaviors**

rule out Dreikurs's goals before considering the newer ones. Certain developmental and systemic conditions will, however, increase the probability that conscious motivations are involved in family interactions: (1) when the children are preschoolers; (2) when there is intense competition between two siblings—especially in two-children families; (3) when one or both of the parents punish severely; (4) when one or both of the parents are excessive worriers; or (5) when the misbehavior is oriented more toward child–child interactions than parent–child interactions.

The Mistaken Notions of Adults with Children

Each of the goals delineated above requires a substantial amount of involvement on the part of parents. Indeed, up until the age of about ten years old, children seeking one of Dreikurs's four goals are essentially oriented toward their parents. When we ask, "Why do parents become so easily locked into repetitive, useless interactions with children?" we are forced to conclude that children can be very powerful beings and that parents must also have some purpose in sustaining the interaction.

Early in Dreikurs's career, he suggested that parents, too, would develop mistaken goals in their constant interactions with children, but he never fully developed the idea (Dreikurs, 1948). Sticking with just Dreikurs's four goals for the moment, it is possible to construct a typology of mistaken notions (or goals) that parallels his formulation as we presented it in Figure 3.1. These mistaken goals account for adult participation in most mistaken interactions with children, as long as those adults (e.g., parents, teachers, or child-care workers) have a sustained relationship with the children and respond to them in repetitive ways. We call these adult goals a *demonstration of adequacy, control, revenge,* and a *demonstration of inadequacy* as an adult with children (see Figure 3.3). As Dreikurs (1948) originally suggested, the goals of adults and children eventually align, locking them into interactive processes that neither really finds productive.

No parent has a child or starts a family with the intent of being dysfunctional. Parents want to be "good" in their new roles, to *demonstrate* that they are at least *adequate* to the job and capable of successful child-rearing. Unlike their newborns, parents will have developed a *style of living* that remains relatively constant across most of their roles and activities. They will usually implement this same style in their approach to children. So how do parents measure their success? The proof, as it is said, is in the pudding. They—and everyone else—look to see how the children are doing.

While early parenting is often consumed with the excitement of a new birth and the daily requirements for survival, growth, and development, it is not all that long before parents start to act in ways they believe will elicit useful behavior in children. Initially, these interventions are designed to promote the appearance of parental or family values: parents may seek demonstrations of harmony, pleasantness, loyalty, politeness, industriousness, achievement and success, activity, or athletic ability, to name a few. The parents may try to create whatever they believe to be an "ideal" child, paying attention to appearance, talent, friendliness, doing things right and proper behavior; their children may always seem to be cooperative in public. A high use of rewards and praise are the most common tactics used initially to elicit desired behaviors. As children become more demanding, however, it is not uncommon for parents to let even five- and six-year-olds do what they want, again giving the appearance that back talk, constant demands, and misbehaviors are normal for these ages.

Children, on the other hand, are terrific observers, and they will develop behaviors and processes that push parental "buttons" and make parents feel that they are required to respond. Adlerian family therapists almost always find that the attention getting and power struggles, the getting and self-elevation processes of children, are directly related to parental or family values.

Even if children were not great observers, parents do a great deal to communicate to children what will "work." Excessive talking has been a particularly common practice in the last quarter century. Parents hope that talking will work so that they won't have to act. They want their children to have "good" reasons for everything, because the parents didn't like the explanation "because I told you so" that they received. As a result, the children of these parents are "parent deaf" as well as becoming excellent debaters. Parents also signal their interests and concerns with excessive supervision, worry, or anxiety. If there are at least two children in a family with a parent who worries excessively, it is probable that one

FIGURE 3.3   Mistaken Notions of Adults with Children

<table>
<tr><th>Goals</th><th colspan="2">Minor to Deep Discouragement</th></tr>
<tr><th></th><th>An Attempt to Stop Useless Behavior in Children</th><th>An Attempt to Elicit Useful Behavior in Children</th></tr>
<tr>
<td>GOAL #1
Demonstration of Adequacy

To feel worthwhile & approved through children's "good" behavior; to be a "good" parent, teacher, or child-care worker; to be successful with children</td>
<td>Excessive talking, Excessive Supervision, Excessive Worry or Anxiety
Criticism; fault-finding (indicating "it's not good enough")
Setting up a lie
Use of punishments (Spanking, yelling, restrictions)
Overprotection
Pampering
Getting involved in the children's fights
Reminding; coaxing; nagging; demanding; lecturing; disparagement</td>
<td>Promoting the appearance of family values (Harmony in the family; pleasantness; loyalty; industriousness; high achievement; success; getting results; being athletic, etc.)
Attempting to create ideal children (Cooperation is simulated)
High use of rewards and praise
Letting children do what they want to do</td>
</tr>
<tr>
<td>GOAL #2
To Be in Control of Children

To gain a sense of power or superiority over the child rather than the situation; to show the child who is "boss"; to be on top</td>
<td>Defensive; stonewalling
Nagging; demanding; lecturing; disparagement
Pleading; yelling; anger and frustration outbursts
Arguing with the child; fighting with the child
Declaring yourself "the boss"
Announcing decisions made for the child
Demanding the child do as he or she is told to do
Extreme overprotection or pampering</td>
<td>Effectiveness with Children Requires Most of These Qualities:

Self-control
Courage & the courage to be imperfect</td>
</tr>
<tr>
<td>GOAL #3
Revenge

To assert power and seek revenge or to hurt back and get even; to overpower with hurt for perceived injury or loss of respect</td>
<td>Contempt; striking back for perceived embarrassment
Name-calling; disparagement
Extreme and severe punishments
Retaliation or hurting statements
withdrawal of love; neglect; rejection
Vicious battles, fights, or arguments
Violent outbursts
Child abuse (physical and emotional)</td>
<td>Self-esteem, self-worth, & self-acceptance
An interest in and acceptance of children as they are
Proactive training of children
Modeling, sharing responsibility
Encouraging children & others
Use of democratic/authoritative–responsive discipline: natural & logical consequences acting without excessive talk emotion coaching staying connected & involved</td>
</tr>
<tr>
<td>GOAL #4
Demonstration of Inadequacy as an Adult with Children

To be left alone and relieved of responsibility; to avoid facing or handling problems with children</td>
<td>Avoid Interaction with child
Disowning responsibility as adult with children (e.g., parent, teacher)
Despair; Giving Up
Saving face by declaring bankruptcy with children
Wanting to get rid of an unmanageable child</td>
<td></td>
</tr>
</table>

child will try to act in line with the parent's needs while the other will give the parent exactly what worries him or her the most. Criticism and other forms of correcting the child are ways of communicating avenues for attention getting and power struggles. It is as if parents are saying, "Do this, and I will respond."

We have worked with families that have placed a high value on honesty, and we often see the parents actually setting up a lie. A parent returns home to find the son's bicycle lying in the driveway. What good does it do to ask the son: "Did you leave your bicycle in the driveway . . . again?" Of course, the child will say, "No." The son is working on a 50–50 chance that the parent will buy the explanation, and he will *avoid* punishment and/or *keep* the parent *busy* with him. But the "honesty" button has now been pushed, and the child is guilty of both bicycle misuse *and* lying.

Overprotection and pampering reflect parental desires to have happy and safe children, but they are done in such a way that children learn quickly to demand service or run from control. Just as getting involved in our children's fights (to promote harmony or achieve "peace and quiet") tells children how to get parents' attention, so does reminding lead to forgetfulness, coaxing to slowness or laziness, and nagging, demanding, and lecturing to parent deafness and active or passive resistance. No amount of punishment (spankings, yelling, or restrictions) does anything other than tell the child that he or she is winning, and that the parent is *losing* in the demonstration of adequacy. It is important to remember that parents get discouraged, too, and the more negative the interaction, the more discouraged, the participants are.

Some parents have a high need for *control* from the very beginning. Other parents may shift to the goal of control as they feel their ability to "handle" their children slipping away. Children, too, can up the ante by initiating power struggles with their parents, even while parents are still seeking to demonstrate adequacy. In the end, *power struggles* and *control* become two sides of the same coin, the mutually reinforcing goals of power interactions. Trying to control the child is an admission that parents have lost two other useful forms of control, self-control and control of the situation. Nothing caps this defeat more than arguing or fighting with the child, demanding the child do as she or he is told, or declaring that the parent is "the boss around here." The anger that the parent feels is augmented by an equally strong feeling of defeat.

Whether sought by children or parents, *revenge* is a goal that always reflects feelings of hurt. In parents, such feelings may follow from a perceived injury or a loss of respect. In either children or parents, seeking revenge is always the devil's goal, because everyone loses: to seek revenge is to dig two graves. Because parents are so much stronger than children are, both physically and psychically, adult revenge tends to overpower. It can come out as contempt or striking back for perceived embarrassment. It can be active, as in name-calling or disparagement, extreme or severe punishments, or passive as in the withdrawal of love, neglect, or rejection. At its worst, emotional, physical, and sexual abuse may reflect an adult goal of revenge. Intense family therapy will almost always be required.

It is seldom that parents totally give up and *demonstrate inadequacy with children* in an effort to be relieved of the responsibility. On occasion, when one parent is super-responsible, the other parent, especially if that parent never really wanted children, may demonstrate inadequacy and remove him- or herself from parenting altogether, avoiding most interactions with children or disowning responsibility for the kids. Some parents with an extremely unmanageable or criminal child also give up and are even open to getting rid of the child.

The mistaken notions of adults with children closes the teleological, interactive loop in our approach to family therapy (see Table 3.2). Together with Dreikurs's typology, Adlerian family therapists can use this conceptualization as a cognitive/systemic map for understanding parent–child relationships. While the goals of children tend to be immediate, adult goals may be either immediate or reflective of the individual's style of living. Mistaken goals are fictional but extremely powerful in organizing personal and family experiences and motivating repetitive behaviors. Helping parents to see how their goals become locked into the children's mistaken goals is often a prerequisite for change in Adlerian family therapy.

Relevant Research

Adlerian psychology and psychotherapy as a whole is one of the more researched and validated models in current use (Sweeney, 1998) with an increase of 37 percent in studies in the eighties over the previous twelve years. It helps that the *Journal of Individual Psychology* (also called *Individual Psychology*) has been developing theory and practice and reporting research findings since before Adler's death. Watkins (1992a, 1992b, 1992c, 1994) reviewed and critiqued Adlerian research, finding strong support for those aspects most related to Adlerian family therapy: birth order and social interest. In addition, the two largest parenting programs in the United States, STEP (Dinkmeyer, D., Sr., McKay, G., Dinkmeyer, D., Jr., 1997) and Active Parenting (Popkin, 1993), are directly related to Adlerian principles. The research related to Adlerian parenting programs has continually demonstrated their effectiveness over the long term and shown them to be methodologically sound (Burnett, 1988).

In the future, the most significant research needs will be for studies that focus on treatment outcomes, comparing Adlerian family therapy with other leading approaches in family systems therapy. In addition, the multicultural assessments of Arciniega and Newlon (1995) need to be extended into effectiveness studies with multiple cultures, especially those related to African American, Hispanic, and Asian communities. Similar studies related to Adlerian approaches with gay or lesbian families are also needed.

Clinical Perspective

Adlerian psychology is a broad theoretical and therapeutic orientation that includes clinicians, counselors, and educators in the full range of the helping

TABLE 3.2   Mistaken Notions of Adults with Children: Narrative Descriptions

	What the Adult Is Saying	What the Adult Is Feeling	New Goals for the Adult	Some Corrective Changes
GOAL #1 *Demonstration of Adequacy* To feel worthwhile & approved through children's "good" behavior; to be a "good" parent, teacher or child-care worker; to be successful with children	I am only a "good" when my child behaves well; I have a place/status if I am seen as a good parent, teacher, child-care worker, etc. if my child needs me	Delighted with "good" behavior; wants others to see good child; a sense of worth as a "good" parent, teacher, etc. or annoyed, irritated, needs child to behave	To be good enough as you are—regardless of mistakes; courage; to allow independence & share responsibility; to separate self-worth from child's behavior	Have the courage to be imperfect; respect the rights of children; give recognition instead of undue attention; emotion coach; give choices; increase order, not control
GOAL #2 *To Be in Control of Children* To gain a sense of power or superiority over the child rather than the situation; to show the child who is "boss"	I only count when I am boss; when I am in control ("I can't control the situation, so I will try to control the child and make the child mind"); when my authority is not challenged or questioned	Angry; provoked; challenged; wanting to assert power or control; a sense of losing the battle to be a "good" parent, teacher, child-care worker, etc.	Self-control rather than child control; to gain power or mastery of the situation rather than the child; admit that you can only control yourself, not the child	Be friendly in the face of child's power; throw in the towel; withdraw from power struggles; solve the problem, don't just end it; act, don't talk; use natural and logical consequences
GOAL #3 *Revenge* To assert power and seek revenge or to hurt back and get even; to overpower with hurt for perceived injury or loss of respect	I am continually being hurt by the child so I will hurt back; I feel "no good" as a parent, teacher, etc. so the child won't feel good either; I'll make the child behave, or he/she will be sorry	Hurt; enraged ("How can the child do this to me?"); wants to hurt back or get even; a feeling of extreme embarrassment caused by the child's behavior	To do things with the child, not against her or him; avoid retaliation; rebuild a positive relationship; return "good" for hurt; maintain personal adequacy in spite of child's provocations	Withdraw; maintain order with a minimum of restraint; encourage; be friendly; invite child into your trust; negotiate; accentuate the positive in both the child and yourself
GOAL #4 *Demonstration of Inadequacy as an Adult with Children* To be left alone and relieved of responsibility; to avoid facing or handling problems with children	Given the situation, I am "no good" as a parent, teacher, etc.—maybe no good at all; I would like to demonstrate that no one else can handle the child either; I have done everything possible & I quit	Despair; wanting to give up; depleted; severe embarrassment and feelings of inferiority or inadequacy in the role of parent, teacher, child-care worker, etc.	Have faith in the child; accept the child as she or he is; act because something needs to be done regardless of consequences or feelings of others	Encourage; encourage; encourage and stick with it; develop a non-demand relationship with the child; have faith in the child even when she or he has none in self; enjoy being with the child

professions. Within this model, there are those who use the construct of psy-chopathology and effectively address the goals, purposes, and lifestyles involved in various types of individual dysfunction (Maniacci, 1999; Sperry, 1995; Sperry & Carlson, 1996). Some of these Adlerian clinicians have extended their psychopathological model into marriage and family therapy (Carlson & Sperry, 1996; Carlson et al., 1997). By far, however, those who do most of their therapy in the models of Adlerian family counseling (Christensen, 1993; Dreikurs et al., 1959), Adlerian family therapy (Sherman & Dinkmeyer, 1987), or Adlerian brief therapy (Bitter et al., 1998; Nicoll, 1999; Nicoll & Hawes, 1984) pre-fer systemic and interactional assessments to individual diagnoses. Indeed, the most common "internal" assessment that Adlerians tend to use in relation to family members is Dreikurs's and Soltz's (1964) term, *discouragement.*

Discouragement is the feeling that one is losing the courage that is needed to face the tasks of life and the requirements of daily living. It is a feeling that can only exist in a social context, when people feel thwarted in their efforts to reach certain ideals or achieve certain goals or purposes. Both parents and chil-dren can become discouraged, and the enactment of behaviors and interactions based on mistaken goals indicates varying levels of individual and systemic dis-couragement. Discouragement always reflects an ambition that is deemed unreachable.

Manford Sonstegard (personal communication, August 1, 1999) was asked to see a little boy and his mother. The young lad, Martin, would run and fall down out of breath. The English doctors could find nothing wrong with him. The boy was one of three children. The eldest brother was a wizard musician; the youngest was a charming and skilled writer; Martin was a middle child. He played English football, and he had been on the school team. He was now having difficulty keep-ing his position, and, as a consequence, he felt endangered. Sonstegard asked him what he was going to do when he grew up, and he replied that "he would play football for England." His answer reflects an ambition not unlike many play-ground basketball players in the United States who dream of growing up to "be like Mike." Few will make it. In Martin's case, his physical symptoms were an escape hatch, a protection born of his discouragement.

Martin's discouragement may seem individual, but it takes place within the contexts of the family, school, and society in which he lives. Martin is growing up in a family where "talent" is the norm, and where it appears to come easily to his brothers. It is extremely likely that there is also a family value related to achieve-ment, communicated by the parents' interest in everything their children can do. Martin feels compelled to meet the highest of standards. His talented brothers have also gone to the same schools and achieved in the same communities in which Martin must thrive. Both internal and external pressures have aligned to force Martin to take a stand, and his assessment is that he is "not up to it." He is discouraged.

A similar assessment can be assigned to all repetitive interactions between adults and children when mistaken goals or purposes are involved. While parents who are trying to *demonstrate adequacy* and children who are *seeking attention* account for relatively low levels of discouragement, those parent–child processes involved in *revenge* are much more serious and reflect extreme discouragement. James Bitter (Carlson & Kjos, 1999) worked with a family in which the mother appeared to be in charge, and the father would withdraw until the noise level or some other irritant got to be too much for him. Then he would intervene, often discouraging the mother, who was struggling to meet the needs of three children. Mother tried to gain *control* by attempting to get each of the children to do things exactly right, and she communicated her intent through excessive talking that most of the children ignored. Michael, the oldest child, developed a pattern similar to that of his father, taking short stabs at fighting with his mother (a power struggle) and then withdrawing to his grandmother's house. The individuals in this family felt discouraged, and they continually found themselves locked in discouraging, yet purposive, interactions.

Adlerian family therapy as a model approaches family assessment with a number of systemic questions that, once answered, reveal both systemic processes and levels of family discouragement. What role does each member play? Are the parents the functional leaders of the family or does some structural realignment need to take place? How happy is each family member with her or his position, tasks, or function? What is it like to live within this family? What is the general atmosphere in the family and what could be added to increase family commitment, social interest, and family harmony (or even joy)? What are the specific problems, issues, or challenges faced by individuals within the family, how are they enacted, and what purposes are served? What are the assets of each family member and of the family as a unit?

Even when families and their members are relatively functional, Adlerians seek to build solid relationships based on mutual appreciation and encouragement, with the parents as leaders and support from relatives and the larger community. Adlerian family therapy can be remedial when necessary, but it is also preventative, seeking to strengthen the psychological tolerance of family members and enabling them to meet life's challenges with togetherness (cooperation) and courage. When individuals fail to develop psychological tolerance, courage, and social interest, they escape into neurosis or psychosis, physical symptoms and disorders, or even personality disorders. Adlerian family therapists see these individual dysfunctions as stylized and patterned difficulties, usually indicating severe discouragement and a retreat from the tasks of life (Adler, 1935a/1996a, 1935b/1996b; Sperry & Carlson, 1996).

Even when severe pathologies have been identified and diagnosed, Adlerians believe that family therapy is at least required as part of the treatment approach. Discouraged individuals are also discouraging individuals, and families are both the most common repository of that discouragement and the best hope for change. No matter how minimal or severe the difficulties, they most often arise in the context of family, and the resources for redirection and reorientation are also usually found within the family. Carlson et al. (1997) have devised an excellent approach to ensuring treatment efficacy with families that involves a careful tailoring of treatment to specific family needs.

The Process and Flow of Therapy

The structure of Adlerian family therapy is founded on the original design of Rudolf Dreikurs (Dreikurs et al., 1959). Adlerian family therapists rely on this structure to facilitate the process and flow of therapy. While this therapy can be conducted with single-unit families quite competently, its effectiveness, with all but the severest of family dysfunctions, is greatly enhanced in an open forum or group setting (Bitter et al., 1998; Christensen, 1993).

In open-forum family counseling, many families come together to join in a psychoeducational experience with a family in focus. The counselor or therapist in these sessions has two clients: the family in focus and the audience. The process emphasizes purposive interactions within the system as opposed to intrapsychic experiences. Little is disclosed that could not be observed by anyone watching the focus family in a public setting. The audience provides a "common sense" check on the process and changes initiated by the counselor. Indeed, the normalization, community support, and encouragement offered by the audience is often more effective in promoting change than any of the therapist's interventions.

Private, single-unit sessions are indicated when severe dysfunctions and confidentiality are prime concerns, e.g., in cases involving family violence or abuse, court-ordered referrals, trauma, crisis, identified psychopathologies, or when a family simply feels more comfortable in a private session. In these cases, the therapist is both a facilitator and a nonjudgmental representative of the human community who seeks to join with the family but also to invite the family to reconnect with a shared humanity. Christensen (1993) has offered the clearest delineation of the flow of therapy.

Meeting the Family

Adlerian therapists seek to make a person-to-person contact with each member of the family that is characterized by mutual respect, friendliness, and an interest in the welfare of each family member. Although the family's concerns tend to surface rather quickly, the initial focus of the therapist is on meeting each person and getting to know the family constellation. Making contact with and valuing family members is the cornerstone to positive change. A human relationship of mutual respect may not be all that matters, but it is the foundation for everything that matters.

Adlerian therapists neither remove themselves from nor impose themselves on the flow of therapy. They lead through a natural engagement that follows from their interest in the family. Adlerian therapy involves a dialogue, a conversation with purpose. It helps if therapists come to family sessions with a clear focus unburdened by other concerns. Beginning therapists may have a tendency to ask internalizing questions, such as "How am I doing?" or "What will the family think of me?" These are the types of questions that distract the therapist from fully meeting each person in the family. It is better to start with "process questions": "What am I noticing?" or "What do I need to do first?" These questions bring the therapist's social interest into the session and start the process of therapy usefully, as an engagement between social equals.

Assessing the Family System

Therapy typically begins with the therapist asking the parents to describe the family constellation, including the names and ages of the children and a consideration of the effects of birth order. The therapist also wants a sense of the impact that any miscarriages, stillbirths, illnesses, childhood defects, or early deaths may have had on the family. Finally, the therapist needs to know if there are any other people living within the family or in relatively constant contact, such as grandparents, aunts or uncles, or other caregivers.

Clarity about the family system is so important that Adlerians seldom proceed to the next step until they are able to describe the system to the family at least verbally and in a manner that helps the family make "sense" out of their life together. Several tools may assist the therapist in developing a picture of the family system. First, by asking each parent to provide three adjectives for each of the children the therapist can often ascertain both the manner in which the children find their place in the family as well as the issues that are important to the parents. The adjectives provided will also suggest the ways in which the children have interpreted their birth position. A family genogram can be used to develop multiple representations of the family from a phenomenological perspective (Sherman & Dinkmeyer, 1987). Making a guess about the family constellation is sometimes used to orient the family to the counselor's thinking model. If the guess is correct in the eyes of the parents, it signals that they are on the same wavelength. If the guess does not fit the parents' understanding of the family, it still gives them a framework within which they can correct the therapist's understanding.

Problem Descriptions

Problem descriptions can emerge while the therapist is still gaining an understanding of the family system, especially if there is one child about whom the parents have their greatest concerns. Sometimes, therapists may actually have to ask if there is anything that either or both of the parents would like to see going better at home. Because family problems will be assessed teleologically in this model, it is essential that specific examples of each concern be elicited. Based on Dreikurs's process for goal recognition, there is a common pattern to the questions that Adlerian therapists ask.

- When was the last time (or a recent time) that this problem occurred?
- How did the problem progress, step by step? What did the child do? Then what did you do?
- What was the child's next response? Then what did you do? (repeated as necessary)
- In the midst of the problem, how did you (the parent) feel?

The information generated by these questions is usually enough to identify the goals of the children's misbehavior. Parents most often respond both externally and internally in the exact manner that the children desire. Child misbehavior will almost always have a direct relationship to parental or family values, family atmosphere, or the mistaken notions held by the adults in the family. These adult stances are most clearly revealed in the disciplinary procedures the parents use.

The Typical Day

There are occasions when the parents are unable to specify a specific problem. In these cases, having parents report on the events that occur in a typical day allows the therapist to isolate specific events that can be explored as purposeful interactions. Asking about a typical day also elicits a wealth of information about parental needs and values, family values, the family atmosphere, and any mistaken notions under which both adults and children may operate. A typical day usually reveals patterns of parent–child interactions. It is highly probable that the parent–child interaction reported in getting the child up in the morning will be repeated at or before bedtime.

Sharing Diagnostic Hypotheses

When Adlerian family therapists identify tentative goals for either children's disturbing behaviors or parental interventions, they share these goals as hypotheses that can be tested through an interview with the children. Adlerians present these hypotheses in the everyday language of the parents and may use stories or metaphors to illustrate the goals that motivate mistaken interactions. When these hypotheses are developed in relation to significant aspects of the family constellation, family atmosphere, or family values, the information often seems to make sense out of what has seemed to the parents to be chaos.

Interviewing Children

Children reveal a lot about their relationships in the way that they enter a room, where they choose to sit, and how they interact before any interventions are made. This is especially true in an open forum. Careful observation gives the therapist hints about where to start.

Adlerians seek to enlist children as partners in understanding the family. A common beginning might be: "Your parents have told us what it is like to be parents in your family, and now I need expert help in order to understand what it is like to be children." While it is common to use part of the interview to reeducate children and redirect mistaken approaches, the most important function of the interview is to test the hypotheses regarding the goals of misbehavior.

Goal disclosure works best in relation to a specific event or misbehavior. It is more effective for the therapist to ask about a particular problem than investigate generalities. "Dad tells me that Jeremy and Annie fight quite a lot, and that the two of you had a fight coming here today." Once it has been established that the children and the therapist are talking about the same event, goal disclosure can begin in a tentative manner that suggests or reveals goals. From an edited excerpt of an Adlerian family therapy demonstration (Carlson & Kjos, 1999, pp. 9–11 [in study guide]):

THERAPIST (TH):   How do you bug the dog?

CHILD (CH):   I pull the tail, the collar.

TH: Do you have any idea why you do that?

CH: Maybe because she does bad things sometimes.

TH: Your idea about that is that maybe it's because sometimes the dog does something wrong and other times it's for something else. I have another idea about why that happens. Would you like to hear it?

CH: Yeah.

TH: Could it be that you sometimes fool with the dog to see how many times you can get your mom to tell you to stop?

CH: Yeah.

TH: And why would that be fun?

CH: I don't know.

TH: I have another idea. Let me try this one. Could it be that sometimes you do it to demonstrate to your mom that she can't make you stop?

CH: Yes, sometimes.

In this dialogue, the goals of attention and power were suggested as the therapist's guesses about the child's goal. While the child acknowledged the goals consciously, Adlerians tend to place greater faith in disclosures that yield a *recognition reflex*, especially in young children. This reflex serves as a confirmation of the diagnostic hypothesis. If there is no recognition of any kind, the hypothesis is rejected, and the therapist must reevaluate and proceed on the basis of new data.

Reorienting the Family

Family reorientation proceeds from an understanding of the essential needs and purposes of the system and the individuals within the system. In general, the first goal of reorientation is *safety and encouragement* for everyone involved. *Caring about the welfare of the family* is the foundation for this goal. People change, grow, and develop from an appreciation of their strengths, in the company of others who have faith in them, and when options and hope are newly realized. *Reframing* and *normalizing family experiences* are often the main avenues for generating such hope.

Systems will change in a positive direction when structured for success and when even one person can disengage from the repetitive patterns that maintain dysfunction. The second goal of reorientation, therefore, is to *establish* or *reestablish the parents as leaders* of the family. This goal is often met by helping each parent to become a support for the other, and to discontinue activities that have consciously or unconsciously undermined the other in the eyes of the children. Sometimes, this process is as simple as learning to "mind your own business." Sometimes, work with the couple's relationship may be necessary before family work can continue.

The third goal of reorientation is to help the family members *unlock the repetitive patterns and mistaken goals or notions* that have maintained ongoing problems. Helping parents understand the mistaken goals of children and confront their own mistaken notions already starts the "unlocking" process. It is extremely difficult to continue interactions once purposes have been disclosed and the unconscious has been made conscious. Because Adlerians want parents to be the natural leaders of the family, we almost always start by helping parents to exercise self-control and to change their roles in adult–child interactions.

When the therapist senses that parents are available for leadership, some form of parent education will be offered with recommendations specifically designed to redirect the mistaken motivations of children. Effective *parent education* based on *democratic* living and *social equality* with children is the fourth goal of reorientation. Task recommendations are usually based on the implementation of natural and logical consequences, encouragement, and/or emotion coaching (see Dinkmeyer et al., 1997; Dreikurs & Grey, 1968; Gottman, 1997; Popkin, 1993).

Families do not change in therapy sessions: they change *between* therapy sessions. To ensure the greatest possibility of success, Adlerian recommendations may address only one problem at a time; and that problem may be the easiest of the parents' *essential* concerns. It is important that the family achieves some success with the initial recommendations so that members will feel encouraged to implement additional recommendations after future sessions. In an open forum, the audience is an excellent resource for parent education. In private sessions, therapists can often lead a discussion that will help the family members to generate their own options for change.

Once recommendations have been identified, the Adlerian family therapist will always seek a commitment from the parents to follow through on implementation. When parents say that they will "try," the counselor helps the parents to reevaluate their commitment to change. Sometimes, too much change has been suggested all at once. Sometimes parents fail to see the relationship between what they will do and desired changes in the children. And, sometimes, parents find it hard to rely only on self-control and to give up their familiar attempts to control the child. When parents agree to implement recommendations for the next week, the first interview is usually terminated.

Follow-up Sessions

In follow-up sessions, Adlerian therapists ask the parents to review the issues, problems, and concerns that brought them into therapy. This review is followed by a restatement of the findings (the goals or purposes motivating parent–child interactions and/or the children's misbehavior). Next, the parents are asked to recount the recommendations that were given in the last session and to report on the results of implementing those recommendations. Adjustments can be made when necessary, and the therapists will often offer additional support as sessions proceed. Both parents and children need lots of encouragement and support while engaging in the difficult tasks associated with meaningful change.

Application to Diverse Family Forms

As with any approach to family therapy, Adlerian therapists recognize that the Caucasian, professional, two-parent-(heterosexual couple)-led "nuclear" family has been designated "normal" in the United States, and many aspects of this society are designed to support this form. Those families that fall outside of this norm often experience discrimination and are expected to cope, regardless of their circumstances, as well as or better than those families that fall within the norm. Adlerians approach those who live in "alternative" family forms as having both external stressors and difficulties that impact the family and internal stressors that can lead to family disturbance.

Single-Parent Families

Carlson et al. (1997), citing Census Bureau statistics, have noted that the number of single-parent families is rising, with 25 percent of all children and 50 percent of African American children currently residing in these homes. These homes may be led by either the mother or father with mothers currently making up the majority of single-parent homes. Even when one parent is absent from the home, however, that parent is not necessarily absent from the lives of children. It is possible for the outside parent to be a support to the rest of the family, but it is far more common for the outside parent to be either lost or another stressor in the life of the family. Carlson et al. go on to note that "60 percent of single women with children under the age of six are employed [and] . . . that approximately one-third of the workforce may be single parents at some point during their work lives" (p. 28).

Many of the external stressors are obvious. Women, being the majority of single parents, earn less money than men in general do, and they will have to make a life for their family with fewer resources. The absent parent will almost certainly have a psychological presence in the family, especially if the parents are recently separated and have not regrouped or made a successful break. Handling work and child care can easily force the single parent into seventy- and eighty-hour work weeks, and that is if adequate child care is available and affordable. Single parents will almost always need outside support systems and specific parenting skills tailored to each family's needs. In many cases, the internal coping skills of the parent may be fine if the person were not totally overloaded with little time for rest or self-care. Helping the parent handle outside stressors and build outside support systems are often essential parts of therapy.

Blended Families

Another family form that warrants special attention is the blended family. While many of these families essentially require a parent and his or her child(ren) to integrate a new "spouse" into the family, most people think of the "Brady Bunch" when blended families are addressed. When working with blended families, Adlerian family therapists pay close attention to the meaning associated with the *blending* of the family. If there is an intact parent–child relationship, what are the expectations that the parent has of the new spouse? What relationship will exist between the new spouse and the child? In general, effective blending requires the new spouse to adopt a less involved and intense relationship with the child(ren), at least initially. How will this new family system and structure relate to the absent parent(s)?

When families blend, it is not uncommon for birth order within the overall family constellation to change. If children are under five or six years of age when the blending occurs, they will tend to adopt a family position within the larger family constellation. A child who was the second-of-only-two may become a middle child or even the youngest of quite a few. On the other hand, children who are in school and older than five or six may retain the birth position they assumed in their original family. In such a case, the blended family can now have two psychologically oldest children, a set of middle children, and one or more babies. If all of the children are older when the family blends and then another child is born, the children will most likely be "hers," "his," and "theirs," with the newborn adopting a very special position that can easily include high levels of pampering and spoiling.

Gay and Lesbian Families

In general, gay and lesbian families experience all of the same family difficulties that occur in heterosexual families, but they are also under an almost constant threat of attack from those who consider homosexuality a "sin" and from others who experience fear when confronted with any family form that is "different-than-we-are." The secrecy that the parents often find necessary for survival can permeate the whole nuclear and extended family, sometimes impeding clear and open communication. Because the discrimination against gay and lesbian individuals is so strong, it is easy to cast family difficulties in terms of this bigotry, but this is not always the case. Sometimes, gay and lesbian families have the everyday difficulties experienced by any family, regardless of form, and they need to solve problems of parenting, communication, structure, and so forth. It is important to ask how the family members are interpreting and experiencing their concerns and how much of their difficulties may or may not be associated with discrimination.

Some families are headed by heterosexual parents, but one or more of the children grows up to be gay or lesbian. Again, because discrimination is real and has real effects, Adlerians believe that all members of the family system will need support. This is especially true when gay or lesbian teenagers start to face their "difference," and feel "on the outside," scared, and often depressed. Indeed, gay and lesbian teenagers are the highest at-risk group for suicide. Any gay or lesbian individual must be in charge of when and to whom they will disclose this essential part of their being, and families are often not the first to hear from their son or daughter on this issue. Family therapists can only support gay and lesbian clients through the process and help families address and integrate what is often new and dissonant information to some members.

Multiracial and Ethnic Families

Like birth order, Adlerians approach *culture* as a vantage point from which to view life. Indeed, the influence of culture may also be as powerful as birth order, because both are givens that remain constant throughout life. Culture-as-an-external-influence is not, however, the determining variable: it is the *interpretation* that each individual gives to culture that is an essential piece to understanding people and the human systems in which they live.

In a given family representing a single culture, there may be multiple interpretations of the influence that culture plays. Immigrant parents, for example, may be experiencing the loss of their former homeland and want to conform to the rules, rituals, and expectations of their culture exactly as they would if they were still "at home." If the couple has a daughter born in the "old" culture, but brought to a new one with a new language and new customs, that child may experience herself as belonging to two cultures (or neither). She may become the link (the translator or interpreter) between her parents and the "new world." Perhaps other children will be born to the family, children who have never directly experienced their parent's culture or homeland. The "new" culture is their only culture.

Each person's interpretation will be correct for that person, but may also be the source of conflict within a system that struggles to keep a place for everyone. With such a family, the Adlerian family therapist seeks to articulate the various individual perspectives and to work with the multiple frameworks within the system. It is also important to remember that discrimination is concentrated in different levels or intensities, depending on culture. Again, discrimination is a *real* outside force, and paying attention to how it is experienced by the family and different individuals within the family is very important to effective treatment.

Additional Therapeutic Interventions

Adlerian therapists use interventions that are unique to Adlerian family therapy. They also integrate therapeutic techniques and strategies that have been developed in other models but fit the basic assumptions and goals of Adlerian therapy. A number of these interventions have been presented above, including typologies for assessing the family constellation and the mistaken goals of adults and children in families; problem assessment, goal recognition, and goal disclosure; uses of "a typical day" assessment in therapy; and reorientation processes. Here, we delineate additional or alternative therapeutic interventions commonly used by Adlerian therapists.

Family Atmosphere

One of the first tasks of therapy is assessing the family. Adlerians often start by getting a feel for the family. What would it be like to be a child in this family? How would I feel parenting these children? How does the family function? What are the rules? Is there acceptance and nurturance in the family or pain and perhaps abuse? What would I learn from father about how to treat women? What would I learn from mother about how to treat men? Would I enter the house and sense joy or fear, happiness or anger and frustration, energetic activity or tenseness or lethargy? Even in the absence of abuse, atmospheres characterized by constant criticism, defensiveness, contempt, or stonewalling will have the most lethal effects on the development of family life (Gottman, 1997). The more painful the family atmosphere, the more necessary it is for the therapist to work on rebuilding positive relationships within the system, and the more likely it is to find parents and/or children seeking power and revenge with each other.

Family Values

When both parents agree and act on the same value, it becomes a *family value*. If both parents are religious, kind to others, believe in education, participate in community activities, these values are treated by the children as "normal" and "expected." It is just as easy for bigotry to become a family value, albeit a negative one, as it is for tolerance, acceptance, and appreciation to reach this status. Whatever the value, Adlerians expect that children will most often seek attention, power, and even revenge in relation to perceived family values. It is as if these values cannot be ignored: Each family member must take a stand for or against the family value. When Adlerians find a whole family that is "good" at a singular activity and when expected birth order differences then disappear, we suspect a family value exists.

Alternative Assessments of the Family Constellation

While most Adlerian therapists rely on the parents to merely describe their children, the process of that description can give the counselor a head start on understanding the dynamics of the family. Parental interactions are often an indication of their family leadership style. Similarly, the adjectives used to describe the children often indicate something about how the children see themselves, how they have interpreted their birth positions, and what the parents find important or difficult about each child. The most complete picture of a family constellation is generated in a hermeneutic genogram that Adlerians use to assess the multiple interpretations that family members have about their family.

Parental interactions emerge quickly even in the easiest of family introductions. One of the parents may take the lead in speaking for the family; the other may participate or withdraw or only comment when he or she disagrees. The therapist is interested in how the couple solves problems together, how they communicate with each other and with the children, and what the reactions of the children are. In a counseling session with Jim Bitter, it becomes clear that, although Glenn, the father, sometimes disagrees with Carol's parenting, he withdraws, stepping in only when matters become chaotic, tacitly supporting the children's disruptive behavior. This is such a common pattern that Michael, the oldest son, has already learned that he can withdraw to his grandparents' house anytime he disagrees with his mother (Carlson & Kjos, 1999).

In this same family, the three terms that mother assigns to Michael are *persistent, a clown,* and *impatient.* The noun descriptor suggests that Michael can be funny and charming when he wants to be, and that he brings joy to his mother on these occasions. The two adjectives, however, suggest that Michael has adopted a position of privilege: He wants what he wants right now, and he will keep at his mother until he gets it. When the therapist wonders why this would work, the first thing that comes to mind is that the parent has given in out of frustration or simple exhaustion. The parent is also probably quite busy, and Michael knows when his mother is at her weakest and therefore most likely to give in.

Genograms have been used in many therapeutic models for both assessment and intervention (McGoldrick, Gerson, & Shellenberger, 1999). They are most often multigenerational maps of a particular family system. *Hermeneutic genograms* are especially useful in tracking the various *interpretations* of family life that exist with a family system. They are ideal for working with visually oriented families or family members, and their use can make it possible for young people, especially adolescents, to see their parents as humans with their own developmental history and their own set of problems.

Adlerians use genograms phenomenologically to assess the family constellation, atmosphere, and values as well as a means of tracking presenting problems and discerning roles, functions, rules, and communication patterns within the system (Bitter, 1988; Sherman & Dinkmeyer, 1987). Indeed, an initial task in therapy might be to ask the family members to generate a family map that best describes the group's picture of the family. Tracking the conversation and assessing the level of cooperation exhibited in the process can be more important than the information contained in the final outcome. Conversely, in cases in which the therapist suspects that multiple family members have very different pictures (and therefore "live" in very different families), multiple genograms may help to delineate the various perspectives from which family members engage in the system.

Adlerians pay particular attention to the adjectives that are used to describe family members. In 1932, Adler suggested that descriptions of family members always revealed a statement about self within relationships.

> there is no character trait without a relationship to others. When the patient says, 'My father was kind,' this means 'he was kind to me.' When he says his mother

was critical, the idea which penetrates is that he attempted to keep at a distance from his mother (Ansbacher & Ansbacher, 1964/1979, p. 194).

Each person's communication about the family has a special meaning that manifests the uniqueness of individuals within the family constellation. The process of mapping, therefore, is as important to understanding individuals as it is to discovering the many aspects that comprise the family system. Listening to individual stories assists the therapist in understanding personal feelings as well as meanings.

Alternative Avenues to Reorientation

We have already mentioned four goals that Adlerians bring to the reorientation process. The most important of these are safety and encouragement, establishing the parents as a leadership team, and unlocking interactions based on mistaken goals or notions. Each of these goals is facilitated when parents feel released from the isolation of family life, from negative judgments, or from the sense that they are alone and without support when parenting.

Normalization is an intervention that often breaks through isolation and negative judgments immediately. It is most easily achieved in an open forum where other families can share their experiences of similar difficulties with the family in focus. Even in private sessions, however, it is often useful to simply tell a family, if it is true, that what they are experiencing is normal and would happen with most families having a similar structure.

> THERAPIST: Now, I want you first of all to know something that you may not know. I am just going to tell you this from twenty years of experience with families. You have a perfectly normal family.
>
> MOTHER: Oh my god.
>
> THERAPIST: It may feel to you at times like all of this is getting out of hand, but any family with three kids who have started with the same value system that your family has are going to have pretty much the same difficulties, because children learn to read parents, and then they figure out what to do (Carlson & Kjos, 1999, p. 34 [in study guide]).

Early recollections are used by Adlerians as a projective assessment (Mosak, 1958, 1995). Even though we have millions of experiences when we are very young, we tend to remember about six to twelve memories that have meaning in our life in the present. These memories serve as stories that remind us who we are, how we see others, what we expect from life and the world. Some of our recollections indicate the ethical convictions we hold, and others reveal the basic mistakes we continue to make. An understanding of early recollections can be especially useful in unlocking adults from their mistaken notions or helping a teenager and a parent understand each other's perspectives.

Family meetings are one of the most common strategies that Adlerians use to help family live and work together. It is a place in which family members can solve problems and make decisions together in a democratic manner, where everyone's input is valued. Family meetings are an excellent place for members to share appreciation and support, learn from natural and logical consequences, plan time together, and develop a sense of self and voice in a safe atmosphere. When parents are ready to fully implement what they have learned from parent education, family meetings are often their best vehicle.

The Therapist as Person: Uses of Self in Therapy

A therapist is a person whose greatest tool is often the human use of self. There are many human characteristics and therapeutic approaches that work quite effectively. Most Adlerian family therapists, however, share five or six qualities in common.

1. Effective therapeutic relationships develop from an interest in the people who make up each family. Family members can sense when a therapist is fully present and interested in their welfare; they experience such a presence as caring, and it automatically constitutes an atmosphere of safety. If every discouraged person who enters therapy can leave feeling encouraged, Adlerian therapists have met their first therapeutic goal. Such encouragement almost always follows directly from the experience of a caring, respectful therapist who has faith in the family and its members and who can engender hope by coconstructing options that have previously seemed beyond possibility.

2. Following from an interest in families and their members is taking time to closely follow the narrative descriptions of each client. In much of Dreikurs's private work, he would separate his interviews into two parts. The first part sought to develop a subjective orientation to the person or family that allowed each client member to fully present his or her concerns and/or life story. The second part took a more objective orientation and developed data that he needed to work psychologically with clients (Dreikurs, 1997). Whether working with individuals or families, there are always meaningful patterns that repeat themselves in the narratives of clients.

3. Throughout counseling or therapy, family members need to feel heard and understood. Therapeutic interventions, skills, and intuition are wonderful assets, but nothing is as valuable as the communication of *empathic understanding*. Referencing an unknown English author in 1928, Adler described the empathy required for therapy: "To see with the eyes of another, to hear with the ears of another, and to feel with the heart of another" (Ansbacher & Ansbacher, 1964/1979, p. 42).

4. Adlerian counselors use a lot of stories and metaphors in family therapy. The open-forum model that Dreikurs first advocated in child guidance and

family education centers practically requires stories as a method of illustrating educational points to the larger audience. Stories and metaphors have the added advantage of influencing families in an indirect manner, allowing family members to consider difficult information or new possibilities without having to defend themselves.

5. Because Adlerian family therapists seek to maintain a positive stance, *reframing* is an essential tool. Adler's original notion was that "everything can always be different" (Ansbacher & Ansbacher, 1956, p. 194). Adlerians use reframing to replace negative references with positive ones, to assign good intentions even to mistaken behaviors and interactions, to change the climate in the family or in the therapy session, to disengage people from power struggles, and to provide encouragement to individuals and the family as a whole.

6. Most Adlerian counselors try to find appropriate avenues to integrate humor in family therapy sessions. The most useful humor follows from an enjoyment of the family or of life in general. Even an enjoyment of the process of therapy is helpful. Humor reduces the burden that clients often feel, lightens their interactions, and opens them to new possibilities. It helps people find connections to each other and to cooperate in the implementation of needed change. For the counselor or therapist, it is probably the single most important quality in the prevention of professional burnout.

Case Example

Jim Bitter met with an intact nuclear family that included the father, Glenn, the mother, Carol, and three children, Michael, Andrea, and Lauren (Carlson & Kjos, 1999). When the children seated themselves, Andrea placed herself at the far end, away from the therapist, with her sister and brother sitting next to each other. After getting everyone's name, Jim started by asking Andrea "How did you get roped into coming?" Even though she did not have an immediate answer, his question served to let her know that he was aware of her presence and that he would not let her get lost.

Turning to the parents, three adjectives for each of the children were requested. Michael, the oldest, was described as *persistent, a clown,* and *impatient.* Lauren, the youngest, was also described as *persistent* and increasingly *impatient,* suggesting an alignment with her older brother, even to the extent that she may be studying his approach. Andrea is described as *hyper,* always *talking,* and *capable of bugging pets and people* in ways that draw attention to her. Another way to describe *impatient persistence* is that "the person is always bugging me." It is not uncommon for children to have learned this approach from the parent who is most bothered by it.

When asked what they would like to see going better, Carol indicates that she would like to have the children, especially Michael and Andrea, listen to her more. She then describes a multitude of ways in which she "keeps at the children," verbally coaxing and reminding until she winds up angry and upset. Carol

Bitter w/ clients

is a parent who tries to control her children with excessive talking, and they respond with parent-deafness. To make matters worse, when the noise gets to be too much for him, Glenn steps in to tell Carol to stop yelling. Carol also has both her mother and her sister criticizing her parenting. It is clear that Carol needs some support in setting appropriate boundaries with her relatives and some help in winning the cooperation of her husband and children.

In spite of their parents' attempts to control them, several goal disclosure processes indicate that the children only *vacillate* between keeping their parents busy with them (attention getting) and demonstrating that they can do what they want (power). They are not dedicated to power struggles, which is a good sign. The children are mostly doing well in school, and, in spite of some really exhausting mistaken interactions, there is really not a "bad" child in the family. It is pretty clear that the parents love and want their children, a point that Jim carefully stresses. Children need to know that they have a useful place in the family always present, just waiting for them.

A typical day reveals many instances when the patterns of control and resistance repeat themselves. It further clarifies how much mother feels a need to be in charge, and how often father escapes to the kitchen, leaving mother to sort things out with the three children. The family atmosphere is at once tense and exhausting. Father sets a masculine guiding line that can be summed up accordingly: "When the going gets tough, the men get going (they withdraw)." Michael has already learned to use his grandparents' house as a place to which he can escape. At the end of the typical day, Jim is able to describe each child's response pattern to mother's talking and imperatives.

"Michael, for one, when he is listening to you, makes one quick determination. Can he do it exactly right and earn your pleasure, or should he get out of the way? And those are the only two decisions he makes. Stay or run.

"Andrea listens to you because you are actually the single biggest help she has. She wouldn't know what to oppose if you didn't say exactly what the right thing was, and then she does exactly the opposite.

"And Lauren. Lauren has this urge to be your baby the rest of her natural life, and she would do anything to keep you happy with her. . . . My guess is that out of that she gets a tremendous amount of service; perhaps, do you still bathe her by any chance?"

From Carol: "Yeah, I do."

Jim starts the reorientation process by giving Glenn two recommendations that are designed to reestablish him as a partner with his wife in the leadership of the family. The first recommendation is to stay out of any activity that Carol begins with the children, especially when he disagrees with how it is going. Helping Glenn "mind his own business" will keep Carol from feeling undermined and reduce the fighting that results between the two of them. The second recommendation is to more evenly split the time that each is responsible for moving the children along: If one of them handles the morning, then the other person will handle the night. Reinvolving the father in the hardest parts of parenting the children is essential to supporting the couple as a leadership team.

It is often difficult for a parent to hear that they must stop talking and learn to act. Jim uses a metaphor to suggest a road that will lead to Carol being more effective with her children. The story of a rattlesnake rattling is linked to Carol talking. "It's when [the rattlesnake] stops rattling that you have to be concerned. . . . As long as you are talking and rattling, [your children] figure 'no problem.' It's when you actually stop and take some action that they pay attention to you." A series of recommendations follows that specifies various ways in which these parents can act without talking. While the recommendations will lead to the children taking more responsibility for their own lives, they are primarily designed to unlock the patterns that have been supported by the parents' goal of being "good" parents and the children's mistaken goals of attention getting and seeking power.

Of all the things recommended, the parents felt that the one thing they could do during the coming week was to "switch off" with the children, each taking responsibility for them at different times. It is significant that they need to reassert their support with each other before they work to improve their interactions with the children. Jim sees a lot of strength in this couple, and he shares his faith in them shortly before the session ends.

Summary

Adlerian family therapy is based on the original contributions of Alfred Adler and Rudolf Dreikurs. Their work with families and children did much to transform parenting and education both in Europe and the United States. Yet, in spite of the fact that their model predated many later developments in family therapy, Adlerian therapy has yet to gain wide attention and influence. Timing being essential to the success of most enterprises, Adlerian psychology and family therapy developed early, when psychiatry and psychology were less than receptive to social psychology and systemic therapy; it had a long latency period and is only now gaining some renewed interest.

> Dreikurs translated Adler's ideas about the need to overcome *feelings of inferiority* by developing *social interest* in a variety of formats, including children's groups, parents' groups, and family therapy groups. His techniques with families combined emotional support and encouragement with interpretations and suggestions about modifying unhappy interactions. He encouraged families to discuss their mutual problems in an open, democratic spirit; and he urged them to institute regular "family councils" in order to incorporate the model of family group therapy into their daily lives (Nichols & Schwartz, 1998, p. 69).

During the last decade, Adlerians have extended the teleological conceptualizations and applications within the model, delineated therapeutic processes for both private and open-forum sessions, and developed brief therapy process and strategies for individuals, couples, and families. With its emphasis on a systemic view of each individual's style of living, Adlerian family therapy is quite capable of moving easily from person to system and back to individuals within family systems. It is a model in need of comparative and effectiveness research studies and a charismatic spokesperson who can give voice and vision to the further development of therapy.

Sources for Training

Training programs and certifications in Adlerian Therapy are offered through a number of different agencies and societies. A membership in the North American Society of Adlerian Psychology (NASAP) is a good starting point. The annual convention will introduce North Americans to a number of different Adlerian applications and will provide members with an opportunity for professional certification. The society also publishes *The Journal of Individual Psychology* four times a year. For more information, contact:

> North American Society of Adlerian Psychology
> 65 East Wacker Place, Suite 1710
> Chicago, IL 60601
> Telephone (312) 629-8801

In addition to training through NASAP, there are a number of Adlerian therapy institutes throughout North America, including sites in Bowie, Maryland, New York City, Ottawa, Ontario, Canada, San Francisco, and Washington, DC. A number of universities have prominent Adlerians who supervise doctoral students, including programs at the University of Georgia, Georgia State University, Baylor University, New Mexico State University, and the University of South Dakota.

The Adler School of Professional Psychology offers APA-approved programs leading to a doctor of psychology (Psy.D.) degree. The main campus is in Chicago, with satellite programs in Fort Wayne, Indiana, Minneapolis, Minnesota, and Montreal, Quebec, Toronto, Ontario, and Vancouver, British Columbia, in Canada. Current program requirements and information are available at:

Adler School of Professional Psychology
65 East Wacker Place, Suite 2100
Chicago, IL 60601
Telephone (312) 201-5900

Weeklong training programs in Adlerian therapy and Adlerian Brief Therapy are available in England and the United States, respectively. For yearly information, contact:

Don Smart
Adlerian Summer Schools
9b Thames Street
Wallingford, Oxford OX10 OHD
England
Ansphone: 01491-835893

or

Dr. William G. Nicoll, Director   (adleriantraining@usa.net)
Adlerian Training Institute
P.O. Box 276358
Boca Raton, FL 33427-6358
Telephone: (954) 757-284

ANNOTATED SUGGESTED READINGS

Bitter, J. R., & Corey, G. (2001). Family systems therapy. In G. Corey (Ed.), *Theory and practice of counseling and psychotherapy* (6th ed., pp. 365–444). Pacific Grove, CA: Brooks/Cole.
An overview of multiple approaches to family systems therapy, including a section on Adlerian open-forum family counseling.

Carlson, J., Sperry, L., & Lewis, J. A. (1997). *Family therapy: Ensuring treatment efficacy.* Pacific Grove, CA: Brooks/Cole.
An excellent overview of family therapy coupled with specific methods for tailoring treatment to various families and concerns and guidelines for treatment adherence and relapse prevention.

Christensen, O. C. (Ed.). (1993). *Adlerian family counseling* (Rev. ed.). Minneapolis, MN: Educational Media Corporation.
The first step-by-step guide to Adlerian family counseling in an open forum.

Dagley, J. C. (2000). Adlerian family therapy. In A. Horne (Ed.), *Family counseling and therapy* (3rd ed., pp. 366–419). Itasca, IL: F. E. Peacock.
A thorough overview of Adlerian family therapy incorporated in one of the best texts on family therapy.

Sherman, R., & Dinkmeyer, D. (1987). *Systems of family therapy: An Adlerian integration.* New York: Brunner/Mazel.
A complete delineation of Adlerian family therapy coupled with chapters by noted Adlerians who have integrated other family systems models into their work.

Sweeney, T. J. (1998). *Adlerian counseling: A practitioner's approach* (4th ed.). Philadelphia: Accelerated Development.
A presentation of every aspect of Adlerian theory and counseling with individuals, groups, couples, and families, including chapters addressing children, adolescents, adults, and the elderly.

Watts, R. E., & Carlson, J. (Eds.). (1999). *Interventions and strategies in counseling and psychotherapy.* Philadelphia: Accelerated Development.
A complete guide to current Adlerian approaches in counseling with excellent chapters by Bill Nicoll, on "Brief Therapy," Robert Sherman, on "Family Therapy," Terry Kottman, on "Play Therapy," and Amy Lew, on "Parent Education."

REFERENCES

Adler, A. (1927/1969). *Understanding human nature* (W. B. Wolf, Trans.). New York: Fawcett.

Adler, A. (1929). *The science of living* (B. Ginzburg, Ed.). New York: Greenberg.

Adler, A. (1930). *The education of children.* New York: Greenberg.

Adler, A. (1931). *What life should mean to you.* Boston: Little, Brown.

Adler, A. (1935a/1996a). The structure of neurosis. *Individual Psychology, 52*(4), 351–362.

Adler, A. (1935b/1996b). What is neurosis? *Individual Psychology, 52*(4), 318–333.

Adler, A. (1938). *Social interest: A challenge to mankind.* London: Faber & Faber.

Ansbacher, H. L. (1988). Dreikurs' four goals of children's disturbing behavior and Adler's social interest—activity typology. *Individual Psychology, 41*(3), 282–289.

Ansbacher, H. L. (1992). Adler's concept of community feeling and of social interest and the relevance of community feeling for old age. *Individual Psychology, 48*(4), 402–412.

Ansbacher, H. L., & Ansbacher, R. R. (Eds.). (1956). *The individual psychology of Alfred Adler.* New York: Basic Books.

Ansbacher, H. L., & Ansbacher, R. R. (Eds.). (1964/1979). *Superiority and social interest: Alfred Adler, a collection of later writings.* New York: Norton.

Arciniega, G. M., & Newlon, B. J. (1995). Counseling and psychotherapy: Multicultural considerations. In D. Capuzzi & D. R. Gross (Eds.), *Counseling and psychotherapy: Theories and interventions* (pp. 557–587). Englewood Cliffs, NJ: Merrill.

Bitter, J. R. (1988). Family mapping and family constellation: Satir in Adlerian context. *Individual Psychology, 44*(1), 106–111.

Bitter, J. R. (1991). Conscious motivations: An enhancement to Dreikurs' goals of children's misbehavior. *Individual Psychology, 47*(2), 210–221.

Bitter, J. R., Christensen, O. C., Hawes, C., & Nicoll, W. G. (1998). Adlerian brief therapy with individuals, couples, and families. *Directions in Counseling and Clinical Psychology, 8*(8), 95–111.

Burnett, P. C. (1988). Evaluation of Adlerian parenting programs. *Individual Psychology, 44,* 63–76.

Carlson, J., & Kjos, D. (Producers & Moderators). (1999). *Adlerian therapy with Dr. James Bitter (Family therapy with the experts: Instruction, demonstration, discussion)* [videotape]. Boston, MA: Allyn & Bacon.

Carlson, J., & Sperry, L. (Eds.). (1996). *The disordered couple.* New York: Brunner/Mazel.

Carlson, J., Sperry, L., & Lewis, J. A. (1997). *Family therapy: Ensuring treatment efficacy.* Pacific Grove, CA: Brooks/Cole.

Christensen, O. C. (Ed.). (1993). *Adlerian family counseling: A manual for counselors, educators, and psychotherapists* (Rev. ed.). Minneapolis, MN: Educational Media.

Dinkmeyer, D., Sr., McKay, G., Dinkmeyer, D., Jr., (1997). *STEP: The parent's handbook.* Circle Pines, MN: American Guidance Service.

Dreikurs, R. (1940, December). The child in the group. *Camping Magazine,* 7–9.

Dreikurs, R. (1948). *The challenge of parenthood.* New York: Duell, Sloan, & Pearce.

Dreikurs, R. (1950). The immediate purpose of children's misbehavior, its recognition and correction. *Internationale Zeitschrift fur Individual-psychologie, 19,* 70–87.

Dreikurs, R. (1957). *Psychology in the classroom.* New York: Harper & Row.

Dreikurs, R. (1971). *Social equality: The challenge of today.* Chicago, IL: Henry Regnery.

Dreikerus, R. (1997). Holistic medicine. *Individual Psychology, 53*(2), 127–205.

Dreikurs, R., Corsini, R., Lowe, R., & Sonstegard, M. (Eds.). (1959). *Adlerian family counseling.* Eugene, OR: University of Oregon Press.

Dreikurs, R., & Grey, L. (1968). *Logical consequences: A new approach to child discipline.* New York: Hawthorn.

Dreikurs, R., Grunwald, B. B., & Pepper, F. (1982). *Maintaining sanity in the classroom* (Rev. ed.). New York: Harper & Row.

Dreikurs, R., & Soltz, V. (1964). *Children: The challenge.* New York: Hawthorn.

Falbo, T. (1977). The only child: A review. *Individual Psychology, 33,* 47–61.

Gottman, J. (1997). *The heart of parenting: Raising an emotionally intelligent child.* New York: Simon & Schuster.

Griffith, J., & Powers, R. L. (1984). *An Adlerian lexicon: Fifty-nine terms associated with the individual psychology of Alfred Adler.* Chicago, IL: AIAS.

Grunwald, B. B., & McAbee, H. V. (1985). *Guiding the family: Practical counseling techniques.* Muncie, IN: Accelerated Development.

Hoffman, E. (1994). *The drive for self: Alfred Adler and the founding of individual psychology.* New York: Addison-Wesley.

Lowe, R. N. (1971). Goal recognition. In A. G. Nikelly (Ed.), *Techniques for behavior change* (pp. 65–75). Springfield, IL: Charles C. Thomas.

Lowe, R. N. (1982). Adlerian/Dreikursian family counseling. In A. M. Horne & M. M. Ohlsen (Eds.), *Family counseling and therapy* (pp. 329–359). Itasca, IL: F. E. Peacock.

Maniacci, M. P. (1999). Clinical therapy. In R. E. Watts & J. Carlson (Eds.), *Interventions and strategies in counseling and psychotherapy* (pp. 59–85). Philadelphia: Accelerated Development.

Maslow, A. H. (1970). *Motivation and personality* (2nd ed.). New York: Harper & Row.

McGoldrick, M., Gerson, R., & Shellenberger, S. (1999). *Genograms: Assessment and intervention* (2nd ed.). New York: Norton.

Mosak, H. H. (1958). Early recollections as a projective technique. *Journal of Projective Techniques, 22,* 302–311.

Mosak, H. H. (1995). Adlerian psychotherapy. In R. J. Corsini & D. Wedding (Eds.), *Current psychotherapies* (5th ed., pp. 51–94). Itasca, IL: F. E. Peacock.

Nichols, M. P., & Schwartz, R. C. (1998). *Family therapy: Concepts and methods.* Boston, MA: Allyn & Bacon.

Nicoll, W. G. (1999). Brief therapy strategies and techniques. In R. E. Watts & J. Carlson (Eds.), *Interventions and strategies in counseling and psychotherapy* (pp. 15–30). Philadelphia, PA: Accelerated Development.

Nicoll, W. G., & Hawes, E. C. (1984). Family lifestyle assessment: The role of family myths and values in the client's presenting issues. *Individual Psychology, 41,* 147–160.

Popkin, M. (1993). *Active parenting today.* Atlanta, GA: Active Parenting.

Selye, H. (1974). *Stress without distress.* New York: Signet.

Sherman, R. & Dinkmeyer, D. (1987). *Systems of family therapy: An Adlerian integration.* New York: Brunner Mazel.

Smuts, J. C. (1926/1996). *Holism and evolution.* Highland, NY: The Gestalt Journal Press.

Sperry, L. (1995). *Handbook of diagnosis and treatment of the DSM-IV personality disorders.* New York: Brunner/Mazel.

Sperry, L., & Carlson, J. (Eds.). (1996). *Psychopathology and psychotherapy: From DSM-IV diagnosis to treatment* (2nd ed.). Washington, DC: Accelerated Development.

Sweeney, T. J. (1998). *Adlerian counseling: A practitioner's approach* (5th ed.). Philadelphia, PA: Accelerated Development.

Terner, J., & Pew, W. L. (1978). *The courage to be imperfect: The life and work of Rudolf Dreikurs.* New York: Hawthorn.

Vaihinger, H. (1965). *The philosophy of "as if."* London: Routledge and Kegan Paul.

von Bertalanffy, L. (1968). *General systems theory.* New York: Braziller.

Walsh, W. M., & McGraw, J. A. (1996). *Essentials of family therapy: A therapist's guide to eight approaches.* Denver, CO: Love.

Watkins, C. E. (1992a). Adlerian-oriented early memory research: What does it tell us? *Journal of Personality Assessment, 59,* 248–263.

Watkins, C. E. (1992b). Birth-order research and Adlerian theory: A critical review. *Individual Psychology, 48,* 357–368.

Watkins, C. E. (1992c). Research activity with Adler's theory. *Individual Psychology, 48,* 107–108.

Watkins, C. E. (1994). Measuring social interest. *Individual Psychology, 50,* 69–96.

4 Strategic Family Therapy

JON CARLSON

Jon Carlson

Brief Description of Theory

In strategic family therapy, the therapist creates what happens in the session and develops a specialized approach for each problem. The therapist assesses the situation and then creates a problem-solving strategy that is *tailored* to each couple or family. The problem is viewed as occurring in a social context and the strategy is specifically designed for that context (Madanes, 1981).

Couples and families are viewed as rule-governed systems and any problems are viewed as having a function within the system. *Symptoms are system-maintained and system-maintaining.* They are also detrimental to the ongoing communication patterns and stop the couple or family from reaching their goals. The therapist focuses on the *present* situation of the couple or family and strives to create a behavioral change. The value of insight or understanding is viewed as less important than behavioral change.

A secondary goal of treatment is to help the couple or family members to move to the next phase in the family life cycle, as well as their own individual life cycles. For example, the stage of a young adult's leaving home is a particularly difficult one for the individual and the family.

Significant Characteristics of Strategic Therapy

Evolution of the Theory

Jay Haley was the person primarily credited with the development of the strategic approach to family therapy. He was strongly influenced by Gregory Bateson and Milton Erickson (Carlson, 2001). Bateson was a research anthropologist studying patterns of communication and cybernetic systems. He had a research grant in the 1950s and was able to hire Haley, John Weakland, and William Fry to join him at the Palo Alto, California VA Hospital. At the VA Hospital, Don Jackson was working on understanding and treating people with schizophrenia. Bateson and Jackson collaborated, which led to the conceptual basis of strategic therapy.

Bateson contributed ideas based on cybernetics, communication, and systems research. Haley was also interested in communications as well as the analysis of fantasy. Weakland was trained as a chemical engineer but was interested in anthropology. Fry was a psychiatrist who was experimenting with humor as a therapeutic modality. Jackson was also a psychiatrist who had been working with schizophrenics and their families and was beginning to develop the concept of homeostasis. Out of this combination came the integration of systems and communications theory.

Jackson founded the Mental Research Institute (MRI) in Palo Alto in 1959. According to Segal (1991), the group came to assume three things: (1) an underlying problem in the family is being exhibited by the pathology of the identified patient in the family; (2) the family behavior is governed by the cybernetic principles of homeostasis, feedback, and redundancy; and (3) treating the family involves changing its patterns of communication.

Haley would spend considerable time visiting Erickson in his home in Phoenix. Erickson was a psychiatrist who used hypnosis and paradoxical instruction to help people who were stuck at different stages in the family life cycle. He believed that problems were largely do to the perception that there is only one solution. Erickson would use various creative "strategies" to help clients behave in more productive ways that generated alternative solutions to their problems.

Erickson saw the therapist as having complete responsibility for the treatment outcome. He believed that the ends or change is what therapy was for and therefore was willing to manipulate, direct, and do what was needed. The "right" way to do therapy was the way that helped clients reach their goals. In 1963, Haley wrote *Strategies of Psychotherapy,* which recorded the creative work of Erickson and sought to demonstrate that paradox was a common element in all effective therapies. Haley wrote several other volumes devoted to Erickson, including *Uncommon Therapy* (1973) and the three-volume *Conversations with Milton H. Erickson* (1985).

To accomplish change required the therapist to have keen powers of observation. This not only included seeing what was maintaining the problem but what resources the client possessed to induce change. Erickson realized that to approach a problem directly created resistance and was frequently a waste of resources and energy. He used hypnosis to deliver strategies such as the paradoxical directive (Haley, 1973). He achieved his therapeutic objectives by:

- accepting and emphasizing the positive (i.e., he framed all symptoms and maladaptive behaviors as helpful)
- using indirect and ambiguously worded directives
- encouraging or directing routine behaviors so that resistance is shown through change, not through normal and continuous actions (Haley, 1963).

Haley left Palo Alto in 1967 to work with Salvador Minuchin and Braulio Montalvo at the Philadelphia Child Guidance Center. From this connection, several basic assumptions of strategic therapy resulted: (1) Families are rule-governed systems that can best be understood in context; (2) the presenting problem serves a function within the family; and (3) the concepts of boundaries, coalitions, hierarchy, power, metaphor, family life cycle development, and triangles are basic to the development of stuck families.

Uniqueness of the Theory

Flexibility is a major emphasis of strategic family therapy. This allows for the therapist to work with a variety of families and their members who display such dysfunctional behaviors as enmeshment, eating disorders, schizophrenia, and substance abuse (Haley, 1980).

It is not necessary for all family members to be present for effective therapy to occur. According to Fisch, Weakland, and Segal (1983), "real change is possible at the individual and dyadic level—that the entire system need not always be involved in lower-order change" (p. 15). By going against the dictum that many family therapists believe, that all members must be present, it is more likely that desirable outcomes will occur.

There is a focus on *innovation and creativity* that was rooted in the early work of Erickson and contemporary practitioners such as Haley, Cloe Madanes, and James Coyne. The goal is to change the perceptions and interactions of the families. Through their "introduction of the novel or unexpected, a frame of reference is broken and the structure of reality is rearranged" (Papp, 1983, p. 22).

Strategic therapy can be *used in combination* with a number of other therapies, especially the behavioral and structural schools. This is probably due to the flexibility of strategic therapy and its focus on changing the presenting problem of the family.

Finally, the *emphasis on the life cycle* is somewhat unique to this approach. Problems and solutions are all related to how they help or hinder the life cycle of the family.

Similarities to Other Theories

The strategic approach is similar to the structural and Adlerian approaches. Each family is viewed as unique with its own rules, norms, and patterns. The social context is emphasized and behavior is maintaining and maintained by the social system. Problems are viewed holistically, with all individual disturbances having a purpose and message from the larger family system. Problems result from faulty thinking and perception of what could be a solution. As the family learns to see the situation differently, the problem is dealt with differently. The therapist is more directive in these models and takes responsibility for planning the therapy. Along with the cognitive–behavioral approach, strategic therapists all believe in the use of assignments or homework and are all present-focused and change-oriented.

According to Corey and Bitter (2001) the points of difference from other methods or uniqueness also include: the emphasis on one problem; the tendency to be too "mechanical" or "technique focused"; the denial of mental illness, including schizophrenia; the very high level of skill required; the short time allowed for treatment; and the lack of collaboration with the family.

Philosophical and Historical Background

Individuals Associated with the Theory

The leading strategic therapists are Jay Haley, Cloe Madanes, and members of the MRI in Palo Alto, including Paul Watzlawick, Richard Fisch, and the late John Weakland. As has previously been mentioned, Haley trained with Gregory Bateson, Milton Erickson, and Salvador Minuchin. The impact of these leaders is evident in the integrative nature of the strategic approach. Haley was the first to pull together the best ideas and strategies from seemingly divergent approaches.

In 1967, Haley left MRI to join Minuchin and Braulio Montalvo at the Philadelphia Child Guidance Clinic. Both Haley and Minuchin give credit to one another in the development of their theories. Minuchin credits Haley with helping him articulate many of the principles elaborated in *Families and Family Therapy* (Minuchin, 1974), while Haley gives Minuchin credit for helping him understand the structure of families described in his *Problem-Solving Therapy* (Haley, 1976). In this book, he used a structural model to apply his strategic interventions.

In the early 1970s Haley left Philadelphia to establish the Family Therapy Institute of Washington, DC with Cloe Madanes. Madanes was known for her creativity in therapy. She had known Haley while at MRI in 1966 as a research assistant, and again in 1971 as a supervisor at the Philadelphia Child Guidance Clinic where she worked with Haley, Minuchin, and Montalvo. Haley and Madanes married for a short time. Now Madanes remains in Washington, DC and Haley has moved to La Jolla, California, where he is in semiretirement, providing supervision and making videos of his work (Carlson, 2001).

The MRI was the leading facility in the early years of family therapy. It was established in 1959 by its founding director Don Jackson, who was consulting with Bateson on a project. He assembled a staff that changed the history of doing psychotherapy: Jay Haley, Jules Ruskin, Virginia Satir, John Weakland, Paul Watzlawick, Arthur Bodin, and Janet Beaven. This group began a family therapy training program and conducted interaction research that led to Satir's (1964) *Conjoint Family Therapy,* Watzlawick, Beavin, & Jackson's (1967) *Pragmatics of Human Communication,* and Haley's (1963) *Strategies of Psychotherapy.* Later, MRI became the home to many others who influenced strategic therapy, including Carlso Sluzki, James Coyne, Steve de Shazer, and Wendall Ray.

Changes, Stages of Theory Development

The strategic approach to therapy reached its height of popularity in the 1980s. Practicing therapists appreciated the clever interventions that could somehow remove problems that were previously viewed as treatment resistant. Near the end of the decade this approach received widespread criticism as being too cold, mechanistic, and manipulative. The 1990s brought an approach that was more interested in collaboration and working *with,* not *on,* families. Elements of strategic therapy still remain: clear therapeutic goals, anticipating the family's reaction to interventions, understanding and tracking sequences of interaction, and using clever directives.

The strategic approach continues to change and develop as it integrates strategies and techniques from other people and approaches. The strategic approach has parented approaches described as brief therapy, problem-solving therapy, solution-focused and systemic therapy. These later approaches have become the basis for the current therapies driven by the managed health care movement.

Relevant Research Related to Theory

The strategic approach has been applied to numerous problems and has generated positive research results. Due to the limited nature of this chapter, the research will not be presented. The reader is urged to read the professional journals, especially the *Journal of Strategic and Systemic Therapies,* published by Guilford Press, for the most recent research, on this approach. Most of the research however, is not particularly extensive and the studies are largely anecdotal or use a case report format.

Clinical Perspective

View of Human Functioning

Strategic therapy is family therapy in which the therapist devises and initiates strategies for solving the family's presenting problem. The strategic therapist is concerned with dysfunctional hierarchies and repetitive sequences of behavior between and among family members that support the presenting problem. The strategic therapist takes responsibility for directly influencing the family in order to bring about change and elimination of the presenting problem. Problems are maintained by ongoing interactional processes, so insight is not a necessary prerequisite for change. Problems cannot be eliminated through understanding alone because the problems are maintained by the ongoing interactional processes. The therapist, therefore, attempts to relabel or reframe the problem rather than producing insight.

If therapy fails, it is the therapist's responsibility. If therapy succeeds, the therapist does not take credit for it, but instead congratulates the family members for their success. Symptoms are viewed as misguided tactics used by one person to deal with another. In strategic therapy, symptoms are seen as interpersonal strategies or efforts to define the nature of relationships. They are embedded in the family's network of relationships. The family system works to maintain homeostasis in interactional patterns, and symptoms can be viewed simply as particular types of behavior functioning as homeostatic mechanisms that serve to regulate family transactions. *Symptom* is a label for a circular set of dysfunctional behaviors that are occurring within a family. Symptoms are not caused. They evolve as the family attempts to find means to establish or maintain family equilibrium, usually succeeding only in making matters worse and becoming the presenting problems in therapy.

As families attempt to master the changes required by normal family life development, problems and, therefore, symptoms occur. Haley described the family life cycle from a systemic point of view. In the book *Uncommon Therapy* (1973), he highlighted the facts that: (1) symptoms are likely to occur at points of transition between stages; (2) some families develop problems because they are not able to make the necessary transition from one stage to the next; (3) when there is a disruption or failure to move to the next stage in the family life cycle, dysfunction occurs; and (4) the failure or disruption occurs because the family is having difficulty mastering the tasks inherent in that stage in the life cycle. The problem, then, is not the identified patient, but the way the family reacts and attempts to adapt to the next stage it is approaching or has entered (Haley, 1971).

The normal developmental processes that most families go through are marked by critical transition points. The courtship period, early marriage, birth of a first child, rearing of the young, departure from home of the children, retirement, and old age all present challenges and critical transition points. Due to losses, the progression is often more complicated for blended and single-parent families experiencing other crises due to loss.

How the Theory Describes Mental Illness

Haley denies the existence of schizophrenia and other mental illnesses. He is a great admirer of schizophrenics and believes that they are very wise and can teach us a lot if they are not drugged too much. He is not interested in labels or diagnosis, but what the person needs to do to get unstuck and what other family members do to keep him or her stuck. He views mental problems as having a purpose and function for the family (Carlson, 2001).

How Does Change Occur?

Strategic family therapists are concerned with four interrelated elements: (1) symptoms, (2) metaphors, (3) hierarchy, and (4) power. Symptoms are viewed as maintaining homeostatic balance in the family system. Symptoms can be seen as a way of communicating metaphorically with the family. (For example, a woman's depression may be her way of communicating her unhappiness with the marriage to her husband or saving him from a workaholic existence by needing him to be at home more.) Symptoms can be understood through hierarchically structured power ladders. The parent should have power over the child and be at the top of the hierarchy. However, in some cases children may develop a symptom, such as poor school performance or trouble with the law, in order to change the power relationship.

The role of the strategic family therapist involves being active and flexible with the family. The therapist works quickly to plan strategies to resolve problems in families. He or she often ignores the family histories and personal diagnosis and focuses on symptoms and behaviors.

The therapist uses four basic steps to insure a successful outcome:

1. defining the problem clearly and concisely
2. investigating all solutions that have been previously tried
3. defining a clear and concrete change to be achieved
4. formulating and implementing a strategy for change (Watzlawick, 1978).

The focus of therapy is on the process rather than content. The methods used in bringing about change focus on breaking up the negative cycles of interaction and replacing them with positive ones that highlight alternative ways of acting. In general, strategic family therapists concentrate on the following dimensions of family life:

- *Family rules*—the overt and covert rules families use to govern themselves, such as "you must only speak when spoken to";
- *Family homeostasis*—the tendency of the family to remain in the same pattern of functioning unless challenged to do otherwise, for example, getting up and going to bed at the same time;
- *Quid pro quo*—the responsiveness of family members to treat others the way they are treated, that is something for something;
- *Redundancy principle*—the fact that a family interacts within a limited range of repetitive behavioral sequences;
- *Punctuation*—the idea that people in a transaction believe that what they say is caused by what others say;

- *Symmetrical relationships and complementary relationships*—the fact that relationships within a family are both among equals (symmetrical) and unequals (complementary);
- *Circular causality*—the idea that one event does not "cause" another but that events are interconnected and that the factors behind a behavior, such as a kiss or slap, are multiple.

Strategies and Techniques

Strategic family therapists use a wide variety of treatment techniques. They view many of the prevailing strategies, such as catharsis and telling people what to do, as ineffective. They believe that behavioral alterations precede thoughts and feelings. Each intervention strategy is tailored or customized to the persons and problems of the family. At the center of this technique-driven approach are six methods.

Reframing.   *Reframing* involves the use of language to induce a cognitive shift within family members and alter their perceptions of a situation. In reframing, a different interpretation is given to a family's situation or behavior. In this process, a circumstance is given new meaning and, as a consequence, other ways of behaving are explored. Reframing does not change a situation, but "the alteration of meaning invites the possibility of change" (Piercy & Sprenkle, 1986, p. 35). For instance, "resistance" may be conceptualized as "persistence" or "stubbornness" or "commitment." In the video, Coyne states:

> TH (40):   "I'm wondering though, again I may be simple-minded on this point and giving him more credit than he deserves on it, but I am wondering are those times when he seems tuned out. Is he being thoughtful about what you are saying?"

Overall, reframing helps establish rapport between the therapist and the family and breaks down resistance. Through the use of reframing, what was once seen as out-of-control behavior may become voluntary and open to change.

Directive.   A *directive* is an instruction from a family therapist for a family to behave differently. "The directive is to strategic therapy what the interpretation is to psychoanalysis. It is the basic tool of the approach" (Madanes, 1981, p. 397). Many types of directives can be given in strategic therapy. They include nonverbal messages (e.g., silence, voice tone, and posture), direct and indirect suggestions (e.g., "go fast" or "you may not want to change too quickly"), and assigned behaviors (e.g., when you think you won't sleep, force yourself to stay up all night). The purpose of these "outside of therapy" assignments is to help people to behave differently so that they can have different subjective experiences. Directives also increase the influence of the therapist in the change process and give the therapist information on how family members react to suggested changes. An example of a directive is to tell parents whose daughter interrupts them, "I want you to talk without your daughter interrupting you." In this situation, their resistance to change may dissolve as they attempt to disobey the directive. On the other hand, if they follow the directive, the therapist can gain more influence in their lives.

Paradox. One of the most controversial and powerful techniques in strategic family therapy is *paradox*. Although there are fine distinctions that can be made, this process is very similar to *prescribing the symptom*. It gives client families and their members permission to do something they are already doing and is intended to lower or eliminate resistance. In the video, James Coyne tells the couple to keep engaging the problem behavior in order to change it.

> TH (87): "So you understand that if we commit ourselves to this course of action, we may be dealing with events that are frequent enough that we won't have to plan them. They will happen anyway. We can be confident about that. But our main goal is not to try to change them but to bring in the details to talk about them and that's where the change occurs."

Jay Haley (1976) is one of the leading proponents of this technique. Paradox takes many forms, including the use of restraining, prescribing, and redefining.

1. In *restraining*, the therapist tells the client family that they are incapable of doing anything other than what they are doing. For example, a therapist might say, "In considering change, I am not sure you can do anything other than what you are presently doing."
2. In *prescribing*, family members are instructed to enact a troublesome dysfunctional behavior in front of the therapist. For instance, parents may be asked to show how they argue with their sixteen-year-old about when he will do his schoolwork and clean his room. They are to continue the argument for the same amount of time it usually takes and to come up with the same impasses.
3. *Redefining* is attributing positive connotations to symptomatic or troublesome actions. The idea is that symptoms have meaning for those who display them whether such meaning is logical or not. In the case of an acting out child, the therapist might redefine her behavior as an attempt to keep her parents together in the marriage by focusing their attention on her.

Ordeals. *Ordeals* involve helping the client to give up symptoms that are more troublesome to maintain than they are worth (Haley, 1984). In this method, the therapist assigns a family or family member(s) the task of performing an ordeal in order to eliminate a symptom. The ordeal is a constructive or neutral behavior that must be performed before engaging in the undesirable behavior. Haley delineates six steps in the process: (1) The problem must be defined clearly; (2) the person must be motivated to get rid of the problem; (3) the therapist needs to select an ordeal; (4) the directive that is the ordeal should be assigned with a rationale; (5) the ordeal is to continue until the problem behavior is gone; (6) the ordeal occurs in a social setting. For example, an ordeal might be to have the client give a present to someone with whom he or she is having a bad relationship—for example, a mother-in-law or ex-spouse—each time the symptoms occur. In essence, the ordeal is always healthy, but is not an activity that those directed to do it want to engage in. The hope is that those involved will give up the symptom in order to avoid performing the constructive behavior.

Pretend.   *Pretend* is a more gentle and less confrontive technique than most of the other procedures used in strategic family therapy. Cloe Madanes (1981, 1984) is identified as the creator of this concept. Basically, the therapist asks the family members to pretend to engage in a troublesome behavior. When a child is afraid, a parent is directed to pretend to be fearful, and the child is directed to protect and comfort the parent. The act of pretending to be afraid helps individuals change through experiencing control of a previously involuntary action.

Positioning.   The act of *positioning* by the therapist involves acceptance and exaggeration of what family members are saying (Piercy & Sprenkle, 1986). If conducted properly, it helps the family see the absurdity of what they are doing. They are, thereby, freed to do something else. For example, if a family member states that her relationship with her father is "difficult," the therapist might respond: "No, it is hopeless" (Watzlawick, 1983).

Clinical Example from Video

In the video, *Strategic Therapy with James Coyne* (Carlson & Kjos, 1998), a same-sex couple is helped to change their views on a long-term problem. Coyne saw each partner alone before bringing them together. He believes that people don't talk together well and that is why they are in therapy. It is hard to expect them to "get better" and talk to one another in order to have therapy and get help. Coyne takes control of the session from the beginning by this maneuver.

In the discussion section, Coyne uses a metaphor taken from the airlines, "That in case of an emergency an oxygen mask will drop from the compartment above. Make sure that your own oxygen mask is adjusted before you start helping others." By using this metaphor, he illustrates the need for each partner to take responsibility for their own behavior before trying to change their partner. This couple had been together for over a decade and was committed, attached, and healthy. Coyne wanted to take advantage of the fact that things in their relationship were overall pretty good, so he could help them resolve some of their annoying behaviors/patterns.

TH (6):   "So right now we have the luxury of not having something pressing."

M1 (6):   "Right."

Carlson w/ clients

TH (7): "And the external pressure outside the stress is reduced for right now. I wonder what might be useful to take advantage of that, to kind of, I don't know, Monday morning quarterback a little bit what's been going on and see what's been useful, and what you might want to consider working on. It would be helpful to me if you would give me a recent example of the kind of communication difficulties that sometimes arise."

He helps each partner to identify the specific sequences that are causing trouble for the relationship.

TH (9): "Can you think of an example that might be a small enough kind of an issue so that this pattern, this process, gets to be the issue and not the detail of it. Some of these things are trivial but they are ongoing."

He continues to focus on the positive and to help the couple have hope that things can and will get better. The focus is on where the couple is as opposed to where they are not!

TH (12): "Despite this style on his part, how have you managed to go, I mean that's an accomplishment for anybody to go twelve or thirteen years or ten years?"

He continues to focus on the positive nature of the relationship and to help the individuals think about things differently.

TH (13): "Sounds like maintenance improvement."

M1 (13): "Right. Overall I think we have a wonderful relationship."

TH (14): "It sounds like you have some insight into this process. Do you have any sense that he does?"

He continues to ferret out the details of the problem.

TH (20): "I see. So he doesn't always get that there is a real communication problem rather than just [you] trying to correct the way he speaks to you."

The therapist helps the partners to understand what is going on in their communication through his careful use of questions.

TH 24: "If I asked him what the most pressing problem was, what would he say?"

M1 (24): "I think that he thinks that I am too short-tempered. Probably that I need to control. I think that really bothers him because I do get real short-tempered."

TH (25): "With him or in general?"

Through questions, each individual begins to look at the problem differently, and to clearly identify what they would like to have happen.

TH (30): "How would he know that it wasn't personal, that he wasn't responsible?"

TH (31): "That would be a useful example to work from a time when indeed that's what he did. That you are allowed to vent, he saw that it wasn't personal, and not only were you able to get on with things, but he was able to get on with things, the day, whatever, without feeling that tension."

The therapist helps to make sure that each partner sees his role in maintaining the problem sequence.

TH (32): "Any sense of contribution that you might make when he is successfully able to negotiate these situations? Anything that you might do that aids him in doing that?"

He continues to notice the positive and builds up the partner when he sees behaviors that will contribute to successful resolution of the problem.

TH (34): "That kind of communication, that's a real achievement for anybody. Is it often you are able to talk with that clarity? That's a real accomplishment."

The therapist continues to "spell out" the pattern so that it can be viewed differently and new responses become possible.

TH (35):   "I mean to put it simple. There are times when you want to be able to communicate with a certain indelicacy, and you'd just as soon that he not take it personal."

M1 (35):   "Right. I want to address my own needs, not be thinking about what he is doing."

TH (36):   "So, maybe I'm moving too quickly, . . . but am I right in that you would feel comfortable, more comfortable if some situation could occur in which you were able to be upset, he was able to hear you out, not problem solve, and not take it personal?"

M1 (36):   "Yes."

TH (37):   "That would be some mark of improvement?"

In this next sequence, the therapist uses a simple reframe to help the individual see his partner in a more positive or less negative fashion. Is it possible that silence is really thoughtfulness?

TH (40):   "I'm wondering though, again I may be simple-minded on this point and giving him more credit than he deserves on it, but I am wondering are those times when he seems tuned out. Is he being thoughtful about what you are saying?"

A hallmark of the strategic approach is the use of carefully placed suggestions and assignments.

TH (48):   "I see. You know, one philosophy is if it's not broke right now, we won't fix it. The other is it doesn't have to be broke to improve things, and I kind of got a sense of wanting to check it out with you that you more operate in the second category, that there is a chance to improve some things, particular[ly] in the sense that you have gotten through a period of stress, and we have the luxury of kind of reflecting on things. Suppose though, as a part of any time that you do some improvements, that it is a matter of some things having to get, there is a bit of disruption. I don't know, just to give an example, getting my floors done. It means that I have to live with a lot of mess with the hope that that's what you have to do to get your floors done. I am wondering if you would be interested in thinking about the relationship the same way, that you would be willing to have some of these incidents occur. In your case, specifically, [are there] instances in which you looked for the opportunity to be upset about something and for you to announce that you are being upset, and you were not asking him to solve it, and you were hoping that he wouldn't take it personal and were able to focus on those things and maybe even not go out of the way to avoid them. Would that be an okay way to proceed?"

M1 (48): "I think so."

One partner leaves and the other comes into therapy. The process continues with similar questions that allow for new perceptions to develop.

TH (61): "So, if he is having a bad time of it, even if it's not personal, it can become your bad time. It will be something you have to do something about."

M2 (5): "Right, right."

TH (62): "Can you think of any time recently, even if it was a small matter. It doesn't have to be a big one. If it's a big one that's fine, too, in which that came up, a specific example. Can you think of a recent time when he was a bit moody or out of sorts?"

The therapist states the obvious to help the individual understand that his partner is not going to stop his behavior and that some alternatives need to be developed.

TH (64): "Now one solution, even if it's a nonrealistic one, would be that he never got upset again. We probably can't count on that one."

M2 (8): "I'd like that though."

With the second partner, the therapist continues to be positive while helping him to view the specific problem sequence.

TH (77): "I guess the thing that I have to keep in perspective, just having met you two, is that you and he have been together for twelve or thirteen years now, and that's no small achievement for anybody. And somehow, at times, he is angry in a way that viscerally, just gutwise, you react to him and, at times, you think out loud in a way that confuses him, but this is a couple that has gone through a lot and has a lot of strengths. It sounds like these are sort of, these certainly haven't been crucial to your surviving as a couple, but nonetheless they are sources of some annoyance. Are things at the point perhaps simply because things are going well in other ways, that you would want to have these sort of things happen as a chance to work on them?"

Before bringing back the other partner, the therapist presents what he hopes will be a successful and acceptable homework strategy.

TH (79): "Well, let me just try this out before I try it on both of you. What if it meant, I don't want to sound like *Mission Impossible,* but what if I offered this assignment, if you are willing to take it, that your job was to watch for opportunities in which he was out of sorts or angry or irritable, and you were inclined to solve the problem for him, and, without giving specific instructions how you are going to resolve that, we look to him maybe getting a better handle on his management of his emotion and you feeling less responsible, and we looked for those things to occur. In fact, we almost took them as opportunities, and the notion is you could then come back and talk to your counselor, about . . . sort of go over those.

M2 (23):   "I think that's . . . "

TH (80):   "So that, getting him upset and you feeling responsible, on one level we can look at, well, that's unfortunate. No relationship is perfect; but instead we could also look at it, well, here's an opportunity to see our reactions, to talk about our reactions, to collect this as an example, and, in some sense, if a week went by without him ever getting angry, that's nice, but it meant that there was nothing to report. So if something happened, it at least gave me something to work on. Is it too uncomfortable, or would you be willing to collect those sorts of things?"

The therapist continues to clarify the problem from this alternate perspective.

TH (83):   "On your part, I am wondering if we could look to opportunities in which you were thinking abstractly, thinking out loud, and he learned to tolerate that that's just the rough draft and that maybe the message is, in the long run, you appreciate that he is concrete, and he needs to come down to that level, but he needs to appreciate that at times you need to think out loud like that. And he should be patient."

With both partners in the therapy room, the therapist outlines the intervention. The therapist is not attempting to remove the pattern but to make it have less of an impact on the couple. He wants the couple to learn how to adjust to one another and learn acceptance.

TH (94):   "Well, we came up with some work for you of sorts. I have work for both of you to do if you are willing to accept this, and it sounds like we can take advantage of the fact that you've been through a rough period and that we can now, having that behind you, concentrate on how can things be improved. Things don't have to be broke for things to be improved. And the burden falls on you if you are willing to accept it from time to time to be irritable, or to be out of sorts, and the idea is that we don't necessarily want you to work up a head of steam just for the benefit of counseling, but from time to time it will happen anyway. And what we are looking for is those incidents to be grist for the mill, something to come in and talk about so each of you gets more of a sense of the other one's reaction. Does that sound okay?"

M1 (56):   "If I understand you, are you asking me to think of an instance and . . . "

TH (95): "No, to wait for the possibility, and so if a week goes by and you are never upset by anything, that could be a great week, but it means that you've had a holiday from the kinds of things, which we all need every now and then, from the kinds of things we are focusing on. If, on the other hand, something happened to upset you and you happened to feel somewhat responsible for that or on edge at a basic gut level at times that affects you, much as you would like it otherwise, it bothers you at that level, and we had a chance to talk about that. So we are looking to collect those. If you never get irritated that's fine. If you do, its something to work on. . . ."

The paradoxical nature of the assignment is highlighted.

TH (96): "It's not too weird that you are asked to go out and be irritable and you are asked to be abstract?"

M2 (37): "We do that anyway."

The therapist helps the couple to see that a good week may be one with problems or one without problems.

TH (103): "Well, if we follow this plan, I won't say go out and have a great week. I'd say have a very good one and have some problems come up that insures we have something to talk about. I hope that's not an odd way of . . ."

The therapist finishes the session with a metaphor about a car needing repairs and how it is necessary to drive the car to find out just what is wrong.

TH (106): "It's almost like if you think about your car having an intermittent problem. You can leave it in the driveway, or you can drive it around and hope the problem occurs so that you can report more clearly about what it is. Particularly when it is the kind of problem we can't necessarily observe when you're in."

If James Coyne had worked with the couple for a follow-up session, he would continue to see each of them separately. At that time, he would check to see what had been happening and how the assignment had worked out. He would ask each person how it set with him, looking for specifics about the interaction. If each one played out his role, Coyne would congratulate them because that would mean that they had something to talk about. His goal would be to insert himself into the couple's life, and, thus, change behaviors because they are, in a sense, being observed. Over time, he would like to see them become more tolerant of each other's behavior while changing their own behaviors.

Summary

Strategic therapy departed significantly from traditional methods of family therapy. It was directly focused on changing the complaint the family brings to therapy. The strategic therapist's model for following the behaviors around the presenting problem allows for a clear understanding of the self-perpetuating sequence of behaviors around the symptom. Once this has been discovered, the therapist develops a strategy to help the family prevent the repetition of the destructive behavior. The plan is to help shift the family organization so that the presenting problem no longer serves a function. The strategic intervention changes the family's perception, which makes different behaviors possible.

Strategic family therapists emphasize the present rather than the past. The family is viewed as being stuck at the present stage in the family life cycle and is having trouble transitioning to the next stage. Strategic therapists give directives or homework tasks to be completed outside the therapy session. By following these directives, the family goes through new experiences that change their perception of the presenting problem. The strength of this approach seems to be the brief nature of treatment.

To Learn More

Read the texts in the References that have an asterisk (*).

REFERENCES

Carlson, J. (In press.) Interview with Jay Haley. *The Family Journal, 9.*

Carlson, J., & Kjos, D. (1998). *Family therapy with the experts: Strategic family therapy with James Coyne.* Boston, MA: Allyn & Bacon.

Corey, G., and Bitter, J. (2001). Family systems theory. In G. Corey (Ed.), *Theory and practice of psychotherapy* (6th ed., pp. 382–453). Belmont, CA: Brooks/Cole.

Fisch, R. Weakland, J. H., & Segal, L. (1983). *The tactics of change.* San Francisco: Jossey Bass.

Haley, J. (1963). *Strategies of psychotherapy.* New York: Grune & Stratton.

Haley, J. (1971). *Changing families: A family therapy reader.* Orlando, FL: Grune & Stratton.

Haley, J. (1973). *Uncommon therapy: Psychiatric techniques of Milton H. Erickson, MD.* New York: W. W. Norton.

*Haley, J. (1976). *Problem-solving therapy.* San Francisco: Jossey-Bass.

*Haley, J. (1980). *Leaving home.* New York: McGraw-Hill.

*Haley, J. (1984). *Ordeal therapy.* San Francisco: Jossey-Bass.

Haley, J. (1985). *Conversations with Milton Erickson* (3 volumes). New York: W. W. Norton/Triangle.

*Madanes, C. (1981). *Strategic family therapy.* San Francisco: Jossey-Bass.

*Madanes, C. (1984). *Behind the one-way mirror: Advances in the practice of strategic therapy.* San Francisco: Jossey-Bass.

Minuchin, S. (1974). *Families and family therapy.* Cambridge, MA: Harvard University Press.

Papp, P. (1983). *The process of change.* New York: Guilford.

Piercy, F., & Sprenkle, D. (1986). *Family therapy sourcebook.* New York: Guilford.

Satir, V. (1964). *Conjoint family therapy.* Palo Alto, CA: Science and Behavior Books.

Segal, L. (1991). Brief family therapy. In A. M. Horne & M. M. Ohlsen (Eds.), *Family counseling and therapy*. (pp. 179–215). Itasca, IL: F.E. Peacock.

Watzlawick, P. (1978). *The language of change*. New York: Basic Books.

Watzlawick, P. (1983). *The situation is hopeless but not serious*. New York: W.W. Norton.

Watzlawick, R., Beavin, J. H., & Jackson, D. D. (1967). *Pragmatics of human communication*. New York: W.W. Norton.

5 Value-Sensitive Therapy

WILLIAM J. DOHERTY

William J. Doherty

Issues of moral personal responsibility and obligation are everywhere in therapy. To divorce or stay married, to move out of state and leave one's children after a divorce, to put one's mother in a nursing home or take her into one's own home, to deceive a potential employer about how long you plan to stay at the job, to allow a flirtation to become an affair, to yield to a new spouse's wishes for your children despite their resistance and your own doubts, these are examples of the moral dilemmas of everyday life. As therapists, we cannot escape them in our work. Our choice is to deal with the moral realm well in therapy, with a conscious model and set of skills, or to deal with it poorly, without a framework of theory and practice. But few of us have received any training in how to engage in moral conversation with clients.

I present here not a model of therapy but rather a perspective on the work of all therapists and a set of strategies for incorporating the moral realm into the practice of psychotherapy.[1] Although my own primary orientation is family systems therapy, readers are encouraged to apply the ideas in this chapter to what-

---

[1]Portions of this chapter have been adapted from Doherty (1995) and Doherty (2001).

ever model of therapy they practice. Because I am not presenting a distinct model of therapy, the outline of this chapter takes a different form from others in this volume.

Let's begin with a core definition. I define the moral domain as behavior that has consequence for the well being of others. *Morality*, as I use the term, deals with interpersonal behavior and its consequences. It seems clear that much of therapy revolves around clients' decisions that have important implications for the welfare of other people: spouses, children, parents, siblings, extended family, friends, coworkers, and the community. As therapists, we cannot avoid dealing with moral issues. Our choice is to deal with them well, with an explicit framework to guide our work, or to deal with them poorly.

The framework I offer in this chapter, spelled out in detail in Doherty (1995), begins with a critique of mainstream psychotherapy, moves to a conceptualization of the therapist as moral consultant, presents a set of techniques for engaging in moral conversation with clients, discusses the videotaped case as an illustration of the model, and deals with a major concern about this model.

Critique of Mainstream Psychotherapy

The heart of my critique is that most models of psychotherapy since the time of Freud have promoted an unbalanced emphasis on individual self-interest at the expense of responsibilities to family and community. I owe much of the framework for my social critique of psychotherapy to social scientists who have written about the modern culture of individualism and consumerism. The most influential, though not the earliest, critique came in 1985 with the book *Habits of the Heart: Individualism and Commitment in American Life* by Robert Bellah, Richard Madsen, William M. Sullivan, Ann Swidler, and Steven M. Tipton. The authors placed psychotherapy at the center of the growing hegemony of individual self-interest in U.S. society. They argued that most psychotherapists unwittingly promote a form of "expressive individualism," which is the cousin of "utilitarian individualism." Utilitarian individualism is the idea that, if individuals are free to pursue their private economic self-interest, the society as a whole will benefit. Expressive individualism applies the same logic to emotional well-being: We can each focus on ourselves, because personal psychological well-being inevitably leads to family and community well-being. At its crudest, expressive individualism is a form of psychological trickle-down economics in which responsibilities to others are reduced to responsibility to self.

The sociologist Phillip Rieff treated these issues prophetically in two important books, *Freud: The Mind of a Moralist* (1961) and *The Triumph of the Therapeutic* (1966). Rieff posited that three "character ideals" have successively dominated Western civilization: (1) the Political Man of classical antiquity (I retain Rieff's prefeminist language); (2) the Religious Man (Judaism, Christianity until the Enlightenment); (3) the Economic Man (Enlightenment through the early twentieth century); and now (4) the Psychological Man, whose goal is self-satisfaction and personal insight in order to master "the last enemy—his personality." Beginning with Freud, according to Rieff, "the best spirits of the 20th century have thus expressed their conviction that . . . the new center, which can be held even as communities disintegrate, is the self" (p. 5). More recently, Cushman (1995) echoed Rieff's critique, proposing that psychotherapy has been the tool of the capitalist, consumerist culture.

As the "therapeutic" increasingly supplants religion as the accepted guide for human conduct, the psychotherapist becomes de facto moral teacher in contemporary U.S. society. The problem with the therapist being seen as a moral teacher, of course, is that therapists have done their best to stay out of the morality business. A cornerstone of all the mainstream models of psychotherapy since Freud has been the substitution of scientific and clinical ideas for moral ideas. There have been exceptions of course, mostly notably in Alderian psychotherapy and in the work of Ivan Boszormenyi-Nagy (1987), who based his model of family therapy on intergenerational ethics. But, by and large, morality has been ignored or pathologized in psychotherapy.

Freud himself put moral conscience in the superego, an often times tyrannical, if necessary, bearer of the traditional morality of one's culture. Freud took morality outside the core personality (the ego), and outside of psychological treatment, and therapists have not put it back in either place since. The result has been a reflexive morality of individual self-fulfillment, with relational and community commitments seen as means to the end of personal well-being, to be maintained while they work for us and discarded when they do not. The often-quoted Gestalt therapy "prayer" penned by Fritz Perls in 1960s illustrates an ideology whose legacy is still with us:

> I do my thing, and you do your thing.
> I am not in this world to live up to your expectations,
> And you are not in this world to live up to mine.
> You are you and I am I,
> And if by chance we find each other, it's beautiful. If not, it can't be helped (Perls, 1969, p. 4).

When I read these quotes for the first time in the mid-1970s, I admired their vision and boldness. Now, I am appalled at their one-sidedness. I have seen too many parents "move on" from their children, too many spouses discard a marriage when an attractive alternative emerged, and too much avoidance of social responsibility under the rubric of "it's not my thing." There is now a widespread reevaluation of the fruits of unfettered self-interest at both the psychosocial and economic levels. Some of the reevaluation comes in the form of a rhetoric of return to an earlier era in which community traditions marginalized women and minority groups, when the pursuit of self-interest (mostly economic) was the privilege of a subset of Caucasian men. But there are many progressive voices of reevaluation, individuals and groups who appreciate what the ideals of personal freedom and the pursuit of happiness have contributed to the modern world, who see the struggle for freedom and equality as, in fact, still unfinished, but who nevertheless believe that mainstream U.S. culture is badly out of balance between private gain (both economic and psychological) and communitarian values and responsibilities.

There are two main reasons for the absence of morality in psychotherapy and for the recent interest in it. For the first six decades or so of psychotherapy's history, therapists could depend on most clients coming to therapy with a clear, albeit too rigid and unintegrated, sense of moral responsibility. Many people suffered from guilt and inhibitions about feelings and behaviors that were entirely human and not harmful to anyone; masturbation comes to mind as an example. A married client considering a divorce could be counted on to have internalized the social stigma about divorce and the moral mandate to remain married until death; the therapist might then help the client see that personal happiness is indeed a legitimate consideration in the decision to stay or leave, and that traditional notions of commitment do not necessarily require prolonged impairment in both parties in order to maintain a deadly marriage. In a world where therapists saw most people as oppressed by cultural norms dressed up as moral principles, psychotherapists could see themselves as agents of emancipation. The clients came with unexamined but powerful moral codes, and the therapists helped them deconstruct these codes and make their own decisions. The moral rules of conventional society, however, could be counted on to provide the scaffolding on which the client could build a more authentic life.

At the start of the new century, however, whatever served as the moral center of mainstream culture seems not to be holding. Massive cheating in the business world and in military academies, decreased but still unprecedented levels of crime and violence, shocking reports of physical and sexual abuse in families, widespread abandonment of children by fathers after divorce or when there was never a marriage—and the justification of each by appeals to personal entitlement, doing one's own thing, or victimization—are examples of trends that undermine any concern that most people in the United States have overlearned a rigidly conventional morality that they must be liberated from by an army of psychotherapists.

James Q. Wilson (1993), a public policy scholar, sums up this point when he describes the context of Freud and other pioneering intellectuals and artists who rejected conventional morality for the pursuit of self-knowledge and self-expression: "[They] could take the product of a strong family life . . . [good conduct] . . . for granted and get on with the task of liberating individuals from stuffy conventions, myopic religion, and political error" (p. 16).

But, like contemporary psychotherapists, these avant-garde leaders were borrowing on what Wilson terms the "moral capital" of past decades and centuries. After one hundred years, the moral capital is depleted and therapists no longer need to see themselves primarily as agents of liberation from an ethic of blind self-sacrifice and inauthenticity. At the cultural level, that battle has been largely won, but the fruits of victory are not as sweet as many of us imagined. Even Rollo May (1992), whose early writings were literate and powerful indictments of living by conventional social roles and obligations, reevaluated the role of psychotherapy before he died:

> We in America have become a society devoted to the individual self. The danger is that psychotherapy becomes a self-concern, fitting . . . a new kind of client . . . the narcissistic personality. . . . We have made of therapy a new kind of cult, a method in which we hire someone to act as a guide to our successes and happiness. Rarely does one speak of duty to one's society—almost everyone undergoing therapy is concerned with individual gain, and the psychotherapist is hired to assist in this endeavor (p. xxv).

I don't want to overstate this case, however. There are still people who have not gotten the message that they have a legitimate claim on selfhood. Women, in particular, have been given cultural permission to pursue personal autonomy only in the last few decades, whereas men have had such permission for much longer. But, by and large, the modal cultural pathology of our day is excessive individualism, not excessive conformity to moral codes.

The Therapist as Moral Consultant on Issues of Commitment

I remember clearly the moment when I could no longer escape the moral dimension of my work as a therapist. I was meeting with Bruce, a forty-year-old man, whose wife, Elaine, had just ended their marriage. Bruce returned from work one day to find that Elaine had tossed his belongings into his car and changed the locks on the house. Overwhelmed and depressed, Bruce came to see me for therapy. He told me he couldn't face the thought of going back to his house to pick up his children, three-year-old Karen and six-year-old Scott, for a visit. Even more intolerable was the prospect of returning alone to his small apartment after bringing them back to their mother. Tearfully, he said that he could not face Elaine after what she had done to him, although he still loved her and wanted to salvage their marriage.

The more Bruce talked the more he began to sprinkle in comments such as, "Maybe the kids would be better off if I just stayed away," and "I think I might need a complete break; maybe I should just pack up and move far away." In fact, a few years earlier, Bruce had lost contact with a child he had fathered with a woman he did not marry. I felt dismayed when he talked about abandoning his children, but my training had only equipped me with responses like, "What do you need to do for yourself right now to get through this?"

The most challenging statements from the traditional therapy paradigm I could offer a client like Bruce would be something like, "I wonder if you have considered the regret you will feel if you take yourself out of your children's lives," or "You may not be in a healthy enough frame of mind right now to make long-term decisions." There is nothing wrong with these statements; I used them in my work with Bruce. But, I also decided to do something decidedly nontraditional—to challenge him in explicitly moral terms. After listening at length to his pain over the end of his marriage, I gently but forcefully told him that I was concerned his children would be damaged if he abandoned them. His reply, "I'm worried about that too, but what kind of father will I be if I am an emotional wreck?" gave me an opening to continue on the track of moral discourse.

Throughout the conversation that ensued, I emphasized how important he was to them, even if he didn't think so and even if he was not emotionally at his best. I told him I could certainly understand that he might need a short time-out to collect himself before going back to his old house and facing Elaine again. But he was irreplaceable to his children, and, in my judgment, they would carry a life-long emotional burden if he simply disappeared from their lives. Finally, I reminded him that his children were not responsible for the marital breakup, and that it simply was not fair that they should be its casualties. I made these points not in the form of a lecture but as perspectives and opinions I offered as the conversation unfolded and Bruce pondered his course of action.

I am not the first therapist to respond this way to clients in a similar situation. Yet, I was struck by how little clinical training I had received on the moral issues I was confronting with Bruce, and I had very good teachers. What mainstream theory of psychotherapy could I look to for support? Like many others, I was trained to avoid "shoulding" my clients, to never inflict the language of "ought" on them. I had been socialized into a therapy profession that, by the 1970s, had developed the firm conviction that "shoulds" entrap people into living life for someone else. The only authentic life was based on heeding the dictates of "I want."

While family therapists are trained more than individual therapists to consider the multiple perspectives of family members, as a practical matter, we also tend to easily lose sight of the moral stakeholders who are not present in therapy sessions. Family therapists are comfortable talking about what clients need and deserve from other family members, but are very reluctant to talk about what clients owe other family members in care, commitment, fairness, or honesty. Being a family therapist does not carry immunity to the cultural ideal of expressive individualism.

To some therapists my pronouncements to Bruce about parental commitment no doubt sound starkly moralistic, but I wanted to make two things very clear to him: I was not neutral on his decision about staying committed to his children, and I was giving priority to his children's long-term needs over his short-term distress. Bruce, with whom I had established a bond of real trust, quickly grasped my point, and moved from whether to stay involved to how to accomplish it. In the end, despite lapses I'll discuss in a moment, he remained a committed father to Karen and Scott, and later reconnected with his child from the previous relationship.

When I describe this case to my colleagues, some point out that I could have obtained the same result—Bruce staying involved with his children—by appealing to his self-interest and emphasizing the guilt and remorse he would eventually feel if he abandoned them. I did, in fact, use these appeals, because I think they are valid. Parents' relationships with their children can be deeply rewarding; when a parent abandons a child it is not only the child who is damaged. However, in dealing with moral decisions I think it is generally a mistake to appeal only to a client's self-interest, even if that appeal "works," because the ethic of personal gain that we thus promote erodes the quality of our clients' lives and, ultimately, the quality of community life.

Expanding the therapeutic conversation beyond the client's self-interest, however, pushes most therapists beyond their training and beyond most psychotherapy literature currently available. In most models of therapy, the lingua franca is self-speak: I want, I need, I feel, I think. Even those who also speak "systems" tend to appeal to individuals in terms of personal cost–benefit analysis. The upshot is that, even if I, as a therapist, happen to believe that a father has a moral obligation to remain in the lives of his children, I am trained to approach clients only in terms of their self-interest. I am not saying that being concerned with clients' immediate needs is an invalid therapeutic concern, but I am arguing that, when that becomes our only consideration, therapy lacks moral and human depth, and therapists end up promoting trickle-down psychological economics.

Stated simply, psychotherapy lacks a conscious moral tradition that can be discussed, debated, and refined. The avoidance of explicit moral considerations, however, has left therapists vulnerable to an implicit moral pedagogy in our work and our writings. Feminists have shown that, if therapists don't have a clearly formulated value system regarding gender relations, they will enforce traditional gender norms in therapy, and the same is true for other value issues: If you don't have a coherent framework of moral beliefs, you will inevitably fall back on good, old-fashioned U.S. individualism, which is, in fact, a far more influential cultural legacy than either Mom or apple pie.

At the same time, it is crucial for therapists to make the distinction between personal values and moral convictions. A good education is one of my personal values, but I am not invested in getting clients to embrace it. Emotional intimacy, based on mutual self-disclosure, is another of my personal values, but I don't pursue it when clients let me know that they are quite content to go through life without a lot of what I might consider "depth" in their relationships. On the other hand, I consider commitment the moral linchpin of family relationships. It is more than a private, idiosyncratic value that I can choose whether or not to promote in therapy. To have professional integrity, I believe I must bring this moral value to bear in my therapy and in my teaching and supervision. To treat commitment otherwise is to play into the very style of thinking that initially led Bruce to consider giving up his kids: Commitment to one's children is just one of a number of competing personal values to be weighed in a values hierarchy of one's choosing.

Although he had decided to remain in his children's lives, Bruce still maintained what I considered a "contractual" idea of being a parent: He assumed that his continued investment in his children should be dependent on what the children gave back. This is an especially tempting line of thought for noncustodial fathers who are trying to decide whether to stay involved or "move on."

Although Bruce set up regular visits with his children, he tended to expect too much cooperation and too great a return of gratitude on his investment of time and energy. His children's misbehavior and "me first" attitude exasperated him, and he sometimes threatened to cut off visitation if they did not start "showing some respect." Describing his struggles with his children, Bruce spoke the same language he might use with a new love relationship that has hit some shoals: "What is this relationship doing for me that I should stay in it?" The language of family commitment as "covenant"—unbreakable, unilateral, unbrokered parental investment—was completely absent. Bruce did love his children, and wanted to remain their father, but he had learned an economic and contractual way of thinking about relationships that was confounding his moral sensibilities.

As might be expected, when Bruce threatened his children with the possibility of ending their visits, they became both more insecure and less cooperative, testing his commitment even more. This pattern changed only after I challenged Bruce's assumption about what kids owe to their parents and are capable of giving to their parents. I told him that young children do not thank their parents very often. The issue wasn't Karen's and Scott's behavior, but Bruce's ability to offer an unconditional commitment to them. It was only once they felt his unswerving emotional investment that Bruce would get the cooperation—and love—he was seeking.

After working with Bruce on his commitment as a father, I myself was changed. I began to see moral issues when previously I had seen only clinical issues. I became more aware of how I had previously promoted a moral agenda of self-interest without being aware of it. For the first time, I was able to translate the insights of social scientists such as Robert Bellah to my everyday work with clients. Take the case of Joe, for example, who came to see me after Bruce had finished therapy.

Another Divorced Father's Commitment

Joe had managed a continued commitment to his two daughters, now eleven and thirteen, for five years after his divorce. But he was caught up short when his ex-wife remarried. Joe was tortured by the thought that another man was going to raise his children and win their loyalty. He became more distant and critical toward his daughters, even warning them that, if he ever learned that they called the new man "dad," they would pay a terrible, unspecified price. The price, as I came to learn, would be his withdrawal from their lives.

Joe's crisis of parental commitment stemmed from his insecurity about competing with another man in his daughters' lives. He was putting his daughters into a terrible bind: disappoint their mother by rejecting her new husband, or accept the new stepfather and risk losing their father. I worked with Joe and his daughters to help him realize that he was a one-of-a-kind figure in their lives, their only father whom no one could replace. After his insecurities became less overwhelming, I helped him see how damaging it was to his daughters when he let his commitment to them rest on how they felt about someone else. The security of noncustodial, twice-a-month father–child relationships is fragile enough without this impossible burden.

From my moral point of view, Joe was doing wrong by his daughters. It is wrong to manipulate children's loyalties the way he did, particularly the threat to use abandonment, the parental version of a nuclear weapon. Joe was not a bad person, but he was lacking sufficient moral fortitude to keep his commitment unquestioned. Of course, he was also lacking a variety of psychological resources to help him through his crisis. His now-deceased father had been inconsistent, his mother had rejected him after his marriage, and his relationships with women were unstable and conflictual. There was plenty to work on clinically. What, then, is the advantage of also describing Joe as lacking moral commitment as a parent? Why not just use clinical language that does not moralize and that keeps the therapist out of the moral judgment seat?

The problem with using only psychological language is that it tends to be long on explanations and short on responsibility. A psychological evaluation of Joe would point to the factors that prevent him from truly committing himself to his children. And the subsequent therapy, perhaps long-term, would try to help him get to the point where he could commit himself fully. In the meantime, of course, his children are being harmed just as surely as if he were abusing them. Sometimes it is necessary to do the right thing before understanding why we have been doing the wrong thing.

The moral dimension added urgency to my therapy with Joe and his daughters. From a moral point of view, he did not have the luxury of delaying change until he achieved more insight, higher self-esteem, or better emotional resolution of his divorce. During the first therapy session I introduced my concerns for the bind his children must be feeling. During the second and third sessions, after listening empathetically and establishing a genuine therapeutic bond with Joe—he knew I cared about him and wanted to help him—I challenged him to take prompt action to undo the damage his stance was inflicting on his children, and to take full responsibility for blackmailing them emotionally.

Earlier in my career, I would have been afraid to challenge someone like Joe in moral terms. What if he collapsed in guilt and shame, or became enraged and dropped out of therapy? What if he agreed in order to placate me, but did not follow through with real change? Somewhat to my surprise, I have not encountered these reactions. The keys, in my view, are caring and timing. When I encourage or challenge a client in the moral realm, I do it with full compassion for the powerful personal binds that can lead us all to compromise our moral beliefs, along with a sense of appropriate timing about when to listen and support, when to raise questions, and when to challenge. In his personal insecurity and his terror about losing his children, Joe was losing his moral compass, which for years had pointed toward commitment to his daughters without loyalty binds with their mother.

My challenge to Joe, and to other clients whom I have worked with in this manner, was to the moral sensibilities he already had. He loved his daughters and would not purposefully harm them. When I showed him the harm he was doing, and invited his daughters into a therapy session to say it for themselves, Joe accepted responsibility without exaggerated self-reproach and immediately set about mending the damage by reassuring his daughters that he would love them always and that they could relate to their stepfather however they wanted. Joe recovered his moral compass and lifted from his daughters a burden they could had not have carried and remained emotionally healthy. And the moral fabric of a family had been resewn with a stronger thread of commitment. Not all cases are as straightforward as Joe's, partly because Joe was a good father who was temporarily impaired by jealousy. I was appealing to a value he held close to his heart: to be there for his children no matter what.

Commitment to Parents and Spouses

The most frequent expression of moral consultation in therapy involves, not a challenge by the therapist, as in the cases above, but rather acknowledgment and affirmation of the client's moral language and moral sensibilities. When a female client whom I was seeing in family therapy reported, during the check-in at the beginning of the session, that she had just come from visiting her dying mother in the nursing home, she added: "I know she was not a very good mother in many ways, but now that she is dying I feel an obligation to be there for her." I replied, simply, "Of course you do." This is a simple affirmation of her moral sensibilities.

An elderly woman, who was learning to be more assertive with her husband of fifty years, came to a session worried about whether she was being "fair" to her husband by being more assertive with him. (He had declined to participate in the therapy.) Ten years ago, I would have suggested to her that fairness was not the issue; rather the issue would be something like her personal sense of power or her use of appropriate assertiveness skills or whether her efforts were paying off in terms of relational change and her own happiness. Now my first response to her moral question was, "That's an important question. What kinds of things are you doing that you think might be unfair to your husband?" After some discussion she came to her own conclusion that she was feeling skittish about her new assertiveness, but that she was not being unfair to her husband by speaking up for herself for the first time. She was not taking advantage of her lifelong companion; indeed, he seemed happier overall these days, although he disapproved of her being in therapy. My point here is that I thought it was important to honor the moral consideration my client broached in therapy, rather than reject that language in favor of clinical language.

One might think that supporting a client's spontaneous moral expressions is a completely obvious thing to do. Unfortunately, it is not. After a professional presentation during which I told the story of how I tried to affirm the woman who felt a sense of commitment to her dying mother, a professional in the audience told me about a similar situation when she herself had been in therapy with a highly regarded therapist during the time her own mother was dying. When she told her therapist of her sense of obligation to help her mother during these last months, the therapist challenged her with the pointed question "What is she to you now?" This is a classic illustration of egocentric therapeutic morality at work:

Every expression of obligation is unhealthy until proven otherwise, and every relationship should be measured by current rewards and costs.

Many therapists would agree that commitment to one's children and one's frail parents are moral issues in therapy, but what about marital commitment? (By marriage, I mean sexually bonded relationships in which two individuals have made a public commitment to be permanent life partners.) The reigning clinical assumption about couples considering divorce might be expressed as follows: Is each partner getting back enough for what he or she is putting into it? Certainly this kind of bottom-line thinking is not only valid, but has particular relevance for women who have historically been discouraged from asserting their self-interest in marriage. Nevertheless, missing from most clinical discussions of divorce is any consideration of moral issues about faithfulness to one's marriage (dare I say it?) vows and responsibility to one's children. The great fear, of course, is that such talk in therapy only serves to entrap people in toxic and even dangerous marriages.

In her book *Uncoupling* (1986), the sociologist Diane Vaughan describes how clients sometimes use therapists as "transition figures" to make an exit from a marriage, particularly when they go to individual therapy. Therapists treating individuals who are in distressed marriages are in a powerful position to encourage or discourage marital commitment. The assumptions embedded in the very language of therapy can move people away from their marital commitment. Every time therapists focus mainly on the questions "What are you getting out of this marriage?" and "Why are you staying?" they are implicitly encouraging divorce based on a self-interested, cost–benefit analysis of what the client is currently deriving from the relationship.

An example of therapists' bias against responsible commitments comes from the experience of a friend. She went to a well-regarded psychotherapist after her husband of twenty-one years (they had three children) announced he was having an affair and wanted a separation. The husband then began to fall apart emotionally and had to be hospitalized shortly thereafter. Just three weeks into this marital crisis, my friend's therapist told her that her desire to work to salvage the marriage reflected an "inability to mourn" and a "reluctance to get on with her life." Fortunately, she fired the therapist and got into marital therapy with her husband; they worked it out together.

I want to be clear here: Self-interest is a valid and even necessary component of a marital commitment decision. My concern is that self-interest is often the only language accepted in therapy when an individual is making the fateful decision about ending a marriage. Many therapists will dismiss as cop-outs a client's statement that he or she is staying married "for the children's sake" or because "I made a commitment for better or worse." These are seen as excuses to avoid confronting a hard decision based on one's own needs. I certainly thought that way during the 1970s and early 1980s, when I would urge clients to focus on their own needs to stay married or get divorced, (the kids will be fine if the parents are fine). I am now willing to recognize and honor clients' moral considerations in the tortuous decision-making process that thoughts of marital separation almost always bring.

The next case illustrates the power of moral commitment in sustaining a troubled marriage. When Judith and Steve came to me for marital therapy, they were at one of the lowest points in a marriage that had seen few high points. Judith was a part-time nurse and Steve was a security guard. After fifteen years of marriage and two children, ages twelve and ten, Judith and Steve were each in therapy, Steve in a group dealing with childhood abuse issues, and Judith in individual therapy focused on her low self-esteem. Each of them was terribly frustrated with the other. Steve, who was beginning to understand the distortions in his family history and his personality, felt Judith alternately abandoned him and treated him like her patient. Judith, who was recovering from years of verbal abuse from Steve, had little tolerance for his complaints about her.

Although the therapy was tough and slow-going, often one step forward and two steps back, I was amazed at their persistence. They were one of the more troubled couples I had worked with, but they stubbornly refused to move toward divorce. Earlier in my career, I might have precipitated a crisis in the therapy—"either make progress or let's quit"—but I found myself hanging in there with them, encouraged by their occasional periods of progress.

After the third or fourth major relapse during the first year of therapy, I told them that I was running out of ideas to help them and asked if they wanted to continue to see me. They both insisted that they did not want a divorce because it was antithetical to the values of their Jewish faith and because it would harm their children. We talked about what sustained their commitment and they explained that their lives centered on the religious rituals, especially weekly Sabbath meals that they held no matter what the state of their relationship. They felt that these rituals provided a glue that helped them stay bonded during very rough periods. Judith and Steve had internalized a powerful and important prescription from their Jewish heritage: The integrity of marriage and family life is too important to compromise without a sustained, energetic, and even stubborn, effort to maintain it. I chose not to pathologize their refusal to give up on their marriage.

I told Judith and Steve that I respected their persistence and courage and that, if they wanted to continue to work on their marriage, I would work with them. This seemed to galvanize them for renewed effort, which produced the longest sustained period of intimacy in their marriage. I did not do anything different in therapy; we just kept working on their ability to identify their needs, negotiate openly and fairly, and keep the children out of their problems. It was like a losing football team deciding its problem was not the personnel, but how hard the team worked.

Judith and Steve emerged from therapy with a marriage that not only was no longer emotionally debilitating, but also had a good measure of joy and satisfaction. I expect I will see them from time to time in the future, to help them over rough spots. They don't have a great marriage and they will always have trouble dealing with conflicts that trigger old vulnerabilities. But they regard their relationship as a "good enough" marriage, one that is grounded in their commitment to each other and to their children, and their mutual determination to make it work even if it is not the marriage they had hoped for in their youth.

I like to present a case like Judith and Steve to workshop participants and ask them if they are neutral about whether people stay married or get divorced. Generally, the students say that they will support whatever direction the clients want to take. But what if the clients are uncertain about whether to separate or to try to fix their marriage in therapy? Are you neutral then? Most say "yes." Then I ask if they are as neutral as they would be on the question, say, of whether a client switches jobs from the county government to the city government, or from IBM to Apple? The latter decisions are lifestyle and career advancement decisions that are generally not fraught with heavy moral weight. The decision to end a marriage, especially if there are dependent children but even if there are not, is a thoroughly moral issue because of past promises made, a life structure in place, and future consequences for many people whichever path is taken.

As therapists, we are moral consultants, not just psychosocial consultants. We should not try to impose our beliefs on undecided clients, but we can advocate in an open manner when appropriate. My own stance on marital commitment, which I use in most cases in which there is not abuse and intimidation, is to tell clients who are considering divorce that I will help them look at their situation and make their own decision, but that I will be leaning in the direction of finding possibilities of restoring the viability of the marriage. I do not conduct a neutral marital assessment, as if their marriage was an automobile I was checking out to help the owner decide whether to repair it or junk it. I will be looking for areas of strength, sniffing for the presence of hope in the midst of pessimism, listening for clues for change. If clients ultimately decide on a divorce, I accept their decision and, if they have children, move on to discuss how they can maintain their commitment as coparents to their children. If they decide to try marital therapy in order to restore their relationship, I tell them that I will be an advocate for their marriage, as well as for each of them individually, and that I will continue to advocate for their marriage until one of them calls me off. In these ways, I define myself as supporting the value of marital commitment, a moral issue about which I am not neutral, in the context of respect for clients as moral agents of their own lives.

Moral Consultation in Therapy: Truthfulness

It seemed an innocent-enough lie. Chad's mother did not approve of his new girlfriend, and Chad, age twenty-one, felt that his mother's underlying agenda was not wanting to be replaced as Chads's first love. He and his mother were recovering from an unhealthy and enmeshed relationship during Chad's adolescence. Chad, who was seeing me for depression, had only recently moved to his own apartment and begun to function emotionally without regular transfusions of support from Mom. With Thanksgiving now approaching, Chad wanted to spend the day with his girlfriend and her family instead of with his mother, but he thought that his mother would be hurt and angry if he did not spend Thanksgiving with her. Chad told me he was considering telling his mother that he had to work all day on Thanksgiving and then would be spending the evening studying for a big exam.

Chad didn't like the idea of lying to his mother, but he also didn't want the grief he would get for abandoning her on a major family holiday. Standard therapeutic discourse would take an entirely pragmatic, and not a moral, approach to his decision-making process. What would he accomplish by deceiving his mother, and what would he accomplish by telling her the truth? What was the likelihood of his mother finding out the truth anyway? Was the risk of discovery and recrimination worth the potential gain of avoiding a guilt-inducing discussion? How badly did he want to spend the day with Stan? How upset did he think his mother would be with the straight story, and how uncomfortable might Mom make it for Chad if Chad told her the truth?

Another standard therapeutic tack would be to express confidence in Chad to handle himself with his mother without resorting to deception. Chad was cowering to a mother who had far less power over him than she had previously. It would be developmentally healthier for Chad to be aboveboard with his mother and take whatever heat comes. He no longer needed to hide his true self.

These two therapeutic stances—the first about risks and benefits of lying and the second about Chad's self-development and self-assertion—are valid and useful ways of helping Chad think through his decision. I called on both stances at various times during our conversation. I thought it would be better developmentally for Chad to take an open stand at this time, and I thought there were serious risks that his mother would discover or intuit the truth, thereby leading to even more recriminations than the truth would bring. I explored with Chad why he was afraid to be honest with his mother about this situation, and expressed my concern for his personal well-being as he contemplated his decision.

But there was more to our conversation than concerns for Chad's fears and personal well-being. I asked him about the possible effects of the deception on his mother and on his relationship with his mother. The effect on his mother was easy to estimate if she found out the truth: She would feel hurt and betrayed and patronized, as if she could not handle the truth. The effect on the relationship could also be serious: a breach of trust and trustworthiness, and an encouragement for Mom, who had not always been honest with Chad in the past, to weave her own tangled web in the future. In other words, lying in this situation ran the risk of hurting his mother and undermining mutual trust in a highly significant relationship.

Mostly I stayed in a low-intensity questioning and exploring mode with Chad, along with an occasional expression of concern for consequences for Mom or the relationship. When he looked past his immediate fear of telling his mother, Chad had no trouble seeing these other dimensions. Indeed, it was partly his concern for his mother and their relationship that had led Chad to consult with me about the decision. He could see that the first lie ("I'm working and have to study") would probably lead to subsequent lies ("Oh, I had an okay day. We weren't busy at work. I didn't miss the turkey. I only talked briefly to my girlfriend today on the phone." And Chad's inquiries about his mother's Thanksgiving would feel disingenuous. Witness the distorting power of deception even if the other person does not suspect or discover the deception. As philosopher Sissela Bok (1979) asserts, lies give power to the deceiver over the one deceived, and patterns of lying inevitably distort and erode human relationships. And this is true whether or not the deceived person knows it.

After Chad came to the decision to tell his mother the truth—a decision I told him I supported and offered to have him tell his mother during a family therapy session—I reinforced his image of himself as a courageous, truth-telling individual. In other words, I addressed the theme of integrity. Integrity is harmony between our moral beliefs and our actions. As Chad had grown psychologically healthier in the past few years, he had learned to be more frank and direct with people in his life. That is partly why he was not comfortable with his plan to lie to his mother about Thanksgiving. When he told me he felt much better about facing his mother with the truth, whatever the reaction, I ended my part of the discussion by saying that I was glad that he had made a choice that was more consistent with his values and beliefs. In other words, I emphasized how he was maintaining his moral integrity, which is one of the responsibilities of adulthood, a realm in life he was just beginning to enter after years of overwhelming emotional dependency. When he shared his decision with his mother in a family therapy session, she took it well and said she was glad her son could be so honest with her.

This may seem like a fairly benign example of truthfulness, but I chose to present it precisely because this is the kind of situation in which therapists have tended to miss the moral dimension. The effects of deception are much more apparent, and the moral issues therefore much more obvious, when it comes to "big lies," for example, about an affair or about the adoption status of a child. I am more interested in exploring the more subtle examples that provide the invisible moral background of routine therapy issues.

Although different schools of psychotherapy take different approaches to the issue of truthfulness, none deals adequately with the moral dimension. Insight-oriented therapies, beginning with Freud, have emphasized truthfulness with self, that is, discovering and honestly facing hidden or repressed dimensions of one's personality. Humanistic and growth-oriented therapies, beginning with Carl Rogers (1965) have emphasized present self-awareness more than mining for hidden historical and repressed truths about the self, and they add the interpersonal dimension of "speaking my truth" to others. They stress honest expression of wants and feelings, but more for the sake of authenticity and self-development than as a moral mandate. The emphasis is on my need and right to express what is true for me, rather than on your need and right to hear the truth from me. The distinction is not a trivial one.

In Chad's case, the psychodynamically or insight-oriented therapist would focus on the underlying personality dynamics of Chad's decision about deceiving his mother. Chad's internal process could be viewed as demonstrating his arrested psychological development. The actual choice of lying or truth-telling might be viewed as insignificant; the therapeutic gold lies in the deeper meaning of his struggle. The question of Mom's needs and rights would not be particularly relevant. My point is not that a psychodynamically oriented therapist would never address the moral dimension of lying, but that the therapeutic discourse generated by the model itself cannot generate such moral discussion. Conventionally trained therapists who deal with the moral dimension of life are not using their "native tongue" as therapists; they are making it up as they go along.

Humanistic and growth-oriented therapists working with Chad would pay more attention to his present decision-making process. One approach would be to help him determine whether he would empower and liberate himself more by telling the truth or by lying to his mother. Because self-expression is aimed primarily at serving personal needs, the therapist might help Chad do a cost–benefit analysis of the issues, with the therapist being neutral about the outcome as long as it promotes the growth of the client. For example, he might decide to not risk lying and harming a relationship that he needs. Or the therapist who believes that authentic truth-telling is generally best for individuals might help Chad define what he wants clearly in his relationship with his mother. From this perspective, Polonius's admonition to Hamlet, "To thine own self be true," can only be fulfilled if we generally tell our truth to others. In either approach—appeal to personal needs or to personal authenticity—the independent moral claims of others on our trustworthiness are absent.

Two other schools of therapy deserve our attention on the matter of truthfulness. Cognitive–behavioral therapists have a here-and-now orientation to clients' decision making. They focus on dysfunctional beliefs and behavioral skills aimed at helping clients maximize their psychological rewards in life. Cognitive–behavioral therapists might question Chad's catastrophic expectations of what will happen if he tells his mother the truth about his Thanksgiving plans. And they might help him learn the assertiveness skills needed to deal straightforwardly with his mother: the ability to say what he wants and to not be deflected by manipulation. As with the other models of therapy, this approach has much to commend it for Chad's situation. But the implicit moral frame is still one of self-interest, even though the therapist might personally hope that Chad ultimately does not think he needs to lie to his mother.

Family therapy is more relational than the individual psychological models of therapy. Most family therapists would be concerned about the effect of Chad's lie on his relationship with his mother. They would advocate for the relationship as well as for Chad. Family therapists would look for the generational patterns of deception and secrets, viewing these as unhealthy for close human connections (Imber-Black, 1993). However, most family therapists would not conceptualize Chad's decision in moral terms, only in relational terms. The implicit moral theory is as follows: People need healthy family relationships and healthy family relationships are based, in part, on honesty. What is missing is family members' *obligations* to each other. Most family therapists use either the language of health and dysfunction or the language of effective or ineffective problem solving, and sometimes the language of personal empowerment, but eschew explicit moral discourse about lying. The family therapist Ivan Boszormenyi-Nagy (1987), on the other hand, does believe that family members have responsibilities to one another because there are moral bonds that connect them. Boszormenyi-Nagy, however, has not written extensively about truthfulness *per se*. Thus, the family therapy tradition provides some of the important elements of a morality of truthfulness in psychotherapy, but so far has not gone far enough in elaborating it.

Why should therapists care about truthfulness and lying? First, some definitions and conceptual distinctions. By truthfulness, I don't mean always speaking what is factually true in a situation. I mean speaking what one *believes* to be true. I might tell you that I will come to your party but not realize that I have an out-of-town commitment. I was truthful with you but in error about my ability to follow through. In other words, there is a distinction between being truthful and speaking the truth. Of course, truthfulness is limited by our self-knowledge and our proclivities for self-deception. But the morality of truthfulness rides on the faithfulness of our words to what we believe.

Belief in one another's truthfulness, according to Bok (1979), is the cornerstone of social relations, without which cooperation and trust cease to exist. She writes: "Trust in some degree of veracity functions as a *foundation* of relations among human beings; when this trust shatters or wears away, institutions collapse" (p. 33). Therapists should be concerned with truthfulness, then, because it is the foundation of trust, without which human relations disintegrate. Truthfulness is not only about personal insight or personal development or psychological gain; it is also the moral foundation of social relations.

I have been using the term *lie* without defining it. In Bok's definition, a lie is "an intentionally deceptive message in the form of a statement" (p. 16). I am lying when I assert something that I do not believe in order to deceive you. Lying, then, is an active process rather than merely hiding from you what I know. Chad would not have been lying to his mother if he had said, "I have other plans" and then declined to be specific. He did not necessarily owe his mother a full explanation of his Thanksgiving plans, but he went farther than concealment when he concocted a false story in order to have his mother believe that his intention would have been to spend Thanksgiving at home. Thus, Chad's story would have been a lie as defined here.

Lying, then, is different from keeping secrets, which has to do with the domain of privacy. Everyone, according to Bok, has a legitimate area of privacy, of experiences, thoughts, and wishes that are not to be intruded on by others. Illegitimate inquiries about one's sexual past are a good example. Truthfulness, then, does not mandate full disclosure of all one's thoughts, actions, and feelings. Given Chad's previous experience with his mother's intrusiveness, if his mother had inquired about how serious he was about this woman friend, he would be justified in either telling his mother that he didn't want to get into it, or in shrugging off her question with an evasive, "I don't know." But going beyond maintaining privacy to manufacturing untrue stories would move him into the domain of lying, turning the tables on the his mother by leading her on. Of course, in everyday life it is not always clear where privacy ends and the other person's right to know begins, as when one's sexual past may have consequences for the current partner's health, or when failing to disclose one's deep dissatisfaction with a marriage undermines the spouse's ability to take corrective action or to protect his or her interests. These are delicate areas of moral consultation in therapy.

In addition to undermining relationships, lying imposes unfair and sometimes oppressive burdens on the one deceived. A lie—and, I would add, an unfair secret—often constructs a sense of unreality, a disharmony between observations, feelings, and intuitions, on the one hand, and the "truth" that the other has convinced us to believe. Rachel Hare-Mustin (1994) critiques a published therapy case in which a woman arrived home to confront a partially clothed husband, another woman dressing herself as she emerged from the bathroom, and a rumpled, semen-stained bed. Her husband maintained vehemently that he had a wet dream and that the woman, the girlfriend of a relative, had just stopped to use the bathroom! The wife felt as if she were going crazy. Their marital therapist dealt with this situation as two people with different "stories" based on their observations and experiences. Hare-Mustin criticized the therapist's handling of the case on feminist grounds of privileging the oppressive story of the husband over the experience of the wife, who, as a woman, has been trained to yield to the authority of males.

From the perspective of this chapter, an additional criticism of the case is that the therapist colluded in the husband's lie by treating his story as having equal truth-value with the wife's. I am not suggesting that the therapist should have told the husband he was lying—such confrontations rarely accomplish anything—but rather that the therapist should have supported the needs of the wife, who was having trouble resisting the power of a big lie. By not supporting the wife's truth-telling over the husband's lying, the therapist contributed to the distortion of her experience and to the oppressive power of the lie. The therapist fell prey to a kind of postmodern fantasy that all stories are created equal, including those of victims and those of perpetrators. Are the truth-claims of historians and Holocaust survivors on an equal footing with the truth-claims of those who deny the historicity of the Holocaust? Heaven help us if they are. Truthfulness is a moral issue in psychotherapy, not just a psychological and interpersonal issue.

Lying is about power and covert self-protection, and truthfulness (within the context of sensitivity) is about sharing power and the willingness to be vulnerable. Ultimately, there is no contradiction between truthfulness as a hallmark of personal authenticity and empowerment and truthfulness as a moral mandate. All the traditional theories of individual psychotherapy support the value of truthfulness for the well-being of individuals. What they miss is the importance of truthfulness in the moral order of relations between people, the notion that others have legitimate demands on us for honesty and that truthfulness is a core element of character. If therapists fail to see the moral dimension of being truthful, then they only help people speak the truth when it will serve their need or promote their personal growth. And they may resort to their own mental calculus about truthfulness and deception in and out of therapy. In either case, the bent needle of truthfulness further tangles the relational web in which we live.

Specific Interventions in Moral Consultation

Psychotherapy is a form of conversation, and moral consultation in psychotherapy can range from the mildest affirmations to the most intense challenges. Following are eight types of responses I have used with clients in dealing with moral issues, listed in increasing order of intensity. I include brief examples drawn from the issue of family commitment. It is important to keep in mind that these moments of moral conversation punctuate otherwise regular clinical interactions. Some of the examples may not be consistent with every therapist's mode of doing therapy; they are not intended to be prescriptive but rather to make more concrete the range of statements related to moral responsibility that are consistent with value-sensitive therapy. Two important principles for the use of the model are: (1) that the more intense the level of moral intervention, the stronger the empathic connection with the client must be; and (2) in dealing with more than one client in couples or family therapy, the therapist should move back and forth between the perspectives of the parties involved.

1. *Validate the language of moral concern when clients use it spontaneously.* A non-custodial father of school-age children was pondering whether to take a job in a city far away form his children. He wondered whether his move would hurt his ability to be a good father to them. I affirmed that, indeed, this was a very important concern.

2. *Introduce language to make more explicit the moral horizon of the client's concern.* The father in the above example proceeded to frame the issue in terms of the possible damage to his "relationship" with his children, a category that does not necessarily encompass the possible harm to the children and the importance of his one-way commitment to them. I sensed that his concern was deeper than his language implied, and I said, "Yes, they may feel that you are walking out of their lives by moving away." My response focused the subsequent discussion more clearly on the needs of the children.

3. *Ask questions about clients' perceptions of the consequences of their actions on others, and explore the personal, familial, and cultural sources of these moral sensibilities.* A woman suddenly left her second husband and moved into a small apartment where her teenage children could not live, leaving them with their stepfather. Her daughter, in particular, was very distressed. After empathetically listening to the woman's story, I asked, "When you were making a decision to leave, how did you think it would affect your children? And how do you think they feel now?" Her answer led to a discussion in which she indicated she had not anticipated the hurt and pain her children would experience and to an exploration of what she could do now to repair the damage.

4. *Articulate the moral dilemma without giving your own opinion.* In the case of the woman who moved out on her children, I arranged a session with her, her children, and the stepfather. (The therapy had been initiated to address the daughter's distress.) After the daughter spoke openly about how rejected

she felt when her mother moved to a place where her children could not live, even part-time, the mother explained that she had felt a need to start a new life and moving to a friend's small apartment seemed to be the most logical way to get out quickly. I then framed the dilemma as follows (speaking to the mother): "So, on the one hand, you've got your strong personal need to leave your marriage right away, and, on the other hand, you've got your children's need to be with you as their mother and to know that you want them." I let the family take the discussion from there.

5. *Bring research findings and clinical insight to bear on the consequences of certain actions, particularly for vulnerable individuals.* Although such information can be presented in any therapy situation, here I am referring to the use of data and theory to influence clients to take a course of action that the therapist considers morally better as well as psychosocially healthier. For example, in speaking to Bruce about whether to leave his children after his marital separation, I described the research data on the importance of regular, predictable contact between fathers and children after divorce. I was summarizing data not as an objective scientist but as a moral exhorter.

6. *Describe how you generally see the issue and how you tend to weight the moral options, emphasizing that every situation is unique and that the client will, of course, make his or her own decision.* A man was contemplating leaving his wife because the marriage had been empty for many years. He had never told her how unhappy he was. He was trying to decide whether to start marital therapy or to end the marriage right away. After exploring his feelings and his thinking, I said something like, "I'll tell you the position I have come to over the years on the question of pulling the plug on the marriage right away versus trying marital therapy. Now, bear in mind that I am a marital therapist, so I am not objective here. But my view is that a long-term marriage is too important a thing to give up on without a serious effort to salvage it in marital therapy. I'm sure there are exceptions, and I can't tell you that you should try therapy or that it will work. But I hate to see a couple break up without at least some consideration of getting help together." He decided to bring in his wife, and in this case the therapy was successful.

7. *Say directly how concerned you are about the moral consequences of the client's actions.* This is what I did with Bruce when he was contemplating a quick move out of town and out of his children's lives. Because time was short, a decision was imminent, and I had a good relationship with him, I used an intense form of moral response.

8. *Clearly state when you cannot support a client's decision or behavior, explaining your decision on moral grounds and, if necessary, withdrawing from the case.* A couple had started marital therapy, and the wife told me privately that she had an ongoing, intense romantic relationship with another man, one that had been sexual but, for the time being (perhaps only for a short time), was not sexual. She did not want her husband to know about it but believed she could give marital therapy a good effort. I told her that I could not accept her decision to participate in marital therapy without telling her husband about

the other relationship, because it would be unfair to him to be in the dark when she and I knew about her divided commitment. Having made the moral point, I also told her that I was confident that the therapy would not be successful in any event if she had an outside lover. The latter remark spoke to the pragmatic consideration I was trained to address, the former spoke to the moral consideration I had to learn to speak up about. After I made a stand about not doing the couples therapy, she decided to tell her husband about the relationship and to end it while therapy continued.

Illustration of the Model with the Video Case

"Cheryl" had been married for seventeen years and had two teenage children. About a year before our consultation, she began an affair with a man she knew professionally. Her job took her out of town about once a month, when she and her lover got together for great sex and conversation. Right now, her lover, recently divorced from his wife, was pressing Cheryl for a commitment to leave her husband and be with him.

I asked about her marriage. She said that her husband was a very good man—kind and loving and supportive—but that the marriage lacked passion for her. She had felt emotionally empty for a number of years. They were doing a good job raising their children, she thought. They rarely argued. Their sexual relationship had been blah for many years, infrequent and unexciting. Her husband had supported her career decisions, although they did not share many outside

Doherty w/ client

interests. In fact, he was so supportive and constructive that she was confident that he would not abandon her or be mean-spirited if she told him about the affair. Although being hurt terribly, he would work to make things better, she said. But Cheryl told herself and me that she deserved more out of life and marriage than she felt she could get from her husband. It was fear of hurting her children that was most stopping her from leaving. They would be devastated, she thought, and their lives turned upside down, especially if she was the one to move out and away to the community where her lover lived.

Cheryl was facing what she called a "churning dilemma." She didn't "fall" into the affair, she noted; she had clearly decided to pursue something she felt she needed and deserved in her life. Her lover gave her an intense and satisfying relationship. Their conversations were deeper and their sex more thrilling. After years of passively accepting a loving but passionless marriage, she felt that she had come alive after being kissed by a man who had been her friend, but soon became her lover.

Every case of moral consultation involves the sorting of values based on an understanding of the facts of the client's situation. As I listened to Cheryl tell her story, I concluded that hers was not an abusive, destructive marriage but rather a supportive and companionate one that seemed to be meeting many of the needs of the children and her husband, and some of Cheryl's needs as well. If Cheryl had told me about her husband's violence, addiction, or chronic irresponsibility, I probably would have come to a different value stance and approached the consultation differently. Instead, my value about moral commitment in marriage permeated my consultation. I saw Cheryl as operating out of what I call a "consumer" approach to marriage, focusing on what benefits she was not receiving from her husband but not on what she was failing to put into the marriage (Doherty, 2001). And I believed there would be serious harm to her children and to her husband if she were to end her marriage at this point. As I listened to her, I reflected on the recent research demonstrating that the children who experience the most harm from divorce are those whose parents have a relatively harmonious but not happy, intimate marriage (Amato, 2000).

Cheryl did hold values about marital commitment and not harming her children or husband. She struck me as a good and sensitive person caught between her conscience and her desires for more fulfillment in her life. But she spoke about her personal desires as if they were constitutional rights, such as freedom of speech, and her emotional needs as if they were biological facts, such as needing vitamin C to avoid scurvy. Our culture teaches us that we are all entitled to an exciting marriage and great sex life; if we don't get both, we are apt to feel deprived. What used to be seen as human weakness of the flesh has become a personal entitlement.

Social historians have shown how psychological individualism has been growing in our nation for more than a century. Its current form is what I call the "consumer attitude," a combination of the human potential movement of the 1970s (with its focus on personal growth) and the market values of the 1980s and 1990s (with their focus on personal entitlement and cutting your losses and moving on if you are not satisfied) (Doherty, 2001).

Although it lurks inside nearly every married person who lives in our culture, the consumer attitude usually does not become apparent until we come face-to-face with our disappointments about our marriage and our mate. That's when we start to ask ourselves, "Is this marriage meeting my needs?" and "Am I getting enough back for what I am putting into this marriage?" In Cheryl's case, she had told herself for years that she was staying in the marriage only for the sake of the children. She had "settled" for a second-class marriage in a world that tells not to settle for second best, because a better product or service is beckoning. Hence, she was vulnerable to the enticements of a new relationship that looked like it could make her truly happy.

During the first twenty minutes of the interview, I focused on helping Cheryl examine the implications of leaving her husband for her own well-being. Using the metaphor of the affair as a tropical island, a vacation paradise that no one can permanently reside in, I tried to undermine the fantasy of a blissful new love relationship that would never encounter the erosion of passion that all long-term relationships must face. I presented a scenario in which Cheryl could see rebuilding her marriage as a positive option for herself, instead of as a sell-out of her core personal needs. Since she will eventually end up on the "big island" anyway, with its daily responsibilities and challenges to a relationship, why not figure out how to have a satisfying marriage with her current husband? Cheryl clearly preferred that option but was doubtful it was possible.

Toward the end of this part of our conversation, Cheryl explicitly said that she had consciously chosen the affair and was no longer "a good girl." I know how I would have handled this comment during the 1970s: I would have encouraged her to challenge the way that society or religion or her rigid conscience were defining her as not a "good girl." I would have supported her heroic efforts to break out of the mold of following other people's expectations for her. Instead, I let her remark pass without comment or follow-up. I wanted to move the conversation to the realm of interpersonal morality—how her behavior and decisions might affect others in her life—rather than focus on her claims to authenticity and rebellion from conventional standards. If we had been able to meet in the future, I would have returned to the theme of her being a good girl or bad girl to see if she could integrate these parts of her identity, but for now I wanted to shift her gaze outward rather than inward.

Although I had been doing implicit moral consultation during the entire interview, through focusing the conversation on the option of retaining her marital commitment, explicit moral consultation began when I inquired about the consequences of a divorce for her children, her husband, and their community. Notice how I first summarized and validated the self-interest aspect of her decision. Here is our exchange, beginning with my words:

> "Okay. So there are two parts of this. One part is where you might have your best chance for personal happiness, to live your life in a relationship so [that] the next part of your life may give you more joy. And then the other part of it is the consequences to different people."

"Yes, I know, I know."

"So let's talk about that part of it."

"The consequences."

"And maybe we can put them [personal happiness and the consequences to others] back together at some place. But, how do you think it would affect your children?"

"Oh, the consequences would be devastating."

During the rest of the interview, I continue to use the central moral consultation strategy, level three (inquiring about consequences for the well-being of others). I also use level four (summarizing the dilemma), and level five (bringing clinical insight or research in a persuasive manner to the conversation).

At a key moment in the interview, I felt invited by Cheryl to lay out a scenario whereby she could put it all together: honor her marital commitment, do right by her children, and still have personal happiness. Here was the key exchange, following my statement that it is possible for couples who work at it to "have the kind of energy and passion that is possible and quite fulfilling, not the new [relationship], but the one that after ten years or fifteen years or twenty years, you say, wow, this is good." Cheryl replied:

"Yeah, see, I can't believe that. It's unbelievable to me that that's possible."

"In your marriage?"

"In my marriage, right. So, keep talking so you can tell me more how to do that."

At this point, I had permission to lay out a path in which Cheryl would end the affair definitively and proceed to tell her husband that their marriage had been in grave danger and that she had had an affair. A while later, when she challenged the idea of telling her husband about the affair, I said that I don't have any rules about this sort of thing, but that my sense in her situation was that this level of honesty would give her husband and her the best chance to make some major changes. I acknowledged that this is an area about which professionals have different opinions.

During the remainder of the interview, I tried to undermine Cheryl's sense of fatalism about whether her husband can change. I did this by challenging her own passivity in the marriage and her unrealistic beliefs about how her husband should respond to her ambiguous gestures about improving the relationship. Toward the end, I repeated the theme that Cheryl, at some point in her life, will have to do the hard work of maintaining an intimate marriage, even if she leaves with her lover:

"And you will have to do the same kind of looking inside to keep that other relationship alive at some point, that you'd have to in your marriage."

"So I might as well do it in my marriage since we've got history in the marriage and it would be hurting so many people."

"That's for you do decide."

"That's for me to decide, yeah."

"But that sure makes sense to me."

Notice that I reaffirmed her autonomy in this important decision. I also quietly affirmed the direction of her decision making, because my position was no doubt quite clear to her anyway. I encouraged her to work through her decision with her therapist.

Whose Morality?

The most common concern I hear about the explicit use of moral discourse in psychotherapy revolves around the question of whose morality should be introduced. Who decides what is right and wrong in any given case or situation? Is the therapist expected to have cornered the market on which actions are consistent with moral commitment and which undermine moral commitment? When is a divorce an escape from one's adult responsibilities and when is it a necessary, though sometimes tragic, act of moral courage? When is placing an elderly parent in a nursing home an act of abandonment and when is it an act of responsibility? Who gets to decide what is right and wrong?

The exploration of moral issues in therapy does not occur mainly inside the head of the therapist playing moral philosopher or moral judge. It occurs in the heart of the therapeutic dialogue, in conversations in which the therapist listens, reflects, and questions, probes and challenges, and in which the client is free to do the same and to develop a more integrated set of moral sensibilities. Morality emerges for all of us from social interaction punctuated by moments of personal reflection. Morality, in the words of the sociologist Alan Wolfe (1989), is "socially constructed."

> Morality thus understood is neither a fixed set of rules handed down unchanging by powerful structures nor something that is made up on the spot. It is a negotiated process through which individuals, by reflecting periodically on what they have done in the past, try to ascertain what they ought to do next . . . Moral obligation [is] a socially constructed practice . . . Morality viewed as a social construction differs from the traditional view of morality as 'adherence to rules of conduct shaped by tradition and respect for authority' (pp. 216, 221).

Those established traditions and authorities have been undermined too extensively to serve as unquestioned arbiters of personal morality in the twenty-first century, except insofar as their precepts make sense to modern men and women. To use an obvious example, all the major monotheistic religions once accepted slavery—now considered a moral evil of staggering proportions—as a practice in keeping with God's will and traditional religious texts. Similarly, governments have manipulated citizens' loyalty and duty to country in order to fight wars that most people now consider unjust. The hard-won battle for personal freedom of conscience in the Western world is not going to brook falling back on an older morality of unreflective rule-following. And psychotherapists would betray their mission if they saw themselves primarily as agents of moral socialization for established traditions.

On the other hand, I do not believe, as some liberals do, that morality is created by each individual out of whole cloth. We are born into families and communities and ethical/religious traditions that shape us and become part of our identity. As Wilson (1993) asserts, moral sensibilities in each individual are formed in the intimate environment of family life in childhood and later through wider interactions. This is not to say that we each cannot distill a personal moral perspective as we mature, but that our moral development and our moral sensibilities are inextricably connected with social interaction. Wilson writes that we are coming "face to face with a fatally-flawed assumption of many Enlightenment thinkers, namely, that autonomous individuals can freely choose, or will, their moral life" (p. 2).

Morality is a communal, as well as a personal, affair. This overemphasis on autonomy and underemphasis on relationships is a reason why Kohlberg's (1991) very influential theory of moral development is not especially useful to psychotherapy, in my view. The theory focuses on abstract moral principles and on the categorizing of individuals' moral reasoning into developmental stages. For purposes of psychotherapy, Kohlberg's work does not deal enough with the affective, interactional, and behavioral aspects of morality—with how people learn, feel, and practice their morality. Even in its main area of moral reasoning, the model has tended to devalue relational thinking, as Carol Gilligan (1982) and others have pointed out. Furthermore, it would be dangerous for therapists to view themselves as leading the client to a "higher" stage of moral development, presumably one occupied by the therapist and not by the client.

Conservatives' rigid rule-following and liberals' excessive individualism and reliance on abstract reasoning, then, do not offer reliable guides for moral discourse in psychotherapy. I believe that a better tradition comes from the early twentieth-century sociologist George Herbert Mead (1956) and other "symbolic-interactionists" who emphasize the social construction of reality. Alan Wolfe's (1987) work comes out of that tradition. If morality is created through social interaction, then psychotherapy can be viewed as a form of specialized social interaction in which current moral beliefs and sensibilities are explored, affirmed, revised, rejected, and new ones created. The therapist, who is also a member of a moral community of social discourse, helps clients reflect on the moral dimensions of their lives. The therapist neither dictates moral rules nor claims to know all the answers, but rather is sensitive to the often delicate interplay of personal, familial, and community needs and responsibilities involved in difficult moral choices.

In the realm of moral responsibility, I do not believe that the therapist's task is to help people think through decisions by means of abstract moral principles that ethicists debate, although these principles have a place in the spectrum of moral discourse. Rather, our major emphasis should be on the lived experience of the client as moral agent, on working through moments of struggle and pain over finding the right thing to do. Just as therapists do not supply clients with feelings and desires, but, rather, help clients discover and work better with them, the same is true for moral beliefs and sensibilities. With few exceptions, clients are able to bring the moral raw material that we work with collaboratively; people are continually explaining and justifying their own behavior and evaluating the morality of others' behavior. The therapist is a consultant in this ongoing process of moral reflection.

Our therapy caseloads are like Shakespearean dramas suffused with moral passion and moral dilemmas. We have been trained to see Romeo and Juliet only as starstruck, tragic lovers, a perspective from which we fail to notice that the moral fabric of parental commitment was torn when their families rejected them for loving each other. We focus on the murder of Hamlet's father and Hamlet's own existential crisis, rather than on Hamlet's mother's abandonment of her grieving son. Commitment to loved ones and betrayal of that commitment are central moral themes in the human drama played out in psychotherapy every day. For Bruce, a searing divorce was the moral crucible in which he forged a new identity as a committed, loving father who could give without counting the returns and remain faithful without weighing the alternatives. From the moment Bruce told me he might abandon his children, I knew that the therapy was about more than psychological and family issues; it was about Bruce's moral integrity and about the moral fabric of a family. That revelation changed both of us. Years later, when I came to the consultation with Cheryl, I knew what I should do as a therapist and a human being. I no longer split my moral self and my professional self.

REFERENCES

Amato, P. R. (2000). The consequences of divorce for adults and children. *Journal of Marriage and the Family, 62,* 1269–1287.

Bellah, R. N., Madsen, R., Sullivan, W. M., Swidler, A., & Tipton, S. M. (1985). *Habits of the heart: Individualism and commitment in American life.* Berkeley, CA: University of California Press.

Bok, S. (1979). *Lying: Moral choice in public and private life.* New York: Vintage.

Boszormenyi-Nagy, I. (1987). *Foundations of contextual therapy.* New York: Brunner/Mazel.

Cushman, P. (1995). *Constructing the self, constructing America.* New York: Addison Wesley.

Doherty, W. J. (1995). *Soul searching: Why psychotherapy must promote moral responsibility.* New York: Basic Books.

Doherty, W. J. (2001). *Take back your marriage: Confident parenting in turbulent times.* New York: Guilford.

Hare-Mustin, R. (1994). Discourses in a mirrored room: A postmodern analysis of therapy. *Family Process 33,* 19–35.

Imber-Black, E. (1993). *Secrets in families and family therapy.* New York: Norton.

Gilligan, C. (1982). *In a different voice: Psychological theory and women's development.* New York: Harvard University Press.

Kohlberg, L. (1991). *The meaning and measurement of moral development.* Worcester, MA: Clark University Press.

May, R. (1992). Forward. In G. R. Vandenbos, N. A. Cummings, & P. H. Deleon (Eds.), *History of psychotherapy: A century of change.* Washington, DC: American Psychological Association Press.

Mead, G. H. (1956). *On social psychology: Selected papers.* Chicago: University of Chicago Press.

Perls, F. (1969). *Gestalt therapy verbatim.* Lafayette, CA: Real People Press.

Rieff, P. (1961). *Freud: The mind of a moralist.* Garden City, NY: Anchor.

Rieff, P. (1966). *The triumph of the therapeutic.* New York: Harper & Row.

Rogers, C. (1965). *Client-centered therapy.* Boston: Houghton Mifflin.

Vaughan, D. (1986). *Uncoupling: How relationships come apart.* New York: Oxford University Press.

Wilson, J. Q. (1993). *The moral sense.* New York: Free Press.

Wolfe, A. (1989). *Whose keeper? Social science and moral obligation.* Berkeley, CA: University of California Press.

6 Bowenian Family Therapy

PHILIP GUERIN AND KATHERINE GUERIN

Philip Guerin

The Theory of Bowenian Therapy

Bowenian therapy is a model of clinical intervention that has evolved over the past forty-five years. The method traces its beginnings to the pioneering efforts of Murray Bowen. As a model of therapy, Bowenian therapy is a multigenerational systems approach based on a series of interlocking concepts and clinical models. These clinical models are used for intervening with dysfunctional children, adolescents, and adults as well as with individuals whose relationships are conflictual. Nichols and Schwartz, in their widely used text, *Family Therapy: Concepts and Methods* (2001), give the following endorsement of its scope and value.

Bowenian family therapy has by far the most comprehensive view of human behavior and human problems of any approach to family treatment. It extends the focus deeper—into the heart and minds of family members—and broader—into the wider family context that shaped, and continues to shape, the life of the family (p. 137).

It is appropriate at this point to consider why there is a need for a distinction between Bowen theory and Bowenian therapy. We believe that the need for this distinction comes from Bowen himself, who clearly emphasized orthodoxy of thinking and practice and did not acknowledge most of what has been published by others based on their understanding of his theory. For example, Bowen, in his own anthology, (1978) and Kerr and Bowen, in their writings together, (1988), did not reference any other article, chapter, or book written by second- or third-generation Bowenian therapists. For this reason, the authors of this chapter, in deference to Bowen, view the work that has evolved from Bowen Theory as existing on a spectrum. At one end exist the most orthodox practitioners of his theory and craft, such as Kerr. In the middle of the spectrum are those who have broadened and modified the concepts and clinical methods, such as Guerin and Fogarty, whose approach will be spelled out throughout the course of this chapter. At the other end are those who use only fragments of Bowen theory or Bowenian therapy, tying the fragments into an otherwise different paradigm. An example of this latter group would be psychodynamic therapists who use a genogram for the working-through process following the completion of a transferential milestone. We will address Bowenian therapy as it has developed across this spectrum over time and as we practice it.

We adhere to a model of Bowenian therapy that has been strongly influenced by, and is, in fact, based on, the concepts of Bowen theory. However, our model has attempted to develop some of the concepts in a clinically practical way and, from the modified concepts, to develop unique models of intervention for working with individuals, couples, and families. In order to understand better the evolution of Bowenian therapy, it is important to be conversant with the original work of Bowen, the diverging pathways of ongoing development, and the previously mentioned specific models of intervention with their emphasis on practical clinical application.

The origination of Bowen's theory began with his clinical work at the Menninger Clinic in Topeka, Kansas, from 1946 to 1954. His research involved direct observation of mothers and their schizophrenic offspring whom he had placed together in small cottages on the Menninger campus for the purpose of his study. At this time, still strongly committed to the principles of psychoanalytic theory and practice, he was hoping to gain a better understanding of mother–child symbiosis. *Symbiosis,* in biological terms, describes a state of existence between two organisms in which each is dependent on the other for the continuation of its existence, thus the term *mutual dependence.* In psychological/systems terms, *symbiosis* describes a relationship state in which individuals form an attachment driven and maintained by anxiety so intense that the independent functioning of each of them is compromised. Observations from these studies led Bowen to the formation of his concept of differentiation. This concept attempts to address the lifetime developmental problem of growing from a state of total mutual dependence in infancy toward increasing degrees of individual autonomy over the course of the life cycle.

Bowen moved his work from the Menninger Clinic to the National Institute of Mental Health (NIMH) in the Washington, D.C. area, where he expanded the Menninger project to further his understanding of schizophrenia. This expansion was accomplished by hospitalizing whole families with a schizophrenic child. It was in this expanded project that he added fathers to the mix and observed how the presence of fathers changed the behaviors of the schizophrenic child and the mother. From this research Bowen expanded the concept of mother–child symbiosis into a consideration of what he termed the "undifferentiated ego mass" of the whole family, a kind of systemwide symbiosis. In addition, his observations of the interactions of mother, father, and child led to the formation of the Bowen concept of triangulation.

In 1959, Bowen left NIMH and went to Georgetown University School of Medicine, where he remained a professor of psychiatry until his death in the fall of 1990. During his tenure at Georgetown, Bowen worked on refining his theory by applying it to less dysfunctional populations, although he firmly believed that schizophrenia remained the "great teacher." While teaching the psychiatric residents at Georgetown in a psychoanalytically oriented department of psychiatry, Bowen attempted to address the problems of transference and countertransference in a different way. For this purpose, Bowen began to research and experiment with the emotional process within his own personal family system. A documentation of this "research" on his own family of origin was first presented at a national family therapy conference in March, 1967, in a paper entitled "Differentiation of Self in One's Family." He published this paper anonymously in James Framo's (1972) edited text, *Family Interaction (Anon.)*, in order to shelter the privacy of family members. Bowen came to believe that, if therapists could learn to operate calmly in the intensely anxious emotional field of their own family of origin, this ability would provide a better facility for avoiding emotionally reactive negative judgments when working clinically with individuals and families.

At Georgetown, Bowen was responsible for the family training of many of the psychiatric residents and clinical staff. Philip Guerin, Thomas Fogarty, and Michael Kerr are, perhaps, the most prominent of the residents trained by Bowen. After their residency training, Guerin and Fogarty left Georgetown and joined the Family Studies Section at the Albert Einstein College of Medicine (AECOM) in New York. Unlike Georgetown, where only the Bowen model of family was taught, at Einstein, Israel Zwerling and Andrew Ferber were assembling a faculty representative of the diversity of thinking and practice in the field of family therapy. While director of training at Einstein, Guerin, along with Fogarty, trained Betty Carter, Monica McGoldrick, Ed Gordon, Eileen Pendagast, and Katherine Guerin. All of them, and Peggy Papp, joined Guerin and Fogarty in 1973 to form the Center for Family Learning in New Rochelle, New York. Kerr remained at Georgetown as Bowen's closest associate, and his clinical work and publications have been reflective of that close collaboration. Among the nonpsychiatrists trained by Bowen was Edwin Friedman, a rabbi in the Washington, D.C. area. He, in turn, trained many pastoral counselors in Bowenian family theory and therapy. The Friedman text, *Generation to Generation* (1985), continues to be very widely used by clergy groups of all denominations throughout the country several years after his death. Fogarty, although influenced by Bowen, was less committed to the multigenerational model, and most of his contributions to the theory have been confined to the nuclear family and the individual. Guerin adhered more closely to Bowen's emphasis on the importance of family of origin work than Fogarty, but was also influenced by Fogarty and the Einstein faculty, particularly Ferber and Albert Scheflen. Guerin and Fogarty have worked, taught, and laughed together, first at Einstein and then at the Center for Family Learning, for more than thirty years.

Guerin's work focused on clarifications and elaborations of the concepts of Bowen theory, as well as the specific application of the theory to the building of clinical models for the treatment of marital conflict and child- and adolescent-centered families and the treatment of the individual from a systems perspective. Nichols and Schwartz (2001) address Guerin's focus on clinical methods of intervention:

> Guerin's sophisticated clinical approach has led to a more differentiated set of therapeutic goals. These goals are derived from highly articulated clinical models developed to deal with problems of children and adolescents, marital conflict, and dysfunctional adults. Guerin's general goals are (1) placing the presenting problem in the context of the multi-generational system by doing a thorough and accurate genogram; (2) connecting with key family members and working with them to calm their own anxiety and level of emotional arousal and, thereby, lower anxiety throughout the system; and (3) define the parameters of the central symptomatic triangles, as well as important interlocking triangles. More specific goals are determined by the presenting problem and which unit of the family (mother and child, nuclear family, marital couple, individual) is the primary clinical focus (p. 152).

Carter and McGoldrick moved off on their own track in 1977, leaving the Center for Family Learning and founding the Family Institute of Westchester. Their work together provided a developmental perspective to Bowenian therapy. They proposed a "family life cycle" (Carter and McGoldrick, 1980) as a backdrop for understanding the development of stress in the family over the years and its role in the production of relationship conflict and symptoms in an individual. "Betty Carter and Monica McGoldrick have done as much as anyone in family therapy to study and disseminate information about normal family development" (Nichols and Schwartz, (2001, p. 146). In addition, McGoldrick added the consideration of culture and ethnicity to the view of the "family relationship system." Carter, working with Papp, Silverstein, and Walters in the Women's Project (Walters, Carter, Papp, & Silverstein, 1988), focused on the importance of gender issues in the study of and clinical intervention with families.

In summary, the Bowenian model of therapy consists of the multigenerational family unit as the context in which to study individuals and their relationship conflicts under the siege of intense anxiety. Fogarty and Guerin each focus on the individual, the dyad, and triangles. Kerr, as the heir of Bowen's legacy at Georgetown, focuses on anxiety, differentiation, and triangles. Carter and McGoldrick focus on the impact of the contextual aspects of developmental stress, ethnicity, and gender issues on the family system.

Murray Bowen and Bowen Theory

The developing concepts of Bowen's theory are documented in his published anthology, *Family Therapy in Clinical Practice* (1978). Bowen designates eight concepts as central to his theory: differentiation of self, triangles, the nuclear family emotional system, the family projection process, emotional cutoff, the multigenerational transmission process of anxiety, sibling position, and societal regression. These same eight concepts are documented by Goldenberg and Goldenberg (1991) and Nichols and Schwartz (2001). The concepts of differentiation, triangulation, and transgenerational transmission of anxiety form the core of Bowen's theoretical contribution.

Bowen's core concept of differentiation consists of two component parts: emotional fusion within the dyad and differentiation of the individual. In his observations on mother–child symbiosis, Bowen recorded alternating cycles of closeness and distance within the mother–child dyad. He hypothesized that sequential cycles of separation anxiety and incorporation anxiety were the primary emotional forces driving the seemingly automatic and reactive relationship patterns. The very interdependent nature of the relationship between mother and child limited the potential for autonomous functioning in both of them. Their behaviors were determined by their anxious attachment to each other rather than by their own internal choices. On a process level, this concept describes the existence of a contagious anxiety that entraps both members of the dyad, thereby determining their behavior in relation to one another as well as their individual levels of emotional functioning. Anxiety in either the mother or child produces an automatic reflexive response in the other. These automatic emotional responses and behaviors describe the fusion or lower level of Bowen's proposed spectrum of emotional functioning. He termed this spectrum his "scale of differentiation," although it was not an actual psychometric measure.

At a higher level on Bowen's scale of differentiation is a high-functioning individual capable of emotional connection without being determined by the anxiety in an important other person or in the relationship. The differentiated self is capable of distinguishing between thinking and feeling and behaves in response to his or her own intellect and judgment guided by principles and opinions, even in the presence of considerable anxiety. This profile of autonomy represents differentiation, which is the opposite of fusion. Bowen's scale of differentiation within the person ranged from the high end of the scale, the differentiation end, to the low end, which is the extreme fusion end. Higher scores indicated an increasing ability to withstand high levels of anxiety while continuing to be autonomous in life choices, including relationship behavior. Lower scores represented emotional fusion, the inability to function autonomously on an emotional level in the face of anxiety. Anxious attachment to others was the automatic response. This kind of attachment can be demonstrated in two ways: either by clinging behaviors in which there is an inability of family members to have an appropriate level of separation from one another or in combative behaviors in which family members fight with each other and then cut off emotionally, using distance as their only way to escape the anxious attachment.

As mentioned, Bowen began his working model of the relationship triangle during the NIMH project after including fathers in the study. The interdependence observed in the mother–child dyad also appeared to be present in the relationships involving fathers. Initially, Bowen expressed the idea of an interdependent triad and compared it to a three-legged stool: the removal of one leg destroyed the essence of the stool. He observed the reactive emotional instability of the fusion-laden dyad and proposed that the transmission of the anxiety in the dyad to involve the most vulnerable other in the relationship system formed a potentially stabilizing but dysfunctional structure called "the triangle." Considered by many to be the originator of the concept of triangulation, Bowen placed heavy emphasis on the relationship–process part of triangulation and little or none on its structural aspects.

Bowen used the triangle as a central part of his clinical approach. He placed himself in contact with both members of a conflictual dyad and worked to remain emotionally neutral while spelling out the emotional process within the conflictual relationship, using a series of "process questions" such as "What about your wife's criticism upsets you the most?" Theoretically, this method was meant to induce a corrective emotional experience for the family members in conflict, allowing them to lower their anxiety and seek more functional pathways of relating to each other. He rarely gave advice or instructions. He just kept asking questions. In fact, he would openly state that the purpose of his questions was to develop his theory further. He even took it to the point of declaring that his clinical connections with people were more about theory development than therapy. The hope in this method was that the people he saw clinically would be able to use this experience with him to calm their feeling system and activate their thinking system and, thereby, develop better ideas themselves about how to manage their emotions and relationships.

Thomas Fogarty and Pursuer–Distancer, the Four-Dimensional Self, and Triangles

When Fogarty moved to New York from Georgetown, his clinical practice consisted of many couples in marital conflict. He spent hundreds of hours dealing with the marital system in the nuclear family. It is not surprising, therefore, that his theoretical contributions began with a focus on the marital relationship. Unlike Bowen, he gave more attention to the development of structural concepts and their clinical usefulness in therapy and paid only passing attention to a therapist's own family work. Fogarty's concept of both the marriage relationship and the individual is a highly structured one. In studying marriage, Fogarty used that portion of the concept of differentiation that deals with fusion and created a structural model of fusion between husband and wife with a blurring and overlapping of the boundaries in the relationship. To this structural model of fusion he introduced the idea of directional movement within the relationship, from which came his construct of the pursuer and distancer. He characterized the emotional pursuer as someone who is open about his or her own thoughts and feelings, readily shares them with others, and expects others to do the same. An emotional pursuer enjoys a lot of relationship time and would like even more in times of stress. The emotional pursuer is very often, but not always, a woman, and she is usually married to a man who is an emotional distancer. Pursuers and distancers complement each other emotionally. The emotional distancer, therefore, does not share thoughts and feelings easily and resents being pressed to talk about feelings or spend more relationship time with the pursuer than is comfortable. In times of stress, the distancer moves toward tasks rather than interaction with people because that is what calms him or her down. The complementarity of emotional styles works well unless there is severe and prolonged stress, in which case the differences between the two partners become problematic.

In his work with the individual, Fogarty again formulated a structural view of the person, which he termed the "four-dimensional self." It includes the lateral dimension, the vertical dimension, the depth dimension, and the dimension of time (Fogarty, 1976a). The lateral dimension of Fogarty's four-dimensional self represented the interactive part of the individual in which movement toward and away from others is formed and operationalized. This dimension was the source from which movement within the relationship developed in the previously mentioned concept of pursuit and distance. Closely connected to the lateral dimension was the depth dimension wherein, Fogarty (1984) hypothesized, was stored the residue of an individual's emotions accumulated over time as a by-product of relationship experiences. Within the depth dimension, Fogarty placed the experience of the existential state of emptiness, a process he believed was a necessary prerequisite to the development of an autonomous self. The vertical dimension contained the occupational and professional potential and actualization of the productivity of an individual. The time dimension had to do with the individual's experience of time, the way in times of stress he or she tended to develop future anxiety or ruminate on the failures and misfortunes of the past. In addition, the time dimension contained a person's basic rhythm and was, again, linked to the lateral dimension's pursuit and distance. For example, an emotional pursuer's rhythm was observed to be erratic, varying between high speed and dead stop, while the emotional distancer was observed to have a much more constant or steady rhythm.

Fogarty's goal in working with the structural model of the individual was to produce a functional emotional balance. He believed the individual should be "centered," that is, in touch with and regulating the appropriate balance among each of the four dimensions of self in his or her life. For example, an individual should not be preoccupied with productivity and nonresponsive in personal relationships or, on the other hand, spend so much time relating to people that other vertical responsibilities are not being met. Drawing on this concept, Fogarty was the first to describe the relationship dance of emotional pursuit and distance in the marital relationship. This concept, more than any other of Fogarty's, has been incorporated into the work of most practicing family therapists.

Fogarty (1976b) also contributed extensively to the development of the concept of triangulation. Again, unlike Bowen who stayed with the emotional process in triangulation, Fogarty focused on the structural aspect of triangulation, especially as it related to the treatment planning. He was, perhaps, the first to focus on the structural aspect of child-centered triangles with his strategies of altering these structures by moving overinvolved mothers away from, and distant fathers in toward, the symptomatic child.

Philip Guerin and the Adaptive Level of Functioning, Triangles, and Clinical Models

When Guerin came to New York from Georgetown, a considerable portion of his early clinical practice involved mental health professionals seeking to study their own families of origin. For this reason, Guerin's contributions to the Bowen family systems model of therapy began with the development and refinement of the genogram as an organizing tool and the coaching of these mental health professionals in their family-of-origin work. While in residency training at Georgetown, Guerin had the privilege of being coached by Bowen in working on his own family relationship system, his own Therapist's Own Family (TOF) work. He took this experience with him to AECOM, where, as director of training in Family Studies, he introduced Bowen theory and TOF work into the Family Training program at Einstein and at various other academic institutions in the New York metropolitan area. As a result of this emphasis and promulgation, TOF work became an alternative to a training analysis for fledgling family therapists. In his TOF groups, Guerin formalized the family diagram used by Bowen and named it the *genogram* (Guerin and Fogarty, 1972).

Because people were sometimes confused by Bowen's concept of differentiation, Guerin shifted his own focus away from Bowen's idea that an individual's level of differentiation is a largely unalterable quantity not subject to much change, even over time. Instead, Guerin focused on increasing what he called an individual's "adaptive level of functioning," which could be raised over time through conscious efforts to change behavior patterns. The focus of TOF work and therapy with clients, therefore, became using conscious effort to modify problematic behavior patterns and neutralizing reactive triangles with the goal of raising adaptive level of functioning.

In his early work with triangles, Guerin made a distinction between "triangles" as a relationship structure and "triangulation" as relationship process. For him a "triangle" is an abstract way of thinking about a structure in human relationships, and "triangulation" is the reactive emotional process that goes on within that triangle. In the structure of a relationship system, there are any number of potential triangles, and the emotional process of triangulation within the triangle can be either dormant or active in varying degrees at any moment in time. For example, at the time a couple presents for treatment, the triangle with their child may have become relatively fixed, so that the mother and child are overly close and the father is in the distant, outsider position. This alignment will shift back and forth over time in response to situational and developmental changes. There will be times when an adolescent boy moves away from his mother's intensity to seek refuge and protection from his more laconic father. At other times, adolescents and young adults attempting to reinforce hard-earned degrees of separation may act out in ways that will drive the parents to a united front. However, in each triangle there seems to be a pervasive and predominant structure to which it inevitably realigns.

Within this triangular structure in times of calm, the reactive emotional process may go dormant awaiting an increase in anxiety to trigger it into active triangulation. *Triangulation* is the term used to describe the emotional process that goes on among the three people who make up the triangle. For example, in a further elaboration of the triangle just described, the father might desire a connection with his child and resent his wife's monopoly of the child's affections; the mother may be angry at the father's distance from her and compensate by substituting closeness with her child. The child, in turn, may resent the father's negative attention and criticism and may move toward the mother but, at the same time, be anxious about the overly close relationship with her. As the emotional process of triangulation moves around the triangle, it can produce changes in its structure. The father may try to reduce his loneliness by moving toward his child or his wife, or the child may try to avoid fusion with the mother by distancing from her and moving toward peers, causing the parents to draw together in their concern for their child.

Thus, triangles can shift their structure at any time in response to the process of triangulation, which has the potential for activation into motion at any given time. As changes do occur, demands are placed on the individuals and on the system to realign in a way that ensures the emotional comfort of the most powerful person in the system and preserves the stability of the system. The concept of the relationship triangle most clearly differentiated Bowen and Bowenian family systems from other theories of human emotional functioning.

Guerin continues to emphasize the importance of thinking in terms of relationship triangles in clinical work, incorporating them in each of his clinical models and emphasizing their overriding importance in systems psychotherapy. He, along with Fogarty, Fay, and Kautto (1996) present an integrated method for the treatment of relationship triangles in their text, *Working with Relationship Triangles: The One, Two, Three of Psychotherapy.*

One area in which Guerin specifically applied the concept of triangulation is in the "sibling subsystem." Bowen's inclusion of sibling position into his eight concepts is based on his appreciation of the research of Walter Toman (1961) on the effect of sibling position and its determinative effect on relationship behavior. Oldests, youngests, and middle children are profiled into patterns of expected behaviors. Furthermore, the position in one's sibling subsystem is seen as potentially influencing a person's marital choice and subsequent behavior patterns in marriage. For example, when a younger brother of an older sister marries an older sister of a younger brother, they continue the dance of their childhood. In addition to this aspect of sibling relationships, Guerin proposed the importance of the sibling cohesion factor and the sibling subsystem triangle. The sibling cohesion factor is defined as the ability of a group of siblings to gather without their parents and discuss important family issues including the positive and negative aspects of their parents. Guerin sees the presence of this factor as a functional strength in families and the absence of it as evidence of intense triangling and splitting between parents and siblings, indicating multiple fixed coalitions within the family. In families with more than two children, the potential for activation of a sibling subsystem triangle exists at all times. In healthier families, the sibling in the outsider position in the triangle will change in response to a variety of stimuli. In less healthy families, if the same child continually lands in the outsider position of the triangle, over time that child becomes more vulnerable to symptom development.

In addition to his contributions to the further theoretical development of Bowen's eight concepts, Guerin has made major contributions in the construction of his clinical models for dealing with marital conflict, dysfunction in individuals, and child- and adolescent-centered families. In Guerin's marital model, the levels of developmental and situational stress affecting the marriage are assessed through the use of the genogram. This information is used to validate for the couple that there has been a documented increase in the stress level of their lives and that this most probably plays a part in setting off and maintaining their conflict. The patterns of movement are documented through a tracking of the couple's patterns of relating in what Guerin has termed the "interactional sequence." Intrigued by Fogarty's idea of pursuit and distance, and working in concert with him, Guerin developed a five-step elaboration of pursuit and distance, the interactional sequence, which is one of the core concepts in Guerin's clinical model for the evaluation and treatment of marital conflict (Guerin, Fay, Burden, & Kautto, 1987). The sequence tracks the movement in the conflictual marital process through repetitive alternating patterns of pursuit and distance until it arrives at a polarized state of fixed distance. This fixed distance is a set up for triangulation to occur. It is characterized by a shutting down in functional communication and an emotional climate laced with hurt, anger, and resentment.

After it has been established with the couple that the patterns of the interactional sequence are operational in their relationship situation, behavioral experiments can then be designed for them to follow before the next session. These experiments do two things: They expose more of the dysfunctional process in the marital relationship and, possibly, make visible to the couple and to the therapist increased options for alternative ways of relating. If the therapist can establish credibility with couples by demonstrating an understanding and knowledge of how marital couples relate and get into conflict, safety may be accomplished within the therapy, which allows for much more open consideration of these issues and even for the management of differences of opinion. If all of this fails to move the relationship toward better functioning, the model calls for investigation and clinical intervention in two areas: covered-over individual dysfunction in one or both spouses, such as a clinical level of anxiety or depression, and the degree of reactivity in the relationship triangles surrounding the marriage. If individual dysfunction is uncovered, the use of medication, cognitive techniques, and coaching sessions are helpful in improving functioning in the dysfunctional individual and demonstrating the effect of the dysfunction on the marriage. It is important in these instances to define the ways the more functional spouse may enable or set off the emotional dysfunction in the partner. To intervene in the triangles surrounding the marital conflict, Guerin and his colleagues Fay, Burden, and Kautto (1987) developed a typology of the relationship triangles of marital conflict. The purpose of this typology is to give therapists a road map for finding the triangles that complicate the goal of successful marital therapy and provide ways of neutralizing the influence of these triangles on the relationship and the therapy. Because the conflict in a marriage relationship often organizes itself around the key issues of sex, money, children, and in-laws, it is also necessary to investigate the place of these issues in their lives.

The goal of the marital therapy is to improve self-focus, decrease emotional reactivity, and neutralize the dysfunctional patterns. If this can be accomplished, the spouses can become better partners, lovers, and companions. As part of this process, they will learn to recognize what they believe in, not just what they are against, appreciate the behavioral idiosyncrasies of self and spouse, and become better able to accept their own assets and limitations as well as those of their marriage.

In addition to his clinical model for working with marital conflict, Guerin has fashioned two other clinical models: one for working with dysfunction in individual adults, the other for child- and adolescent-centered families. The individual model begins with an assessment of the symptom profile of the dysfunctional family member. Attention is paid to the individual's developmental history including developmental tasks from early infancy through adolescence and young adulthood. These include entry into school, separation from home and family, and choice of marital partner. In addition, any significant physical or emotional illnesses, medications used presently or in the past, educational achievement, and occupational history are assessed. When this assessment of symptom profile and developmental track record has been established, the dysfunctional individual and the symptoms are contextualized in the multigenerational family system and occupational system. In this way, the relationship system factors that may play a part in the development and sustaining of the dysfunction can be discovered as well as the number and source of potential supportive relationships. A major part of this process is the definition of key relationship triangles that are an active part of the dysfunctional process in the surrounding system. The treatment plan for such cases is twofold. One part is the focus on the amelioration of the symptoms of anxiety, depression, attentional problems, substance abuse, and so forth. This is done through the use of psychotropic medication, cognitive techniques, and twelve-step program participation, where indicated. The second part of the treatment program is uncovering and working on the underlying relationship process and any other hindrances to improved productivity and relationship connectedness.

The authors collaborated on the following case, which is a good example of the integration of medication, education, and systems psychotherapy in a young man with anxiety, attention deficit disorder, and educational deficits. In the case of Charlie, a tall, awkward, and shy young male whose attentional difficulties had been diagnosed in middle school, there had been no "follow through" because both Charlie and his parents were anxious about the use of a stimulant medication. They also didn't place much credibility in the excellent behavioral recommendations made by the psychologist at the time of the evaluation. In the absence of treatment, in spite of his high intelligence, sincere desire to learn, and intense, although inconsistent, academic efforts, Charlie's educational deficits continued to mount. He continued to lose self-confidence academically and socially. His parents continued to be anxious, frustrated, and worried about their son, which created more pressure for him. Finally, Charlie's superior IQ couldn't override his untreated Attention Deficit Disorder and learning problems any longer and he was asked to leave college for a year because of his low grades. Charlie presented for therapy to one of the authors, demoralized, depressed, and isolated from his peers.

There were several aspects to his treatment plan. The therapist believed Charlie needed to have a trial on medication to help him with his attentional problems, a place to talk about his depression, his avoidance anxiety about his academic work, and his low self-esteem brought about by his failures. He also needed help dealing with his cumulative academic deficits in the skill subjects and his well-meaning but overanxious parents. In addition, a plan for connection with other young adults during this year off from school was considered important. Finally, he needed to learn about his attentional disorder and all its ramifications in his personal and relational life in order to begin a behavioral program that will help him to take charge of his own situation like the competent young adult he wanted to be.

Treatment was twofold. The psychiatrist provided stimulant medication for his attentional problems, and the therapist began a combination of psychotherapy and tutorial study in the skill subjects of mathematics and English usage. The therapist's first career as a high school mathematics teacher provided a background for this combination treatment. She has found that a focus on academic struggles is an effective segue into psychotherapy of the emotional factors. During these sessions, the educator/therapist would focus on skill development interspersed with discussion about Charlie's frustration, anxiety, feeling stupid, and so on. There was also frequent discussion of exactly what Charlie needed to do behaviorally to take charge of his life and be accountable to himself for developing a daily structure that he would need to be able to continue functioning well when he went back to college. He was also encouraged to make sure he found ways to spend time with friends his own age. Several meetings with Charlie and his parents spelled out for everyone in the family exactly what Charlie is responsible for and what his parents must continue to leave as his responsibility in spite of their parental anxiety. Following six months of treatment, Charlie left for school on medication, knowing much more mathematics and English usage, with an academic plan for the semester, feeling much better about himself, and pleased with how he had managed his year off. The triangle with his parents was effectively neutralized, at least for the time being.

This case began with the clinical presence of a dysfunctional young adult, but, like the demonstration family, fits into Guerin's model for working with child- and adolescent-centered families. This model is called "Trees, Triangles, and Temperament" (Guerin and Gordon, 1986). It uses genograms to identify the number and quality of available relationship options and the level of developmental and situational stress in the three-generation family system. It proposes a typology of the child- and adolescent-centered triangles to assist the therapist in finding and defining the relationship triangles that may be contributing to the child's symptoms. Finally, the model also assesses the goodness of fit between the individual child's temperament and the family's expectations for children born or adopted into their system. The model is based on seven key assumptions.

1. A child is born into a family with certain constitutional assets and limitations. Among the limitations is a genetic predisposition for the type and severity of physical and emotional symptoms he or she may develop during a lifetime.

2. Whether or to what degree these vulnerabilities will emerge over time depend on (a) the basic functioning level of the family system around the time the child is born, (b) how well the child's temperament fits in the family and his or her sibling position in the family, and (c) the amount of internal and external stress the family must absorb and dissipate over its life cycle.

3. Symptoms will develop when the amount of unbound, or free-floating, anxiety in the family has reached a critical level, that is, beyond the relationship system's ability to bind, diffuse, or dissipate it.

4. The driving force for this anxiety will be the development of cluster stress. This is the coming together of a series of transition times in a quantity sufficient to shake the emotional equilibrium of the family. A classic example of this is the family that is all at once going through the turmoil of adolescence, midlife crises, and grandparental aging and death.

5. A vulnerable member of the family will absorb the excess anxiety, thereby developing a symptom.

6. The vulnerable individual most likely to absorb and act out the family's anxiety is the most isolated, invalidated family member, with the least functional leverage in the system.

7. The symptom serves the function of binding the excess anxiety in the system, allowing the family to maintain its organization or to reorganize and continue functioning.

In the video demonstration family, the daughter was born with physical abnormalities that defined her both as a source of anxiety and as an organizing locus for anxiety from other sources. We don't have a lot of factual information about the family's basic level of functioning other than the disclosure about the father's alcohol abuse, a sense of chronic distance in the marriage, and the closedness of communication around the older brother's death. The daughter's shyness and nondisclosing nature and emotional distance seem not to fit with her mother's fantasy about a daughter and a mother–daughter relationship. Given the clinical situation, it would be easy to hypothesize that the daughter, as the most vulnerable family member, is the projective object of the parental anxiety, is isolated and invalidated, and lacks much in the way of functional leverage in the family. Her only power is through her distance, her withholding of communication, and her symptoms. Clearly, from the interactional play of the demonstration interview, she is caught in an intense triangle with her parents. A further review of this case, the interview, and the treatment plan will be discussed later in this chapter.

Clinical Techniques in Bowenian therapy

The major techniques used in Bowenian therapy include the genogram, the process question, relationship experiments, neutralization of the symptomatic triangles, coaching, the "I-position," and displacement stories.

1. The **genogram,** which is also known as the *family diagram,* was first formally named and described by Guerin in Guerin and Fogarty (1972), elaborated on by Guerin and Pendagast (1976), and further developed by McGoldrick and Gerson (1999). It is an organizing tool that documents the developmental and situational stressors in a three-generation family system. In addition, it is used to record factual data on physical and emotional illness in family members. Relationship conflicts and cutoffs as well as viable relationship options are noted, along with key triangles that surround the presenting symptom. The function of the genogram is to collect comprehensive information about individuals and the family in a short time and to serve as a road map for the development of a treatment plan. It is important to remember that the process of collecting the information is sometimes therapeutic in and of itself. On completion of a genogram, family members will often say, "It never occurred to me how all of those events fit together."

2. The **process question** is the major technique employed by the interviewer while obtaining the genogram and tracking the relationship process. It is also used to help manage and neutralize the triangles of the case, including the potential therapy triangle that may develop between the therapist and the various family members. The process question is a question aimed at calming anxiety and gaining access to information on how the family perceives the problem and how the mechanisms driving and maintaining the

problem operate. If process questions and validation by the therapist decrease the anxiety, people are better able to think clearly. This clarity allows them to discover many more potential options for managing their problems. In addition, they are more open to experimenting with modified patterns of relating that the therapist suggests. The information gained from the process questions also aids the therapist in creating appropriate behavioral experiments for the family. The purpose of these experiments is to challenge individual family members to behave in a different way within the context of a particular relationship. They are instructed to monitor their own emotions and the impact the experiment is having on the relationship. It is hoped that these experiments will break the cyclical nature of the problem and expose underlying emotional processes that can then be understood and dealt with more effectively.

3. **Relationship experiments** are behavioral tasks assigned to family members by the therapist to first expose and then alter the dysfunctional relationship process in the family system. Part of the process of therapy in this model is using process questions to define repetitive patterns of relating and to track the direction and intensity of distance and pursuit in the relationship. Once these patterns of relating and movement are defined, relationship experiments can be constructed. For example, Paul is a forty-five-year-old successful lawyer and father of three children. His wife, Jill, divides her time among domestic management tasks, being chief emotional consultant to Paul, and three days a week of paralegal work for one of Paul's friends. Their oldest daughter, Julia, is struggling through the adjustment to her first year of college. Paul misses his oldest daughter and can't find a way to talk about it. In fact, he flat out denies that he misses her most of the time. Instead, he takes his anxiety and converts it into intense telephone movement toward his daughter with nightly phone calls to her campus phone to inquire about her well-being and her academic progress. Paul, Jill, and Julia initiate clinical consultation during the semester break of her freshman year following the arrival of her first semester grades in all of their 2.3 GPA glory. As the consultation defined and tracked the process, an initial relationship experiment was designed.

In this experiment, father was to call Julia only twice a week. During these calls he was forbidden to ask any questions about her academic progress, but was to have a conversation based on other information, such as talking about himself and his struggles at work or other points of mutual interest. For example, they both loved tennis but hadn't played with each other for more than a year. They agreed to play at her university courts once a month and also to attend an indoor tennis tournament in New York City. Julia was to focus her energy on setting up her own priorities and function accordingly, keeping in mind the fairness doctrine of accountability for expenditure of family funds and honest academic effort.

Father and daughter were given a Saturday appointment for three weeks into the second semester. At that appointment, Paul reported his considerable angst at trying to carry out his experimental role. He found himself anxious, often with nothing to say to Julia. But it was getting better, even to the point that he and Julia were able to laugh at his "slips" into asking "taboo" questions about her grades. For her part, Julia reported experiencing relief from her father's previous pattern of daily telephone calls, but noticed a gradually increasing uneasiness in herself. She was now able to talk about missing home, being insecure about fitting in at school, and feeling unsupported by her mother, whom she experiences as not critical, but often cold. In spite of this experience of emotional discomfort, her academic efforts were improving somewhat. In addition, as the process in the triangle began to shift, there was an uncovering of emotional difficulties between Julia and Jill. The definition of the dysfunctional triangle is an outgrowth of this relationship experiment. When assigning a relationship experiment, family members are instructed by the therapist to use as much conscious effort as necessary to accomplish the experimental behavior. They are instructed to observe their own internal emotional reaction as well as the observable impact on the relationship. This process supplies an ongoing experience of the connection between an internal emotional state and relationship behavior.

4. The **neutralization of the symptomatic triangles** is the authors' method for the management and neutralization of reactive emotional triangles. This five-step process includes finding the triangle, defining the triangle's structure and the flow of movement within it, reversing the flow of movement within the triangle, exposing the emotional process and, finally, dealing with the process and moving toward improved functioning.

   Closely linked to the management of the central symptomatic triangle is the potential therapy triangle among the family members and the therapist. If the therapist can remain free of the emotional reactivity in the therapy triangle, the family members will be better able to reduce their own reactivity and begin to think more clearly about themselves and their situation. In the case of Paul, Jill, and Julia, the therapist could have become reactive to Paul's boundary intrusion with his daughter and could have become critical of him or become overly supportive and enabling of Julia. Falling into either of these traps would do nothing but perpetuate the family's dysfunction. Any attempt to form relationship experiments in the face of an active therapy triangle is fraught with distortions and overcorrections, and doomed to failure.

5. **Coaching** is a Bowenian therapy technique that is used when highly motivated individual family members have attained a reasonable degree of self-focus, can be in charge of their own internal emotional reactivity, and can read the predictable relationship patterns in their system with some facility. With these conditions in place, the therapist offers some options that might be tried as a change from the robotlike usual patterns of behavior. The "coach" tries to help the player predict the responses to exercising such an option and the hoped-for results if it is "successful." Coaching is "supportive" insofar as it

encourages and reflects confidence in the player's courage and skill. However, in this model, the coach is careful not to "rubber-stamp" reactive acting out masquerading as a conscious effort toward change situations. Coaching does not foster dependence on the therapist; in fact, it should accomplish the opposite. As "coachable" individuals become more skillful at these experiences, they become capable of making highly creative functional changes in their own emotional systems with only minimal input and review from the coach. When Jennie came to therapy because of her major depression, she was emotionally isolated amidst the highly anxious controlling family system of her in-laws. Money was tight and Jennie was at home with three children under the age of five. She was not permitted by her husband to have anyone take care of the children except his parents, who lived nearby. Although her father-in-law was often helpful, her mother-in-law was frequently not available to help and resented the time her husband spent with the grandchildren and her daughter-in-law. Jennie's own parents were dead and her married brothers did not live near her. Almost all social time was spent with her husband's family; her husband rarely, if ever, sought to have time alone with her. As her mood improved with the help of an antidepressant, she began to see the factors that had contributed to her situation. At the therapist's suggestion, she began to have her husband, Tony, deal directly with his mother instead of always going through her. When her mother-in-law called to ask about Tony, Jennie would call him over so that he could talk with his mother directly. In addition, she encouraged him to spend time with his family at their house and bring the children with him, but she did not always go along. When she did visit, she stopped giving advice to anyone in his family and listened a lot. Although her extended family members were at a distance, she made a concerted effort to see them if she could, often without her husband's cooperation or support. As her children enter school, she is becoming active on school committees and is establishing a network of friends who can help each other out with child care without incurring any expense. Her parenting is more creative and, at the same time, she is setting better boundaries with her children. If she believes that she is doing something for herself that is functional, something that reduces her isolation or connects her with friends, she is now able to do so without her husband's approval. With the assistance of medication, Jennie's depression and anxiety decreased. Relieved of the emotional burden of her depression, Jennie was able to feel less the victim and begin to develop clarity of self-focus. This emotional freedom enables her to see the maze of triangles that were entrapping her. Now she can make functional use of coaching to neutralize these triangles, give herself a way out of the maze, and provide an increased number of functional relationship options.

6. The **"I-position"** is a nonemotionally reactive, clearly communicated statement of opinion and belief. In a situation of increased tension and emotional reactivity, it often has a stablizing effect for one person to be able to detach from the emotional furor and step into an " I-position." In Bowenian ther-

apy, family members are encouraged to take functional "I-positions." Therapists can model this technique in clinical situations or coach family members in the art of its execution. In a marital therapy case, there can often be extreme pressure on the therapist to solve the problem, take sides on a difference of opinion, or convince the other spouse to change. For example, the therapist may be implicitly or explicitly asked to convince the other spouse to see the wisdom of parenting the children in a certain way. In this marital conflict situation that involved conflict around parenting styles, it would be important for the therapist to be able to take an "I-position." An example of the implementation of this technique would be the following statement: "In my opinion, it is important for parents to be open and clear with one another about their differences in philosophy and style of parenting. Then parents are able to work out differences in a way that allows for a united parental front when that is the reality, but also permits a difference of opinion between parents with support for the parent who began the problematic negotiation with the child in the first place."

7. We use **displacement stories** extensively in the form of films or videotapes. Telling stories, or asking "just suppose" questions about fantasied solutions, are also powerful ways of reducing defensiveness in the family. "I Never Sang for My Father" is one of the many films used over the years to teach people about the emotional process in their own families without raising their defensiveness. Joe is a thirty-seven-year-old attorney whose mother has died recently and whose irascible father is now in a nursing home. Joe came to therapy because he was having difficulty getting over his mother's death and even greater difficulty dealing with his father now that his mother is no longer present to protect the two men from each other. Somehow it is easier for Joe to watch Gene Hackman, the middle-aged son in "I Never Sang for My Father," struggle with his difficult widowed father than for Joe to accept the therapist's observation that he had been overclose to his mother and too distant from his father over the years. Joe paid close attention to Gene Hackman's relationship to Melvin Douglas, his screen father, as that connection deteriorated after his mother died because the son had never built a direct relationship with his father, but had always gone through his mother. From his experience watching the displacement film, Joe was able to accept the challenge of making a different type of connection with his father before his father died or slipped into "speechless senility." He began this experiment by making planned visits to his father in the nursing home. During these visits, Joe would concentrate on keeping his own anxiety in check while sitting silently with his father or engaging him in conversations about his father's youth and early adult life experience. In the beginning, the father remained irritable and irascible in his cynical response to the son's presence. At one point he even commented to the son, "I bet you wish that your mother was here and that I was dead." To which the son replied, " That may be your wish, Dad, but it never even occurred to me."

Sustained effort on the son's part over several months began to modify the climate in the relationship between the two men. One day the father said that his major regret in life was that he did not know his children better and that he wasn't sure they knew or appreciated all that he had done on their behalf. To which the son replied, "It's never too late to start trying, Dad." Although this exchange of honest feelings certainly did not wipe out thirty-plus years of contentious interchange between Joe and his father, it did represent a potential new beginning. In our experience, it is not unusual for the use of displacement material in the context of a positive therapeutic relationship to produce these kinds of results.

At this point we have reviewed the history and the development over time of the conceptual framework and techniques of Bowenian therapy. In addition, we have described in some detail how we would approach several types of clinical situation. Now let us step back from the theory and clinical technique and take a brief look at how this model views mental illness and the process of change, as well as its range of application in clinical situations.

With respect to mental illness, it is important to remember that Bowen theory began with the study of schizophrenia. From that study evolved Bowen's scale of differentiation, on which he placed those individuals with schizophrenia on the lowest levels and those individuals capable of independent thought in the midst of intense anxiety and intense emotional turmoil at the highest level. In the authors' version of the Bowenian model, individual dysfunction of a biological, psychological, or combined nature does exist as a clinical reality. Thought disorders such as schizophrenia, and mood disorders such depression and anxieties of many kinds, are a by-product of individual genetic and psychological vulnerability. The relationship support surrounding the symptomatic individual participates in this emotional process in two ways. On the one hand, the combined level of developmental and situational stress and the premorbid level of functioning of the family contribute to the circumstances that produce the expression of vulnerability in the individual in the form of symptoms. On the other hand, the same relationship system potentially offers the structure of relationship connection and support that can be of significant help in ameliorating these symptoms, decreasing morbidity and improving prognosis. The characteristics of family systems that are helpful to decrease the morbidity of mental illness include openness of communication, acceptance of individual differences and conflict, and flexibility of response to developmental and situational demand. Unhelpful characteristics of the family system include the opposite characteristics of closedness of communication, rejection of individuality and differences of opinion, and rigidity of response. The goals for the individual would be freedom from symptoms, the ability to be productive at work, have functionally connected relationships with others, and a sense of personal well-being.

Therapeutic change in Bowenian therapy is defined as a decrease in intensity and duration of symptoms of anxiety and depression and a decrease in emotional arousal in individuals and in emotional reactivity in relationships. There is a deintensification of active relationship triangles, a decrease in projection and blaming, an increase in self-focus in the individual, an improvement in the opening of communication around toxic issues, and an increase in available relationship options. Although there may be several members of a family system present at any given therapy session, we believe the process of change begins individually, outside the therapy session. Waiting for others in the family to change so that things will be easier for you leads to no change at all. One of the basic beliefs of Bowenian therapy is that, if one person in the family system can maintain enough self-focus to change in the direction of improved functioning, others in the family system will follow. The beginning of change in the individual is brought back into the therapy interaction where it is processed and reinforced. This process of change then continues to be demonstrated in the naturally occurring relationships in the family. The therapist is the coach and catalyst to this process rather than the transferential focal point. Change in a relationship conflict would be all of the improvements in the individuals listed above plus a significant reduction in the amount of conflict in the relationship, accompanied by an increase in the satisfaction with that relationship.

Bowenian family therapy may be used across the diagnostic spectrum with psychoses, anxiety disorders, major clinical depression, cognitive and attentional difficulties, and all manner and forms of relationship conflict. As a therapist working with this model, it is possible to incorporate biological and behavioral interventions, and use twelve-step programs to assist in the management and alleviation of symptoms. In addition, techniques from other family systems models, such as narrative therapy, may be used to facilitate the elaboration of underlying relationship symptoms and process. Although this

Guerin w/clients

model is often viewed as working best with affluent, middle-class, two-parent families, we believe this to be a somewhat prejudiced view. Remember, this model began in clinical work with psychoses (Bowen, 1978), has elaborated specific modifications to be used with single-parent and blended families (Pendagast, 1983), and, from an early time in its history, paid attention to cultural, racial (McGoldrick & Garcia Preto, 1984), and gender issues (Walters, Carter, Papp, & Silverstein, 1988).

Having reviewed the history of Bowenian therapy and its major concepts, we will illustrate how the theory is applied in a clinical situation. The following section shows, through the use of the video demonstration interview, how Bowenian therapy is actually used.

The Clinical Interview

The family on this demonstration tape is adult-child focused. "Adult-child focused" means that the presenting symptoms reside in an unmarried adult who presents to therapy as part of her family of origin. The symptom bearer is an adult child, aged thirty-two, brought to therapy by and with her parents. A young woman with physical and developmental difficulties from birth, she is still living at home with her parents. The mother works outside the home and appears, at best, unhappy. The father, who retired at a fairly early age, appears angry, controlling, and intimidating by nature. An older brother has died in the recent past, but the family declares death to the visiting therapist who insists on talking about that brother rather than talking to their daughter and getting her to discuss her problems and what can be done about her situation.

In order to clarify the method behind the therapist's behavior in this session, we will attempt to do three things. First we will show the link between the theoretical concepts elaborated earlier in this chapter and the clinical method used. Second, there will be an elaboration of the techniques of Bowenian therapy as they are employed. Third, the process of the interview will be tracked and integrated with the theory and clinical methodology. Finally, we will consider the logical pathway for follow-up therapy with this family.

The first goal of the interviewer is to engage the family in the joint endeavor of alleviating their pain and gaining more control over their problems. There is an attempt to make a connection with each member of the family. This is done by assuming the position of a calm, interested, compassionate investigator. As the session moves along, an attempt is made to understand how they define the problem and to validate for them their emotional experience. In addition, the therapist attempts to avoid a control struggle with the father and to stand clear of the fallout left behind from previous interviews. In other words, he is attempting to make a connection with all three family members and to avoid activating the preexisting therapy triangles. At the same time, the therapist is trying to determine the pathway through which the family will allow him access to their lives and the relationship process of their family system.

In the beginning of the interview, the father's anger and need to control are palpable. The potential traps for the therapist are manyfold. The therapist can be controlled and paralyzed by the father's anger and need to control, or confront the anger directly, risking that the entire session will be absorbed by the fallout from his confrontation or, even worse, the father might leave the session. True to the model, the therapist uses a series of process questions aimed at neutralizing the father's anger. That is, he has as calm a discussion as possible while putting the father's anger on the table as an open issue. The additional agenda of the therapist in this initial exchange of comments is to probe this closed system by addressing the issue of emotional safety. How safe is it to talk about emotionally loaded things in this family? The implied message emphasizes the importance of somehow making it safe to talk about difficult issues in the therapy in order for that safety to carry over to the family system outside of the therapy session. The following segment of the videotape addresses the issue of emotional safety in the family and in the therapy session.

TH: "Do you let your parents know what it is about each of them that bugs you? Do you know what it is about each of them that bugs you?"

D: "No."

TH: "If you knew, would it be safe to tell them?"

D: "I don't know. I really don't know."

TH: "I mean if your dad behaved in ways that really bugged you, would it be safe for you to say, 'Daddy, when you do this it really upsets me, makes me angry and makes me want to . . . '?"

D: "I can try that one."

TH: "Would it be safe?"

D: "I can try that one. I haven't tried that yet."

TH: "No? How come?"

D: "I don't know."

TH: "Is your dad an easy guy to talk to?"

D: "Ah, sometimes."

TH: "What's that mean? I mean, when is he and when isn't he?"

D: "Well, when he is hurting and real, real angry, no. No. I just back off."

TH: "So, when he is in a good mood and he's kind of light and stuff, then you can talk to him."

D: "Yeah."

TH: "And can you tell him negative stuff about him when he is in that kind of mood? Not angry but . . . "

D: "I don't know. I haven't tried yet."

TH: [To Father] "She's said she's never tried it. Would it be safe?"

F: "I don't know. What could possibly be negative about me?"

TH: "Oh, oh, you can't even think what it possibly might be?"

F: "No!"

TH: "No?"

F: "Oh, Lord, it's hard to be humble."

TH: "Can you sing that for us? That was a good country and western song."

M: "He used to sing it very well."

TH: "Be straight with me now. Could you take negative feedback?"

F: "Oh, probably."

TH: "Would it be easier to take from Pam or from Judy?"

D: "Yeah, let me try that one."

F: "It all depends on what it is. When you say negativity . . . "

TH: "Well, if they say, 'Dad, you've got too hot a temper and you scare me and you intimidate me,' would you be able to hear that?"

F: "Oh yeah, I mean I used to be a lot worse. A lot."

TH: "Is that because you've been working on it or because you just got older and have mellowed?"

F: "No, I think I got older and mellowed out, and I worked on it. I used to drink a lot. Many years ago."

TH: "And so that would kind of, you were an angry drunk."

F: "Yeah, yeah. And since I quit drinking I think I've been a lot mellower and everything else."

M: "Well, it's been many, many years though."

F: "Yeah, well, it's been many years. Yeah, I get angry you know like anyone else does, I would assume."

In this segment, as mentioned earlier, the therapist takes the issues of emotional safety, open communication, and the father's anger and gently but factually presses the father and daughter about the presence of these issues in the family, attempting by this to open communication and begin the process of detoxifying and neutralizing these issues. If this can be successful, it will become safer in the therapy session and at home to discuss more openly emotionally charged topics. Otherwise, these toxic issues get buried, building negativity and tension. An indication that the therapist is being somewhat successful in establishing therapeutic safety is seen in the father's disclosure of his anger and alcohol abuse in the past and his improvement in the present. As you can see from this segment of the interview, learning the art of asking process questions is critical to using the Bowenian method of intervention. However, not all questions in the interview are aimed at elaborating or uncovering process. Some are what we call "information questions" aimed at the elaboration of the facts. For example,

TH: "How often does Pam go with you [to their vacation house for the weekend]?"

TH: "So, Pam, what do you do if you stay at home?"

TH: "What do you do for fun?"

TH: "What kind of dog do you have?"

These questions serve the purpose of opening a closed system and replacing overanxious distortion with a more factual representation. A third type of question is what we term a "suppose question." These questions displace the content to a "what if" scenario that allows the family to respond more openly by diminishing their defensiveness, as the next segment of the interview illustrates.

TH: "What would happen if you won a lottery and part of it was that you got to have your own condo, you know. And so fully furnished . . . "

D: "Let's go guys . . . "

TH: "You'd bring them with you? Yeah. You don't listen to them, you plug your ears, but you'd bring them along?"

D: "Yeah."

TH: "Now, you know when you are talking to a psychiatrist and you say that ['Let's go guys'], they are liable to say maybe you have a problem separating, you know. What do you think?"

D: "Sure, I'd rather stay home."

TH: "Yeah? Now that's a problem, or should everyone just sit back and accept that?"

D: "I don't think that's a problem."

The "just suppose" question is a variant of the displacement story technique described earlier. It provides a fantasy alternative as a way of uncovering and documenting underlying individual and relationship process. In this instance, it documents the degree of anxious attachment present in the family. The therapist offers the daughter the fantasy of freedom and she automatically, in just a heartbeat, elects to bring her parents along. This maneuver accomplishes the parents' goal of continuing to focus on the daughter, while simultaneously allowing the therapist to define the level of the separation difficulties inherent in this family system.

Another critically important part of the successful engagement process is the therapist's avoiding triangular traps. As has been mentioned, from the beginning of the session the therapist is making his way through a maze of relationship triangles. In this instance, the therapist chooses to attempt to avoid being triangled by being open to the family's discussion, hearing their message—talk to our daughter, don't focus on our son's death. In addition, he doesn't jump to defend the previous five "bad guy" therapists or contend that he will somehow be better than the one "good guy." One process question from the transcript exemplifies this detriangling method.

Following the family's discussion of their preceding experiences with visiting therapists, the therapist asks: "So maybe you don't even need to be here today?"

With this question the therapist distances himself, avoids selling himself and criticizing the other therapists. The family responds by endorsing the potential usefulness of the consultation. After some success at engaging the family the therapist turns to the central dysfunctional triangle of father–mother–daughter and begins his investigation of its structure with one simple process question: "Do you think Pam has a kind of, you know, just as much a relationship with you as she has with your wife?"

It is clear from the structural set up, and the positioning of family members in the room, that the father and daughter are linked in alliance with the mother on the outside and unhappy about it. The therapist tries to nudge the direction of movement in this triangle by urging the mother to close the distance with her daughter on her daughter's terms and for the father to cease his efforts to promote the relationship between these two women and let them get on with it themselves. This entails not only an attempt to change the direction of movement in the triangle, but also proposes using the technique of relationship experiments in order to break the dysfunctional sequence.

> TH: "Maybe she thinks you worry about her too much. Do you?"
>
> M: "Well, I worry about her, yeah. But you know the way things are out there, you know, nowadays, you can't say, you can't worry too much. Like when she comes home at night, if she comes in late, I always tell her to make sure she wakes me up, you know, so I know she's home."

The therapist, having begun the investigation of the father–mother–daughter triangle, moves first to the mother and then on to the mother–daughter relationship.

> TH: "Would you say you're an anxious mother?"
>
> D: "A worrywart!"
>
> M: "No, I don't walk the floors."
>
> TH: "You go to sleep anyway."
>
> M: "I do go to sleep."
>
> F: "She goes to sleep but she's not sleeping. Do you have children [to the interviewer]?
>
> TH: "Do I? Sure."
>
> F: "I don't know how old they are, but when they're out late, you go to bed, you're sleeping, but when that door opens . . . "

M: "Yeah, but you know I'm a very light sleeper. I hear all sorts of noises and stuff."

TH: "Now, you know while we've been talking both Judy and Pam get tearful. I'm not sure what the tears are connected to. [To the father] Do you know?"

F: "I don't know. I think Judy really wants Pam to love her, to be a pal with her, and with Pam, I don't know, and Pam is just embarrassed to talk about it, and she is doing something that she doesn't want to do, so she will get very teary-eyed, and she's sorry that she's acting that way towards her mother, but she is still going to do it."

TH: [Addressing the mother] "Is Adrian right about what you are tearful about?"

M: "I don't know. I cry very easily. I can watch a movie and sit there and cry, and it could be the funniest movie in the world, but I still cry."

With her last comment, the mother boxes the therapist out.

TH: "So we shouldn't pay attention to those tears?"

The therapist accepts and reinforces the distance.

M: "Not always, no."

The therapist presses on.

TH: "Is there a difference between when you cry just because you are a sentimental person and when you cry because there is something really pinching your insides?"

M: "Oh, yeah."

TH: "How can we tell the difference?"

M: "I don't know."

TH: "Can you tell the difference?"

M: "I could probably tell the difference myself, yeah."

TH: "Do you let anybody in on it?"

M: "No, I just hold it into myself."

F: [To wife] "I caught you a couple of times."

TH: "Everybody holes up unto themselves. Everybody goes off into their box, right? Pam does. She says, 'Leave me alone.' Mother says it, and you do, too. How come?"

M: "It's easier that way."

TH: "It's easier. What makes it easier, Judy?"

M: "Well, there is no fighting, no arguing, or . . . "

TH: "So, if you start talking about what's upsetting you, then the fight would ensue?"

M: "Well, it might if it was something said that . . . "

TH: "You mean if it was critical or . . . "

M: "Yeah, if it was something, yeah . . . "

TH: "But suppose it was just sadness or upset . . . "

At this point the therapist pokes gently at the sadness, loneliness, and sense of loss in the family without mentioning the dead brother.

M: "Oh, I think we can talk about that. I think we talk about that if it was something sad or something . . . "

TH: "So, if the tears are coming from frustration and anger, and it's frustration and anger with somebody else and you try to talk about it, then it's not safe. But if it's because there has been a loss, or your feelings have been hurt, or you are frustrated because things are not going well at work, then you can talk about that."

M: "Probably, yeah."

TH: "Now, what Adrian tells me is that you have upset feelings. I'm not sure they aren't hurt, that you and Pam somehow can't have the kind of connection you would like to have with your daughter. Is that accurate?"

M: "Well, I, yeah, I . . . "

The therapist pushes the mother to move toward her daughter and communicate directly with her.

TH: "And have you told Pam about those?"

M: "I've asked her, you know, to do things with me and . . . "

TH: "Have you told her about your feelings?"

M: "Oh, I think so."

TH: "Has she, Pam? Do you remember?"

D: [grunt]

The therapist checks out the daughter's availability and openness to change in mother's direction of movement.

TH: "Would you prefer her not to tell you?"

D: "Prefer her to tell me."

TH: "Would you? So, if she were to tell you, 'It really upsets me that you and I can't find a way to be connected and have fun together and be comfortable together.' You want her to say that? [To mother] Do you believe her, Judy?"

M: "No."

TH: "Why not?"

M: "Because if you knew Pam, she can sit here and tell you exactly what you want to hear."

TH: "Is that what she's doing right now?"

M: "Mhmh."

D: "No."

F: "A lot of it."

D: "No."

F: "There is a lot of it that's sincere, but there is a lot of it that, because this is what she thinks you want to hear."

TH: "Pam?"

D: "No, no, no, no, no, no."

To this point the session dealt with extrafamilial triangles involving the previous six visiting clinicians, and has been defining the structure and process of the central symptomatic triangle involving father, mother, and daughter, and proposing ways in which the mother might experiment with change. The therapist now very gently opens the issue of the brother's death by returning to the previously discussed topic of loss.

TH: "I don't want, I don't wanna dwell on this. I just want to ask a question about it because I know you've dealt with some of it in the other session. Is it easy for you guys to sit around and talk about the losses that you've had in your life, like when the grandmothers died and when your son died and stuff, or is it hard?"

F: "Everybody but my son."

TH: "That one's kind of a no-no."

F: "That's a tough one."

TH: "Real sensitive. Have you worked on getting that less sensitive or have you just left it in its compartment?"

F: "We just put it away and let it be there."

TH: "Do you think it would be a negative to take it out of the compartment and work on it, or . . . ?"

F: "I think it would be."

TH: [Therapist to mother] "Okay, would you agree?"

M: "Well, we talk once and a while about the good times we had together with him."

D: "But that's it."

M: "We remember things that we did together."

The therapist chooses not to press on here leaving further exploration for another day. In the final phase of the session, the therapist uses the triangle with Pam's geriatric friend Jesse. In doing this he challenges the mother to face the reality of her daughter's movement away from her and toward Jesse and for the mother to learn from it, even to the point of studying Jesse's methods. Having done this, the therapist returns to the parents' agenda and broaches the topic of Pam's social phobia and gives Pam total responsibility for dealing with it. In this way, he hopes to relieve the mother of some of her guilt and feelings of responsibility for Pam's isolation while challenging Pam to take on the social phobia and do something about it.

TH: "Hey, Pam. I'm going to tell you something. You ready? I have a hunch, now it's only a hunch, but I have a hunch that one of the reasons you don't kind of move out a little bit more and find things to do with people your own age is that you, you're a little bit scared, and I think you ought to work on that. I know it is not easy for you to talk about these things, but it might help to have somebody, and maybe you can talk to Jesse about it, and Jesse can help you with it. But I think that it would be worth it for you to start working on that. Does that make any sense to you?"

D: "Yes!!"

As the interview draws to a close, the therapist moves to reinvolve the father.

TH: "I haven't figured out anything for you to do, Adrian. That's not good, is it? I'm going to let you off the hook. You guys got any questions? Because we gotta stop. Okay, I want to thank you for coming to meet with me."

M: "Thank you for coming. You came a long way."

TH: "Yeah, but it's been enjoyable sitting and talking to you."

M: "No, we'll keep trying."

TH: "You gotta remember what I said now. Everybody going to remember?"

D: "Try to."

TH: "Okay. I'll be checking up on you. Take care."

M: "Thank you very much."

In this demonstration interview we have seen an attempt made by the therapist to:

1. engage and connect with each family member;
2. make it safer in the therapy and safer in the family to address the family's phobic areas, which are the father's anger, the mother's loneliness, the toxic

issue of the brother's death, the daughter's restricted and unfulfilling life, and the parents' marriage;

3. operate and neutralize the relationship triangles as they presented themselves;
4. define the symptoms and begin to propose a change in the direction of movement in the central symptomatic triangle between mother, father, and daughter.

Hopefully, all of this forms the beginning beachhead for the ensuing therapeutic journey. If there were a follow-up session the next week, the therapist would probably begin the session by checking in with the family to see if they had tried his suggestions. He would ask Pam if she had done any thinking about what was going on. He would check with the mother to see if she had thought about Jesse's method and why that worked with Pam and her method didn't. He might ask the father if he felt left out because he didn't have any assignments. He would then ask them what they wanted to work with in that session and he would expect that they would go back to Pam. He wouldn't be surprised if little or no change had occurred between sessions.

In our experience, the theory and clinical methodology of Bowenian therapy as presented in this chapter offer a framework for understanding individual dysfunction and intense relationship conflict in the context of the multigenerational family system. The clinical methodology presents multiple pathways for assisting symptomatic individuals in alleviating their pain, improving their functioning, and reducing the conflict in their relationships. To date, none of the concepts or models of intervention has withstood the scrutiny of concept validation by psychometrically sound measures, nor have they been subject to controlled outcome studies. To our knowledge some of the best attempts to date rest in the work of David Chabot, a Bowenian therapist at the Center for Family Learning, who is currently involved in research on Bowen's concept of differentiation and Fogarty's concept of the pursuer and distancer. As developed by Bowen, the scale of differentiation measured two aspects of his core concept: the lack of emotional autonomy due to anxiety and the level of emotional fusion in dyadic relationships. The Chabot Emotional Differentiation Scale (Chabot & Takagishi, 1999) attempts to measure the part of Bowen's differentiation concept that deals with the emotional fusion in dyadic relationships. The measure is a self-report questionnaire designed to assess the interpersonal aspects of an individual's level of emotional functioning in a variety of situations, stressful and nonstressful, conflictual and nonconflictual. As a relatively new measure, only pilot testing information is available on reliability and validity. However, data at this time indicate acceptable levels of reliability and validity, subject to further studies.

Chabot and his associates at Fordham University Graduate School of Psychology have also attempted to operationalize Fogarty's concept of the emotional pursuer and distancer in the marital relationship in their thirty-six-item self-report measure, the Chabot Pursuer Distancer Movement Scale (Chabot, 1998). It is based on the theoretical assumptions that pursuit and distance are not direct opposites and that pursuing and distancing behaviors are specific to a given relationship.

The scale measures behaviors within a relationship in conflictual and nonconflictual times. From the six studies completed to date, this measure evidences solid reliability and validity. The direction of further work includes identifying more components that distinguish emotional pursuit from emotional distance and developing a measure to capture pursuit and distance in a parent–child relationship, as opposed to the marriage relationship.

If Bowenian therapy hopes to remain viable, further attempts must be made to validate its concepts and demonstrate positive clinical outcome. Guerin and Chabot have addressed the question of the future viability of family therapy in general at the conclusion of a chapter on family systems theory and therapy in the *History of Psychotherapy* (1992), a volume written in celebration of the American Psychological Association's one hundredth anniversary. In our opinion, their appraisal of the future of Bowenian therapy remains accurate.

> One of the most important questions for the future of the family therapy movement is what will happen as the old guard of pioneers moves on and a new generation steps forward. How much of an attempt will be made to elaborate further some or all of the concepts developed in the first 40 years? If family theory is to continue to develop as the conceptual basis of a comprehensive model for understanding the individual's emotional functioning in a relationship context, several eventualities must occur. There must be a sophistication and refinement of the characteristics of functional compared with dysfunctional relationship systems, a systematic model of the individual including a continuum linking his or her "inner and outer space," and a model for tracking dyadic interaction and triangle formation. The goal of these family concepts and models would be the development of an integrated system of interventions that would enhance the ability of a therapist to steer relationship process toward better functioning both for individuals and for the family systems as a whole. If this is not forthcoming, family therapy may become more like group therapy—a clinical modality to be used at specific times in response to specific clinical indications in conjunction with, or in lieu of, traditional psychodynamically based individual therapy (Guerin and Chabot, p. 258).

REFERENCES

Anonymous. (1972). Differentiation of a self in one's family. In J. Framo (Ed.), *Family interaction* (pp. 111–173). New York: Springer.

Bowen, M. (1978). *Family therapy in clinical practice.* New York: Jason Aronson.

Carter, B., & McGoldrick, M. (1980). *The family life cycle.* New York: Gardner.

Chabot, D. R. (1998). Emotional pursuit and distance. Invited seminar, Division 43, American Psychological Association Annual Meeting, San Francisco, CA.

Chabot, D. R., & Takagishi, S. C. (1999). An examination of young adults as they separate from their parents: A six-factor approach. Unpublished research, Fordham University, NY.

Fogarty, T. F. (1976a). Systems concepts and dimensions of self. In P. J. Guerin (Ed.), *Family therapy: Theory and practice* (pp. 144–153). New York: Gardner.

Fogarty, T. F. (1976b). Marital crisis. In P. J. Guerin (Ed.), *Family therapy: Theory and practice* (pp. 325–334). New York: Gardner.

Fogarty, T. F. (1984). The individual and the family. In E. Pendagast (Ed.), *Compendium II: The best of the family* (1978–1983), (pp. 71–76). New Rochelle, NY: The Center for Family Learning.

Framo, (1972). (Ed.) Family interaction. New York: Springer.

Friedman, E. (1985). *Generation to generation.* New York: Guilford.

Goldenberg, I., & Goldenberg, H. (1991). *Family therapy: An overview,* Pacific Grove, CA: Brooks/Cole.

Guerin, P. J. (Ed.). (1976). *Family therapy: Theory and practice.* New York: Gardner.

Guerin, P. J., Jr., & Chabot, D. R. (1992). Development of family systems theory. In D. K. Freedheim (Ed.), *History of psychotherapy: A century of change* (pp. 225–260). Washington, DC: American Psychological Association.

Guerin, P. J., Jr., Fay, L. F., Burden, S. L., & Kautto, J. (1987). *The evaluation and treatment of marital conflict: A four-stage approach,* New York: Basic Books.

Guerin, P. J., & Fogarty, T. F. (1972). Study your own family. In A. Ferber, M. Mendelsohn, & A. Napier (Eds.), *The book of family therapy* (pp. 83–133). New York: Science House.

Guerin, P. J., Fogarty, T. F., Fay, L. F., & Kautto, J. (1996). *Working with relationship triangles: The one, two, three of psychotherapy.* New York: Guilford.

Guerin, P. J., & Gordon, E. (1986). Trees, triangles, and temperament in the child-centered family. In H. C. Fishman and B. L. Rossman (Eds.), *Evolving models for family change: A volume in honor of Salvador Minuchin* (pp. 158–182). New York: Guilford.

Guerin, P. J., & Pendagast, E. (1976). Evaluation of family systems and the genogram. In P. J. Guerin, (Ed.), *Family therapy: Theory and practice* (pp. 450–464). New York: Gardner Press.

Kerr, M. F., & Bowen, M. (1988). *Family evaluation: An approach based on Bowen theory.* New York: W. W. Norton.

McGoldrick, M., Pearce, J., & Giordano, J. (1982). *Ethnicity in family therapy.* New York: Guilford.

McGoldrick, M., & Garcia Preto, N. (1984). Ethnic intermarriage: Implications for therapy. *Family Process, 23*(3),

McGoldrick, M., & Gerson, R. (1999). *Genograms: Assessment and intervention.* New York: W. W. Norton.

Nichols, M. F. & Schwartz, R. (2001). *Family therapy: Concepts and methods* (5th ed.). Boston, MA: Allyn & Bacon.

Pendagast, E. (1983). The multiple-marriage family. In E. Pendagast (Ed.), *Compendium II: The best of the family (1978–1983),* (pp. 200–204). New Rochelle, NY: The Center for Family Learning.

Toman, W. (1961). *Family Constellation.* New York: Springer.

Walters, M., Carter, B., Papp, P., & Silverstein, O. (1988). *The invisible web: Gender patterns in family relationships.* New York: Guilford.

7 Feminist Family Therapy

DIANE KJOS

Cheryl Rampage

Feminist family therapy is a relatively new idea in the field for family therapy, and its growth can be related to the women's movement of the late sixties and early seventies. Although Virginia Satir was considered an early pioneer of family therapy, little attention was paid to the feminist perspective until women such as Rachel Hare-Mustin and Peggy Papp begin to challenge traditional family therapy. Feminist family therapy is more an attitude toward or way of thinking about families and family therapy than a defined theory or clinical approach to family therapy. It was characterized as "the application of feminist theory and values to family therapy" by Goodrich, Rampage, Ellman, and Halstead (1988). As such, it is practiced by family therapists from a number of theoretical perspectives. The growth of this approach to family therapy was influenced by several factors. The first, and probably the most significant, was the women's movement, which gave voice to gender differences and brought women's issues to the fore. The second, fueled by the growing number of families headed by women and the concurrent recognition of gay and lesbian families, was the emergence of a new idea of what constitutes a family. The idealized "normal family" of mother, father, and 2.5 children became more myth than reality. This, in turn, called for alternate ways of viewing and working with families. The third is the increase in the number of women among family therapists, counselors, and clinical psychologists. This increase may well have contributed to the fourth factor, an increased awareness of the physical and sexual abuse of girls and women.

A concurrent increased sensitivity to women's issues brought an awareness that women's development, needs, and issues were different from those of men. Traditional family therapy was criticized for being dominated by male therapists, for the failure to incorporate research related to women in the development of theory, and for its reliance on a systems perspective that often did not give voice to a feminist perspective or recognize individual differences within gender identity. Kaschak (1992) accuses family systems therapists of typically approaching families as "regulated, well-governed systems, like computers, or as hierarchical, executive-run systems, like businesses" (p. 17). She further notes that male therapists have tended to attribute the source of problems in the family as coming from the mother's overinvolvement or enmeshment with the children.

With the rise of feminism came an awareness that family therapy was influenced by a set of assumptions that followed traditional, but becoming less accepted, gender roles in mind. The traditional family was based on the assumption that men were essential for the well-being of women and responsible for taking care of the financial and safety needs of the family. Women, on the other hand, were responsible for the relationship and expected to take care of the home and children while men provided for the family. Women who worked outside the home were seen as doing so only because of a financial necessity, not because they felt this work fulfilling. Men who opted to stay home and do "women's work" were out-of-step and somehow not "normal." The value of the male was, and often still is, based on his financial success and recognition. However, from the feminist perspective, privilege and responsibility are shared and the well-being of both the male and female are based on a shared relationship and one's ability to care for others. The feminist family therapist works toward a coequal relationship, with family roles based on personal strengths.

Marriage, traditionally, fills different needs for men and women. For women, marriage has provided safety and a sense of identity and self-esteem. For men, marriage is a way of fulfilling physical and emotional needs. Kaschak (1992) contends that marriage seems to be more effective in meeting the needs of men than those of women. However, women are often more likely to initiate family therapy because, as Bernard (1972) notes, women seem to be more concerned about the relationship, while men may be more dependent on the relationship.

Another, and significant, argument for a feminist approach to family therapy is the growth in the number of families headed by women. In 1998, 23 percent of all children lived in a female-headed household (U.S. Census Bureau, 1999). For black and Hispanic families, the percentage of female-headed households is even higher, 51.9 percent for blacks and 26.9 percent for Hispanics. The role of the single parent is different from that of either parent in a two-parent family, and the lack of a parent may be seen as the cause of or contributing to problems with the children in the family. Female-headed households are also more likely to be lower-income or poverty-level households and, while nonresident fathers may be expected to contribute financially to their children's needs, the resident mother is expected to provide full-time child care while earning an income sufficient to maintain the family. The economic value of child care is probably best exemplified in the relatively low pay that child-care workers receive. In 1998, the median hourly earnings of child-care workers was $6.61. (http://stats.bls.gov/oco/ocos170.htm)

Early in her session with Rampage (1999), the single mother brings up her concern about the absence of a father in her son's life and how that might be affecting his behavior and success in school.

> M (6): "Yes. And you know I didn't know, you know, if that was starting to have an effect on him even though his father hasn't been around since he was a little over one. I didn't know if that was, you know, because he is a boy he is getting older, and you know, the fact that he is in school and all these other kids, you know, maybe their fathers pick them up or they talk about their fathers, you know, playing baseball with them or something, that it may be affecting him in some form or fashion" (p. 8).

Early approaches to feminist family therapy emphasized the practice of family therapy from a feminist or gender-sensitive perspective. Therapists were encouraged to pay attention to how they viewed male and female roles in the family and how this might be influenced by their own perspectives of gender- and age-appropriate roles and behaviors. While this was a shift from family therapy that had, theoretically, supported traditional gender roles, more changes were to come as feminist family therapy evolved from a therapy approached with gender awareness to a therapy based on a feminist theory of family and a consciousness of how traditional gender roles are related to problems families bring to therapy. Thus, feminist family therapy became more than family therapy for families in which a significant male figure was absent, and is now seen as a theoretical approach that incorporates specific conceptualizations and interventions that emanate from feminist research and literature, the feminist perspective, and a sensitivity to the power differential between men and women. Rampage (1999) notes that feminist family therapists "will look at how power gets expressed, how it gets used and how it might impact the problem that the clients are having."

Hare-Mustin (1978) identified areas of family therapy in which a feminist orientation is important: the contract, shifting tasks in the family, communication, generational boundaries, relabeling deviance, modeling, ownership and privacy, and the therapeutic alliance with different family members" (p. 185).

Braverman (1987) in "a beginning attempt to formulate the considerations which would underlie a feminist-sensitive approach to treatment, whatever the particular technique being employed" (p. 8), suggests seven values or considerations for the feminist family therapist.

1. understanding the impact of a patriarchal system on both men and women, and acknowledging that the social and political contexts (e.g., lower salaries for women, numerical scarcity of women in positions of power, etc.), as well as the family context, have a significant influence on the problems of women;
2. recognizing the limitations of traditional theories of psychological development based on a male model of maturity;
3. familiarity with women's problem-solving processes, which tend to focus on connection and relationship, rather than on logic, abstraction, and rationality;
4. understanding that the "personal is political," that is, motherhood, child rearing, and marriage are not simply life-cycle events, but institutions that carry particular sociocultural legacies for women;
5. a sensitivity to the biological effects of the female life cycle (including menstruation, adolescence, pregnancy, childbirth, and menopause) on women's symptom presentation and interpersonal relationships;
6. understanding women's sexuality and sexual responsiveness so that confused and mistaken notions, such as the exclusivity of vaginal orgasm, are not perpetuated;
7. valuing women's relationships with each other as a special source of support, different from their relationships with men (pp. 8–9).

The feminist family therapist is an agent of social change in that she maintains an awareness of how family therapy might support or maintain a woman's subordinate position in the family system and strives to develop, support, or strengthen an egalitarian relationship within the family. Gender issues such as traditional family roles, as well as traditional male and female roles and expectations, are all issues for discussion and exploration in feminist family therapy.

In a survey of self-identified feminist family therapists in Illinois, Whipple identified five general themes. These included nonhierarchical client–therapist relationships, including gender as an issue in therapy, encouraging egalitarian relationships, affirmation of the female experience and values, and social activism or empowerment of clients (Whipple, 1999, pp. 2–13). While one or more of these themes may appear in other forms of family therapy, taken as a whole they serve to characterize feminist family therapy.

The feminist family therapist establishes a coequal or nonhierarchical relationship with the client family. The feminist family therapist develops a contract or understanding with the family to achieve what the family wants to achieve in therapy. The coequal relationship reflects the therapist's belief that the family is the expert on the family, while the therapist is the expert on helping families work more effectively. Thus, therapy becomes a collaborative process with shared leadership and a cocreated contract for therapy. The clients "are engaged in discussions about expectations for therapy, specific strategies, gender roles, family structures, and justice in everyday family activities" (A. L. Gosling & M. Zangari, 1993).

In this collaborative process, the therapist avoids labels that tend to pathologize the family or any members of the family. Rather than identifying an "identified patient" or "IP" or the family as "dysfunctional," the therapist works from the perspective that the family shares a problem and, with the therapist's consultation, will be able to devise a way of handling the problem.

The feminist family therapist pays attention to the balance of power in the family. Goldner (1985) contends that "the family therapist is really the last in a long line of professionals from whom women have sought legitimation and power" (p. 38). In the process of therapy, the therapist works to maintain a coequal balance of power that recognizes the unique contributions of each family member. The feminist family therapist uses skills such as immediacy and mediation to assure that each individual is heard and that everyone's perceptions and ideas are validated. This is especially consequential in a family in which control is a primary issue. The therapist is also aware of how external power factors affect the family. These might include expectations of parents or other family members, demands and expectations of employers, religious beliefs, and society as a whole.

The feminist family therapist pays attention to roles and structure within family. The traditional family structure, and, indeed, societal expectations, define specific roles for men, women, and children in the family. The male has traditionally had responsibility for providing the larger share of the income, for maintaining the yard, exterior of the home, and the family car. The female was responsible for child care, the interior of the home (except for major repairs), and providing family meals. With these traditions in mind, the feminist family therapist recognizes that it may be difficult for the husband to accept the fact that his wife is the primary breadwinner or for the wife to admit that the major housekeeping tasks fall to her husband.

Feminism, as a movement, is often criticized as being "antimale" and "antifatherhood." Ideally, in feminist family therapy, the focus is "profamily," with individual roles based on personal strengths. This allows both partners, as in same-sex couple relationships, to employ their individual strengths.

The feminist family therapist is aware of the role sexism plays in diagnosis of psychological problems. In feminist therapy, the therapist recognizes the clients' strengths and avoids diagnostic labeling. The therapist is alert to how gender and gender roles relate to problems within the family and recognizes how these roles, based on societal expectations and traditions, function to create power discrepancies between the husband and wife. For example, although the wife, like the majority of women in today's society, works outside the home, she may make less than the husband and, therefore, may be seen has as having less economic value to the family and, therefore, be entitled to less respect for her contribution. The husband, as the primary "breadwinner," may be seen as having the right to make all or most of the major family decisions. If, as in some cases in which the wife brings home the larger income, there may be issues around the husband's view of self and his status in the family.

The Practice of Feminist Family Therapy

Because feminist family therapy is primarily based on a set of principles about gender and how gender plays a role in relationships, the feminist family therapist could be working from any of a number of theoretical approaches. Thus, the practice of feminist family therapy involves the use of basic therapeutic skills that are important to all forms of family therapy as well as attention to gender and gender-informed beliefs and practices within the family system and society itself.

Thus, the important difference between feminist family therapy and other forms of family therapy lies in the application of feminist principles in the therapeutic process. Hare-Mustin (1978) identifies specific areas of intervention in which a feminist orientation is of particular importance: the contract, shifting tasks in the family, communication, generational boundaries, relabeling deviance, modeling ownership and privacy, and the therapeutic alliance with different family members" (p. 185). In this process, the therapist is consistently aware of how gender differences and perceptions about gender relate to the family's presenting issues.

Walters, Carter, Papp, and Silverstein (1988, p. 26) suggest the following guidelines for a feminist approach to family therapy:

1. Identify gender messages and social constructs that condition behavior and sex roles;
2. Recognize the real limitations of female access to social and economic resources;
3. Be aware of sexist thinking that constricts the options of women to direct their own lives;
4. Acknowledge that women have been socialized to assume primary responsibility for family relationships;
5. Recognize the dilemmas and conflicts of childbearing and child rearing in our society;
6. Be aware of patterns that split the women in families as they seek to acquire power through relationships with men;

7. Affirm values and behaviors characteristic of women, such as connectedness, nurturing, and emotionality;
8. Recognize and support possibilities for women outside of marriage and the family;
9. Recognize the basic principle that no intervention is gender-free and that every intervention will have a different and special meaning for each sex.

Family Therapy Skills and Feminist Family Therapy

Wheeler, Avis, Miller, and Chaney (1978) identify three skills that are important to all forms of family therapy: develop and maintain a working relationship, define the problem, and facilitate change.

In *developing and maintaining a working relationship,* the feminist family therapist works with a basic background of feminist thought, understanding the impact of gender-role socialization on both genders. She is aware that men and women tend to view problems in different ways. Men are likely to see problems and issues in terms of power and control while women consider relationships and connection to others. Thus, the therapist needs to use a range of skills to build a relationship with each member of the family in terms of that family member's perspective while simultaneously building a relationship with the family as a whole. Family members, though they may not agree, come in with a fairly clear idea of who is at fault, and the therapist needs to take care to hear and acknowledge each family member's perspective without attributing blame. The underlying hypothesis of why someone is at fault may differ, based on each individual's perspective. Thus, during the relationship-building phase, the therapist is aware of the differing needs and attitudes of each family member and how gender may influence these needs and attitudes.

> Nine-year-old Jim has been acting out in school and teasing his younger sister until she cries. Jim's father suggests that the problem is a lack of firm discipline. He reports that his job requires a lot of travel and his wife just 'coddles' Jim too much. Jim's mother, on the other hand, believes that Jim misses his father and that his acting out is a result of his father not spending enough time with him. She says she tries to give Jim 'quality time' but that it just doesn't seem to be enough.

In this situation, the therapist may recognize that both the mother and father are "right" in their perception of the problem without blaming either parent or any innate or learned gender differences that influence their perceptions.

During the process of building a relationship with the family, the feminist family therapist works from the basis of an equal rather than a paternalistic or an "expert" relationship. The contract for therapy, whether explicit or implicit, is based on a mutual agreement between the therapist and the family and may

Rampage w/ clients

include goals, arrangement for treatment, and an agreement on "rules" for therapy. This helps the family "begin to understand how rules regulate the behavior of family members" (Hare-Mustin, p. 185). The therapist also sets and/or demonstrates guidelines for communications that will allow each member of the family to participate. Thus, the therapist may ask that family members not interrupt each other or speak for other family members. She may need to help individual family members be more specific about thoughts and feelings, or to articulate the feelings related or specific behaviors or incidents. Early in her session with a single mother and her son, Rampage (1999) asks the son what would happen if he wanted to talk to his mother about his feelings.

TH (18):   "But how about if you wanted to talk to her now or later on tonight and you wanted to tell her something about how you were feeling, if you were feeling sad or angry or worried about something? Could you talk to her about that?"

C (10):   "Mmhm."

TH (19):   "Yeah? What do you think Becky? Does he talk to you about problems when he is upset or sad or worried?"

M (9):   "Sometimes. Ah, he's, usually if something really upsets him, you know, he'll tell me, but he doesn't bring up about his dad too much, you know, voice his concerns. [Okay] And that's what I am thinking, wondering if, you know, there may be things going on but he just doesn't know how to express it. [Mmhm] You know, I thought maybe the counseling or something, you know, might help to draw it out" (pp. 10–11).

In *assessing or defining the problem,* the feminist family therapist pays attention to the effect power differentials, gender-based expectations and behaviors, and social and cultural influences have on the definition of the problem. For example, while one might expect the family structure to be patriarchal, the opposite may be true. In some cases, the mother is the head of family, with the father either absent or not active in the family dynamics. Throughout this process, the therapist avoids labeling or diagnostic "jargon," focusing on family dynamics, individual family roles, and the impact of socialization on the family's perception of the problem.

The feminist family therapist recognizes that each family member has a view of the problem, that each viewpoint might be different, and that each viewpoint may be influenced by the individual's gender identity and relative status in the family system. The therapist might ask each family member to talk about the problem from his or her perspective and then explore, with other family members, how that individual's viewpoint might be different from that of someone of the opposite sex or someone with a greater or lesser status in the family.

Issues of employment and family income may also be important areas to explore in assessing the problem. While those who do full-time mothering and home management, whether male or female, would disagree, there is a general perception that mothering is not a *real* job because it does not contribute to the family income.

When *facilitating change,* the feminist family therapist is aware that there may be gender-based differences in how family members approach problems and pays attention to both the thoughts and ideas each family member has about a problem as well as the attendant feelings and behaviors. The therapist will need to be aware of the balance of thoughts and emotions and help individual family members express both their ideas and feelings about a subject. The stereotypical ideas that males are rational and logical and females reactive and emotional may not always hold true. However, it is important to recognize and access both the "thinking" strengths and the "feeling" strengths of each family member.

> Bill and Sandy came for counseling after the loss of their first child, who was stillborn. Bill reported that they were referred by someone at the hospital and he thought it would help Sandy. Bill maintained that his primary concern was for Sandy, who was clearly grieving the loss of the child. He, on the other hand, said 'What is, is and there's nothing we can do about that, so why get all upset.' The counselor acknowledged Bill's ability to see the situation from a rational perspective while noting his real concern for Sandy and wondered aloud about what kind of thoughts he had about the idea of being a father.

The therapist will also pay attention to behaviors that support gender inequities and maintain stereotypical gender roles as well as behaviors that recognize the individual strengths of each family member regardless of gender. How are tasks assigned in the family? What happens when changes occur in the family structure? What if the father loses his job or the mother needs to take on more responsibility at work? Are expectations of the children's behavior, contributions to home life, or educational attainment based on gender? Rampage (1999, pp. 14–15) talks with Nicholas about chores:

> TH (65): "We were talking before about chores, and you said, Nicholas, you told me you clean."
>
> C (37): "Mhmm."
>
> M (33): "He'll clean anybody's house."
>
> TH (66): "He will? Yours too, his house, will he clean?"
>
> M (34): "Well, he'll clean, he cleans. Yeah. There are plenty of Sundays [Oh my] when I've gotten up and he's already, you know, dusted and done the glass table tops and stuff."
>
> TH (67): "Well, I am impressed. Can I just tell you that? You are the first six-year-old person I've ever met who spontaneously cleans the house."
>
> M (35): "And he loves to vacuum. He wants his own vacuum."
>
> TH (68): "Well, that I understand. My little boy loved to vacuum, too. That's a neat invention for kids."
>
> M (36): "Right now he wants a $300 vacuum."
>
> TH (69): "Well, he has good taste. Maybe a $300 vacuum ought to run itself. But you get up in the morning sometimes and clean the house before your mom even gets up?"

In the process of facilitating change, the feminist family therapist works to: "Minimize hierarchy in the family by (1) consistently questioning male dominance and female subordination when they occur; (2) valuing women's work in the family; and (3) challenging rules or patterns which seem to be gender specific" (Wheeler et al., 1985, p. 145).

> After the sudden death of his father, fifteen-year-old Tim was told, in one way or another, by his uncles and others that he was the "man of the family now." Tim took this to heart and began to attempt to discipline his younger siblings. He questioned his mother about how much she was spending and talked about dropping out of school and getting a job.

The therapist is also aware of and identifies stereotypical behaviors that occur in the session and models alternative behaviors when appropriate. For example, the therapist comments on the female's tendency to report how her partner feels about the problem while the male finds the need to explain what his partner "means" when she talks about the problem. Through this process, the therapist may help family members learn skills to negotiate differences, identify key issues before they become problems, value differences attributed to gender, and communicate more effectively with each other.

Feminist Family Therapists as Agents of Change

Feminist family therapy, because of its emphasis on an egalitarian relationship between client and therapist, and the view of knowledge as being socially constructed, has been said to incorporate postmodernism and social construction in therapeutic practices (Bievier, de las Fuentes, Cashion, & Franklin, 1998) and to use the narrative approach introduced by Michael White (Gosling & Zangari, 1993). It is an approach to therapy that has grown out of a social movement with feminist family therapists acting as agents of social change. "The context of feminist therapy is more political in nature than the idealistic and virtually unattainable neutrality that many family theories promote" (Dankoski, Penn, Carlson, & Heckler, p. 97). Given the political nature of this approach to family therapy, the feminist family therapist is not neutral when it comes to gender issues. Rather, she acts as an agent of change, striving to promote gender equity and equality for all, not just in families, but in society as a whole. Within this theoretical orientation, the feminist family therapist may embrace or adapt components of other approaches to therapy. What defines feminist family therapy is not style or representative interventions, but the political and social beliefs and attitudes of the therapist.

REFERENCES

Bernard, J. (1972). *The Future of Marriage*. New York: World.

Biever, J. L., de las Fuentes, C., Cashion, L., & Franklin, C. (1998). The social construction of gender: A comparison of feminist and post modern approaches. *Counseling Psychology Quarterly, 11*(2), 163–179.

Braverman, L. (Ed.). (1988). *Women, feminism and family therapy.* New York: Howorth.

Dankoski, M. E., Penn, C. D., Carlson, T. D., & Heckler, L. L. (1998). What's in a name? A study of family therapists' use and acceptance of the feminist perspective. *American Journal of Family Therapy, 26,* 95–104.

Goldner, V. (1985). Feminism and family therapy. *Family Process, 24,* 31–37.

Goodrich, T. J., Rampage, C., Ellman, B. and Halstead, K. (1988). *Feminist family therapy: a casebook.* New York: W. W. Norton and Company

Gosling, A. L., & Zangari, M. (1993). *Feminist family therapy and the narrative approach: dovetailing two frameworks.* [On-line]. Available: http://chd.Syr.edu/Faculty/goslingpub.html

Hare-Mustin, R. T. (1978). A feminist approach to family therapy. *Family Process, 17,* 181–194.

Kaschak, E. (1992). *Engendered lives: A new psychology of women's experience.* New York: Basic Books.

Lewis, J. A. (1992). Gender sensitivity and family empowerment. *Topics in Family Psychology and Counseling, 1*(4), 1–7. Aspen, CO: Aspen Publishers, Inc.

Myers-Avis, J. (1986). Feminist issues in family therapy. In F. P. Piercy, D. H. Sprenkle, & Associates (Eds.), *Family therapy sourcebook* (pp. 213–242). New York: Guilford.

Rampage, C. (1999). *Study guide and interview transcript for family therapy with the experts: Feminest therapy with Dr. Cheryl Rampage.* Boston, MA: Allyn & Bacon.

U.S. Census Bureau. (1999). *Statistical abstract of the United States: The national data book.* Washington, DC: U.S. Department of Commerce.

U.S. Department of Labor. (2000). Preschool teachers and child care workers. *Occupational outlook handbook.* [On-line]. Available at: http://stats.bls.gov/oco/ocos170.htm

Walters, D., Carter, R., Papp, P., & Silverstein, O. (1988). *The invisible web: Gender patterns in family relationships.* New York: Norton.

Wheeler, D., Avis, J. M., Miller, L. A., & Chaney, S. (1989). Rethinking family therapy training and supervision: A feminist model. In M. McGoldrick, C. M. Anderson, & F. Walsh (Eds.), *Women in families* (pp. 135–151). New York: W. W. Norton.

Whipple, V. (1999). Feminist and family therapies: Continuing the dialogue. *ICA Quarterly, 147,* 2–13.

8

The Satir System

JEAN A. MCLENDON AND BILL DAVIS

Jean McClendon

Theory Overview

Some months before her death, Virginia Satir (1916–1988) stated, in her uncanny, simple and straightforward manner, "I was responsible for putting life into therapy" (King, 1989, p. 28). Satir developed a model for making contact with a client's inner essence so that the uniqueness and universal human hungers of the person could be validated. As a result of many years of observation and practice, Satir generated a model called The Human Process Validation Model, which reflected her key beliefs about what she knew it meant to be "fully human." Most importantly, she believed that all people have the necessary resources for growth. For Satir, the work of therapy is to assist with the midwifery of a person's third birth, "the point in time when an individual accepts responsibility, privilege and the risk that comes with becoming one's own decision maker" (Satir, n.d.).

Although not an academician, Satir was an eager learner, avid reader, and skilled tester of ideas. Intuitive hunches, when they met her rigorous laboratory experience for truth and relevance, became hypotheses that led to her theoretical beliefs and concepts. These beliefs convey Satir's understanding of the universality of emotionality and her understanding of the therapeutic process (Satir, Banmen, Gerber, & Gomori, 1991). As she demonstrated in front of the thousands of people who came to learn her theories and methods, the success of her system was not dependent on a person's or family's particular culture, circumstances, gender, age, sexual preference, type of dysfunction, or severity of problem.

Though many believe its success was due to the "magic of Satir," practitioners of the model now know that it is the concepts and skills operationalizing her core beliefs that make this system effective in working with clients and systems.

Self-Esteem

Satir never veered from her conviction that the level of a person's self-esteem determines, in large part, the quality of a person's performance, health, and relationships. Above all else, she wanted to help people raise their self-esteem. The centrality of self-esteem gives Satir's theory a holographic nature. A therapist can engage at the intra- or inter-levels of a client's life and still land squarely on the issue of self-esteem. Engaging directly with self-esteem invariably leads to the world of outward communication, the external manifestation of what one thinks and feels on the inside.

Communication

Satir divided the universe into three components: the self, the other(s), and the context. Communication that dismisses or denies one or more of these components is reflective of low self-esteem at that moment in time. Authentic communication that expresses internal valuing and consideration for all three components is the form of communication that Satir sought for herself and those with whom she worked. She termed it *congruent communication*. It meant that there was integrity or alignment between the inside and the outside, balance and harmony between and among the components, and choice for when, how, and what could be expressed. For Satir this meant "being in one's flow."

Satir observed that there are four primary forms of incongruence, or low self-esteem communication stances: placating, blaming, superreasonable, and irrelevant (Satir, 1988). Low self-esteem contaminates how one views oneself, other(s), and context, thereby coloring how people perceive their past, present, and future. These stances, when sculpted into physical caricatures, convey vividly the mind–body–spirit connection of the Satir System (McLendon, 2000).

Primary Triad

Low self-esteem also taints the perceptions people have about the four human phenomena that Satir postulated explained people's behavior and pain: a person, a relationship, an event, and change. Understanding these mental and operating modes gave Satir a direct and deep understanding of the person (Satir, n.d.). Low self-esteem creates a hierarchical view of the world in which conformity, linear thinking, dominant–submissive relationships, and rejection of change are common and accepted. On the other hand, high self-esteem generates appreciation for each individual's uniqueness, relationships based on equal valuing of the people involved, a systemic thinking pattern for explaining events, and change experienced as natural and an opportunity for growth.

The self-esteem and the associated interpersonal process patterns of the adult caretakers of children affect a child's self-esteem more than anything else. Though she did not deny genetic influences, Satir followed the belief that self-esteem evolves from the relative proportion of constructive to destructive interaction experiences arising from the parental pair in a triadic relationship with the child. She emphasized that children's experiences in the primary triad (father, mother, child) provided the essential source of identity. On the basis of their learning experiences in the primary triad, they determine how they fit into the world and how much trust can be placed in relationships with other people (Satir and Baldwin, 1983).

Before Satir's death, sperm, egg, and uterus donors, single parenting, and same-sex unions were not uncommon. A child could have the experience of life with the egg and sperm donor. Or, if the child was missing a parent—biological or not—Satir thought that the fantasies and rumors about the parent penetrated the psyche of the child, contributing to identity formation. The actual adult caregivers transfer massive amounts of information about coping with one's humanness. Especially in the early years, this adult behavior, influenced by the familial, social, and cultural histories of caregivers, serves as the dynamic container in which children develop their own personhood.

Change

Satir recognized that awareness did not equal behavior. It could open the door for choice; however, healthy choosing required practice and support. Her theory of change reveals the emotional processes associated with interrupting a system's status quo. She offers a map for traveling the territory of change, which helps clients understand their change process (Dodson, 1991). The map underscores the need for the therapist to give support and information about what the client is apt to experience. The client can deal more effectively with the pain and anxiety of chaos if it is understood that those are normal feelings associated with the change process. Patience and compassion are needed, especially when the client has an awakening experience and doesn't yet know that considerable time and energy will be required to fully and effectively integrate and put into practice the new possibility. It is time for celebration and gratitude when a new status quo is created that has more health and less cost. Because the new homeostasis is naturally impermanent, Satir's approach sought to teach people how to master the ever-present process of change, rather than to help them solve a particular problem.

Therapist–Client relationship

Employing a systems and communication, humanistic, family-of-origin, action-based approach, Satir challenged the profession to become more holistic, experiential, spiritual, personal, and loving. She believed that the outcome of therapy was directly related to the quality of the relationship that the therapist established. Treatment in this system is truly an interactional process. Inside the therapy room, the client's problems and possibilities, with the therapist as a guide, are presented in a milieu designed to create emotional safety that is sufficient to support risk taking to learn new ways to see, feel, touch, think, speak, and behave. Satir wrote, "I consider myself the leader of the process in the interview but not the leader of the people" (Satir, 1964, p. 251). "The process still—and always—is the relationship between you and me, here and now" (p. 243). In a courageous way she adds, "Very little change goes on without the patient and therapist becoming vulnerable" (Baldwin & Satir, 1987, p. 22).

Philosophical and Historical Background

When World War II ended, there began a great opening for exploring more about human relationships and communication. In addition to the need for effective psychiatric treatment for returning soldiers, there must also have been a hope that people could learn a different way to be in relationship. It is in this social and medical context that the seeds of family therapy took root. The founding decade is generally thought to be the 1950s (Goldenberg & Goldenberg, 1991).

Family Therapy Categories

There have been, and continue to be, efforts to categorize the various theoretical family therapy models. Beels and Ferber's classification in 1969 divided the forerunners of the new family therapy profession into conductors and reactors. Conductors were noted for their aggressive, public, charismatic personalities, and the strong value systems they used in their work with families. Satir's practice of teaching people how to live placed her clearly as a conductor. Other conductors included Nat Ackerman, Sal Minuchin, and Murray Bowen. Reactors entered families by playing different roles at different times. This group was subdivided into the analysts and the systems purists. Analysts included Carl Whitaker, Ivan Boszormenyi-Nagy, James Framo, and Lyman Wynne. Jay Haley and Don Jackson were classified as system purists: astute observers who used paradox to manipulate the power structure of the family. Though both groups used control, the conductors used direct ways and the reactors indirect, paradoxical ways (Beels & Ferber, 1969).

Philip Guerin, Jr. placed Satir with Don Jackson and Jay Haley as communications and structural family therapists, given their colleagueship and association with Gregory Bateson and his pioneering research on communication at the Mental Research Institute. Guerin further suggested that strategic and structural therapy were derived from their work (Guerin, 1976).

L'Abate and Frey classified therapists on the dimensions of emotionality, rationality, and activity: the E-R-A model. They placed Satir and Whitaker in the E-school because they paid so much attention to how feelings are dealt with in the family system (L'Abate & Frey, 1981). However, Parkison felt that such classifications had overlooked therapists who were influenced by the existential, phenomenological, and human potential movement. He believed they were due a separate category and called it "experiential/humanistic." Satir and Whitaker were the most recognized of them (Parkison, 1983).

In the mental health field, by the midfifties, family therapy practitioners and researchers were finding increased opportunities to gather and collaborate. There was an extended professional family in the making, and Satir was central. For example, Ivan Boszormenyi-Nagy was a resident in Satir's family therapy residency training program in Illinois (Duhl, 1983). James Framo notes that he began working with Ivan Boszormenyi-Nagy in 1957 (Framo, 1976). Peggy Papp, along with numerous other nationally recognized family and group therapists, speaks of being influenced by Satir (Guerin, 1976).

Theory Development

Satir grounded her ideas about human relationships in general systems theory (biologist, Ludwig von Bertalanffy), psychoanalysis (Sigmund Freud, Alfred Adler, Harry Stack Sullivan, Carl Jung), communications theories (Don Jackson, Gregory Bateson), and beliefs about human relations grounded in Martin Buber's I–Thou concepts. She made use of a rich mix of ideas to help her clients move to higher levels of functioning. Her theories and methods were tested widely as she traveled across the planet demonstrating her system with people of vastly differing circumstances and cultures.

Four developmental phases describe the growth and establishment of the Human Process Validation Model. The early phase, 1916–1941, is the *foundation* period. The middle phase, 1941–1964, reflected *innovation*. The late phase, 1964–1988, saw *expansiveness*. The fourth and current phase suggests *sustainability*, and is reflected by the work of Satir's students and their students. The model is linked to Satir's personal history and the issues and shifts that took place in the mental health profession and the larger societal context of her time. If one includes Satir's postcollege public school teaching and years as a school principal in her professional career, then she developed her model of therapy over a span of almost sixty years.

Through the experience of the powerful connections that she was able to make with people, Satir knew that people come together through their similarities and grow through their differences. Over the decades, she attracted people who resonated with her belief system and recognized the sageness of the ideas in her model. In this context, founded on connection, differences emerged that opened Satir to new awarenesses and learning, and led to further development and empowerment of the model. The generativity from being with others helped Satir describe the factors inherent in her incredible skills of connecting with people and families, which in turn helped others actualize their own abilities to make connection.

Foundation

The early phase includes the influences of her birth family, college life, and work in the public schools as a teacher and principal. She reports that, at age five, she wanted to be a "children's detective on parents." "I didn't quite know what I would look for, but I realized a lot went on in families that didn't meet the eye. There were a lot of puzzles I did not know how to understand" (Satir, 1988, p. 1). The embedded puzzles of her childhood about family life and the "how comes" of adult relationships were early driving forces that remained compelling as she searched to understand people and the myriad ways they express their uniqueness. As the eldest child in a Wisconsin farm family, she had many opportunities to hone her leadership, creativity, and helping skills. Bouts with serious and unexplained childhood illnesses, and being larger than all of her peers, must have increased her sensitivity as well as her distaste for prejudice and attitudes.

Satir's first formal experience in the business of helping others began during her college years at Milwaukee State Teachers College when she worked at the Abraham Lincoln House. "I did all kinds of stuff there. I started a nursery school; I did a play group; I did a dramatic group with young adolescents. Some of them were older than I was" (Russell, 1990).

She resisted categorizing her approach in much the same way she resisted labeling her clients. She was asked in her senior year of college to write a paper on "crippled children." Satir responded, "I can't do that; I have to write a paper on children with crippling conditions" (King, 1989, p. 20). The seeds of acceptance and hope and a vision of growth and possibilities were already evident.

Innovation

During the middle period, Satir entered and established her centrality to the new field of family therapy. At this time, the mental health field was male-dominated and followed the medical model of "disease." She became the "Columbus of family therapy," the people's therapist, author, and teacher. Her formal initiation into the field began when she enrolled in the master's degree program at the School of Social Service Administration at the University of Chicago in

1941. Although her innate abilities were becoming shaped into professional competence, it was her creativity, compassion, and common sense that stands out. Talking about her work at the Chicago Home for Girls, her training placement, Satir says,

> What they needed was to feel some connection with themselves and with life and with family, and they had horrible feelings about themselves. One of the things I did was to develop some puppets. Then I had them use those—one puppet for themselves and some for their parents—and I had these puppets talk to each other. I don't know why I left that, but anyway that was an innovation. I suppose the adaptation I made of that is the role playing I do now in the simulated family (King, 1989, p. 22).

Virginia Satir saw her first family in 1951 in her Chicago private therapy practice. It took little time for her to realize that her clients were able to make gains during therapy sessions, but regressed to their former self-defeating behaviors in the presence of their families. This, of course, was consistent with ideas she had begun to develop as a school teacher when she realized that she needed to know the families of her students in order to leverage support for their learning. In her private practice she also noticed that it was not uncommon for one member of the family to make changes only to see another member become the one with the problem. Detective that she was, Satir studied this phenomenon by meeting, interviewing, and then involving family members in therapy sessions. Her eyes were opened. Unbeknownst to her, while she was in the initial exploratory phase of working with whole families, others were also beginning to see the futility of successful work with individuals absent their families.

During this phase, Satir established the first family therapy residency training program at the Illinois State Psychiatric Institute in 1955. She shared with Michael Yapko, PhD, in an interview for the Milton Erickson Foundation Newsletter, that she had seen close to 500 families by the time she joined Don Jackson and others in 1959 to establish the Mental Research Institute. "I didn't know it then, but I had seen more families in the world than anyone else by that time" (Yapko, 1988, p. 3). She made her first European presentation in Vienna, Austria, in 1961, and published her groundbreaking book, *Conjoint Family Therapy,* in 1964. In this book, she articulated cutting-edge concepts about symptoms being the manifestations of the the pain of dysfunctional family dynamics. She also presented the value of her innovative experiential exercises as tools for working with families. "If one uses the growth model, one must be willing to be more experimental and spontaneous than many therapists are. The necessity of flexibility in technique and approach, including particularly direct, intimate contact between patient and therapist, is thought to be basic" (Satir, 1964). Her systemic approach was clearly contributing to the evolving mental health profession; at the time, however, her passion for an orientation toward health and connection, and away from pathology, set her apart and ahead of her colleagues.

Expansiveness

By the end of the late developmental phase, 1964–1988, Satir's theories were being taught to a wide audience of human service professionals and laypeople alike. While continuing to consolidate her theories about change and human functioning, she openly linked the effectiveness of her approach with spirituality. In a 1985 *Common Boundary* interview with Richard Simon, she says, "It is something you can call 'spirit,' 'soul,' or whatever you want. In any case, it is there and the only thing that really changes people is when they get in contact with their life force. That is the essence of self-worth." She not only expanded her theories to include spirituality, she expanded her influence with a head-on thrust into global activism. Satir was certain of what she had been observing, and she wanted to share it with the world.

Directing the Training at Esalen, California's premiere growth center at Big Sur from 1964–1969 gave Satir an open, supportive, and safe setting that was nonclinical and nonresearch-based. She used this freedom to experiment beyond what she had theorized and written about in *Conjoint Family Therapy*. She became more firmly convinced of the connection between the mind–body–spirit. Techniques evolving from her belief system were taking on more clarity and form: family reconstruction, parts parties, the mandala, and so forth. (Satir et al., 1991). Founding the International Human Learning Resources Network in 1969 was a way to support the cross-fertilization of ideas among people who were onboard with her and her growth model. The large numbers of psychotherapists being influenced by Satir was underscored when, in 1970, the Group for the Advancement of Psychiatry surveyed practicing family therapists and asked them to rank the major figures in the field according to their influence. In order they were Satir, Ackerman, Jackson, Haley, Bowen, Wynne, Bateson, Bell, and Boszormenyi-Nagy (Group for the Advancement of Psychiatry, 1970). There was great resonance in middle America for her theories about communication, relationships, health, and the significance of feelings. She talked openly and plainly to North Americans. In *Family Circle's* 1971 featured interview by Fred Warshofsky, she says, "The best way to cope with our inhibitions is to deal with the feelings we have and not give them 'good' or 'bad' labels. The problem is not with having feelings—it depends on how we use them" (p. 42). *Peoplemaking*, published in 1972, became both a household guide to healthy family living and a textbook for family therapists. The vastness of applicability of her ideas was further recognized when Phil Donahue featured her on his television show in 1979. There she taught people in the United States that the problem is not the problem . . . it's the coping.

Not only did she challenge the profession to move toward a focus on strength and health, she was not reticent to discuss the importance of spirituality in healing. She was on a different path from her early days as a private practice clinician. No longer limited by the requirements, norms, and politics of her profession, she became a teacher of peace and congruence to the larger world.

Needing more support for her work and mission, she founded the Avanta Network in 1977 by inviting about thirty-five people to join her for a month to explore how this important work could go forward. Many of that original group continue to teach, share, and use her growth model to help heal families, groups, and nations. Consistent with her solidly based humanistic orientation and desire to share, she did serve a term as President of the American Humanistic Psychology Association beginning in 1982. Though at this point she rarely attended the the large professional conferences, when she did there was resounding appreciation and interest in what she had to teach. Her influence to the profession was soundly acknowledged when amazing numbers of people, with standing room only, came to hear her speak at the 1985 Evolution of Psychotherapy Conference in Phoenix, Arizona. *Time* magazine (Leo, 1985) quotes a colleague of Satir: "She can fill any auditorium in the country." Her global influence was confirmed in 1986 when she was selected as a member of the International Council of Elders, a society developed by the recipients of the Nobel Peace Prize. Similarly, she served on California's Commission to Promote Self-Esteem and Personal and Social Responsibility, chaired by John Vasconcellos. She did her last international training in the former USSR in late spring of 1988, just months before her death on September 10.

By the time of her death, what had initially separated her from her profession, a focus on health, was becoming more accepted. But she threw the profession another curve and challenge before leaving when she connected health and self-worth with spirituality. In a January 23, 1988, interview by Sheldon Z. Kramer, Satir explains:

> The most powerful thing I think is growth. The organisms in the world are geared always constantly toward growth. . . . The seeds for me are a manifestation of spirituality. A plant wants to get its head out and then it wants to flower. . . . For me vitality and self-worth are related to health. That is the manifestation of our spirituality (Kramer, 1995, p. 10).

With the work of Satir's students and their students, a new phase is underway. These individuals and groups seek to further explicate Satir's work and to make it more sustainable for future therapists. Lynn Hoffman, nationally recognized family therapy professor at Smith College School for Social Work, writes that Satir was a voice so ahead of her time that only now can it be heard (Hoffman, 1998). Though not limited to those mentioned here, these are people who studied with Satir extensively and who are either writing and/or teaching the system in its most current form. They apply the Satir System in many different settings and contexts, i.e., from therapy to teaching to consulting. This group includes: Teresa Adams, Lynn Azpetia, Michele Baldwin, John Banmen, Jim Bitter, Barbara Jo Brothers, Judy Bula, Laura Dodson, Paula Englander-Golden, Jane Gerber, Maria Gomori, Lori Gordan, Hugh Gratz, Karen Krestensen, Sharon Loeschen, Jean McLendon, Anne and Bill Nerin, Sharon Wegscheider-Cruse, Gerald and Dani Weinberg, and Joan Winter.

A new generation of Satir teachers who never met Satir are adding to the model and translating it into useful applications for work with a wide range of clinical and organization situations. Specifically, Bill Davis, Tom Fahy, Sheri Hanshaw, and David Keil, faculty to the Satir Performance Development Program, sponsored by Avanta and the Satir Institute of the Southeast, reflect the highest level of competence and creativity at both demonstrating the power of the system and teaching it to others. The programs are under the direction of Jean McLendon, and information about them can be found at <www.satirsystems.com>.

Therapist Stance

Satir used the idea of within–between–among to discuss connection, the core competence of Satir System practitioners. To begin, the therapist needs to be connected with her own internal parts. This centering process enhances the therapist's resourcefulness and her ability to help the clients claim and utilize their own internal resources. Connection and access to resources is a theme that is always operating in the following therapy session with a boy and his mother. Resourcefulness is the "R" in McLendon's articulation of the R.E.C.I.P.E., which serves as a frame of reference in looking at this therapy session.

> Satir's six primary strategies are provided in 'recipe' form, beginning with the following basic ingredients: Resourcefulness, Empowerment, Congruence, Inner System, Patterns, and Externalization. Satir's therapeutic tools (the mandala, meditations, sculpting, communication stances, family mapping, inner child work, and the self-esteem maintenance kit) are added to each of the basic ingredients . . . (McLendon, 2000).

In the video, before the work with the clients, the therapist talks about the importance of breathing as basic to tuning in with herself, gathering her resources "within" before meeting the clients. She can then make the "between" connection of the therapist with the client.

For Satir, the simplest model of the human reality is self–other–context. After connecting with herself, the task of the therapist is to establish connection between self and other, all the while taking conscious steps to establish safety in the therapy context. Satir believed that, when a therapist connects with the inner essence of a client, their self-esteem is enhanced, and that self-esteem is the driving force for positive change.

Eye contact, body position oriented to the client, volume and tone of voice, gestures, attentiveness, active listening, and reflection of the person's statements and body language, all help establish contact between the therapist and the client. Many of these are observable in the first minutes of the video. For example, the therapist empathetically reaches out to the boy when she validates his experience of anger and helps him connect the body sensations associated with feeling anger.

TH (6):   "You grit your teeth, and you just want to hit them for no reason. That does sounds like anger doesn't it?. . . . That you are trying to figure out and you are trying to cope with and you are trying to understand. That takes a lot of courage to say 'I'm angry' and I would like for it to be different. Don't you think?"

This is the first of many affirming statements from the therapist as she works with the boy and his mother.

Within the first minute of meeting, the therapist is already introducing resourcefulness to the child by asking him what it is "you wanted to have happen for you," a reference to the wishing wand in the self-esteem maintenance kit. The resources of the self-esteem maintenance tool kit

> are a golden key to open the door to the unknown and to new possibilities; a wishing wand to help surface hope and desire; a courage stick to provide the strength to change; a yes–no medallion to support healthy boundaries and self-care; a detective hat to analyze and sort out input and options; and the wisdom box . . . which represents the inner, grounding guidance available to all humans (Satir et al., 1991, pp. 293–298).

Later in the session, the heart, which has been added to Satir's original kit because it reminds us of our ability to love, will become instrumental in the boy's awareness and possibilities for change. It is apparent that the mother has used her yes–no medallion regarding her marriage; that she has a knowing in her wisdom box that time heals and that her son had his wisdom box and golden key in knowing to ask for help; that both have used the courage stick to take care of the grandmother during her illness and death; and they have their detective hats with them for exploring possibilities for the future. The therapist continually affirms the strengths that the son and mother show individually and in their dyadic relationship.

Safety is enhanced for the clients when, throughout the session, they are able to claim their own experience. The boy has a chance to talk about his anger, his feelings about his brother, and both have their pain for the loss of the maternal grandmother. To be able to talk about their pain in each other's company, to have it witnessed and honored by the other and by the therapist shows the importance of relationship as a medium for healing and for growth to happen.

Doing the family mapping during the session not only provides active participation for the clients, it makes things concrete and an easy reference for all participants. Beyond that, it is also an honoring of Satir's Five Freedoms:

> The freedom to see and hear what is here,
> Instead of what should be, was, or will be
> The freedom to say what you feel and think,
> Instead of what you should
> The freedom to feel what you feel, instead of what you ought
> The freedom to take risks on our own behalf,
> Instead of choosing to be only "secure"
> and not rocking the boat (Satir et al., 1991, p. 243).

The family map recreates the story of the clients' history and brings it into the therapy room where it is used to discover what has been, to generate awareness, and to suggest possibilities for realizing the wishes of the clients. The unfolding of the map offers many opportunities to deepen the connection between the therapist and the clients. As the therapist guides the clients in the process, the clients guide the therapist into their world. The map is an empowering (the first E of recipe) visual representation that helps illuminate the interpersonal process patterns (the P of recipe) within the family. The narrative technique of family mapping grounds the therapist and clients in the territory of the family's connections, legacies, and culture, which further anchors the therapist and the clients with the Others and Context of their world.

It is empowering in that it expands the boy's view of himself, to see that he is not alone, that he lives in the context of relationship and is connected to a system that has experienced significant loss. For both of them, the clients' experience of the mapping helps them reconnect with the vitality of the connections in their lives. The map is a presence in the room, just as the therapist, the boy, and his mother are.

Therapeutic Interventions

Satir was one of the earliest and strongest proponents focusing on the strength and health of the client, rather than the pathology orientation of conventional psychiatry and psychology. As a way of helping the therapist work with clients to access these, Satir developed the ideas and techniques of the self-esteem maintenance tool kit, the five freedoms, and family mapping, among others. With these concepts always in mind, the therapist works with the map of the family to explore their personal territory. In this process,

- She helps ground experiences in the body (TH [4]: "Where do you feel it in your body?;" TH [5]: "Do you feel it is your shoulders or your stomach or your thoughts?;" TH [6]: "You grit your teeth, and you just want to hit them for no reason?");
- She reflects back to them the experiences they each had (TH [27]: "Okay. So that would help you if you could understand what you're angry about?");
- She highlights their losses and the pain associated with them (TH [32]: "Well, you have had two big losses. I'm thinking about your brother not being with you, and not having your father.");
- She affirms their strengths and courage (TH [6]: "That takes a lot of courage to say I'm angry and I would like for it to be different.");
- She orients them to the idea of coping as the issue rather than the problems themselves (TH [6]: "That you are trying to figure out and you are trying to cope with and you are trying to understand.", TH [39]: "So how did you deal with, let's put your anger up here. You're saying you're not so angry anymore, so we will just put a little bit. How did you deal with yours?");

- She helps them discover meanings behind their feelings (TH [12]: "And so he is angry too. Are you all angry about the same thing?");
- She explores their histories and who their models were (TH [7]: "Do you know anybody else that's angry?"; TH [30]: "So how to help Jonathan in his feelings. How are you doing with yours?");
- She stresses the importance of a support system (TH [42]: "Who supported you?");
- She remarks on the specialness of relationships (TH [48]: "Were you pretty special to her? Let's see, if we were going to show a real special line, what do you think about purple? And we will show a nice big line between you and Lorrine.").

Within the first ten minutes she has established a working relationship with the son and his mother.

The loss of the grandmother is painful, and the mother cries. The therapist remarks to the boy, "Is it hard for you to see your mother crying because her heart is so full of her relationship with her mother?" (TH 56). His response, "It makes me want to cry, but I know I gotta get over it" (C34), opens the door to work with him at a deeper level. The therapist has a very rich response to him that speaks beautifully to the humanness and power of the Satir Human Process Validation Model.

C (35):   "It's like I can't go my whole life thinking that my grandma is going to come back."

TH (58):   "Right. Because she won't come back. But you must have wonderful memories to bring her back with. And you have a big kind of hole in your heart to not have her. It hadn't been that long ago really. Again, I'm just thinking about the, the losses for you. To lose your granny, your brother, in different ways, and your father. That's a lot Jonathan. That's a lot to have to handle as a little boy. You know? You know how I feel about your tears? They just seem so healthy and so wholesome. And so real. And I'm glad that you can have your tears, and I hope it's okay for you to have your tears, too. Because, you know, sometimes underneath a lot of anger is a hurt. Like a, a hole in your heart. Does that make sense to you? Seems like it does. Like there is a little, little boy inside, about, I don't know, maybe about this little [therapist picks up puppy], and he has gotten hurt, and he's inside of you, and what I hear is that you are trying to get him to be [a] "big boy," tough, you know. Get on with your life, you know. Ah, get past those tears. But this little guy still lives inside of you, like a little girl does inside of you [therapist looks at mother] that lost her mother. That's real. Is it okay with you if I talk about you having a little girl inside of you?"

M (36):   "Yes, it's okay."

The idea of the Inner Child is well known in therapy circles today. Many of the ideas that guide people in working with the inner child, and the techniques that are used, are based in the work of Satir. This interaction among the three participants sets the stage for the later introduction of the heart from the self-esteem maintenance kit and the puppy and dolls to represent the inner children. This represents externalization, the second E in recipe. One outcome of externalization is that often people will take greater ownership of that which is being externalized.

The therapist initially attended to her own inner system (the I in recipe) before she met the client and his mother. Connection with the Self is the foundation for manifesting congruence (the C in recipe) when one then meets Others. It is when the inner system (Self) of the therapist and the inner system (Self) of the client can make contact and experience the connection with the inner system of the Other that the partnership of the therapeutic relationship will be experienced so that, within the context of therapy, work can happen.

> Meeting the inner system of an individual or couple is the strategy that connects the therapist to the client system's essence and universal desire to connect and contribute. Satir had many techniques for entering the inner domain, perhaps none more important than her full expression of genuine interest. For Satir, therefore, change does not happen unless contact is made (Satir & Bitter, 2000, p. 97).

Throughout the video, the therapist continually expresses interest to the boy and to the mother, demonstrating in every physical and verbal way that she is attending to their story, to their experience, and that she cares about them and their lives. One way that she affirms the partnership aspect of this therapeutic process is through the frequent use of "thank you" to the clients for their contribution.

McLendon w/ clients

The therapist externalizes the inner system of the client when she gives the following picture:

> TH (74): "Well, I want to give you a picture that I have about your challenge. Do you know, ah, the word *challenge,* like if something's a challenge? It's like if you had to climb a, a big hill and you had a lot of weight on you, that would be like a challenge, and that's kind of what I think you have. This is the picture I have [picks up heart]. Here it is right here. This is like the little one inside of you [holds out puppy], okay? And this like his heart [places heart against puppy], and his heart is sad. But he is not supposed to be sad. He is supposed to be big . . . "

Through the use of the puppy to represent his inner child and the heart, which is part of the self-esteem maintenance kit, the therapist is giving the client a vivid externalization of his inner process in dealing with hurt. She has laid the groundwork for this with the visual representation of the map, which is the outcome of having heard from him, his mother, and the therapist about the many losses he has known in his young life. Additionally, she has made the reference to hurt and to the heart on multiple occasions,

> TH (56): "Is it hard for you to see your mother crying because her heart is so full . . . ?"
>
> TH (58): "And you have a big kind of hole in your heart to not have her . . . Like a, a hole in your heart."

As in TH (74): above, the therapist concretely establishes for the boy the connection between his losses and his pain. She further develops this theme through the rest of the session, and she articulates for him what his challenge will be to lead him to the wish he expressed for himself at the beginning of the session.

> TH (76): "It would be very hard. It would be very hard. So here's my idea. My idea is that you have to take this little one [hands puppy and heart to boy], and you have to let this little one know that you are going to be there with him and that it is okay to be sad when you're unhappy and when you feel lonely, when you miss your brother, when you wonder where your dad is, when you think about your grandmother. I bet you saw her suffer. And when you think about how special she was. It seems like to me that we need to find a way for this little one inside of you to not have to pretend because I think when you have to pretend, it probably makes you angry. It probably makes you real angry to have to pretend something that's not true for you [Five Freedoms]. What do you think about that? What do you think would have to happen for you to have more freedom to just be with your heart? What do you think would help?"

One of the things that the therapist has helped the boy and his mother recognize more fully is the degree of loss that they have experienced, and also to discern the pattern for dealing with pain in the family system. She has illuminated that for them in their dialogue and in the map. Now they know that they have dealt with pain through the use of support and the passage of time for the mother, and that the boy has dealt with it by trying to put it aside, to ignore it, to repress it.

The challenge for a new coping is there. The mother responds with her hope for her son's new coping,

> **M (48):**   "Just be allowed to be and feel I guess what he's feeling and express it. Be able to express it. Ah, he didn't know what it was. You know, it's like those things were there, but I guess he'll have a better understanding of what's causing it and feel free-er to express what's going on, and I guess it's my job to get him the help to get through it."

She can serve as a model and a resource for him in doing something different.

All of this leads to a beautiful summary for the boy and his mother in which the therapist pulls many aspects of the session together, that helps the boy understand anger, part of his wish at the beginning. He can see the relationship between pain, coping, anger, and how hurt can be coped with differently in the future. Once again there is further externalization of the inner process by introducing the little girl dolls for the mother and therapist. In claiming her own little girl inside, the therapist continues the congruence that she has practiced during the whole therapy session.

> **TH (86):**   "Yeah. But a little understanding from a man could go a long way for Jonathan because you know it's like you have a similar job here. This could be your little girl. Mama has a little girl inside of her too [hands doll to mother]. So you have this little girl and she has a heart that has to be taken care of [hands heart], and of course, ah, me, too [therapist gets own doll]. I have a little girl inside of me too, and you know, she has hurts and disappointments and stuff that I have to deal with. I'm just thinking that you, Janice, you seem to do such a wonderful job of being able to be where your heart is, and that's so wonderful for you to see [looks at boy], and I suspect at times it may feel a little overwhelming, I don't know . . . [looking at boy] So I suspect if you don't figure out how to love that little one and have, have a good open heart to yourself, that you probably are going to clench your jaws and find your muscles tight and have to express it some way."

The therapist continues expressing interest in the clients, validating their experience, and affirming them as people with their own resources. The genuineness of her concern and caring for them has been a powerful element of the whole therapy session. Near the end of the session, she learns more about them and expresses appreciation for who they are and for their assets as individuals.

> TH (90):   [To the boy] "You are a very wise young one. You, I know when you have that ability to know what you're feeling, it gives you choice about what to do. If you didn't know that you were feeling angry and you just went around punching, all you would do is get in trouble, but to be able to know it and ask for help is just so impressive. . . ."
>
> TH (97):   [To the mother] "I thank you for listening to your son with such attentiveness. You are a very good mother."
>
> TH (99):   [To the boy] "So, I would like to say goodbye to you and goodnight to you, and can I shake your hand and tell you, 'You are very special'?"
>
> TH (100):   [To the mother] "You are a very special woman."

In this brief session of thirty-five minutes, the therapist has either used as a frame of reference for herself and/or shared with the clients directly or indirectly the elements of Satir's six primary strategies, the "recipe": the Resourcefulness of the self-esteem maintenance kit, in particular, the wishing wand, courage stick, and the heart; Empowerment of the Five Freedoms; Congruence of self–other–context, especially as demonstrated by the therapist's own connecting with her parts, her own Inner System, and then bringing all of that into connection with the clients' Inner Systems, especially the inner child; the Patterns of loss and pain in the family of origin; and, Externalization to enhance ownership of life, choices, copings. This was all facilitated by use of Satir's Family Mapping, which provided a frame of reference for the unfolding of the process.

"The first task of the therapist is to make full contact with the individuals who make up the family, to build safety and hope, and to assess the status quo" (Satir & Bitter, 2000, p. 97). The therapist recognized opportunity consistently throughout the session, and this continues at the end regarding the heart that the boy was holding with the puppy.

> TH (102):   "And I'll take these little ones. They have become more special because they've been here with you two. [To the boy] Yours has a heart sound, did you notice? You know what, maybe you should take this home with you. What do you think?"
>
> C (48):   "Yes."
>
> TH (102):   "What do you think? Do you think it would help, that you would remember about your heart and about your losses and about how it's okay to feel sad when you're sad, you don't have to cover it up with being tough and angry? What do you think?"
>
> C (49):   "I guess. [Therapist gives heart back] Thank you."

Research

Unfortunately, there is a dearth of research about the Satir system and its strategies. Fortunately, however, Satir's therapeutic approaches and the results of her strategies are found in Dr. Joan Winter's dissertation. Dr. Winter compared and contrasted the therapeutic strategies and outcomes of three great theorists and therapists: Virginia Satir, Murray Bowen, and Jay Haley. Unlike her peers, Satir had no training or clinical program near the research project. She had to bring her therapist team together from around the country. This constraint required Satir to develop a brief therapy model.

Winter's findings indicated that the Satir (5.1%, $n = 3$) treatment group had fewer premature terminations than the Haley (60.9%, $n = 28$) and Bowen (36.5%, $n = 19$) groups. The Satir group completed therapy with the highest number of families (88.8%, $n = 56$), followed by the comparison group (59%, $n = 36$), the Bowen sample (57.9%, $n = 33$), and then the Haley (26.5%, $n = 18$) treatment group. In general, and more importantly, regardless of the group tested (identified client, mother, or father), all family members being treated gave the Satir therapists higher satisfaction scores than those given to the Bowen and Haley clinicians (Winter, 1993).

Research is needed to find therapists whose work is primarily influenced by Satir. Follow-up studies could then be done to find out how these therapists are using the Satir System in their practice today.

Sources for Training

Although there is no certification program at present, there is training available in the Satir System.

AVANTA, the Virginia Satir Network, is an international educational organization. Membership information should be directed to Avanta's Executive Director at 2104 SW 152nd Street, Suite 2, Burien, WA 98166. The phone number is 206-241-7566. E-mail: <avanta@foxinternet.net> Web site: <www.avanta.net> Avanta makes information available on Satir affiliates and training throughout the world.

The Satir Institute of the Southeast, Inc. produces a subscription newsletter, and, with Avanta, sponsors Satir System training workshops throughout the year. For information, contact the office at 87 South Elliott Road, Suite 203, Chapel Hill, NC 27514. The phone number is 919-967-2520. E-mail: <admin@satirinstitute.org> Web site: <www.satirinstitute.org>

Resource Centers

Archives: Library, Oral History Program
University of California
Santa Barbara, CA 93106
805-893-3062
Contact David Russell

Institute for Families in Society
University of South Carolina
Columbia, SC 29208
803-777-3290
Contact Miriam Freeman, PhD

Chapel Hill Satir Resource Center
87 South Elliott Road, Suite 203
Chapel Hill, NC 27514

REFERENCES

Baldwin, M., & Satir, V. (1987). The use of the self in therapy. *Journal of Psychotherapy, 3*(1), 17–25.

Beels, C., & Ferber, A. (1969). Family therapy: A view. *Family Process, 8,* 280–332.

Dodson, L. (1991). Virginia Satir's process of change. *Journal of Couples Therapy, 2*(½), 119–137.

Duhl, B. (1983). *From the inside out.* New York: Brunner/Mazel.

Framo, J. (1976). Chronicle of a struggle to establish a family unit within a community mental health center. In P. Guerin (Ed.), *Family therapy theory and practice* (pp. 23–29). New York: Gardner.

Goldenberg, H., & Goldenberg, I. (1991). *Family therapy: An overview* (3rd ed.). Pacific Grove, CA: Brooks/Cole.

Group for the Advancement of Psychiatry. (1970). *The field of family therapy.* (Report No. 78). New York: Author.

Guerin, P. (Ed.). (1976a). Family choreography in *Family therapy theory and practice* (pp. 465–479). New York: Gardner.

Guerin, P. (Ed.). (1976b). *Family therapy: The first twenty-five years in Family therapy theory and practice.* New York: Gardner.

Hoffman, L. (1998, April). Setting aside the model in family therapy. *Journal of Marital and Family Therapy, 24*(2), 145–156.

King, L. (1989). *Women of power.* Berkeley, CA: Celestial Arts.

Kramer, S. Z. (1995). *Transforming the inner and outer family.* New York: Haworth.

L'Abate, L., & Frey, J., III. (1981). The E-R-A model: The role of feelings in family therapy reconsidered: Implications for a classification of theories in family therapy. *Journal of Marital and Family Therapy, 7,* 143–150.

Leo, J. (1985, December 23). A Therapist in every corner: Harmony was the goal, but participants seemed out of tune. *Time [Behavior], 126*(25), 59.

McLendon, J. A. (2000). The Satir System: Brief therapy strategies. In J. Carlson & L. Sperry (Eds.), *Brief therapy with individuals and couples* (pp. 389–346). Phoenix, AZ: Zeig, Tucker & Theisen.

Parkison, S. C. (1983). Family therapy in C. E. Walker (Ed.), *The handbook of clinical psychology: Theory, research, and practice,* vol. 2 (pp. 1009–1027). Homewood, IL: Dow Jones-Irwin.

Russell, D. E. (1990). Conversations with Virginia Satir. Santa Barbara, CA: University of California, Santa Barbara Davidson Library Special Collections.

Satir, V. (1964). *Conjoint family therapy.* Palo Alto, CA: Science and Behavior Books.

Satir, V. (1972). *Peoplemaking.* Palo Alto, CA: Science and Behavior Books.

Satir, V. (1988). *The new peoplemaking.* Mountain View, CA: Science and Behavior Books.

Satir, V. (n.d.). *The third birth.* [Bound notes]. Burien, WA: AVANTA.

Satir, V., & Baldwin, M. (1983). *Satir step by step: A guide to creating change in families.* Palo Alto, CA: Science and Behavior Books.

Satir, V., Banmen, J., Gerber, J., & Gomori, M. (1991). The Satir model: Family therapy and beyond. Palo Alto, CA: Science and Behavior Books.

Satir, V., & Bitter, J. (2000). The therapist and family therapy: Satir's human validation process model. In A. Horne (Ed.), *Family counseling and therapy* (3rd ed., pp. 62–69). Itasca, IL: F. E. Peacock.

Simon, (Winter, 1985). Life reaching out to life: A conversation with Virginia Satir. *The common boundary between spirituality and psychotherapy* (3)1.

Warshofsky, F. (1971). Ideas for living. *Family Circle, 4*(11), 42.

Winter, J. E. (1993). Selected family therapy outcomes with Bowen, Haley, and Satir. Unpublished dissertation, College of William and Mary, Williamsburg, VA.

Yapko, M. D. (1988). An interview with Virginia Satir. *Milton H. Ericson Foundation Newletter, 8*(3), 11–13, 15–16.

Zimmerman, J., & Sims, D. (1983). Family therapy. In C. E. Walker & M. C. Roberts, (Eds.), *Handbook of clinical psychology*. New York: Wiley.

9 Solution-Oriented Therapy with Families

STEFFANIE O'HANLON AND BILL O'HANLON

Bill O'Hanlon

In family therapy, often only one or two family members are very motivated for treatment and the rest are along for the ride, at best, and conscientious objectors at worst. However, less-than-motivated family members can be the best collaborative therapy trainers. They will notice if you haven't heard and acknowledged all the points of view, whether you are allowing unhelpful interactions to proceed too long without interruption, if you are more eager to have the family in treatment than they are to be there, and, finally, if you know anything about how to solve the problem they came in with. Solution-oriented therapy offers a collaborative approach that allows you to ally with even the most reluctant clients. Solution-oriented therapy also offers an effective way to address the additional challenges that occur in family therapy: figuring out who should show up and what they should change. There are multiple and sometimes conflicting perspectives, experiences, and goals.

When Steffanie took her first job in the family unit of a community mental health center, she had a next-door office mate, Gary, who would drop by between sessions and recap the progress of his latest case with his usual refrain: "vini, vidi, vici" (loosely translated: *they* came, *they* saw, *they* conquered). Steffanie and Gary, despite their advanced training in psychodynamic psychotherapy and family systems treatment, often felt stymied about how to proceed. "Okay, so the family is triangulating. Do we do a structural or strategic intervention or do we talk about projective identification? And what about the fact that the family was referred by the social services, doesn't really want to be here, and is resentful of most anything we say or suggest." This chapter will show you how to use solution-oriented techniques and actually have fun while you're doing it.

What Makes Therapy Collaborative?

We start creating a collaborative context by recognizing the expertise of family members and giving their ideas and preferences as much weight as our professional training and knowledge. We view our role as consultants. We have lots of ideas based on our education and experience to bring to the family, but they are the only ones who know what is happening in their lives, what they are concerned about, what ideas and actions will work for them, what feels respectful, and what feels disrespectful.

Families frequently come to therapy prepared to be blamed for their difficulties or rescued from them. We try to move them from these unhelpful postures and empower them to be active participants in bringing about change. We assume that the family has strengths and seek to utilize and incorporate these rather than focus on pathologies and deficits. On the other hand, we acknowledge that families can damage one another through abuse, neglect, and other interactional processes. At these times, we confront and intervene in such destructive patterns. We endeavor to do this in a way that doesn't blame or presume bad intentions, but invites family members to adopt alternative behaviors and interactions.

Families are an active part of the treatment planning process. They are consulted about goals, directions, and their reactions to our methods of therapy throughout treatment. We make the process of therapy clear and accessible. This includes making diagnostic procedures, conclusions, and case notes understandable and as free from jargon, theoretical, or technical terms as is possible.

We try to ask questions and make speculations in a nonauthoritarian way, giving families ample room and permission to disagree or correct us. For example, if we were going to talk to the family about clear lines of authority and decision making, we would bring up the idea as a possibility, rather than a truth. We might say, "One of the theories of family therapy has an idea that it is very important for the family hierarchy to be clear. If it isn't, according to this idea, it tends to generate problems. For example, if grandparents are somehow taking over for the parents or undermining parents' rules or policies with kids, it can cause problems with either the marriage or the children. Some families and some cultures do it differently; there is no one right way. Do you think the rules and lines of authority are clear in your family? We have seen some things that make us think there may be some confusion in the hierarchy. Is it important to you that they be clear? What do you think?" We give multiple options and let the family coach us on what fits for them. If we have an idea, strong personal opinion, or perception, rather than keeping it hidden and unspoken, we make it public by noting it in the conversation, but clearly as our personal point of view or perspective and not as a statement of fact about the family. We are wary of what we call "theory counter-transference" (Hubble & O'Hanlon, 1992), imposing our beliefs and therapeutic values (and favorite diagnoses) on the family. We don't view ourselves as having special knowledge about the best way for the family to live life after therapy is concluded or the manner in which they should resolve the concerns that brought them to therapy.

We also extend this collaborative stance to our work with other helpers who may be involved with the family. We respect their treatment and contribution and invite them to cooperate by inquiring about their views of the situation and the outcomes they expect from treatment. If they are willing, we ask them about how we might help or, at least, not interfere with their treatment. We want to note that this does not mean that we always accept or support everything other helpers do. Our first loyalty is to our client(s). If we feel the other therapist/helper is imparting harmful or discouraging ideas, what we typically call "impossibility stories," to the family, we gently and subtly challenge those unhelpful ideas by first acknowledging their possible validity and then introducing alternate perspectives, for example, "So the discharge planner at the hospital said Johnny would always need to live in a structured setting because of his schizophrenia. You agree for right now that he should be in residential treatment following discharge, but lots of things can happen down the road (medication changes, independent living programs, and so on) that may make other living situations more workable."

Philosophical and Historical Background of the Approach

The solution-oriented approach derives in part from the work of Milton Erickson, the late psychiatrist. Erickson had a unique combination of pragmatism, an interest in how to rapidly solve problems, a belief that people could change (he wrote about the "seething forces of change that exist in families"), an appreciation of resources and abilities people have, and a systemic/anthropological perspective on human issues.

Solution-oriented therapy shares some assumptions and working methods with Haley's strategic therapy, with the MRI brief therapy approach, with Goolishian and Anderson's "problem determined systems therapy" (which later evolved into the Collaborative Language Systems approach), and with the Milwaukee solution-focused approach.

Solution-oriented therapy is rooted in the tradition of social constructivism, i.e., that human experience is heavily influenced, if not created by, social interactions and language. Instead of seeing people as set or fixed by their genetic or biochemical parameters, by their family or history, or by the contingencies in their current environment, people and problems are seen as changeable. The therapist's beliefs, as reflected in his or her language and interactions with clients, create the likelihood of certain problem definitions and courses of therapy. For example, if the therapist believes that therapy must be long-term to be effective and lasting, that belief will influence clients' feelings and expectations for problem resolution. Or, if the therapist believes dreams are the royal road to therapeutic change, talk of dreams will dominate. If the therapist becomes enamored of a new diagnosis, such as multiple personality, many of his or her clients will appear to have that diagnosis. Unless the therapist is aware of the creative and socially influential potential of these beliefs, he or she will think that problems are being discovered in an objective manner during the assessment process.

What's the Evidence that This Is a Useful Approach?

We think that the state of psychotherapy and psychotherapy research has reached the stage where medicine was when physicians were putting leeches on people and thinking that what they were doing was scientific and modern, so we offer the following list with some trepidation, suspecting that it will seem primitive to readers in the not-too-distant future.

- In well-designed psychotherapy studies, distinguished by experienced therapists, clinically representative clients, and appropriate controls and follow-up, brief therapy has been shown to be as effective as longer courses of treatment (Koss and Butcher, 1986), "Research on brief psychotherapy," [pp. 627–670] in Garfield and Bergin (Eds.) *Handbook of Psychotherapy and Behavior Change.* New York: Wiley.
- Average duration of therapy is five to eight sessions in both private practice and community mental health centers, regardless of the theoretical orientation or techniques used by the clinician. Clients generally expect to stay in therapy about six to ten sessions and no longer than three months. (Garfield, 1978; "Research on client variables in psychotherapy," in Garfield and Bergin (Eds.) *Handbook of Psychotherapy and Behavior Change.* NY: Wiley; Taube, Burnes, & Keesler, 1984; "Patients of psychiatrists & psychologists in office-based practice: 1980," *American Psychologist,* 39: 1435–1447; National Institute of Mental Health, 1981; "Provisional data on federally funded community mental health centers, 1978–79," U.S. Gov. Printing Office; Howard,

Kopta, Krause, & Orlinsky, 1986). "The dose-effect relationship in psychotherapy." *American Psychologist, 41:* 159–164.

- Seventy-five percent of those clients who benefit from therapy get that benefit within the first six months in therapy. The major positive impact in therapy happens in the first six to eight sessions, followed by continuing but decreasing positive impact for the next ten sessions. No one form of psychotherapy is demonstrably better than others for the wide range of clients and problems (Lambert, Shapiro, & Bergin, 1986; "The effectiveness of psychotherapy," in Garfield and Bergin (Eds.) *Handbook of Psychotherapy and Behavior Change.* NY: Wiley. and Smith, Glass, & Miller, 1980).

- Emotionally disturbed children and their families who received a brief assessment and a follow-up interview showed more improvement (closer to the goals set by the therapist at the initial session) in a four-year follow-up study than those families who had time-unlimited psychodynamic therapy or time-limited (twelve-session) psychodynamic therapy (Smyrnios & Kirkby, 1993). "Long-term comparisons of brief vs. unlimited psychodynamic treatments with children and their parents," *Journal of Consulting and Clinical Psychology, 61,* pp. 1020–1027.]

- Several studies have indicated that one session is the most common length of treatment (30 percent in one study, 39 percent in another, and 56 percent in another) across the range of clinicians, whether biologically oriented psychiatrists, psychoanalysts, or eclectically oriented therapists. Surprisingly, follow-up research indicates that a large percentage (78 percent in one study) felt that they got what they wanted and that their problem was better or much better from that one session (Pekarik & Wierzbicki, 1986; Talmon 1990). "The relationship between expected and actual psychotherapy duration," *Psychotherapy, 23:* 532–534.

- Research done through the Milwaukee Brief Family Therapy Center on solution-focused therapy showed that 77 percent of the clients felt they had met their treatment goal and 14 percent thought they had made progress toward their treatment goal. In an eighteen-month follow-up of 164 cases, 51 percent reported their problem was still resolved and 34 percent reported that the problem was not as bad as when they started therapy (85 percent then thought they experienced long-term improvements). All of these clients, who presented with diverse problems and from diverse ethnic populations and genders, received less than ten sessions of therapy (average of three sessions) (Research done by Dave Kaiser and reported in M. S. Wylie, M. S. (1990). "Brief Therapy on the Couch," *Family Therapy Networker,* 14: 26–34, 66.

- Research done in Sweden found that 80 percent of the clients completing solution-focused therapy accomplished their stated treatment goals; average length of treatment was five sessions (Andreas, "A follow-up of patients in solution-focused brief therapy," Paper presented at the Institution for Applied Psychology, University of Lund, Sweden.]

- The more "solution-talk" (discussion of solutions and goals by clients) in the initial session, the more likely the client was to complete therapy (versus dropping out) (Shields, C. G., Sprenkle, D. H., & Constantine, J. A. (1991). "Anatomy of an initial interview: The importance of joining and structuring skills," *American Journal of Family Therapy, 19,* pp. 3–18.
- Therapists who were given a twelve-hour training program in brief therapy obtained lower rates of attrition (unplanned/nonmutual treatment termination) and recidivism (return for treatment) and higher success rates than nontrained or self-trained therapists. The therapists in the study ranged from beginners to experienced therapists and the results held among all skill levels. However, once experienced therapists accepted the value of brief therapy, their effectiveness increased. (Burlingame, Fuhrman, Paul, & Ogles, 1989). "Implementing a time-limited therapy program: Differential effects of training and experience," *Psychotherapy, 26,* pp. 303–313.]

Who to See?

For therapists, a primary and crucial question in family therapy is identifying which members to see. When family therapy was new, there was a rigid insistence on seeing *all* the family members or refusing to take the case. Families were always to be seen together, both in order to assess and intervene in the systemic interactions and to avoid supporting the individual view of the problem (that the problem arises from psychological processes within an individual). This has softened over the years, so therapists are now faced with the dilemma of deciding when they should agree to meet with part of the family and when it is important to hold out for everyone to attend. We prefer to see whoever is motivated to seek therapy or make change, or whoever is upset. Typically, this is the person who is making the phone call, but it might include a large supporting cast as well. We ask ourselves a number of questions to ferret out the most likely participants: Who is complaining or alarmed? Who thinks there is a problem? Who is willing to pay for therapy and/or do something to effect change? Whose concerns will constrain or affect therapy? Who is pushing for change?

Sometimes we start with one person and end up with many. Sometimes we start with a whole family and break down into smaller subsets. If a mother is calling and is concerned about appropriate limit setting with her fourteen-year-old daughter and says no one else in the family is concerned or wants to come, we would be willing to meet with Mom alone to do "family therapy." Later we might try to involve other family members if it seemed important. Or, in another family, if Dad says he doesn't like the way he responds to his son's "mouthing back," we might just see Dad. Of course, we prefer, if possible, to see whoever is affected by the complaint. For example, if a father is calling about conflict between mother and daughter, we would like to see all three because, although mother and daughter are fighting, Dad is concerned about the escalation of the conflict.

We find individual sessions helpful in family therapy. Sometimes crucial information emerges (such as reports of abuse or other concerns that a family member is afraid to speak about in front of other family members). Sometimes having so many people present makes it hard to focus the conversation, and we find ourselves struggling just to manage the conversation or prevent conflicts from exploding. Individual sessions also provide an opportunity to coach an individual, whether it be a parent or child, on how to change their response without having to attend to the potential defensive response of another family member. We find this particularly helpful with teenagers, who often need a forum in which to discuss legitimate concerns, but usually do so in such a provocative manner ("They never let me do anything, they are too *&%#ing strict") that they are not heard. We can, and often, do family therapy with only part of the family, usually with the motivated part of the family. It isn't necessary to get the whole family to attend therapy to bring about a change. Who will attend is often determined by the goal or agenda that has been set. The more inclusive of various members' concerns the agenda is, the more likely reluctant family members will attend. We will talk more about how to set inclusive goals.

What to do about those clients who are mandated/required to attend therapy? We see them even if it seems they are not motivated, and then we negotiate goals or a focus that is relevant to them. Steffanie used to work in a psychiatric hospital with adolescents. Most of them did not want to be there, let alone comply with the rigorous rules. What they did want was to get out of the hospital and to get out as quickly as possible. Treatment would focus around what the teens needed to do to demonstrate to and convince skeptical hospital staff, family members, and whoever else was involved (school personnel, youth services, parole officers, etc.) that they were ready to leave the hospital and handle their problems in a different way. In such cases, it is important to acknowledge up front that clients don't want to be there and also to hear the reasons behind their not wanting to participate in therapy. This approach also works with parents who are being forced into treatment. Bill saw a parent whose child had been removed from the home by child protective services. She was accused of having burned her son with cigarettes, and she protested her innocence. She had seen a variety of helpers but none had, in her view, listened to her. Bill listened to her experiences with protective services, the various therapists, and her frustration about wanting her child back in a way that the client perceived her position was acknowledged. Then Bill and the client were able to come up with a plan that allowed her to maintain her innocence and fulfill the requirements for safety that protective services had set.

There seems to be an inverse effect in that, the more motivated certain family members are, the less motivated the others will be. In her private practice, Steffanie got to be known as a specialist in adolescents and she saw this phenomenon quite frequently. One or both of the parents would be very eager about therapy and the teenager was very miserable about being dragged in. The teen didn't want to speak and either communicated this through sullen glances or direct pronouncements of his or her unwillingness to participate. Steffanie would casually commiserate (acknowledge) that they didn't want to be there or speak. She would tell them that it was okay with her, that the teen could just hang out and be silent if he or she wanted, and Steffanie would speak with whoever had brought them (typically a parent) as they were clearly the most concerned. And if something came up that the teen wanted to clarify or add, he or she could speak up but it wasn't necessary. At this point, there would be a sigh of relief and the tension/hostility would decrease significantly. Usually, within five to ten minutes, the adolescent was jumping in to rebut the parent's description of the problem. If, on the other hand, the teenager was reluctant to attend treatment and refused to even attend one session, Steffanie would suggest that the parent go home and tell the teen that part of what was going to happen in therapy was renegotiating rules and consequences in the house, and that the therapist [Steffanie] was concerned about offering the teen an opportunity to represent him- or herself and to talk about other changes he or she would like to see happen in the family as well. Usually the teenager would show up for the next session. To make therapy palatable for reluctant attendees, therapists need to find out what motivates them and link therapy to that. It is also important to find out what turns reluctant family members off and stop doing that (e.g., giving them the sense they are to blame, repeatedly asking them about how they are feeling, etc.). What makes therapy relevant and interesting for them? Because they may be feeling dragged there to begin with, the therapist needs to be careful to structure the session to minimize the likelihood that they will feel misrepresented or blamed and to ensure that prolonged unhelpful interactions do not occur. If the reluctant client is a child or teen, he or she can often be motivated by the possibility of having a say in renegotiating rules and consequences, getting a parent to stop some unwelcome behavior like nagging or yelling, and, of course, receiving increased privileges. This often motivates reluctant spouses as well. If they have a sense that real change can occur and that it isn't just going to be a gripe session, they are usually more willing and, often, more enthusiastic participants.

Many people ask about whether we see children individually. We generally don't see children in individual therapy. Steffanie began her career doing play therapy and working under the child guidance model (children are seen separately from parents; often, each family member has his or her own individual therapist). Generally, the change that happens with this approach is long in coming, if at all. And, when a child is able to make change in individual psychotherapy, it does not always transfer into the family context unless the family has changed its interactional patterns. We have both found it more effective and respectful to coach parents and families to develop strategies to directly solve their own problem than to rely on a third party to influence the emotional and behavioral lives of their children. When we do first sessions with families, we may speak briefly with the children separately to enable them to express things they have to say privately, and to get a sense of their resources outside of the immediate family context.

We do tend to see adolescents in a combination of individual and family therapy, usually because most adolescents have individual concerns and express some desire for more individual sessions after they become engaged in treatment. We rarely see younger children in individual treatment, again primarily when they want to be seen alone and have a specific personal problem to work on. For example, both of us might see a child individually to do hypnosis or EMDR for a focused problem, such as a school phobia or bedwetting or a trauma. We also see children individually when parents, school, or court insist on it and our efforts to dissuade the parents from individual sessions have been futile. (Sometimes a parent just won't believe that change is credible and will last unless we see the child individually and discuss Little Ken's anger.) When we do meet with kids individually, we talk with them about whether they think there is a problem and get their ideas about the problem. We say things like, "We are meeting because your parents are concerned about your anger. They think it's a problem. Do you think it's a problem? Does it make things hard at school or with friends? Or does it cause you to lose out on things you want to do? Do you want to do it differently or is it okay for you?" We typically use these sessions to build rapport and gather information to build interventions for the family.

What Do You Work On?

When families come into therapy, they are typically demoralized and entrenched in a process of speculation and blame about the causes and reasons for their difficulties. Traditional family therapy sometimes inadvertently reifies the situation by initially replicating these same conversations (pathology/blame-based). Further, traditional family therapy sometimes requires that the first three sessions be used for gathering information about family history and etiology of the problem before intervention can begin. Families are often frustrated by this process and the therapist feels hamstrung, unable to act until all the information is collected. This is akin to checking in to a hospital with acute appendicitis and having the staff tell you that they want to gather a lot of insurance information and history before giving you treatment. Solution-oriented therapy focuses on clients' goals for treatment and almost always starts the intervention process in the first session.

Complaints and Goals: Focusing and Finding Mutually Agreeable Directions

Solution-oriented therapy focuses on the family's complaints and goals. It is vital that the focus that comes *from* the family, not from our theories or from some normative model. We get that information from the family. For example, a family may come in complaining of a child's temper tantrums and we may observe "triangulation" in the family interactions, but if it is peripheral to the problems and goals we are trying to focus on, we wouldn't bring it into the spotlight or challenge it. *Many families triangulate but do not have problems that bring them to therapy.* Unless the family members are concerned about triangulation or it is part of the problem as they express it, we do not pursue such "theoretical" problems. (If, for example, triangulation is either demonstrated over time to be a contributing factor or an impediment to reaching the treatment goal, then we address it directly.)

To determine the complaint, again we ask ourselves and the family members a series of questions. What is bothering someone enough to get him or her to seek or get sent to treatment? What is he or she complaining or alarmed about? When has the complaint occurred? Where has it occurred? What are the patterns surrounding or involved in the complaint? How does the person, the customer, or others involved in the situation explain the complaint?

With families and couples, there are typically multiple complaints, usually at least one per person and sometimes several per person. We try to acknowledge and address each complaint and combine them into mutual complaints and goals on which to focus our inquiries and interventions.

We ask each person what he or she is here for and what he or she wants to accomplish. Needless to say, each person has a slightly or vastly different perspective on the situation, so finding or creating mutual goals is a way to harmonize multiple complaints.

Acknowledging, tracking, and linking are ways to coordinate complaints and goals. We acknowledge each family member's perspective by restating it in the least inflammatory way possible that still acknowledges and imparts its meaning and feeling. We link these statements by using the word *and* as it builds a common concern rather than opposing or competing needs and goals. For example, "Dad, you become concerned that Pete is getting depressed and may make another suicide attempt when you see him hanging out in his room. So you go and check on him. And Pete, you feel like you're on 'fifteen minutes checks' and want your Dad to back off. And so you guys get into it. And then Mom, you hear them winding up and feel like you need to cool things down. So Dad, you want to be reassured that Pete is okay. Pete, you want some space. And Mom, you don't want to have to be in the middle of these fights." We not only acknowledge and link, but track the complaint as well by giving descriptions of actions or sequences of behaviors that are occurring. The intent is that the family jump in and clarify any misperceptions or areas of discomfort until a mutually agreeable description emerges. Once we have a commonly agreed-on description, we begin to flesh out the direction and goals for treatment.

It's important to balance acknowledging the difficulty the family is experiencing without allowing them to become too discouraged in the process. There is nothing more demoralizing than going to a therapist's office and having the same old arguments with no better outcome (and paying a lot of money to do so). One of the ways we do this is by going back and forth between getting descriptions of concerns and problems on the one hand, and eliciting descriptions of better moments (exceptions to the problem and more compassionate, helpful ways of viewing the situation) on the other. We also usually ask clients what they have already tried to solve the problem, so we don't try to use a broken wheel. We also acknowledge their efforts and expertise, as well as how seriously stuck and discouraged they are.

In gathering information, it is important not to crystallize or reify the problem. Feelings and concerns are not set in stone. We notice that, in the process of gathering information and filtering out problematic stories, family members' feelings or ideas about the complaint often change, sometimes radically. One of the ways this transformation occurs is by getting people to translate vague and blaming words into action descriptions (Hudson and O'Hanlon, 1992; O'Hanlon and Wilk, 1987). If "poor self-esteem" is the complaint, we ask for a specific description of what "poor self-esteem" and "good self-esteem" looks like in that family. Does it involve eye contact when speaking, a certain tone of voice, asking for what you want, or other components? The key here is to get a description of the actions or processes involved in the expression of "self-esteem." If someone is complaining about a "messy house," we find out what that means for that person or that family. Is it papers in piles or no piles of paper, passing the white glove test, clothes on the floor, clothes on the bed or chair, instead of hung up in the closet, or something else altogether? Families (and many therapists, we might add) tend to use words like *communication, self-esteem, depression, trust, behavioral problems* and *underlying anger,* which are very general. In addition, we like to find action correlates for feelings ("Tell me what kinds of things she does when you get the sense she's upset with you" or "How does he show you that he is sad but hiding it?").

Another element of involving family members in setting the direction and focus of therapy and in developing mutuality is to collaboratively define goals for the therapy and for the family. How will family members know when therapy has been helpful enough to terminate or when the agreed-on results have been achieved? What are the first signs that will indicate (or already have indicated) progress toward the goal(s)? What are the final actions or results (in videotalk, seeable, hearable, checkable terms) that will indicate that this is no longer a problem? How will we know when therapy is done, when it has been successful? It is important, if possible, to get goal descriptions in specific videotalk terms. This helps to ensure that goals are achievable, not utopian. Achievable goals consist of clients' actions or conditions that can be brought about by clients' actions (for example, parents could ask that the child spend two hours per night doing homework or that the child raise his or her grade to a B in a particular subject). These goals include time elements: how often (frequency), when (date/time/deadline), and how long (duration). We help guide the family to define the goal to achieve agreement of what constitutes final resolution of the therapy concern or enough progress to terminate or take a break from therapy. We also help family members translate labels or theoretical concepts into action descriptions. If we are unable to define goals in action terms, we attempt to get the family or family members to rate the problem on a scale and then select a target number that will indicate success on that scale.

Sometimes we are asked by supervisees or participants in training how to get family members to be specific when they persist in stating the problem or the goals in vague language despite the therapist's efforts to be specific. We often "prime the pump" by providing multiple-choice answers that are slanted in the direction of being more specific. This technique usually leads to family members either choosing one of the provided options, which is specific, or giving a similar specific that has not been provided. Sometimes we get family members or families to get specific by asking them to teach us how they "do" their problems. We have several ways to do this.

- Get people to teach you how you could reproduce the problem if you tried to create it.

    If I were going to get into a conflict with you, how would I go about it?

    Teach me your method for getting your parents to let you out of consequences.

- Get details of the thoughts, feelings, sensations, fantasies, actions, interactions, and contexts when the problem typically happens.

    Tell me what kind of thoughts go through your mind just before you run out of the room.

    What do you notice in your experience as you are getting upset with your father?

- How would the person or family make the problem worse or better, if they could?

    If I was going to learn how to make the arguments even worse than they are, what would I have to do if I were you?

    Is there anything you have done that seems to help avoid a conflict or make them a little less intense?

We also want to note that certain circumstances dictate that we superimpose our goals on the family instead of letting them set the agenda. In situations where there is indication of homicidal or suicidal plans or actions, sexual assault or violence, and certain other legal and ethical issues, stopping these activities becomes the immediate treatment goal regardless of whether or not family members see that goal as crucial or relevant. For example, if, in the course of discussing her depression, a client discloses that her son has been sexually abusing other children, safety for those children becomes a primary focus of treatment, at least temporarily. We continue to work collaboratively, explaining our legal and ethical responsibilities, and engage our clients in taking the necessary steps to report offenses, develop safety plans, or arrange hospitalizations, and so on. However, we will act unilaterally if they are unwilling to work collaboratively. Both of us, however, have had good success in having families call and report their own abusive behavior to child protective agencies when invited to do so in a respectful and nonblaming way.

O'Hanlon w/clients

Intervening: Acknowledging Experience and Changing Views, Actions, and Contexts

Next, we will take up how we organize our thinking for intervening in families. We use four areas for intervention in family therapy. These are: *Experience, Actions, Stories,* and *Context.* Table 9.1 summarizes these areas.

Within *experience* lie all the inner aspects of people's lives, their feelings, fantasies, sensations, and their sense of themselves. All of these are things that happen inside our experience, that are unavailable to others unless we somehow, through words, art, or gestures, communicate it to them. We suggest that therapists just acknowledge, value, and validate experience. Let people know their experience has been heard and not judged as wrong or invalid. Let them know that they are valued as people and that they have valid experiences. This is the realm of acceptance, not change (although communicating that acceptance may, of course, lead to change).

We always start out by acknowledging what the family is experiencing. The family needs to know that you, the therapist, get not only the content of the problem but also understand the emotional weight or resonance it has for them. This is fundamental for the rest of the treatment process, and for some families this *is* the treatment. Steffanie had a client that came in for one session to tell her about a rape that she had experienced several years before. She had never spoken about it and just wanted someone to hear her experience. In a follow-up phone call the woman said she went home and told her husband as well. She felt able to move on with her life. Most clients, however, need more than acknowledgment. They not only need to be heard and validated but then given help to begin actively making changes to solve the problem. Acknowledgment may last anywhere from five minutes to many sessions. If clients don't feel heard and understood, you will not be able to move on to the other stages in therapy. If acknowledgment is all you offer, it won't be enough for most families. But if we feel, as therapists, that we are starting to experience lack of cooperation or hostility in the treatment, we stop and move back into acknowledgment.

TABLE 9.1   **Areas for Intervention in Family Therapy**

Experience	Views	Actions	Context
Feelings	Points of view	Action patterns	Time patterns
Sense of self	Attentional patterns	Interactional patterns	Spatial patterns
Bodily sensations	Interpretations	Language patterns	Cultural background and propensities
Sensory experience	Explanations	Nonverbal patterns	
	Evaluations		Family/historical background and propensities
Automatic fantasies and thoughts	Assumptions		
	Beliefs		Biochemical/genetic background and propensities
	Identity stories		
			Gender training and propensities

Steffanie saw a family in which the nine-year-old son had been referred by his family physician for behavior problems following his diagnosis and surgery for a chronic ongoing medical condition. The family agreed with the physician that Joe's temper tantrums were a problem and wanted to change his behavior. However, when we began to discuss ways for the family to respond to temper tantrums, Dad would begin to shift around in his chair. After observing this several times, Steffanie told Dad she felt she wasn't being helpful in some way and asked for his comment. Dad said that the discussion was about things that *they* could do to manage Joe differently, but that he thought that there was something Steffanie could do to "fix Joe." That opened up a discussion about how Dad saw the problem and what he thought needed to happen. He spoke about how he managed Joe before his illness and his wife's concern that disciplining Joe now might interfere with Joe's willingness to report his physical symptoms (which were important to manage his illness). The Dad hoped that Steffanie could make Joe behave so that there would be no ambiguity about whether the family was doing it correctly or not. Once Dad's expectations and concerns were acknowledged and responded to, therapy proceeded quickly and smoothly, with Dad's full cooperation. If Steffanie had continued on without acknowledging Dad's discomfort or had she interpreted it as resistance, therapy might have stagnated or bogged down completely.

The next three columns in Table 9.1 define the realm in which change occurs. Here, we focus on three areas of change: *changing the viewing of the problem, changing the doing of the problem,* and *changing the context surrounding the problem.*

In these three areas, we search for patterns: both the problem and solution patterns. What are the problematic views that family members hold about themselves, their family, and each other? For example, are there patterns of blame that persist in the family view of the problem situation? What are more helpful supportive, change-enhancing or change-inviting views? What are the problematic action or interaction patterns that occur within the family, between family members, or with others? What are more helpful action and interaction patterns? And, finally, what are the aspects of the context that are conducive to change and results, and which aspects of the context hold people back or keep them having problems?

We try to change the habitual ways people think about, attend to, or see the problem—changing the "viewing" of the problem—and to change the habitual ways people have been acting and interacting in the problem situation—changing the "doing" of the problem. Some years ago, the brief therapist John Weakland told Bill, "Life is just one damn thing after another. Therapy can't change that. But people who seek therapy are no longer experiencing that—life for them has become the same damn thing *over and over and over.*" Our task as possibility therapists, then, is to help people get from a situation in which life has become the same damn thing over and over back to a life in which it's one damn thing after another. People will always have some problems, but what discourages and disempowers them so is struggling unsuccessfully with the same problem over and over.

To the ideas of assessing and changing the "doing" and the "viewing," we have added changing the context of the problem. As therapists, we have become much more aware of the influence of culture, gender, biochemistry, and other contextual aspects on people's problems. Problems do not occur in a vacuum. We believe that contextual aspects are influences (not causes) and that there are both problematic and helpful contextual influences. A family member may have a biochemical context that suggests a predisposition toward obsessiveness or schizophrenia, but that does not *cause* him or her to act in a particular way. For example, one may be subject to hallucinations, but that does not *cause* one to run down the street naked or hit someone. Or just because a man is from a cultural tradition in which males are trained not to express feelings doesn't mean he is or will always be unable to express feelings.

We search for helpful contextual patterns as well as identify problematic contextual patterns. For example, we might say, "So there has been quite a history of alcohol abuse and dependency in your family. Dad, three of your uncles died from drinking in their thirties. Mom, your mother was a secret drinker until a few years ago. Tell us this. How did your mother stop drinking, Mom? And Dad, who in your family didn't succumb to the invitations of alcohol?" Or, "Because we don't know much about Pakistani culture, perhaps you can help us with this. When there has been violence between a couple, how does it typically stop, if it does, in Pakistani culture? What aspects of the culture support violence between couples and what aspects of the culture challenge or restrain violence in those situations?"

TABLE 9.2   **How to Intervene in the Four Areas**

Experience	Views	Actions	Context
Give messages of acceptance, validation, and acknowledgment. There is no need to change or analyze experience as it is not inherently a problem.	Identify and challenge views that are: Impossibility Blaming Invalidating Nonaccountability or determinism. Also: Offer new possibilities for attention.	Find action and interaction patterns that are part of the problem and that are the "same damn thing over and over." Then suggest disrupting the problematic patterns or find and use solution patterns.	Identify unhelpful and helpful aspects of the context, then suggest shifts in the context around the problem (e.g., changes in biochemistry, time, space, cultural habits and influences, etc.).

Changing the Viewing of the Problem

When families enter therapy, they often have stories (ideas, beliefs, hypothesis) about each other or the problem. These stories tend to be rigid and divisive. Stories are unhelpful when they get in the way of change or get a bad reaction from other family members. When families come for therapy, we typically find that someone in the family has unhelpful stories that have become part of the problem. We have identified four typical problematic stories. These beliefs may be held by anyone interacting about the problem: the family, the therapist, or the referral source.

Impossibility stories

In impossibility stories, clients, therapists, or others in their lives often hold beliefs that suggest that change is impossible.

He has ADHD and can't control his behavior.

She'll never change.

She is just like my mother.

Blaming stories

Stories of blame assume or view oneself or others as having bad intentions or bad traits.

He's just trying to get attention.

It's all my fault.

They are trying to drive me crazy.

Invalidating stories

Ideas of invalidation lead to clients' personal experience or knowledge being undermined by others.

He needs to express his anger about his father's death.

He's too sensitive.

You're too emotional.

Deterministic stories

Stories of nonchoice or deterministic stories suggest that someone has no choices about what he or she does with his or her body (voluntary actions) or has no ability to make any difference in what happens in his or her life.

If that teacher knew how to handle a classroom, Kate wouldn't have these problems at school.

I was raised in a home where silence was the way to express anger, so when I get angry, I stop talking and go my own way.

If she didn't nag me, I wouldn't hit her.

We challenge or cast doubt on problematic stories in three ways:

1. *Transform the story by acknowledging and softening or by adding possibility*
   Validate the current or past problematic points of view but add a twist that softens them a bit or adds a sense of possibility. For example, a parent may say of her son, "He doesn't care about our family. He just wants to do anything he feels like doing, regardless of the pain it causes us." One could respond by acknowledging the feelings and point of view of the parent, but reflect it back with a softer, less globalized sense to it. "So a lot of the things he's been doing have given you the sense he cares more for himself than for you or the family." Or another reflection could add a sense of the possibility that things could change in the situation in the future: "So you'd like to see him doing more things that show that he can put the family above his own interests at times."

2. *Find counterevidence*
   Get the family or others to tell you something that doesn't fit with the problematic story. For example, "Gee, you tell me that he's out of control, but now you're telling me that his teacher said he kept his cool when another boy taunted him in class." Or, "So, you tell me that you were raised in a family in which the only way to express anger was violence. But I'm curious. When you get angry, you typically hit your wife and your son, but when you get mad at work, do you hit your boss or the customers?"

3. *Find alternative stories or frames to fit the same evidence or facts*
   Give the facts a more benevolent interpretation. "You get the sense he just wants to do anything he wants when he wants to do it, but my sense is that

he's trying to find a way to be independent and make his own decisions. When you come down hard on him, the only way he can see to show he's independent is to rebel and resist you, even if it gets him in trouble." Or, "You think your father hates you because he grounds you, but I wonder, if he didn't care for you, he'd just let you do what you want as long as it wasn't a hassle for him."

Changing the Doing of the Problem

Insanity is doing the same thing over and over again and expecting different results.
—Rita Mae Brown

There are two main ways to change the "doing" of the problem:

1. Identify and alter repetitive patterns of action and interaction involved in the problem; and,
2. Identify and encourage the use of solution patterns of action and interaction.

Identifying and Altering Repetitive Patterns of Action and Interaction Involved in the Problem

The first way to change the "doing" of the problem is to interrupt or disrupt repetitive patterns involved in or surrounding the problem. Ways to do this are:

1. change the **frequency/rate** of the problem or the pattern around the problem;
2. change the **duration** of the problem or the pattern around the problem;
3. change the **time** (hour/time of day, week, month, or time of year) of the problem or the pattern around the problem;
4. change the **intensity** of the problem or the pattern around the problem;
5. change some other **invariant quality** of the problem or the pattern around the problem;
6. change the **sequence** (order) of events involved in or around the problem;
7. **interrupt** or otherwise prevent the occurrence of the problem;
8. **add a new element** to the problem;
9. **break up** any previously whole element of **the problem into smaller elements;**
10. have the person **perform the problem without the usual accompanying pattern** around it;
11. have the person **perform the pattern around the problem** at a time **when he or she is not having the problem;**
12. **reverse the direction of striving** in the performance of the problem (paradox);
13. **link the occurrence of the problem to** another pattern that is **a burdensome activity** (ordeal);

14. change the **body behavior/performance** of the problem.

> Bill had a family come to see him that was having a classic problem: Father and daughter would argue, while Mother felt caught in-between, trying to get both of them to be reasonable and occasionally finding herself called on to be the judge of who was right. After some discussion, we decided that the next time there was an argument between father and daughter, they would have to go out into the back yard with water pistols, stand back to back while Mother counted ten paces for each of them to walk, and then turn and fire until the gun was out of water. Mother was then to tell them who was the winner of the duel. This led to much laughter and good-natured dissipation of tension that allowed them all to sit down and have much more helpful discussions about the problem at hand.

Identifying and Encouraging Solution Patterns of Action and Interaction

In addition to disrupting the problem pattern, usually we seek to discover and highlight solution patterns. These are efforts and behaviors that any or all family members have done in the past to solve the problem or to make the situation better. It is important to evoke a connection to the solutions, not merely convince families that they are good competent people by pointing out to them that they have, at times, acted in resourceful ways in the past or that they must have the best of intentions. We are not trying to be cheerleaders for the family, but to ask questions and gather information in a way that convinces us and highlights for them that they have the resources to solve their problems. To this end, we have used a variety of methods for evoking solution patterns.

> **One of the ways is to ask families to detail times when they haven't experienced their problems when they expected they would.** This includes asking about exceptions to the rule of the problem. It is important to ask about this area in a way that both helps the families notice that there are exceptions and to make it likely that they will increase the solution patterns in the future. In part, that means asking about what anybody *did* differently in the exception situation. Otherwise, one might find out about exceptions but in a way that implies that there is nothing anyone can do to make it happen again, such as "I was in a better mood that day." Asking questions that evoke action descriptions is more helpful in this regard: "So usually his coming home after curfew would lead to a big argument. How come it didn't go that way last night? What did anybody do differently last night from the usual drill?" "What is different about the times when you are getting along (there are dry beds, he does go to school, and so on)? How do you get that to happen?" "Have you ever had this difficulty in the past?" If yes, "How did you resolve it then? What would you need to do to get that to happen again?"

Another way to evoke solution patterns is to find out what happens as the problem ends or starts to end. What is usually the first sign the family or family member can tell the problem is going away or subsiding? What will the person or the family be doing differently when their problem has ended or subsided from what they are doing when the problem is happening? "What happens or what did you do to *get* her to stop the temper tantrum?" "What did you do to *get* the fight to end?"

We also search for other contexts of competence for the family members or the family as a whole. We ask about areas in the family's life that they feel good about, including hobbies, areas of specialized knowledge, well-developed skills, or places and times when they get along or solve problems. For example, "What subjects do you like best in school?" "What kinds of things do you do for fun?" "What do you do for a living?" For example, we might find out that, when they are on family trips, things go better. What is different then? we might ask. Everyone has clearly assigned roles and tasks; Jimmy plans the route and is the navigator. Mom makes the hotel reservations and coordinates meals. Dad is the driver and Sue is the GameMaster. She organizes games to play that everyone likes and that pass the time. Then we see if we can translate any of this situation to the problem that brought the family for therapy. "So, could we use the same team effort with everyone having an assigned role and task to help Jimmy get along with other kids better without getting into fights?"

Another way to elicit competence is to get families to tell us about others that they know who have faced similar problems and resolved them successfully. A variation on this method is to ask families to tell us what they would suggest to another family or another child troubled by the same situation. Interestingly, when asked in this one-step-removed way, many children and families have lots of good ideas and wisdom that can be tapped to solve their problems.

> Bill saw a family in which all six children were having problems of one sort or another. The parents had just successfully completed some marital therapy and they had decided the children could use some help. The family was very religious and the kids often felt out of place in their schools and had a tough time making friends. Several were depressed and some were taunted by other children at school. As we discussed this issue, it came to light that the oldest daughter had recently begun to make friends and had become more socially skilled and happy. She had previously been shy and depressed. When I showed some interest in this recent change, the Mother mentioned that her history was similar to her daughter's. She had been shy and awkward socially, not due to religion, but due to her shame regarding the severe abuse and dysfunction in her family of origin. She had never wanted to make friends with anyone for fear they would discover the terrible things that were going on in her

home. She had also felt so different from others that she had been shy. I asked her how she got over it and she said she had finally left home and gone to work, where she was forced to interact with others on a day-to-day basis. She had started to realize that she wasn't so different from others and gradually made friends and got less shy and more secure. The daughter who had recently overcome shyness chimed in that she had also made the change in the same way. She had gotten a job and had begun to be around people other than her family. That led to her making friends and overcoming social awkwardness and isolation. From there on, it became an easy matter to have the mother and oldest daughter become expert consultants to design a program to help the younger ones end their isolation and awkwardness much earlier than either of them had. Regular nonschool/nonchurch activities outside the family were planned for each of them.

As a last resort, if we can't find any other way to identify and elicit solution patterns, we may ask why the problem isn't worse. Compared to the worst possible state families or people or this person could get in, how does the family explain that it isn't that severe? This normalizes and gets things in perspective as well as eliciting things the family does when they finally succeed in confronting the problem. "Joann has failed three of her classes. How come she didn't fail them all?" "Things get loud, but they haven't gotten violent, as far as I've heard. How do you keep things from getting physical, even though tempers are flaring?"

Changing the Context of the Problem

By *context*, we mean the aspects of the person's world that surround the problem but aren't necessarily directly involved in the problem. This includes time patterns (when, how frequently, and for how long the problem happens) and spatial patterns (where the problem typically happens). Because these two patterns overlap with the categories in changing the doing, we will skip them here and focus on the other aspects of the context. These include cultural background and propensities, family/historical background and propensities, biochemical/genetic background and propensities, and gender training and propensities. We assess what kinds of patterns and views come from each of these influences that support the problem or make it likely to arise. We are careful not to imply that these influencing factors are causal. That is, being from certain cultural backgrounds or families of origin doesn't determine how one turns out, in our view. Likewise, having a genetic or biochemical propensity for depression or schizophrenia does not of necessity make one depressed or schizophrenic. The situation is more complex than that. While we assess the problematic aspects and patterns of the contextual influence, as in the doing and viewing, we also assess the solution aspects of the context.

Bill was teaching a workshop in England and a participant came up after the first day's presentation to say she had enjoyed the material, but had a question. "I work in a battered woman's shelter," she said, "with a mixed group of women, some British in their background and some Pakistani immigrants. I can usually get the British women to at least acknowledge that they are in a bad situation, but the Pakistani women seem resigned to their situation. They have told me that if they leave their husbands, they will be dead, either from lack of support among their fellow Pakistanis or from murder that will go unsolved. What would your solution stuff say to that?" Bill replied that *he* wouldn't have the answer, but thought that the Pakistani women might have some answers. He suggested that, when she went to work that night, she get a group of the women together and ask them to be her consultants. She should ask, "How does domestic violence get successfully dealt with in Pakistani society?" After much discussion (in which it was generally agreed that it rarely gets dealt with successfully), several women knew of one instance in which the violence was successfully stopped. It was sometimes stopped when the woman who was being beaten told her family of origin of the situation and her father and brothers called on her husband and threatened to beat him if he continued to abuse the woman. Of course, it didn't always work, but when something worked, that was it. When one of the women wondered out loud how this new-found realization could help any of them, because most of their families of origin were back in Pakistan, another woman got a small smile on her face and said, "Yes, but my family is coming to visit here in Britain next month."

The point of the story is that, in every cultural, gender, biochemical situation, there are problematic patterns and influences as well as solution patterns and competence. Instead of just doing a genogram to find the patterns of addiction that run through the generations, it is also important to do a "solutiongram," which can detail the strengths and counterproblematic patterns that run through the family history. "So, you've told me that all of your father's brothers were alcoholic, three of them dying in their thirties from alcohol-related diseases. What I am curious about is that other brother who stopped drinking when he was fifty and your grandfather, who stopped drinking when his wife died. How do you think they did that and do you think you have inherited any of those abilities?"

Another way we use the context is to normalize and highlight strengths. If a person starts to understand that, given the context in which the problem occurred, many people would experience, think, feel, or do something similar, it often lessens shame and feelings of isolation. For example, knowing that women have been socialized to take on the emotional or physical maintenance of relationships or families is often helpful to the woman who feels guilty if she doesn't do the dishes or leaves on a business trip, when she wouldn't have the same reaction if her male partner did the same things. Or a man might be complimented on his withstanding his gender training and staying home with the infant, despite his guilt for not being a "good provider" for his family.

Solution-Oriented Interviewing with Families

As we watch our work on video, we have noticed that we typically use seven strategies during the interview to accomplish the therapeutic ends. Here is a summary of these strategies with an elaboration of why and how each is used.

1. *Summarize, validate, and soften*

   This strategy ensures that the therapist is listening adequately, as well as validating each person without taking sides. In addition, through slight word changes, the therapist can soften what might be a blaming or discouraging communication from one partner to another.

2. *Self-disclosure/storytelling*

   This strategy has several functions. One is to join and more equalize the relationship (we all have issues and struggles in relationships, not just clients). Another is to normalize by helping families realize that others may have the same kinds of issues, points of view, or feelings. The last element of this strategy is to suggest new possibilities for actions or points of view.

3. *Identifying and tracking problem patterns*

   This strategy, often combined with getting specific, helps the therapist understand what the couple or one partner is concerned about and how he or she experiences the problematic situation. In addition to getting an idea of the problem, the therapist is searching for typical patterns in the problematic interactions or situations.

4. *Identifying and tracking solution patterns*

   This strategy, again often combined with getting specific, is used to evoke and highlight more helpful actions and points of view related to the problem based on the family's past experience.

5. *Suggesting possibilities*

   This strategy offers ideas from the therapist's experience that might be helpful in the future, either based on what the family has said so far (usually derived from the solution patterns) or based on some ideas the therapist has. It is important to give these suggestions in a tentative manner, not to impose them on families. But it is just as important not to leave the therapist's ideas out of the conversation in the name of neutrality or a nonexpert position.

6. *Getting specific/action descriptions*

   This strategy involves getting the couple to tell the therapist about specific incidents and actions, so the therapist can understand the couple's situation without having to project or interpret as much as would be necessary with more vague descriptions. This often involves the use of what we call "videotalk," that is, having family members describe the situation as if it could be seen and heard on a videotape.

7. *Naming classes of solution or problems and initiating searches*
This strategy involves using vague, general words or inquiries to facilitate the evocation and organization of problem or solution categories or specific incidents that could be examples of those categories.

Promoting and Provoking Change between Sessions

Someone once asked Bill after he had given a presentation on therapy: "I'm not clear. Are you of the opinion that change mostly takes place in the session or between sessions in therapy?" Bill's succinct reply was, "Yes," which drew a laugh but was actually quite serious. Solution-oriented therapy uses both arenas, in session and between sessions, to promote change.

We often give clients action plans or ideas to remember to further the changes we have begun in our office meetings with them. We put a premium on getting families to do things or notice new, more helpful things in their lives. These assignments are experiments that both provide the opportunity for change and mastery and provide more information for the therapist. We design those assignments collaboratively with our clients and use carboned forms to both facilitate follow-through (they are more likely to be remembered and carried out if they are written down) and follow-up (we are more likely to remember to ask about the task if we have a copy in the chart and they are more likely to take further assignments seriously if they see we follow up).

We heard about an experiment that a physician carried out some years ago. He dictated his medical notes after seeing each patient and then arranged for the notes for half of his patients (randomly chosen) to be sent a copy of the notes in a letter form and the other half to receive nothing in the mail (except the bill, of course). Follow-up indicated that the patients who received the letter perceived the doctor as more competent and thorough and the care they received as much better than the patients who received no letter. The care given was no different, only the letter. We recommend sending follow-up letters not only to enhance clients' perceptions of clinicians' services but to further therapeutic gains as well. The letters can summarize progress made in the session, reinforce new perceptions, and urge families to follow through on the tasks agreed-on in the session. Another way to carry out between-session changes is to do individual sessions with one or more family members between the conjoint family sessions.

Summary

- Create a collaborative environment.
- Determine who to see and what to work on early in the process of therapy.

- Acknowledge the feelings and points of view of various family members.
- Focus on changing the viewing, the doing, and the context.
- Disrupt or change problem patterns of viewing, doing, and the context.
- Evoke solution patterns of viewing, doing, and the context.
- Keep change going between and outside of sessions with letters, tasks, and individual sessions.

Family therapy is fraught with a myriad of pitfalls and possibilities for change. Many therapists spend their careers avoiding or dreading these sessions and their characteristic flashpoints and reluctantly hostile participants. Solution-oriented therapy offers a collaborative problem-solving approach that provides a way to transform these sessions from dreaded encounters to powerful (and enjoyable) means for effecting change with children's or family problems.

Further Resources and Training

Currently, there are no certificate programs for brief solution-oriented therapy. Intensive training courses with supervised practice are available through Possibilities, 551 W. Cordova Rd., #715, Santa Fe, NM 87501, USA, 505.983.2843, fax 505.983.2761, E-mail: PossiBill@aol.com; Web site: http://www.brieftherapy. com. Visit the Web site for more information on books, tapes, and training seminars.

REFERENCES

Bertolino, B. (1998). *Therapy with troubled teenagers: Rewriting young lives in progress.* New York: Wiley.

Bertolino, B., & O'Hanlon, B. (2001). *Collaborative, competency-based counseling and psychotherapy: A basic manual for interviewing, intervention, and change.* Boston, MA: Allyn & Bacon.

Bertolino, B., & Thompson, K. (1999). *The residential youth care worker in action: A collaborative, competency-based approach.* Binghamton, NY: Haworth.

Cade, B., & O'Hanlon, W. H. (1993). *A brief guide to brief therapy.* New York: Norton.

Dolan, Y. (1991). *Resolving sexual abuse.* New York: Norton.

Durrant, M. (1993). *Residential treatment: A cooperative, competency-based approach to therapy and program design.* New York: Norton.

Durrant, M. (1994). *Creative strategies for school problems.* New York: Norton.

Furman, B., & Ahola, T. (1992). *Solution talk: Hosting therapeutic conversations.* New York: Norton.

Hubble, M. A., & O'Hanlon, W. H. (1992). Theory countertransference. *Dulwich Centre Newsletter,* 25–30.

Hudson, P. O., & O'Hanlon, W. H. (1992). *Rewriting love stories: Brief marital therapy.* New York: Norton.

Levy, R., O'Hanlon, B., with Goode, T. (2001). *You can't make me!: Successfully managing strongwilled, oppositional and defiant children.* Emmaus, PA: Rodale.

Metcalf, L. (1995). *Counseling towards solutions: A practical solution-focused program for working with students, teachers, and parents.* New York: Center for Applied Research in Education.

O'Hanlon, B. (1996). *Do one thing different.* New York: William Morrow.

O'Hanlon, B., & Bertolino, B. (1998a). *Even from a broken web: Brief, respectful solution-oriented treatment of sexual abuse and trauma.* New York: John Wiley and Sons.

O'Hanlon, B., & Bertolino, B. (1998b). *Invitation to possibility-land: A teaching seminar with Bill O'Hanlon.* Philadelphia: Brunner/Mazel.

O'Hanlon, B., & Hudson, P. (1996). *Stop blaming, start loving.* New York: Norton.

O'Hanlon, B., & Wilk, J. (1987). *Shifting contexts: The generation of effective psychotherapy.* New York: Guilford.

O'Hanlon, S., & Bertolino, B. (1998). *Evolving possibilities: Bill O'Hanlon's selected papers.* Philadelphia: Brunner/Mazel.

O'Hanlon, W. H. (1987). *Taproots: Underlying principles of Milton Erickson's therapy and hypnosis.* New York: Norton.

O'Hanlon, W. H. & Weiner-Davis, M. (1988). *In search of solutions: A new direction in psychotherapy.* New York: Norton.

Schultheis, G., O'Hanlon, B., & O'Hanlon, S. (1998). *Brief couples therapy homework planner.* New York: John Wiley and Sons.

10 Brief Sex Therapy

DOMEENA C. RENSHAW

Domeena C. Renshaw

Brief Description of Theory

Sexual problems are as old as humanity. Causal theories included witchcraft, divine punishment, and brain degeneration. Havelock Ellis, a British physician, had to publish his six-volume *Studies of Sexual Psychology in Germany* in English because no publisher in Victorian England in 1905 would do so (Ellis, 1942). In the late nineteenth century, Sigmund Freud's psychoanalytic theory hypothesized that unconscious conflicts (beginning in childhood) caused many somatic complaints and included sexual problems of all kinds (Brill, 1938). He emphasized that sexuality (libido) was a natural drive with constant constraints (parental, social, moral, and legal), but did not suddenly appear at puberty. It was lifelong, from birth to death, and shaped each individual's personality. Besides childhood sexuality, Freud's other major original theory was of unconscious thoughts that formed an essential level of human motivations and behaviors. Preconscious thoughts were retrieved with some effort. Unconscious thoughts reached awareness only in dreams, slips of the tongue, art forms, or free association. They were disguised pleasure pursuits and included sexual, aggressive, and dependency tendencies. The unconscious was modified by learned personal controls and social–religious beliefs. Although opposed and contested, Freud's theories started a significant intellectual movement in U.S. thought. It became respectable to study psychology alongside neurology. Freudian ideas, such as castration anxiety, penis envy, dominant mother/weak father, and so forth, were discussed for years in psychoanalysis but did not reverse the patient's sexual symptoms around erection, ejaculation, or intercourse.

Religious factors in the West contributed to shame and guilt around nearly all sexual thoughts, fantasies, and expressions outside (as well as, at times, within) marriage (Green, 1992). Research into human sexual behavior was rare before the 1940s but emotional reactions were high. Alfred Kinsey's surveys of thousands of men and women in the 1940s and 1950s caused an uproar against sex research, but, for the first time, the studies provided objective evidence of the sexual expression of average adults in the United States and, subsequently, the Kinsey Institute for Sexual Research at Bloomington, Indiana, was formed (Kinsey, et al., 1948; 1953).

In the 1920s, a gynecologist–obstetrician, R. L. Dickinson, in Cleveland, was impressed with the number of marriages in which both partners were totally ignorant of their genital structure (Dickinson & Prerson, 1925). To assist them, he constructed life-size anatomical wax models of the pelvis and genitals, and then instructed such couples about sex. This is the first recorded conjoint (couples) sex therapy. William Masters, M.D., a reproductive specialist at Washington University School of Medicine, Department of Obstetrics and Gynecology, St. Louis, Missouri, was amazed, like Dickinson, at his women patients' lack of knowledge of their own genitals. He decided to devote a sabbatical to the study of those he thought would be women's sexual experts, namely, prostitutes. In face-to-face interviews, with the help of police in each city, he realized that these "ladies of the night" were no more well informed than his Midwest patients. He returned to the medical school and set up a clinical lab, the Reproductive Biology Research Foundation, to study sexual responses of 350 volunteer adult men and women in 1954. This research led to careful, reliable physical and physiological information at both subjective and objective levels of human sexual responses in both sexes (Masters & Johnson, 1966). Next, for five years he studied the clinical treatment of sexual inadequacies of 510 couples. This was his original two-week method, called "brief sex therapy" (Masters & Johnson, 1970).

Significant Characteristics of the Theory/Evolution of the Theory

The background of sex therapy is that, despite ancient superstitions regarding the magical, diabolic, or punitive causes of sexual symptoms, evolving treatments by primitive healers were not effective (Bullough, 1976; Tannahill, 1983). Medical awareness by the end of the nineteenth century speculated that genetic, degenerative, organic factors caused the many sexual symptoms patients brought to their physicians. A wide range of medications, electrical gadgets, and even surgical techniques were unsatisfactory as treatment (Holbrook, 1959). Freudian theories of unconscious conflict factors seemed to offer a promise of cure through psychoanalytical "talk therapy," but with years of such treatment the symptoms persisted (Brill, 1938).

Dickinson's sex education provided to couples in the 1930s helped many couples and inspired gynecologist William Masters to study sexual responses of men and women in a lab setting and scientifically document their similarities and differences. He was well informed on psychoanalytic theories. He was also impressed that psychiatrist Joseph Wolpe had, in the 1950s, successfully applied relaxation and behavior therapy to assist a few women to become orgasmic (Wolpe, 1958). He also knew that urologist, James Semans, had used a brief behavioral method in the mid-1950s, a penile "squeeze technique" with woman-on-top coital position to effectively reverse years of premature ejaculation problems (Semans, 1956). Alfred Kinsey's door-to-door U.S. studies in the late 1940s and 1950s had shown that both sexes were willing to discuss their sex practices. A decade of indifferent results from hormone replacements in women and men had not been of significant help with sex problems.

The need for sexual symptom help was confirmed when Masters proceeded from the sexual lab studies to brief (two-week) conjoint sex therapy after he had done a physical and genital examination (Masters & Johnson, 1970). A two-member sex-therapy team was said to offer each partner understanding, support, and representation by a same-sex therapist. This reduced the two-to-one polarization that might occur when a solo therapist sided with a particular partner. Many modifications of the Masters–Johnson model of sex therapy have evolved in the past three decades and include various nonphysician professionals and individual, group, even hypnosis sex therapy (Araoz, 1982). Countless unorthodox offers to help patients with sex problems have also been marketed.

What Makes This Theory Different or Unique?

Brief sex therapy in the Masters–Johnson Foundation model had specific features.

- It was brief (two weeks of daily, thirty-minute visits to the therapists).
- The couple stayed in a nearby hotel in St. Louis.
- It was conjoint (both partners were patients).
- Single patients with no collaborative partner were assigned a "replacement" partner (surrogate) to talk to, hold on to, learn from, to receive from and to give to. This was the most sensational and controversial part of brief sex therapy.
- A general physical plus a sexological examination of the genitals in the partner's presence was a mandatory part of the therapeutic sex education.

- The naturalness of sex was emphasized to reduce sexual shame.
- Therapeutic behavioral reinforcement (sexual exercises) were prescribed to be practiced in the privacy of the couples' bedroom. They would then return the next day and report their problems and progress.
- Directive sex therapists gave specific explicit behavioral sexual exercises for each partner and both partners together (unlike psychoanalytic therapy, in which the therapist was nondirective).
- Two therapists, one male and one female, conducted the treatment together.

How Is the Theory Like Others?

Physical and sexual examinations are done daily by all physicians—family physicians, internists, gynecologists, urologists, and endocrinologists—to exclude genital causes of the presenting sexual symptom. If indicated, they then provide medical or surgical treatment, e.g., hymenotomy for pain during intercourse or antibiotics for vaginal discharge, which may cause intercourse avoidance.

Philosophical and Historical Background

Ancient Times

Primitive art dating back more than several millennia depicts sexual contact and fertility in animals and humans. Written history from 1000 B.C. reveals sexual customs and behaviors. Women were regarded as property of a father or husband; men were free to have several partners; children were the property of the father; and prostitution was accepted as part of life (Tannahill, 1982).

Ancient Greece and Rome accepted homosexual contacts between men and boys after puberty, but sex between men and prepuberty boys broke the law and exclusive adult homosexual partners were frowned on, so there were mixed messages. There was a strong emphasis on marriage and family. Judaism in the Old Testament, and specifically in the Ten Commandments (Exodus 20:13), forbade adultery as sinful. Homosexuality was also condemned (Levitucus 18:22 and 21:13). However, in the Song of Songs, the pleasure and joy of sex was elevated, not discouraged or shame-ridden. Christianity also set many constraints around sexuality. Procreative marital sex was acceptable but sinfulness shrouded all other sexual expressions. In the ancient East, sexual attitudes varied, from the Hindu acceptance of sex as part of divine worship to some characterized by natural openness, for example, in China, Japan, and India. Women were seen as subservient and prostitution prevailed. Within nearly all cultures and societies, marriage is a legally and socially sanctioned union between a husband and a wife that accords status and inheritance to their offspring and is regulated by laws, beliefs, customs, and attitudes that prescribe the duties of partners.

In the Christian tradition, all recreational sex was considered forbidden and sinful in Europe. The nude human form crept into religious art forms as cherubs, angels, and dying martyrs. The predominance of Catholicism was challenged in 1517 by Martin Luther, a German ex-priest, later by John Calvin, a French ex-priest, and King Henry VIII of England. The Protestant Christian faith resulted from this movement of "reformation." Many splinter Protestant groups then formed. None showed sexual celebration or political and religious tolerance. In 1621, the Puritans left England and landed in search of political and religious freedom at Plymouth Rock, Massachusetts. Dogmatic prohibitions about sex prevailed and sexual inhibitions have not since disappeared. Some communities formed with polygamy as part of their religious beliefs (e.g., Mormons and Oneidans) but ran counter to the federal law of monogamy (Nordoff, 1966).

Contemporary Roman Catholic theologians since the 1970s no longer condemn masturbation and oral sex as perversions or heinous sins, instead regarding them as amoral realities where each individual must make his or her choice in the circumstance. Sex offence laws exist in each U.S. state as well as in federal laws. Some are centuries old and have rarely been used, but such laws condemn acts between consenting adults, e.g., anal sex. For people raised in strict orthodox beliefs, without an understanding of the now known normal range of sexual behaviors, anxieties and guilt may pervade a couples' relationship, particularly if one partner holds different and more liberal beliefs and wants to practice alternatives to traditional man-on-top intercourse (Boteach, 1999).

In this decade there has been a surge of conservative "born-again" Christians. They have affluence, higher education, are materialistic, and live active lifestyles, but live with a sexual silence that matches that of the Puritans, despite the contemporary eroticized media. Their rigid and restrictive sexual attitudes are a therapeutic challenge.

Changes, Stages of Theory Development

The Masters–Johnson Foundation brief sex therapy was centered in St. Louis, Missouri. They trained six or seven special dual-sex teams from different parts of the United States, hoping for an identical format of physical/sexological examinations, two weeks of daily thirty-minute couples' visits, and home exercises, to gain a similar 80 percent symptom-reversal rate. The therapist pairs included at least one physician from a specialty, gynecology, family medicine, or psychiatry, with an allied licensed health professional. Ideally, this therapeutic model resembled a business franchise. But adhering to the format was difficult. For the couple, it entailed two full weeks in a hotel with thirty-minute daily visits to the sex therapists. The rest of the days were spent as if the couple were on vacation. This turned out to be very costly for two working partners, and difficult therapy to provide in their hometown. The trained therapists could not command the high fee of the Masters–Johnson Institute nor was there enough patient volume to make a good income. These teams did not attain national recognition or sustain an "only brief sex therapy" practice.

What did occur was that the Masters–Johnson books, dull reading as they were (to ensure that no hint of prurience could be attributed to the authors) became best-sellers in a dozen languages. Literally hundreds of doctors, counselors, and therapists studied them and attempted to graft them onto their practice of infertility, gynecology, family medicine, endocrinology, urology, psychiatry and psychology, family therapy, social work and so on. Some even adopted hypnosex therapy (Araoz, 1982). They recommended segments of the books to their patients to read, to apply at home, and then return for a follow-up. No accurate studies exist of follow-ups to find the actual number of either therapists or people seeking sex therapy that resulted worldwide. In the United States, due to the explicit format in the Masters-Johnson writings as well their workshops, recommendations for behavioral home sexual exercises allowed thousands of psychologists, counselors (including pastoral counselors), social workers, family, and marriage therapists to enthusiastically adopt brief sex therapy and weave it into their regular style and method of clinical management and treatment. The number of physician sex therapists in the United States is small because it has been too time-intensive. Nonetheless, Masters–Johnson brief sex therapy has been modified to allow for elective training of medical students, postgraduate physicians, nurses, social workers, counselors, psychologists, and priests and ministers (Renshaw, 1995, 1996). These professionals will not run exclusive sex therapy practices but they are sexually educated and comfortable about discussing and responding to their patients' sexual questions.

What rapidly became apparent was that the demand for sexual help was large. However, no medical subspecialty or licensing exists for sex therapy. There is no established curriculum, nor board examinations to regulate the basic knowledge and clinical skills that physicians, nurses, and family therapists need. Anyone can (and does) set himself or herself up as a sex therapist. Many abuses have ensnared vulnerable patients and, of course, always hit the headlines. The public and other professionals still seek sex information but remain guarded about sex therapists.

Self-designated individuals have set themselves up as "sexual surrogates," with business cards to pass out. This is indefensible in the era of AIDS and HIV+. The risks to both patient and so-called surrogate are high for sexually transmitted diseases as well as for AIDS. For a woman "surrogate," her additional risk, due to multiple patient partners, is greatly increased for cervical cancer. Some states (Florida, Oregon) have prosecuted a sexual "surrogate" under prostitution laws. The use by Masters of women "surrogates" (thirteen Foundation women volunteer employees) was the most controversial and sensational part of their therapy (Masters & Johnson, 1970, 1980). In the experimental phase of the Foundation's treatment, there were several single insecure men with premature ejaculation. There was not yet enough study and knowledge about premature ejaculation, so volunteer employees were "indoctrinated" about a male's sexual function and his sexual fears so they could then provide psychological and sexual support and help him reverse his symptom. That program of surrogates abruptly ended in the 1970s for legal reasons.

Today, sex therapy for premature ejaculation is provided for a partnerless solo male patient by suggesting masturbation and then self-penile squeezing while he is on his back. This helps him to relax and control the ejaculation. He lasts longer, builds sexual self-confidence, and then can request that his partner at home be on top for coitus. It works well and has helped over forty men in the author's practice.

More recently, new antidepressants, SSRIs (specific serotonin reuptake inhibitors), that cause the unwanted side effect of delayed ejaculation among men and delayed orgasm among women, have been deliberately and successfully used for men with resistant premature ejaculation, e.g., sertraline (Zoloft) 25 mg to 50 mg used two to four hours before intercourse, not daily. This treatment can be of definite help. Several other SSRIs have been used with similar success (Keller, Hamer, & Rosen, 1997; *The Medical Letter*, 1992; Seagraves, 1998).

Since the 1960s, clinical urologists have been in the forefront of sex research and treatment of impotence or erectile dysfunction (ED) (Goldstein & Rothstein, 1990). The search for penile rigidity began when a surgeon removed a rib and inserted it into the patient's soft penis. Soon it was discovered that blood phagocyte cells absorbed this rib (as a foreign body) within twelve to eighteen months. Solid silicone (Small Carrion) penile implants were invented. They were reasonably priced and many patients had them inserted after radical prostatectomy. However, there was then a constant, embarrassing semierection, so patients always had to wear a tight truss in public.

Next, when a man's penis unexpectedly became erect when a defective Foley bladder catheter was inserted, a Texas urologist invented inflatable penile implants. He placed a reservoir of silicone fluid in the abdominal wall that could be activated by air pumped from a valve in the scrotum. This pressure moved the silicone fluid into hollow cylinders implanted in the cylindrical left and right penile crurae. A mechanical erection resulted, and it could be inflated in private. Deflation of the erection made a defizzing sound, so the patient needed a private place and time to do so. Ejaculation occurred only if he could do so before the penile implant surgery. Each potential recipient needed to be told that that there might be no orgasm for him. The capacity to please his partner is often of great joy and pride to a sensitive lover who wishes to share his partner's pleasure even if he cannot ejaculate. If he is insensitive, he might urgently try to ejaculate and continue pumping for two hours, bathed in sweat, and exhausted. One patient ignored his partner's requests to stop. His upset wife said, "I'm raw," and went to a gynecologist with painful, swollen, inflamed genitals.

The price for an inflatable penis, which ranged from $6,000 to $12,000, occasionally was covered by VA hospitals and some insurance. The side effects of the implantation were also costly: leakage of the silicone reservoir, twisting and blockage of the lengths of tubing, erosion (it is a foreign body) and infection. This could necessitate extubation, another costly surgical procedure. But patients with erectile dysfunction (ED) taught their physicians how important erections were to many men of all ages when they continued to seek costly ED treatment (Lue, 1992).

Refined, improved silicone implants with single cylinders and a smaller reservoir were produced, but urologists had many hundreds of patients with ED and they continued to research the feasibility of penile injections. Unbelievably, men by the thousands were willing to endure the pain of having papaverine combinations, with enhancers such as phentolamine, regitine, or prostaglandin (E), injected into their penises which, after twenty to forty minutes produced a chemical erection that lasted twenty to thirty minutes. Sometimes, it resulted in priapism (a long, sustained erection that lasted over three hours), which could be destructive to the tissue of the penis. The patient was warned that this was a medical emergency for which he would need a counteracting injection of norepinephrine into his penis. Surgery was, at times, necessary to treat the priapism.

The patient who accepted penile injection therapy was taught how to inject the medication and given a prescription for it. The reckless celebrated with papaverine parties with friends. One pharmaceutical company invented single disposable kits that were more convenient, accurate, and penis friendly, but shots are shots. Eighty percent of the men given penile injection therapy were capable of having erections. The bad effects for some were fibrosis and a curved penis. The same chemicals were next packaged for insertion into the urethra to be absorbed. Only about 40 percent of these worked, however, for many patients, the chemicals caused a burning pain in the penis. Pain is not conducive to sexual arousal for men or women.

The search continued for a better, easier treatment for the estimated 40 million U.S. men with impotence. Vacuum erection devices (V.E.D.), by prescription, were marketed in the 1980s. The noninvasive pump worked empirically to draw blood by vacuum suction into the penis where it was retained by an elastic band around the root of the penis. This provided sufficient rigidity for penetration of an accepting cooperative partner, but the man could ejaculate only after the ring was removed. A thirty-minute limit for the band was emphasized because it blocked circulation. The negative side effects? The method was unromantic (although the inflation process could be done in private before coitus), and caused discomfort, numbness, and discoloration (temporary) of the penis. If the patient left the elastic ring on because of forgetfulness, having drunk too much alcohol, or falling asleep, gangrene of the penis resulted. Although rare, this has been reported. Some nonprescription pumps were also marketed.

Since the 1998 arrival of Viagra, (Goldstein, 1998), four of the five companies that manufactured V.E.D.s closed down. However, for cardiac patients who require nitrate medication, yet have ED, and want to engage in intercourse, the V.E.D. may still be a valuable prescription. The price is moderate (close to $400).

In the 1980s, soon after heart bypass surgery became frequent, vascular study of the penis began on a large scale. By the mid-1990s, however, penile blood flow tests were challenged as not sufficiently accurate. Bypass revascularization microsurgery, which can take up to eight hours (with a resulting cost of $40,000) brings the inferior epigastric artery from the abdominal wall to the penis. Postoperative thrombosis and a reported success rate ranging from 20 to 80 percent has made its usefulness questionable. The surgery is now performed only on young males after severe trauma, such as a pelvic fracture. The majority of men over fifty years with arteriosclerosis are poor candidates for this procedure. Another controversial surgical procedure was ligating (or tying) penile venous leaks (similar to varicose veins), after study of the penile cavernosa by cavernography. Restored potency results range from 28 percent to 73 percent, and the procedure is still viewed as "experimental."

In England, in about 1990, a study was being conducted for cardiac chest pain with a drug called sildenafil citrate, a selective enzyme inhibitor of nitric oxide that acts to dilate the coronary blood vessels. It did not seem to lessen the chest pain. However, at the end of the study, the male patients were not returning the unused pills, and one nurse asked a patient why. He replied with a smile that it worked "below the belt." She passed this on to a physician at the pharmaceutical company involved. For some reason the company was slow to act, and it was seven years before they carried out the necessary ED studies. They were surprised by the results and the billion-dollar "miracle" drug sildenafil citrate, now packaged in the blue diamond-shaped pill was called Viagra. There was much unexpected free anticipatory media fanfare and endless jokes in the United States before its release in April 1998. In fact, because of the publicity, smiles, and cartoons, the very word *Viagra* brought laughter. Ten-year-olds cured a fallen cowboy with Viagra in their school play! (I have said the blue pill should have been bright yellow with a smiley face!) There was a rush for prescriptions, not only by affected men but also by their women partners, because they, too, were silently affected by their partners' ED (Renshaw, 1981). Because Viagra increased blood flow for older men, it was dubbed the "youth pill." Although Viagra was not approved for women, both sexes hoped it would work for women as an aphrodisiac or as an "orgasm pill." It did not, despite a few dramatic placebo reports. The studies on women and Viagra showed disappointing responses: The effects were no better than a placebo (577 women) (Basson, MacInnes, Smith, . . . 2000; Shen, Urosevich, & Clayton, 1999).

Many questions arose. All Viagra tablets, whether in doses of 25 mg., 50 mg., or 100 mg., were priced at $10 each. Some insurance companies allowed six pills per month, some did not. How would it impact couples? That depended on each couple. For some, both partners were joyous. Preliminary love play was essential to obtain the restored erection. If the woman was relieved that her partner no longer had erections, she might complain: "I'm so dry at fifty-nine, but he comes home at sixty-five with six Viagra pills. If I don't play along he'll find a young partner. What's there to boost my desire?" Extra lubrication and hormone replacement usually worked to reduce her pain during intercourse. Physician or counselor encouragement can also help because the woman is now free of pregnancy concerns and she can more freely enjoy lovemaking. Therapeutic encouragement to use fantasy for arousal can reverse the stereotype that sex is only for young people. Many seniors are still very sexual (Brecher, 1982).

Some men were concerned about reported deaths after the use of Viagra. Of the millions of Viagra prescriptions, only sixty-nine deaths were verified as occurring within four to six hours after intercourse. With no medication at all, 0.6 percent of coitus efforts are reported to result in a coital death (Derogatis, & King, 1981). The mechanisms of some of the Viagra deaths were related to overdoses (three to eight times the 100 mg. maximum dose) or the use of nitrate medication for heart problems at the same time (contraindicated). None of the deaths could be categorically blamed on sildenafil.

Sometimes a patient reports that "Viagra didn't work." Absence of foreplay or conflict between a couple will require some intervention and repeated instruction about preliminary love play and then a retrial of Viagra. In these cases, the success rate with Viagra is 70 to 80 percent. Competing erection pills have been under study and will certainly hit the market. Herbs and over-the-counter "cures" of various kinds, salves, inhalers, and so forth, are constantly advertised, but all require caution to avoid harmful effects and interactions with needed medication.

Meantime, while the urologists were evolving their new potency subspecialty, many gynecologists (reproductive subspecialists) had been working to reverse women's fertility problems by artificial insemination, in vitro fertilization, or surrogate motherhood, interventions that required elaborate legal contracts. Can infertility cause sexual dysfunctions? The answer is yes. The urgency, sense of emptiness, and pressure to conceive may result in anxiety, depression, self-blame, partner blame, or turn lovemaking into mechanical baby-making with tears and grief every time a woman's menstrual period dashes her hopes for a pregnancy. These possible reactions should be mentioned by the infertility clinician to the couple in order to prevent or deal with problems if they surface during fertility treatments.

Female hormone levels have been measured and adjusted without major desire escalation for the thousands of women who were seeking help for low libido. Addition of testosterone was controversial, but used in the late 1970s, and it is again being used (Tuiten, et al., 2000). The blood level of testosterone in women is barely detectable, 0 to 70 ngm/cc (in men it is 250–1200 ngm/cc), yet testosterone patches or combination pills were given to women, sometimes with tragic effects such as unwanted virilization and suicide. Is there such a thing as a *tiny* dose? Always, without exception, before any attempt to use androgen, no matter how little or how briefly, an early morning (before 9:00 A.M.) blood testosterone level should be done for the woman patient and, only then, used if indicated. The blood test, however, is rarely done.

There are no accurate statistics on how many women have low desire or hypoactive desire (HSD) or no desire. The symptom is not gender-specific. Hundreds of men also present for sex therapy with low desire (Katz & Jardine, 1999). It is not unusual to blame the marriage for HSD: "It started after we got married" or "after the second child." Work may also be offered as a factor: "The problem began when I got a promotion." Overload, fatigue, role change, early sexual trauma, and taking each other for granted are all possible issues to be raised in treatment (Maltz,

1991; Renshaw, 1989). Lack of sexual fantasy can cause HSD. When there is no longer courtship or pursuit of each other, no compliments, no smiles, or anticipatory thoughts of being together, but only predictable couples' routines, the sexual excitement may subside. Keeping those special fantasies of past sexual highs are the most reliable aphrodisiacs or desire triggers for each person.

To mimic men's vacuum erection devices, there is now a new, small, vacuum battery-operated device for the clitoris called "Eros." It is the size of a computer mouse, has a thumb-sized "cap" to fit over the clitoris, and it provides suction, vibration, and pulses when turned on. It has to be physician-prescribed, has been FDA approved (2000), and sells for about $360. Will women pay so much? Will their partners give them one? It is not returnable in the age of AIDS. Will insurance companies pay? Will some women refuse it, even as a gift? Perhaps. Eros has no aphrodisiac powers, but if, indeed, the claimed sensations and clitoral swelling can enhance vaginal lubrication, then women may experience climax. If they use it with their partner present, it could bring them closer so that he can share and enhance her pleasure.

Another change that evolved at the Masters–Johnson Foundation was beginning to study and treat symptomatic homosexual couples with the same brief two-week sex therapy (Diament, 1989; Masters & Johnson, 1979). Other therapists also do gay couple brief sex therapy.

Relevant Research Related to Theory

While it did not focus on couples in sex therapy, a sociological study of close to 6,000 couples was conducted that encompassed heterosexual married, cohabiting, unmarried, also gay, and lesbian couples in the sample (Blumstein & Pepper, 1983). It provided a valuable follow-up to the Kinsey studies of the 1940s and 1950s. In 1994, another sociological study by the University of Chicago group headed by E. O. Lauman et al., *The Social Organization of Sexuality: Sexual Practices in the United States*, revealed that 43 percent of women and 31 percent of men reported sexual dysfunctions. The high number of people with problems made headlines. Gynecologists and family physicians confirm that women today present with almost as many sexual symptoms as do men.

Clinical Perspective

View of Human Sexual Functioning

Individual sexual responses occur from conception to death, whether they are expressed or not. In utero, ultrasound can detect the penis of a male fetus and even note the tiny erections. In countries like Pakistan and India, this early detection has made it lethal for a female fetus, because, due to the cost of a dowry for her to marry, the upset mother will cross the street to a legal abortion clinic and so prevent the birth of a daughter. Another underemphasized sexual fact is that *not* expressing one's sexuality is quite normal. Both sexes can choose abstinence or celibacy. There will be no physical harm to the celibate man or woman. Permanent control of other vital functions, breathing, eating, sleeping, urinating, and so on, will kill the self. Not so for sex. Celibacy only prevents a future generation.

Sexual responses in both men and women are there twenty-four hours a day, recurring in a diurnal rhythm, even during sleep. Each individual will recognize, ignore, control, or express sexuality in complex, learned ways, depending on the culture, the family, or religious beliefs. From infancy onward, the rights and wrongs are taught and learned of nudity, dress, privacy, cleanliness, and genital touch, what is allowed or forbidden. Personal autonomy begins when a child expresses sexual pleasure privately despite parental or other sanctions. Masturbation is now known to be natural and normal. However, because it has been labeled as gross, sinful, or perverted, some will struggle with anxiety and guilt, particularly those raised with the "new wave" of restrictive beliefs during the 1990s. A physician's best gift to his or her community is to educate religious leaders about scientific sexual facts, because masturbation, even today, can be regarded with ignorance and cause inappropriate guilt. Masturbation is essential as a diagnostic test for an impotent male and a necessary part of assisting a nonorgasmic woman to explore her path to orgasm and to share the information with her partner so they can enjoy improved closeness and mutual release (Renshaw, 1995).

The *Diagnostic and Statistical Manual of Mental Disorders* (1994), Fourth edition, lists the sexual symptoms that present for treatment.

Men

Primary impotence (male virgin)—302.74
Secondary impotence (psychogenic)—302.74
Physical impotence—607.84
Premature ejaculation—302.75
Delayed ejaculation—608.89
Dyspareunia (pain on intercourse)—302.76
Hypoactive sexual desire—302.71

Women

Primary anorgasmia—302.72
Secondary anorgasmia—302.72
Dyspareunia (pain)—302.76
Vaginismus—306.51
Hypoactive sexual desire—302.71

For both

Unconsummated marriages (not listed in *DSM-IV* or ICD-9)
Sexual aversion/anxiety—302.79

(Vroege, Gijs, & Hengeveld, 1998).

Sex therapy does not conflict with theories of mental illness. Specified diagnostic criteria for each emotional illness are to be considered and can be identified at the same time as a sexual dysfunction (Renshaw, 1975, 1981, 1987, 1997). Are there mental conditions in which sexual symptoms are more frequent? Most certainly, yes. Substance abuse, including alcohol and street drugs as well as prescribed sedative, hypnotic, anxiolytic, antidepressant, antipsychotic, antihypertensive, cardiac, seizure, and several other medications, may result in hypoactive sexual desire, impotence, delayed ejaculation or orgasm, and dyspareunia (if there is dryness of the vagina as a reaction).

In the Masters–Johnson 1960s phase of researching sexual responses, men and women with both physical and/or emotional illness or medications were excluded. However, many patients with emotional illness have a sexual symptom that may predate their diagnosis and treatment. Sometimes a new sexual symptom may result from a helpful medication being used for anxiety, depression, anorexia nervosa, or some other emotional problem. Sex therapy can proceed by providing sex education about the sex symptom as well as the emotional condition and the sexual side effects of the needed medications. It is useful for the patient to get a pharmacy printout regarding the medication's side effects and check under "genito-urinary" to see whether libido, orgasm, erection, or ejaculation effects are listed. Anxiety will be a factor with a patient of either sex who has an aversion or pain disorder (usually anticipatory rather than actual pain). If uncertain, the non-physician sex therapist can refer the patient for a genital examination to exclude newly occurring physical factors. Patients with major depression, bipolar illness, chronic anxiety, and psychosis in remission have all done well with brief sex therapy. It is unkind and unethical to exclude them from therapy.

Substance Abuse

If couples present for sex therapy with alcohol abuse in remission, they do as well as other couples, but the residue from previous hurts around alcohol excess must be discussed and resolved. When current alcoholics (especially those who combine alcohol with prescribed psychotropics, which enhance the effects of alcohol) enter a brief sex therapy contract, management is usually complex and difficult (Renshaw, 1975). The same is true for people who use street drugs: pot, cocaine, and crack. If used on and off or regularly during sex therapy, such drugs aggravate the problems. The video, *Family Therapy with the Experts: Sex Therapy* (Renshaw, 2001) shows how alcohol and drug use can result in marital and sexual problems.

Jennifer, in her twenties, volunteered the couple for the interview. However, her husband, on disability leave for knee injuries, at the last minute failed to show up. She was disappointed and upset but, determined to seek help, packed her infant with his stroller into the car and came without her husband. What was the symptom which she presented for help? There had been no sex for over two years, since the pregnancy was confirmed.

Renshaw w/ clients

It is noteworthy that neither she nor her husband had a mechanical sexual symptom. Jennifer's husband would have been diagnosed with HSD (Hypoactive sexual desire, 302.71) and substance abuse alcohol/cocaine dependence (303.9 + 304.2), if and when he revealed these. But it was Jennifer, a sexually non-symptomatic partner, who presented for sex therapy. She showed no emotional or mental illness. For her, the correctly applicable diagnostic code is *309.9* (adjustment reaction of adult life). Yes, she had tears; yes, she had anxiety, anger, and sadness; but all of these symptoms were normal and of insufficient severity or duration to make another diagnosis. During the one-hour interview, she displayed adequate perspective and awareness to predict that these feelings of anxiety and upset would reverse if the marriage could be restored. She did not want or need medications. Because daily sex had been a vital aspect of their closeness, its loss was devastating to her, and she was looking for a way to restore it. Her upset resulted from the fact that she loved her husband and he loved their baby, but he had refused couples' therapy after he promised but refused to continue after only one visit. She had left him for a few days but this had not caused a change in his behavior. A second separation and her threat of divorce had resulted in his promise for cooperation in marital counseling, which he had broken. Now he said, "Get a divorce."

Her history revealed that, after her pregnancy was confirmed, her husband slept on the couch. They had copurchased a home and lived together over a year before that happened. They had partied and both had used alcohol together. She stopped drinking alcohol immediately when she knew she was pregnant. They then went to Las Vegas for a few days and, on impulse, they got married there. "We wanted the house more than a big wedding." The wedding ring, however, did not change his sexual avoidance. Unknown factors for the absent partner in Jennifer's case need to be identified: Did he feel deceived or tricked by this pregnancy? Did the condom tear or was the birth control pill stopped? Did he think intercourse during pregnancy would harm the baby? Did he realize how hurt/rejected Jennifer felt when he refused her overtures for sex? Did Jennifer ever turn down his overtures for sex? When he stayed away all night, where was he? How much was he drinking? Was he using any drugs? What? How much? Did he have erection problems? Desire problems? How frequently per week was he masturbating? Were there police problems? Money problems? What did he see as his biggest problem? Does he love Jennifer? And the baby? How does he think things can be improved at home? Is there another sexual partner?

As the interview proceeded, Jennifer revealed that she was raised in a turbulent home where an alcoholic father repeatedly beat her mother, who several times left with Jennifer and her brother but returned to him. A younger sister was born. Jennifer saw herself as her caretaker because her mother worked three jobs and finally divorced. At age seventeen, she left home, got beauty culture training, and "did a lot of crack. I thought nothing of it. But one day I just quit" (the crack and those friends). She mentioned, at the very end of the interview, that she regretted telling "so much of my past" to her husband, whom she now thought was on drugs, not alcohol, because, as she herself had used both, she could recognize the signs of cocaine use. For a while, she had followed him at night to check if he was having an affair and found none, and her husband's best friend told her there was not another woman. Because she had struggled with self-blame, it was possible, she worried, that he had been attracted to crack after hearing about her experiences. With further visits the question of how the husband got into cocaine needs to be asked.

If she is correct and he is on cocaine, that dependence is well known, after a brief "sexual high," to result in sexual apathy. Instead, the user engages in an enduring and intense obsessive pursuit for more cocaine. It is a truly destructive addiction with compounded medical risks due to the unknown chemical additives in street drugs. The cost of abuse escalates, as do risks of police raids or arrest.

Jennifer is bright and feels as though she grew up early, at 12, due to family chaos and rupture. She met her husband in a bar; they became social and sexual playmates and then decided to become solid citizens and copurchased a home. Both worked and went to classes but kept separate monies. Motherhood occurred and then marriage, which was a major life change for Jennifer. She stopped drinking alcohol.

For her husband, the change had different results. He totally withdrew physically from sex and from their bedroom, and Jennifer feels that he now emotionally rejects her. Yet, she says he is a "great father." Although he is now on work disability and awaiting more knee surgery, he is in a construction union and receives full pay. The layoff has not been positive. He refuses to tell her how he feels. She admits to provoking fights with him to get some response but these have not helped. "I need to talk. He doesn't." Gender differences are clear-cut for this couple.

His supportive family knew nothing of their problems until the day of this interview. Currently, her divorced father had returned to Illinois, has an apartment, and remains in A.A., dry for some years now. He loves her, her husband,

and the baby and has been very supportive. On her second separation, she stayed with him and they are now close. Her mother is still a strength for her but her mother's home is crowded with grandparents, aunts, and her challenging sixteen-year-old sister. Jennifer stayed with her mother during the first separation, but it was too noisy there. Her mother was Jennifer's standby and support during the delivery, C-section, and her return home. Her mother understands addiction and loves her son-in-law.

How does sex therapy fit into this case? Jennifer chose this subspecialty by saying there was a major sex problem. There is no way to bring in the absent partner in this case until he is ready, albeit reluctant. The sex therapist's task is to get as explicit a sex history as possible. Jennifer was clear that neither of them had symptoms and that both had previously enjoyed their almost daily sex until the pregnancy. The husband might not regard his deliberate avoidance as a sexual symptom. After he withdrew sexually, she said she would approach him but was repeatedly rebuffed. "You get used to doing without it."

This would have been a good time to inquire about the frequency of Jennifer's masturbation. Did she have inhibitions around it? The sex therapist could reassure her that masturbation is both a natural and a normal release of sexual tension, which could make her less vulnerable and less angry at her husbands' sexual refusal or avoidance rather than allow the build up of sexual tension. Although she had now told her mother, her father, and her father-in-law about their need for couples counseling (correctly so), she still showed much hurt and anger. On this first interview she had a great need to talk and to seek affirmation. The masturbation question could wait for discussion on follow-up, but it should not be neglected by the therapist because it is a significant part of the complete sex history, and could possibly help as she tries to restore the marriage.

What also unfolded was that, on some occasions, the conflict between them would lead to blows and hair pulling. However, she minimized the severity because she considered it less violent than what she had witnessed between her parents. Domestic violence has recurred in this generation so the therapist must be concerned about perpetuation of it in their son's life. Is she a battered wife? She denied this, saying that she had provoked some of the fights. "Non-violence" is a clear rule to emphasize in couples' therapy, which includes sex therapy. The stereotypic defense of the perpetrator by the battered spouse, her leaving and returning, are aspects that Jennifer shows ("I'm sure I provoked it"), so the alert therapist will record this information and check on further risks of violence e.g., "If you do X, how might your husband respond?" "If he is high on drugs, would he hurt the baby?" "Could you take the baby and go to your father's home again for safety?" "How safe are you now?"

How Change Occurs

The difficulty at this point is that Jennifer describes a standoff, her husband's sustained withdrawal and avoidance. The most recent crisis was her telling him the day of the interview that she had phoned his father for help, which she says he saw as a betrayal that angered him. Could her father-in-law (who is close to his grandson and to Jennifer) persuade her husband to try some counseling? Sometimes that is possible. The best friend might also be an ally, someone who could convince her husband to confront the cocaine/alcohol use. Jennifer's father tried to get the husband to go with him to A.A., but he refused. Addiction to substances is a tenacious disease. Sometimes it takes a crisis—facing death of oneself or a close person (the baby, Jennifer, or a parent)—to precipitate a decision to change. Jennifer's threat of divorce didn't work as she hoped it would. Occasionally, job loss or a religious conversion can be a reality test to make someone aware of how severe the impact of their behavior is on others.

Meantimes, individual counseling (fortunately, Jennifer has good insurance coverage) can help her to remain in a healthy "holding" pattern herself, stay on her job, nurture the baby, and keep growing. At this point she, in fact, does not see divorce as an option. She will probably support him during the next knee surgery and rehabilitation, which might hamper his drug seeking. His return to work might further help if it restores his self-value. He may relent without couples' therapy and return to the marital bed, as her mother did a generation ago. The individual therapist must discuss birth control and carefully remind Jennifer of the catastrophic reaction her husband had to this pregnancy to prevent a recurrence.

Range of Application

Sex therapy will be limited if the husband's substance abuse persists. Later, there may be medical (brain) sequelae from whatever street chemicals he abused or, if he abused only alcohol, there could be liver damage. Such medical problems would have been picked up at his surgery and anesthesia workup. Jennifer did not report any educational, police, or emotional problems in her husband before their marriage that might interfere with sex therapy. He managed to get his artisan training and Union card—both strengths—as well as being a good parent and his needing to please his father.

Application to Various Diagnoses

If Jennifer presented with distress, such as high anxiety or depression that disturbed her sleeping, eating, hygiene, baby care, or work at home or at the beauty shop, then the possibility of a diagnosis of depression, panic attacks, and so on would be made with the appropriate medication prescribed. She had no learning disorders or prior conditions such as schizophrenia or bipolar disorder. If they existed, then the therapist should discuss the prescribed medications, how compliant Jennifer is as a patient, what side effects the drugs might cause, and how regular her medical follow-ups are. The sex therapy counseling would continue if Jennifer is stable. If she goes off her medications, then the therapists can help by asking her to consent to talk to the physician, and even have her call from the therapist's office to get her medication renewed and make a follow-up appointment.

If Jennifer had a sexual problem such as anorgasmia, then sex education would be the sex therapist's task, along with suggested reading, so Jennifer can practice at home (Barbach, 1991; Renshaw, 1995). Dyspareunia (pain during intercourse) would not have surfaced after the baby's birth due to Jennifer's husband's avoidance of sex. If there was pain, the therapist would strongly encourage her to return to the obstetrician–gynecologist specifically to check on this complaint. It was a long difficult breech (legs first) delivery that finally required a Cesarean section, so there was no episiotomy, which can cause coital pain during the first sexual activity after birth.

If her husband has developed erectile dysfunction (ED) or impotence, he needs referral to his primary doctor for a checkup. The cocaine or alcohol or the combination could cause reversible ED. It will take six to twelve weeks after he stops using drugs for erections to return.

Application to Diverse Family Forms

Consideration for Current Constraints

For about two years, Jennifer reports an emotional and sexual divorce in a superficially intact marriage with a sexually avoidant substance-abusing husband. She has been faithful, and her husband may also be faithful. This will be an issue to explore if and when he presents for solo or couple therapy. If she divorces, her emotional healing will take time, and trust will have to be rebuilt. It will take *time*, lots of time, until she will feel safe enough to relate to a new person. This can be discussed in individual therapy.

Relationship to Past

Jennifer volunteered her own childhood history of a turbulent and ruptured home and family due to her father's drinking, with her mother leaving and returning. Also, she had herself been on crack cocaine plus alcohol, and quit both substances. These early experiences have been stored, not denied. This has given her hope that her husband can change, too, as did her own father, although he ended up divorced. She wants to avoid divorce and says she plans now to remain in her home.

Therapist Stance, Style

Nature of Family–Counselor Relationship

Jennifer volunteered for a "one-time consultation" for this video interview as a couple when recruited by the counseling agency where she sought help. She felt in crisis and was pleased that her husband agreed. At the last minute, he took off. She was upset and cried but pulled herself together and came with the baby. Does this happen in everyday practice? Not infrequently. The inflexible thera-pist will say sorry, I only see couples for sex therapy. The flexible therapist will use the visit to assess, evaluate, and determine how to help the patient who presents.

The first interview cannot be thought of as "only data gathering." It is always that plus therapeutically relating to another in the professional custom and style of each therapist. Jennifer was reassured that she was intact mentally and relieved that she was listened to. Jennifer was open, not guarded, coopera-tive, verbal, descriptive, and intensely emotional, showing no hint of secrets, and apologetic for crying, but mentally intact and alert. The capacity to relate is a true personality strength. It is absent in autistic, psychotic, oppositional children, and in schizophrenic, paranoid, or narcissistic adults. Jennifer related warmly and well. Her report of close family relationships confirms this. She should do well in therapy.

My Mind Was Saying

Jennifer has lived a tough life. She was eight years old when her baby sister arrived after she and her seven-year-old brother returned with mom from Cali-fornia to their father, who was still drinking. Mother started working three jobs, so Jennifer became "little mother" at home for the next four years, until the vio-lence resulted in divorce. With her mother and siblings, she moved in with her grandmother. She managed her schooling but the bustle in the home drove her out on her own at 17. She was in beauty school training, and explored crack and the bar scene. She quit crack but continued alcohol. She met her husband in a bar and was strongly attracted by the undivided attention he gave her. Their sex was good and frequent. Both were hardworking. She suggested buying a house. He agreed. My self-talk said: It started with strong sexual attraction, alcohol, and play. Then their work ethic grounded them. Both birth families accepted the new partner. Jennifer was the leader: to buy the house, to get married in Vegas. Her husband went along.

The pregnancy question remains unclear. His reaction is dramatic and one she cannot control. He did not suggest abortion; she was clear about that. He has not rejected the baby. The pregnancy may be a deceit or a misunderstanding. Clar-ification is needed. It could be a path to reconciliation for them. Adjustment for all three in this new family will be enhanced if there is harmony instead of resent-ment, blame, and conflict

My self-talk also hoped that his surgery might require a medical workup as well as temporarily stopping the possible substance abuse. My medical self-talk was concerned about withdrawal reactions if he had complications, and that the surgeon should be told about the alcohol/drug use. This would be an ethically difficult issue for the counselor, but it could be raised with Jennifer, who could tell her husband to let the surgeon know about his drug or alcohol use before the operation to prevent the complications of withdrawal reactions.

Specific Interventions Related to Sex Therapy

Sex education from therapist to patients remains the most important assistance for sexual problems. Today, thirty years after the research on the sexual responses of men and women, millions have not read or heard of the Masters–Johnson studies.

Sometimes sexual symptoms result in unconsummated marriages of up to twenty-three years' duration. Loyola University has treated 158 of these. Occasionally a woman presents in a second unconsummated marriage, the first having been annulled. These women are a special challenge in treatment.

At any age, from in utero to the senium, orgasm is defined as a buildup of vasoneuromuscular genital tensions that culminate in a peak, with a sudden discharge of tensions, tonic–clonic muscle contractions of all large and small muscles of the body, followed by a return to the preexcitement state. During sexual arousal, there is an increase in heart rate, respiratory rate, blood pressure, and muscle tone, penile erection, and vaginal lubrication. The stimulus may be oneself (masturbation or fantasy), another person (same or opposite sex), or another species (animal). It must be emphasized in therapy that, for male and female, the phases or stages of the sexual responses are similar, but the average timing of the cycle is much longer for women (see Figure 10.1). This information allows the anorgasmic woman to be patient with herself as she learns her own responses. All people can be born with similar genital apparatuses, but capacities to be aroused and to respond differ. This latter capacity depends on an intact brain, spinal cord, peripheral and autonomic nerves, plus muscles, blood vessels, and end organs, as well as the individual's personality and his or her response to external erotic stimuli, whether sex is pleasurable, painful, or conflictual.

Sexual expression is the only instinct in which deliberate, sustained control or even complete suppression does not result in a threat to the life of the individual, as would cutting off breathing, eating, sleeping, elimination, or circulation. This fact must be considered in cases where "loss of desire" (HSD or Hypoactive Sexual Desire) is the presenting complaint. HSD must be carefully differentiated from selective, deliberate nonfunction with a particular partner as with Jennifer's husband. Is there desire with another partner or solo (masturbation)? That would be selective or situational HSD.

At times the avoidance is denied and more difficult to modify because the individual voices helplessness, "I want to feel sexual but I cannot." What is the clinician's responsibility here? Firstly, to exclude possible organic causes, although these are rare: myxedema, pituitary tumor, Addison's disease, severe anemia, radiotherapy, or medications, including barbiturates, antihypertensives, chemotherapy, SSRIs, or antipsychotics. If present, treatment of the disorder, or a change of drug or dose, may reverse the HSD. If there is no medical problem, conflictual factors within the individual must be sought or between them as partners. On occasion, beneath the alleged HSD is a sexual dysfunction or libido difference amenable to brief directive sex therapy. The subsequent relationship growth may be quite rewarding to the sex therapist.

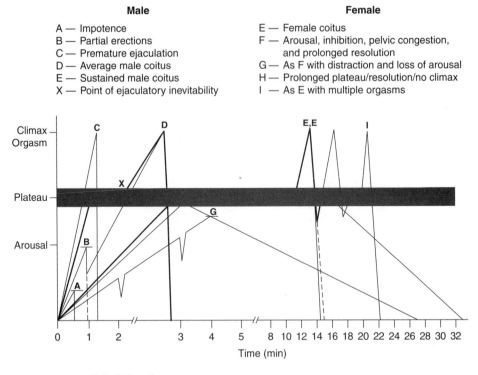

FIGURE 10.1 Coital Graph

An exceptional standard of excellence and professionalism is demanded of those who make ongoing contributions in this field. Those therapists who seek inappropriate sexual solutions or gratification for self in this sensitive, intimate, and demanding specialty can only bring discredit to the discipline and disaster to their patients and themselves. A supervised training experience in sex therapy for professionals allows for open discussion of the therapists' sexual feelings, enhances their growth, and prevents inappropriate intrusion of the therapists' own discomfort into the patient's therapy. The use of two therapists as part of training assists their learning by allowing, during supervision, on-site peer feedback about the clinical behavior of each when they were with the patient couple (Renshaw, 1996), but two therapists are often not cost-effective or possible. Much candor, flexibility, and exchange is demanded between members of a dual therapy team. Solo therapists can also do good counseling and intervention.

The methodological underpinnings of what has been called "The New Sex Therapy" are worth examining. The new therapy comprises a breakthrough in the treatment of sexual dysfunctions, even those of long duration, through brief behaviorally oriented directive outpatient sex therapy, which lasts from two to seven weeks. Masters and Johnson have been much criticized for being "simplistic," "mechanical," "cookbook," and "unscientific" (Zilbergeld & Evans, 1980), but their described sexual therapy techniques do work! The immediate results show that this method is effective. Follow-up, although very difficult, is essential for careful, ongoing scientific evaluation of the long-term outcome.

The basic principles of sex therapy are wholesome medical practice. First, an extensive medical, personal, and sexual history for each partner of a committed couple must be taken. Next, both individuals must have a careful physical examination from head to toe. Special patient education should be provided during the genital examination. Finally, the therapist must manage the couple's progress by giving them home directives for more open, affectionate sexual exchanges and improved communication. Masters and Johnson introduced two important clinical innovations:

1. Brief sex therapy over five or six visits with an individual or a couple;
2. Specific sexological examination of each patient, symptomatic or not, by the responsible physician, in the presence of the spouse.

The solo therapist in practice can request that a routine physical examination include a sexological examination when a sexual dysfunction presents to provide personal patient sex education in full light with a mirror for self-viewing in the presence of the partner, or with a nurse chaperone for a female solo patient. This removes the cloak of myth, mystery, and misinformation about the genitals. The sex therapist can promote acceptance by emphasizing ahead of time that the sight and sensation of the sexual organs are natural, normal, respectable, and potentially pleasurable.

In follow-up visits it may be necessary to explain comfortably, explicitly, and sometimes repeatedly, to the couple or individual patient about sexual anatomy and physiology, especially the asynchronous timing of male and female sexual organs in all the phases of sexual responses, using a basic visual aid (Figure 10.1). Also, the sex therapist should allow them to discuss any mistaken beliefs that may be causing shame, anxiety, or guilt.

Sex therapy suggests, and sometimes even prescribes, instructions for the couple to practice in the privacy of their own bedroom. This is permission-giving from a trusted authority. The goal is to involve both partners in pleasurable, relaxed exchanges and to break old, maladaptive, unsatisfactory sexual and communication patterns. Pressure to perform, penetrate, or be penetrated is avoided in the early weeks of sex therapy by suggesting different, less negative, relaxing nongenital body touch and massage, which will lead to more enjoyable affectionate and sexual responses. The positive reinforcements are effective because each partner has pleasant personal reactions and receives additional pleasure from the partner's pleasure as well and the approval of the sex therapist.

Even in 2001, about 80 percent of patients presenting sex problems still have faulty sex education and respond well to the opportunity for accurate sex information provided in sex therapy. Also, the careful elimination of possible physical causes and, if there are no medical problems, being told they are normal is reassuring.

Patients may seek permission and encouragement to explore and enjoy their closeness, affection, and sexuality at home, even those who regularly watch X-rated
movies. There is also value in recommending conservative self-help books for the
patients to read for enhanced sexual learning. (See Self-Help Books at the end of this
chapter.) However, in about 20 percent of the cases there may be many layers of
severe unresolved interpersonal problems between a couple, above and beyond
their sexual problems. Whether sex is the primary problem and conflict secondary
may be merely an academic question by the time they seek help. There may be
immediate sexual symptom reversal, but conflicts and distance will recur between
them unless they find a successful way to resolve daily conflicts. Sex therapy has
rapidly attained a popular acceptability, so that many patients view it as preferable
to psychotherapy, and deny a need for marital or individual counseling.

A great deal more than behavior therapy occurs in the intimate exchange of
sex therapy. Trust is built toward the sex therapist as a credible, concerned authority who will focus on the relationship. Reassurance, direction, and permission to
change, to express affection, and to be sexual are all provided. Destructive partner
exchanges are interpreted to the couple, often repeatedly. When there is resistance
to resolving their maladaptive way of relating, the therapist becomes a third party
who mirrors and models, so that their communication can improve. A few sessions may result in profound positive change.

At the risk of oversimplification, the alert sex therapist who treats sexual
dysfunctions can look for common contributing factors:

- clinical depression (which may require adequate antidepressants) and common fears: anxiety about impregnation, infection (herpes, VD, AIDS), pain,
  concern about sinfulness, the size of the penis, the adequacy of sexual performance, risking a possible coronary or stroke during coitus, and so on.
- emotional conflicts: anger at self or at each other, bringing up during lovemaking old remembered conflicts or current ones, or other resentments
- alcohol in excess (perhaps the most common worldwide cause of the first
  episode of secondary impotence in males); it can cause high anxiety and fear
  of future failed performance, with resultant psychogenic impotence
- drugs (whether legitimate, over-the-counter, or "recreational"), which may
  cause chemical impotence or anorgasmia

A sex therapist can do extra reading about the variety of ways in which different people, cultures, religions, and ages express and control their sexuality to
avoid misinterpretation of a patient's sexual beliefs and preferences or simply
ask: Where was this belief learned: family, country, religion? For each culturally
bound individual, early sexual learning results in sanctions or prohibitions that
may be retained for life. New learning may alter these. For some the ideas remain
fixed.

Interpersonal expression in sexual exchange is the ultimate outcome of all the
attitudes of the total person: toward self and others; toward pleasure, pain, time,
and performance; and toward beauty, ugliness, right, wrong, joy, or guilt. These

antecedent factors emerge in a careful sex history. Without this personal background for each patient, the sex therapist cannot bring a therapeutic perspective to understanding the sexual complaint and assisting in symptom removal.

Finally, differentiating between functional and physical sexual dysfunctions may be done inexpensively with a diagnostic clinical trial of a few weeks of modified sex therapy. The couple's affectionate relationship may be improved and their sexual alternatives broadened. Specific lab tests to prove an organic base for impotence or HSD are complex and difficult despite modern technology (Masters, Johnson, & Kolodny, 1995).

For many medical conditions, such as stroke, open-heart surgery, post-prostatectomy or hysterectomy, diabetes, hypertension (although medication may be causative), and dialysis, sexual dysfunction may be tragically and needlessly fixed when a patient in the post-acute phase inquires about a sexual problem and is erroneously informed by a physician that it is "due to the disease." However, the sex-related symptom may be transient and due to medications or anxiety about the possible sexual effect of the surgery or illness. Giving accurate sex education to a patient is doing preventive sex therapy. The extra thirty minutes taken for patient education by the physician will greatly enhance rehabilitation and recovery. For a man or woman, love play and intercourse must be within his or her level of exercise or discomfort tolerance.

Sex clinics are too few and often overloaded. Patients with a reversible sexual symptom are often self-referred; they may be on a waiting list for months and may say, "My doctor told me not to waste your time and my money to come for sex therapy." That is not necessary. Brief sex therapy today merits a diagnostic trial.

When and How Interventions Are Best Applied

 In clinical practice, the best time for intervention is when a patient or couple presents to a therapist for help with a specific sexual problem, when people invite us into their lives. It may also be when a colleague refers a patient to a sex therapist for a specific sexual problem, for example, when a gynecologist sends a patient (sometimes unwillingly) because of lack of orgasm. The patient may object, "There's nothing wrong with my mind!" This is not uncommon. Sometimes it is the partner of someone with a symptom of sexual dysfunction: "It's not my problem! It's his/hers." The task of the sex therapist then becomes that of acknowledging that sometimes a patient complies with a referral to please the physician, and asking why she thinks the gynecologist sent her, what suggestions the physician had for the complaint, and what self-help she has tried thus far. For the partner of the individual with symptoms of sexual dysfunction, the sex therapist will do best by acknowledging that it may seem unnecessary to be there for a partners sex problem, but that a symptom always involves both persons and working as a couple could be a shortcut to reversing the problem. In addition, a different perspective may be offered by the nonsymptomatic partner to help the person with symptoms and the therapist.

There are times in regular psychotherapy when complaints of sexual symptoms surface. The therapist's task is to give attention to the sex problem, get details of the onset and duration, and ask what factors are considered operative or causative, for example, medications, alcohol or street drug use, conflict in a couple, job change, money, or police problems. "What's your idea about what caused this problem?" Often a patient comes with a problem but also carries the answer within. Then sex education can be provided, with suggested reading and practice at home, and return visits to discuss the outcome.

Specific Instructions for Implementing One or More Interventions

For sexual symptoms, with or without physical problems, a diagnostic trial of brief sex therapy can be a highly effective way to reverse the problem.

Couples' Conflict around Sex

- Obtain full personal, medical, and sexual history for both people.
- Discuss conflict resolution as the process of negotiation and compromise.
- Outline their power struggle.
- Provide sex education.
- Encourage normal sexual fantasy during foreplay as a way to attain preliminary arousal, for example, "Discuss your courtship and your remembered feelings during your first phone call or before your first date."
- Suggest activities they can engage in at home. Instruct them to take a long shower or bath together or soap, towel, or rub lotion on each other. Nongenital foreplay can be suggested for sensual stimulation rather than sexual (sensate focus). This will allow relaxation, reduce pressure to perform, reveal to each person how light, medium, or firm skin touch feels so both can enjoy loving foreplay and deliberately delay intercourse for two weeks. Both are encouraged to talk about their arousal, to be honest and open, and to ask each other to stimulate less or more, to kiss, to play. Only in later sessions (third week) do they proceed to genital touch, then to intercourse (fourth week) with ten minutes of foreplay (total body massage). Extra lubrication (saliva, KY jelly, Astroglide) might also be used for comfortable penetration (Renshaw, 1995).

Individual Sex Therapy for a Woman with Anorgasmia

Many women seek help in solo sex therapy if they've never had an orgasm. They may have faked it for years but now want to learn how. They may have read dozens of romantic novels, but not used those fantasies in bed. Fantasy is an essential part of preliminary sexual arousal.

Treatment must be individualized, but very often the woman needs to become more aware of her own body and her own sexual responsiveness, and the therapist should encourage the woman to explore her own sensual potential. Everyone has erectile tissue in the earlobes and the turbinates of the nose (which is why heavy mouth breathing is characteristic of arousal), as well as the nipples and clitoris. The whole skin is richly endowed with sensitive nerve endings, particularly the mouth, lips, feet, genitals, and fingertips. She can explore and massage herself with a large towel during and after a shower. For women, or men, masturbation normally produces a more intense response than intercourse because partners must adjust to each other's reactions. Objective studies comparing coitus and masturbation in the same person show that, during masturbation, the heart rate, blood pressure, breathing, and muscle tone are all more rapid. Women need to know this.

Arousal during masturbation follows all the same stages of arousal during intercourse. The subjective feeling is different, however, without the personal closeness of coitus and without a penis separating the vaginal walls. The pubococcygeus muscle shows a response pattern of contractions both when stretched by the penile shaft and when orgasm is achieved by masturbation. A vibrator is harmless, nonaddictive, and can assist a primarily nonorgasmic woman to experience orgasm. More intensely than can be accomplished with touch, it stimulates the vibratory sensory nerve endings of the periosteum covering the pelvic bones. (A vibrator should not be used in the tub nor inserted way up into the rectum because it may sometimes require surgical removal.)

Oral sex, given or received, is a natural variant of sex play, and has been for as long as humans have recorded eroticism in their drawings and artifacts. Needless guilt has been associated with this activity, which many men and women enjoy but may, in sexual ignorance, regard as frighteningly perverted. Many women desire cunnilingus and easily climax this way. A patient, however, may assume that the act is undesirable or tedious for her partner. Many men are aroused by performing oral sex, and comfortable discussion about oral sex will clarify the partner's false assumptions and dispel anxiety. Due to early attitudinal learning, the patient may have difficulty being the initiator of sex, yet her partner may welcome her advance, viewing this as a boost to his sexual self-esteem. Occasionally, when the partner is sexually insecure, he may misinterpret overt sexual expression as an excessive demand or wonder suspiciously how she learned all of these new techniques. Most women's magazines report these and she should simply tell him so. Discussion between the two and with the sex therapist is the key to solving such problems. Extra reading, her growing awareness of her sexual responsiveness, and her willingness with her partner to add variety to lovemaking can help both the patient and her partner to grow in intimacy.

Video Case Example

If, somehow, Jennifer brought her husband with her for sex therapy, I would begin by spending fifteen minutes with them as a couple, acknowledging that he has come, that this affirms that he cares for Jennifer, and I would ask him what kind of a contract or commitment he wants to make. And I would ask if, at the end of this visit, he would review the session. Then I would have them face each other, and ask if they're willing to just touch each other's fingertips. To Jennifer I would say: Look at your husband and tell him what you remember about your very first meeting. What attracted you to him? To the husband I would say: Tell Jennifer what you remember about your first meeting. What attracted you to her? This literal getting-in-touch with their hands and eyes often reduces tension and can affirm positive feelings between them.

Now, because it is necessary to take the husband's personal, medical, and sexual histories, Jennifer would be asked to leave for thirty minutes and perhaps, given some relevant reading. After assuring the husband of the confidentiality of what he tells me, I would do a thorough history. He might be guarded or open. At the end of this interview, I would ask him if there are aspects of it that he doesn't want shared, and reassure him that I will not do so.

Jennifer could then return to integrate as best as possible what can be summarized of husband's history. If he gave a "share nothing" instruction, that must be respected. In this case, I would summarize by saying, your husband talked. He does not want to share this information at present, but he did come today and that is positive. At least he has checked me out as a therapist. I would then ask Jennifer if I can summarize for her husband what she told me on her first visit. If she agreed to this, I would then briefly outline for him her early history, her meeting him, the pregnancy, and his move to the couch.

At this point, I would tell them: The crisis of the pregnancy is still a mystery to me. You were living together, had bought the home together, and were having sex daily. What birth control were you using? Both may reply or only Jennifer. The third ear and eye of the therapist must be alert to their interaction as well as the husband's reactions to this question. If they start to argue, with each blaming the other, much will be learned to mirror back to them about the dynamics of the hurt, anger, and disappointment that caused such a major rift between these two when she became pregnant.

It is worth remarking to the reader that a man's withdrawal before ejaculation (coitus interruptus), is an ancient, highly unsuccessful form of contraception, but people still believe that it works, and it accounts for thousands of unwanted accidental pregnancies in A.D. 2001. Also, condoms can rupture, or the contraceptive pill can be irregularly taken. The obvious assumption of the therapist is that, for this husband, the pregnancy news was upsetting or negative. If the reason emerges, it is more likely to be resolved than if it remains undealt with.

Next I would complete the summary of Jennifer's story by mentioning the Las Vegas marriage, mention each family's acceptance of the new bride and groom, and ask questions such as, Did they give you a party? Then I would tell the husband that Jennifer sees him as a good father." After discussing the husband's job suspension as a stressor and Jennifer's worries about another woman or cocaine use, I would say: "Jennifer admits that to get you to talk she has picked fights but that has not been good. She loves you and wants to be with you. Could you commit to five visits together?" Sometimes a brief, limited contract seems more possible than open-ended therapy. Can he make the deal and break it? Yes. That has been his pattern. But, as a born optimist, I would hope for the best and will have done my best by making the offer.

I would end this session having them touch fingertips again, and ask him to tell her what he wants to happen at home this week and have Jennifer do the same. Then I would say: "I would like you to sleep in the same bed, no intercourse at all. Just talk to each other this week, and we can go from there. You have a lot of positive qualities to work for in this marriage. Your little boy is ten months old now. He's watching and learning. I don't want him to learn that parents yell at each other or that daddies sleep on the couch." If this couple does return, I would let the husband determine how far and how fast he feels able to proceed. He is a reluctant patient, but sometimes miracles happen.

Summary

Strengths of Sex Therapy

Until 1970, an important aspect of human behavior was obscured by scientific ignorance and therapeutic neglect or ineffectiveness. Surveys in the past sixty years in the United States have consistently shown that a large percentage of men and women admit to sexual dysfunctions. Finally, a bright, dedicated researcher, William Masters, from a respected medical school, spent a few decades of his life studying and documenting human sexuality, its problems, and possible treatment. Previously, sex, a natural, everyday function, was "too delicate" and embarrassing to discuss. But it has now become accessible and manageable. Many other physicians and medical schools have followed, and produced more research, teaching, and remedies. One positive result has been that the work has stood up to scientific duplication both in the United States and abroad.

In the sixteenth century, Montaigne, the French essayist, remarked, "There is an A, B, C ignorance that precedes knowledge and a doctoral ignorance that comes after it." Every open-minded scholar discovers, as a study proceeds, that the more he or she knows about a subject, the more there is to learn. It is not only in the West that this paradox is noted. Chinese philosopher Lao-tze, in about 550 B.C., wrote: "To the ignorant man, a tree is a tree and a river is a river. To the learned man, a tree is not a tree and the river is not a river. To the wise man, a tree is a tree and a river is a river—but they are not the same tree or the same river that the ignorant man sees." How do these observations relate to the scientific study of sex? Twentieth-century medicine has gradually emerged from complete ignorance about human sexuality, and thousands of professionals worldwide have now found it possible to weave sex therapy into their various practices and to help their patients with sexual problems.

Limitations of Sex Therapy

Antisex people still exist everywhere, including in schools and colleges. They object to the very word *sex* and object to sex education, sex topics, sex clinics, sex therapists. Every sex therapy clinician, therefore, must be prepared for possible antisex senti-ment, be able to acknowledge it, invite the individuals to examine the programs that are offered, and even suggest some reading. Sexual medicine is a newly arrived stepchild among medical practitioners. Sex therapists must, therefore, recognize the fact that sensational headlines await any misstep or accusation of unprofessional behavior. Work of quality and excellence are always essentials in the healing profes-sions, but even more so in the field of sexuality. Suspicion of therapist–patient sex is ever-present. Such behavior is unethical and will cost a professional his or her license and more. Because of such realities, sex therapists need to be aware of certain pitfalls and limitations that can affect the feasibility of therapy.

1.
   a. *Limitations in the sex therapist:* insufficient sex education, clinical skill, and awareness of chemical side effects or of the sexual impact of medical illness. Also, the comfort of the sex therapist determines the comfort of the patient. That comfort comes from knowledge, practice to gain the skill, and the atti-tude or belief that treatment of the sex symptom will benefit the individual.
   b. *Time:* For all overloaded people, therapists and patients, devoting the necessary time to therapy is a major limitation. All seek the quick fix, so a pill (magic) seems preferable to taking the time needed to undo years of accumulated problems. Time is costly, and no one wants to pay for it. Sex therapists may give up for this reason.

2. *Limitations in the patient/couple:*
   a. Severe psychopathology:
      - active psychosis
      - active paranoia
      - severe depression
      - acute substance abuse
      - severe personality disorders (too rigid to change in brief therapy)
      - recurrent lying
      - domestic violence
      - persistent domestic violence

   b. Severe acute physical pathology for example, coronary disease not yet reha-bilitated, congestive heart failure, painful arthritis, severe stroke, and so forth

   c. Refusal of one partner to attend (as with Jennifer):

   If the attending partner attends alone then sex therapy can be done and practiced at home if the absent partner will cooperate, which sometimes happens. If the absent partner refuses then masturbation is recommended for home practice. Under no circumstances should the therapist suggest that the patient seek another partner because the sex therapist may be found liable for "abetting alienation of affection." We live in litigious times.

d. Deep resistance of one/both partners can limit change. At a superficial level, they seek help, but the message is "help us but don't change us." They may both be invested in their current disequilibrium because it is customary, and change is difficult. The underlying theme may also be "even seven weeks of sex therapy couldn't fix us, therefore, let's forget sex or try divorce." Therapists can only take a patient as far and as fast as each is willing to go. The patients define the sex problem and invite us into their lives. Treatment (change) occurs at home between them, and we cannot force them to comply.

3. *Limitations in the office/clinic:*
   No fancy chairs, lighting, or settings are needed. The essential atmosphere is people relating to people in a helping way. Privacy and confidentiality are critical. Heavy costs will, of course, limit patient attendance. Few insurance companies pay. Refusal to approve a sex clinic at a hospital or institution will be a major limitation. The sex therapist will need to persuade, educate, and reassure those in power that sex therapy is needed by the community. Sex therapy is a scarce service, of value to the institution as a provider of subspecialty care. Because many couples are both working, an evening sex clinic conveniently allows both partners to attend after 5:00 P.M. and makes productive use of space vacated after regular hours. A stern secretary or a security person will provide a chaperone so there is no risk of accusation of patient–therapist sex. An office in the home of a solo therapist may be perceived as a risk for a solo patient, but a spouse can serve as a chaperone.

Implications for Further Research

For further research the subspecialty of sex therapy must first survive. Creative efforts to obtain funds for sexual research will no doubt continue as will genuine unfunded clinical research to improve current treatments to reduce negative consequences, including sexual ones [e.g.: prostatectomy, episiotomy and hysterectomy techniques.] Where there are possible profitable outcomes, more research is being done to market "drug-induced orgasms" for both sexes, with the lucrative trailblazer Viagra to inspire pharmaceutical companies. But Viagra is not an *aphrodisiac.* Researchers will still pursue that "holy grail." In my estimation, there are many millions of women (and/or their partners) who would gladly purchase an *orgasm pill* in our hurried culture.

Men with delayed ejaculation are fewer in number than anorgasmic women, but they can be truly distressed. The symptom has thus far somewhat defeated chemical efforts to relieve it. With improved understanding of male erections, ejaculation study is also under way. The largest groups of men and women with symptoms of sexual dysfunction are those with HSD (hypoactive sexual desire). They very commonly present for sex therapy, and, for patients treated in the Loyola Sex Therapy program, that designation covered a variety of underlying factors. For over half (52 percent) the HSD was not global but situational; namely, the patient masturbated regularly but did not approach the partner for intercourse. Conflict, deliberate control, and pregnancy/impregnation avoidance were some of the reasons noted at the conclusion of treatment. The symptom reversal rate of 80 percent was similar to that of other presenting symptoms. Chemical causes were determined in about 24 percent due to needed medications. For example, antidepressants are a leading and well-known cause of sexual dysfunction. Understanding this connection is a relief to many patients. Some decided to discontinue or change the medication with the approval of their prescribing physician. Others can make love before they take the medication or use more fantasy or a vibrator. Pharmaceutical research continues for a refined antidepressant without unwanted sexual and weight gain side effects.

Sexual fantasy is a very important aspect of sexuality in great need of research (Kronhausen & Kronhausen, 1979). For many people who present for sex therapy, the question about sexual fantasy evokes a "never" response. Sometimes fantasy education is necessary, which in itself indicates approval from the therapist. This research is "soft," due to the subjective nature of responses, but efforts must be made, through outcome studies, to measure the objective physiological responses to fantasies, e.g., vaginal lubrication, erections, ejaculation, and so on. There will be inevitable limitations because of sample selection, age, informed consent, ethnicity, race, and culture, and all will have to be factored in. There is also the question of researcher bias and lack of random selection because of the self-selection bias introduced by those who volunteer for such research. Physiological research into sexual responses must continue, particularly due to advances in our knowledge of hormones, enzymes, and genetics, which may soon reveal a spectrum in libido levels that may be the result of circulating hormones rather than retaliatory responses between conflictual partners.

The effect of our global reach on the Internet is definitely affecting relationships and the availability of sex education and of erotic images. These are all essentials that require survey and study.

Sociological and demographic surveys will undoubtedly continue worldwide. An important question to ask is whether better sex education for children in the 1990s will achieve lessened sexual dysfunctions by 2010.

It will be every clinician's task to keep up with current research, whether by survey, case report, or new sexual drug releases, and to evaluate how the knowledge can assist present and past patients.

It is perfectly ethical to review past cases, for example, men with ED, to discuss Viagra and suggest they visit their primary physicians for evaluation and trial. Usually the patients contact us, but it is also good practice to send a note or to leave a message to call to maintain confidentiality about new aids. For example, telling a nonorgasmic woman who can afford $360 for the new Eros device could help her if her doctor will prescribe it, but it may be upsetting information for a woman on Public Aid who cannot afford it. If patients try a new method, the sex therapist's own task is to keep some details of the patients' response, either positive or negative, for personal research. Such information influences whether to recommend the method to other patients.

Questions to Consider

1. How valid do you think the results read in a journal or magazine are compared with your experience?

2. Should you get further information from an author or pharmaceutical company or the Internet?

3. Some college students might question instructors about doing a sexual research project. How would you evaluate the proposal for its scientific value?

4. What social/clinical/academic value is served by a particular case report, survey, or research study (e.g., the video of Jennifer's interview)?

Specialized Training Opportunities and Certification

The Masters–Johnson Foundation closed completely several years ago. Treatment of patients and training professionals to do sex therapy is no longer available there.

Very few programs offer clinical training. Those that remain must be carefully examined by each potential trainee for their cost and the quality of supervised clinical experience with patients with sexual problems to develop the skill and comfort for the practice of sex therapy.

- Attending a workshop even for forty hours, is not clinical training. Nevertheless, there are many workshops offered in the United States and abroad, but they vary greatly in quality.
- The value of certification or a diploma is something the trainee should check out carefully. Neither are licenses. In addition, a certificate from another country is often not recognized in the United States. There is no such thing as a sex therapy *license* as there is for psychologists, social workers, and nurses. "Certification" does not mean that an examination was passed or that the owner has a license. In some cases, a diploma or certification may indicate little more than the number of hours of attendance. The family therapist *license* on the office wall may be much more meaningful and reassuring to a patient because the license guarantees a code of ethics, accountability, and standards of practice.

The Loyola University Sexual Dysfunction Training Clinic is designed for a medical school whose students will be or are M.D.s and R.N.s. It does not offer a license or a diploma; only an attendance certification is given. It is both an academic (fifteen hours) and a clinical experience (seven weeks, thirty-five hours) with a patient couple, supervised on-site. It is an excellent learning and treatment method. The trainees must already have a masters degree to apply and will later get their medical or social work/nursing/psychology degrees through other examinations and training. Finally, they will be licensed in their specific discipline in the state in which they practice.

Sex therapy remains a patient- and buyer-beware arena, a concern to professionals who must guide and protect patients. There are several sexology associations that have many members and sometimes publish a journal. But membership only means membership. Each individual's license reports his/her discipline. Most are enthusiastic professionals who attend the meetings, write articles, and do good research and clinical work. Many are accessible on the Internet.

> *Kinsey Institute:* (E-mail) Kinsey@indiana.edu
> Web site: http://www.indiana.edu/~kinsey/education.htm provides details about training there.
> *A.A.S.E.C.T.* (American Association of Sex Educators, Counselors and Therapists): (E-mail) AASECT@Worldnet.att.net
> *S.S.S.S.* ("Quad S" Society for the Scientific Study of Sex): (E-mail) The Society@Worldnet.att.net
> Web site: http://www.ssc.wisc.edu/ssss
> *S.S.T.A.R.* (Sex Society for Therapists and Researchers):

Each explorer will find a great deal of Internet information in addition to that listed here.

Resources for Further Study

Sexual medicine journals have flourished, but, in the past ten years, many have ceased publication due to lack of funding and advertisers. STD (sexually transmitted diseases) and AIDS journals now attract more pharmaceutical advertisers. *Medline* searches will locate many references. The *Ovid* Web site will lead to psychology references. Masters, Johnson, and Kolodny (1995) provide fifty-eight pages of references, articles, and books. Bookstores devote special shelves to books with sexual titles, with new publications daily covering child and senior sexuality.

Self-Help Books

Barbach, L. G. (1975/1991). *For yourself: The fulfillment of female sexuality.* New York: Doubleday.

Boston Women's Health Book Collective. (1975/1994). *Our bodies ourselves: A book by and for women.* New York: Simon & Schuster.

Botwin, C. (1985). *Is there sex after marriage?* Boston: Little, Brown.

Goldberg, H. (1976). *The hazards of being male.* New York: New American Library.

Maltz, W. (1991). *The sexual healing journey.* New York: Harper Collins.

Masters, W., Johnson, V., & Kolodny, R. (1986). *Sex and human loving.* Boston: Little, Brown.

Paul, J. & Paul, M. (1983). *Do I have to give me up to be loved by you?* Minneapolis, MN: Compcare.

Renshaw, D. C. (1995). *Seven weeks to better sex.* New York: Random House.

Zilbergeld, B. (1992). *The new male sexuality.* New York: Bantam.

REFERENCES

American Psychiatric Association. (1994). *Diagnostic and statistical manual of mental disorders* (4th ed.). Washington, DC: Author.

Araoz, D. L. (1982). *Hypnosis and sex therapy.* New York: Brunner/Mazel.

Basson, R., Mcinnes, R., Smith, M. D. (2000). *Efficacy and safety of sildenafil in estrogenized women with sexual dysfunction associated with female sexual arousal disorder. Obstet Gynecol 95*(4 Suppl), 54S.

Blumstein, P. W., & Pepper, P. (1983). *American couples.* New York: William Morrow.

Boteach, S. (1999). *Kosher sex.* New York: Doubleday.

Brecher, E. (1983). *Love, sex and aging.* Boston: Little, Brown.

Brill, A. A. (1938). *The basic writings of Sigmund Freud.* New York: Modern Library.

Bullough, V. H. (1976). *Sexual variance in society.* New York: Wiley.

Derogatis, L. R., & King, K. M. (1981). *The coital coronary. Archives of Sexual Behavior 10,* 325–335.

Diament, L. (1987). *Male and female homosexuality, psychological approaches.* New York: Hemisphere.

Dickinson, R. L., & Prerson, H. H. (1925). Average sex life of American women. *JAMA 8,* 1113–1117.

Ellis, H. (1942). *Studies in the psychology of sex* (2 Vols.). New York: Random House.

Goldstein, I., & Rothstein, L. (1990). *The potent male.* CA: Body Press.

Goldstein, I., (1998). Oral sildenafil in the treatment of erectile dysfunction. *New England Journal of Medicine 338,* 1397–1404.

Green, R. M. (1992). *Religion and sexual health.* Boston: Kluwer.

Holbrook, S. (1959). *The golden age of quackery.* New York: McMillan.

Katz, R. C., & Jardine, D. (1999). The relationship between worry, sexual aversion, and low sexual desire. *Journal of Sex & Marital Therapy 25*(4), 293–296.

Keller, A. A., Hamer, R., & Rosen, R. C. (1997). Serotonin reuptake inhibitor-induced sexual dysfunction and its treatment: A large-scale retrospective study of 596 psychiatric outpatients. *Journal of Sex & Marital Therapy, 23*(3), 165–175.

Kinsey, A. C., Pomeroy, W. B., & Martin, C. E. (1948). *Sexual behavior in the human male.* Philadelphia: Saunders.

Kinsey, A. C., (1953). *Sexual behavior in the human female.* Philadelphia: Saunders.

Kronhausen, R., & Kronhausen, E. (1979). *Erotic fantasies: A study of the sexual imagination.* New York: Bell.

Lauman, E. O., (1994). *The social organization of sexuality: Sexual practices in the United States.* Chicago: University of Chicago Press.

Lue, T. (Ed.). (1992). *Book of impotence.* England: Smith-Gordon, Nishimura.

Maltz, W. (1991). *The sexual healing journey.* New York: Harper Collins.

Masters, W. H., & Johnson, V. E. (1966). *Human sexual response.* Boston: Little, Brown.

Masters, W. H., & Johnson, V. E. (1970). *Human sexual inadequacy.* Boston: Little, Brown.

Masters, W. H., & Johnson, V. E. (1979). *Homosexuality in perspective.* Boston: Little, Brown.

Masters, W. H., & Johnson, V. E. (1980). *Ethical issues in sex therapy & research.* Boston: Little, Brown.

Masters, W. H., & Johnson, V. E., & Kolodny, R. C. (1995). *Human sexuality* (5th ed.). New York: Harper Collins.

The Medical Letter. (1992). Drugs That Cause Sexual Dysfunction—An Update. *Medical Letter Drug Therapy 34,* 747.

Nordoff, C. (1966). *The communistic societies of the United States.* New York: Dover.

Renshaw, D. C. (1975). Sexual problems of alcoholics. *Chicago Medicine, 78*(10), 433–436.

Renshaw, D. C. (1981). Coping with an impotent husband. *Illinois Medical Journal, 159*(1), 29–33.

Renshaw, D. C. (1987). Sexual therapy for psychiatric patients? *British Journal of Sexual Medicine,* 34–39.

Renshaw, D. C. (1989). Treatment of sexual exploitation—Rape and incest. *Psychiatric Clinics of North America, 12*(2), 257–277.

Renshaw, D. C. (1995). *Seven weeks to better sex.* New York: Random House.

Renshaw, D. C. (1996). Profile of a sex therapy clinic in 1996. *Journal of Women's Health, 5*(5), 481–487.

Renshaw, D. C. (1997). Women's reactions to partners' pornography. *African Journal of Sexology,* 11–12.

Renshaw, D. (2001). Sex therapy. In Carlson, J. & Kjos, D. *Family therapy with the experts.* Boston: Allyn & Bacon (videotape).

Seagraves, R. T. (1998). Antidepressant-induced sexual dysfunction. *Journal of Clinical Psychiatry, 59*, Suppl. 4, 48–54.

Semans, J. (1956). Premature ejaculation. *Southern Medical Journal 49*, 353–8.

Shen, W. W., Urosevich, Z., & Clayton, D. O. (1999). Sildenafil in the treatment of female sexual dysfunction induced by selective serotonin reuptake inhibitors. *Journal of Reproductive Medicine 44*(6), 535–341.

Tannahill, R. (1982). *Sex in history.* New York: Stein & Day.

Tuiten, A. (2000). Time Course Effects of Testosterone Administration on Sexual Arousal in Women. *Archives of General Psychiatry, 57,* 149–153.

Vroege, J. A., Gijs, L., & Hengeveld, M. W. (1998). Classification of sexual dysfunctions: Towards DSM-V and ICD-II. *Comprehensive Psychiatry, 39*(6), 333–337.

Wolpe, J. (1958). *Psychotherapy by reciprocal inhibition.* Palo Alto, CA: Stanford University Press.

Zilbergeld, B., & Evans, M. (1980). The inadequacy of Masters and Johnson. *Psychology Today, 14,* 29–43.

11 Object Relations Therapy

JILL SAVEGE SCHARFF AND DAVID E. SCHARFF

Jill and David Scharff

Brief Description of Theory of Object Relations Therapy

Object Relations Family Therapy is based on object relations theory, a contemporary approach that integrates psychoanalytic understanding of the individual with group psychology, systems theory, and developmental psychology. The family is viewed as a small group with the task of supporting its members at various stages through the life cycle, and carrying the culture of the community in which that family lives. The family functions as a system of roles and relationships—between the parents as a couple, parents and children, siblings, and the extended family—in multiple daily transactions in various combinations. Beyond that conscious level of interaction, however, the role relationships operate with even greater complexity at the unconscious level.

Significant Characteristics of the Theory

Object relations family therapy takes its theory base from modern relational psychoanalytic theory and from the classical principles of technique handed down from Freud. We listen to the unconscious themes by attending to words, gestures, and the quality of silences. We listen not just with our ears but with our own unconscious, tuned to material that is being communicated to us. We note the resonance in ourselves with the material that family members are consciously and unconsciously expressing, and, from our own experience, we develop a sense of what they have gone through and what they require the important people in their lives to experience, in order to feel understood. We call this "working in the transference and countertransference." That is to say, from our own experience we develop a model of the family's transference to us. By *transference*, we mean the projection onto us of all their hopes, fears, and longings about the relationship that we may provide in our role as therapists. Our experiences and our understanding of the family then leads to an interpretation geared toward developing insight, understanding, and growth.

We offer a therapeutic relationship that is not directive and yet is not as remote as the blank screen approach of the classical analyst. We are interactive, and yet we always follow the unconscious direction of the family. We create an environment similar enough for old patterns of relating to important figures in the family of origin to be recreated, and yet different enough to allow them to be detected by us. These patterns of interaction occur over and over again, giving us plenty of time to recognize them, point them out, and understand the defensive reasons for their occurrence. We bring a capacity for providing this kind of psychological holding environment for sharing with the family in their experience through tolerating anxiety and loss. The gap between the family's experience of us as being like the early objects of their dependency, love, and aggression and their experience of us as new objects in the here and now is a space for understanding and growth. In this reflective space, they can look back at the past, observe the present, and write a new script for the future.

Evolution of the Theory

Object relations family therapy was first described by Jill and David Scharff (1987a). It is an approach to the family that is built on analytic theory of small groups and of marital dynamics. The theory of object relations family therapy is different from family systems theory in that it takes the unconscious into account (Slipp, 1984). It values insight as a necessary precursor for change, and it believes in making the unconscious conscious. It does not subscribe to paradoxical instructions that can bypass or trick the unconscious into submission, because it believes that the most effective adult development rests on a trusting access to the unconscious, which enriches conscious life as soon as there is no longer a need to fear and defend against it. It is like individual psychoanalysis in that it reaches a level of depth not commonly seen in shorter-term directive family systems approaches, and in that it uses transference and countertransference (D. Scharff, 1989b). It is unlike it in that it deals with the actual interpersonal relationships in the family context, as well as with the internal object relations set of each individual and the shared internal object relations set of the family group. It is like small group therapy in that it works with the group and with group dynamics, but it is unlike it in that it does not deal with a group of strangers. But, people with a history and with a future together. Each person in this group is a significant other.

Philosophical and Historical Background

This theory is built on the work of Henry Dicks, who integrated concepts from Fairbairn and Klein. To his basic system, we have added some insights from Winnicott and extended them to the functioning of the small group by using the theory of Bion. Fairbairn (1952) gave us a theory of personality that did not depend on Freudian instinct theory. Instead, he saw the infant's motivation as deriving from the wish to be in a relationship. To a family therapist, this makes a great deal of sense. He thought that psychic structure developed from the infant's attempt to cope with the various experiences during the necessary stage of human dependency on the mother. He thought that the infant took in good and bad experience in relation to the mother and stored it inside the self as pieces of psychic structure called "good and bad objects" with which the ego (the executive part of the self) would have to deal. His greatest contribution to modern relational theory was to notice that the ego itself became split by the need to relate to these different aspects of the object, while preserving a generally good enough view of the object for the ego to feel secure and well related. Unsatisfactory parts of the object were split off and repressed into two main categories of internal object relationship. An internal object relationship is an interactive system of a repressed part of the ego, part of the object and the affect that connects them. The two major systems are the exciting object system and the rejecting object system. Closer to consciousness remains the central ego and the aspect of the object that was good enough, connected by feelings of satisfaction and hopefulness. All of these systems are in dynamic relation.

Next to be considered is the Kleinian concept of projective identification (Klein, 1946, 1975), a mental mechanism for ridding the self of anxiety-provoking affect that arises from the interplay of the forces of the life and death instincts. To deflect the death instinct, Klein said, the infant puts angry feelings into the mother and then misidentifies her as the source of the rage, and then experiences her as a persecutory object that has to be dealt with by taking it inside the self. To keep the life instinct safe, the infant also projects good feelings into the mother, identifies her as a caring object, and then takes that in as well. We recognize death anxiety when the object cannot contain the self, and we attribute it to constitutional insufficiency of the self, overwhelming circumstances, inadequacy of the external object, or a mismatch between the needs of the self and the capabilities of the object. We do not attribute death anxiety to a death instinct. Nevertheless, we use projective identification as a linking concept for explaining how the ego relates to the internal object inside the self and in interaction with significant others, such as the mother, the spouse, or the therapist.

Henry Dicks (1967) used Klein's concept of projective identification to amplify and extend Fairbairn's view of the individual personality as a system of parts in dynamic relation to understand the unconscious fit between the personalities of spouses. He noted that, when two partners fall in love, this dynamic relation extends itself to a melding of the two personalities. A marital joint personality is formed in which the partner relates to repressed internal object relationships in the spouse as if they were in the self and either attacks them there or cherishes them, depending on how this part of the self was and is experienced. In the good marriage, these parts of the self that are found in the self will be allowed to emerge and become more integrated with the conscious personality, but in the marriage that is not successful, these repressed parts of the spouse will be more thoroughly condemned than before (Scharff & Scharff, 1987b, 1991). The solution, then, is submission and giving in to pathology or leaving the marriage for a new setting in which to rediscover the self in association with a loved one.

Our view of the family as a small group system also owes a great deal to Bion's study of small working groups (1959, 1962, 1967). We regard the family as a small group with two main tasks. First, it has the task of supporting its members through the life cycle. This task takes various forms at different stages of life. For instance, when the children are infants, the family needs to take care of their dependent needs. The needs of the toddler, however, are quite different from those of the lap baby, and issues of autonomy rather than issues of dependency come to the fore. Second, the family provides the intimate relating that each of its members' needs.

Bion described how the work of a group can be supported or subverted by subgroup formations, which he called "basic assumption group processes." He noted three major types of subgroup formations, all of them due to groupings between members of the group who join together to express an attitude toward the leader. These take the form of dependency, fight or flight, and pairing basic assumptions. The dependency subgroup expresses the longing to be taken care of by the leader. The fight or flight expresses the wish to subvert the authority of the leader and obstruct or get out of the task, while pairing expresses the wish to be the one to have a special relationship with the leader, to the exclusion of others.

In the family group, fight and flight formations are dominant when the children reach adolescence and the parents need a capacity to tolerate this in order to let their young people separate. In earlier years, however, dependency is a dynamic that fosters the family's ability to care for young children. We see normal pairing and normal jealousy when the young child is excluded from the parental bed room, but when sexualized pairing occurs between a child and a parent instead, then we see abnormal envy. The need for a secure pair is vested in the parents, but the pairing of a child with a parent, in actual or fantasized sexual interaction, has a disruptive effect on the task of the family.

Winnicott (1958, 1965, 1971) studied the mother–infant relationship extensively during his work as a pediatrician and child analyst. He noted two aspects of mother: the environmental mother and the object mother. The environmental mother provides the arms-around holding that keeps her child safe and ensures going-on being. The object mother is there for doing, for intimate direct relating, eye-to-eye relating in gaze interactions, vocal cooing, and loving touch. We extend this view of the infant's mother to conceptualize the role of the family in providing emotional holding and intimate relating for its members of any age. It also gives us a metaphor for our functioning as therapists who promote being and doing through the psychological holding environment that we provide and through our availability for core affective exchanges.

Research

Dicks's theory was introduced to the United States by Shapiro, Zinner, and colleagues in their research at the National Institute of Mental Health (NIMH) in the 1960s (D. Scharff, 1989a; Shapiro 1979; Zinner & Shapiro 1972). They extended Dicks' use of the concept of projective identification to refer to a tendency in families to identify the adolescent as the part of the self that was causing the most trouble. Other orientations have referred to this adolescent as the "scapegoat," the one who is seen to embody all that is bad and destructive in the family's life. There is an attempt to isolate this quality, locate it in one person, and then expel that person from the family because of sickness or delinquency. They developed a form of family therapy called the "group interpretive approach to family" that was based on the interpretation of this projective identification in the family so that repressed aspects could be reintegrated into the family without cost to one individual. That research ended in the early 1970s as NIMH became more preoccupied with biological research.

At this point, the most useful research to help in our thinking about families comes from object relations research (Westen, 1990) and from infant and adult attachment research (Slade, 1996). Westen's research in object relations confirms many but not all of the tenets of object relations theory. Westen and others show that the affective quality of the object world, the capacity to distinguish between self and other, and the ability to invest in self and other are shaped in the preoedipal years, and the affective tone of the object world is set in interaction with the mother. They do not confirm the idea of the oedipal complex as the final defining moment of personality development. Research shows that object relations are not finalized by the oedipal stage, but continue to develop from immature dependency to mature respect and love until adolescence, and, we would add, continue to grow and change through adult life experience with work, friendships, relocation, marriage, and raising children.

Attachment patterns are closely related to object relationship structures, and so the findings of attachment research are highly relevant to elaborating new object relations theory, applying it to technique in clinical work and conceptualizing therapeutic action. As clinicians, we can use attachment theory during assessment and in treatment. We use it in assessment when we evaluate attachment strategies, strengths, and weaknesses in the family's capacity for relating, and we alter our technique so as to engage them. We use it in treatment to guide us in adjusting the therapeutic relationship to suit them, and in developing a focus for the therapeutic work.

Attachment theory helps the clinician to be aware of the need to provide a secure base through regularity of attendance, attention to boundaries, fees, and monitoring of personal reactions to keep a clear space for psychological work. It helps us to be on the lookout for attachment themes and patterns and to detect the predominant organization and structure of attachment. We can view our participation in therapy as a dynamic interplay between the therapist's attachment organization and the patients' (J. Scharff, 1998). We are working not just with the past and its expression in the present, but how it will play out in the future, not just in the family now, but in the next generation.

In our view, however, therapists are more than attachment objects. Therapy consists in being available to be used as an object—of attachment and detachment, of desire and disgust, of hate and denigration, of envy, and so on—and becoming aware of it. Then the therapist actively interprets the experience of being used as this necessary object with whom to replay in dynamic interaction the internal object relationships as they come to light in transference–countertransference.

The Clinical Perspective of Object Relations Therapy

Object relations therapy addresses human functioning as an expression of individual intrapsychic fields interacting with each other, with the group, and with the culture. These individual intrapsychic dimensions are constructed from genetically given constitutions interacting with experience. Mental illness results when constitutional factors impede learning from experience or when environmental factors overwhelm constitutional capacities for adaptation. An individual's symptom is an expression of an internal object relationship, and the index patient is the symptom of a disorder in the family system of internal object relationships. Change occurs through interpretation of unconscious conflict between repressed object relationships within the self and between the self and others in the family. Projective identifications are recognized and eventually taken back into the self. This relieves the external object of the burden of being perceived according to old formulas and enriches the self.

Applications of Object Relations Therapy

The object relations therapy approach adapts well to various modalities and to the treatment of various conditions. Because the theory derives from the study of the mother–infant relationship as it is revealed in the transference, and because it deals with the interpersonal enactment of intraspychic conflict, the object relations approach works with individuals, couples, families, and groups. It works with families of any socioeconomic class or ethnic origin, because, being devoted to following the family's thread and working for the family's own goals, it is not imposing any particular way of doing things. It tends to be thought of as a long-term method because of its analytic underpinnings. Certainly, it is most effective for those who can invest a couple of years in a type of treatment geared, not to symptom removal, but to growth and development. Nevertheless, we feel that it is also applicable to short-term therapy, serial brief therapy, and single-session consultation, because it reveals the issues in depth, which, even if they cannot be fully addressed in the time available, are then identified and the family can choose whether or not to proceed with adequate therapy (Scharff and Scharff, 1998; Stadter, 1996).

In families dealing with conditions such as schizophrenia, object relations family therapy deals effectively with the family's projective identification into the ill family member, but it has to be combined with antipsychotic medication, work rehabilitation, and psychoeducational approaches. In eating disorders, we work on the meaning that food has to the family as well as to the anorexic or bulimic individual (Ravenscroft, 1988). Food is often viewed as an exciting object that stimulates a repressive action from the rejecting object system. In phobia, the situation to be avoided is seen as representing an object that is feared because, if it is engaged with by the ego, the engagement will stimulate an affect-filled internal object relationship that returns from repression.

The object relations approach, which applies well in marital therapy to show how the two personalities become intertwined at the level of the internal object relationships, is also useful when the couple has sexual dysfunction. The genitalia are viewed as a projection screen for an unacceptable internal object that cannot then be related to by the self or the partner (D. Scharff, 1989a). When the couple is gay or lesbian, the approach deals with projective identification between partners, who, being of the same sex, have a self-similar body that houses the object of their desire and also drives the replay of the internal object relationships.

Therapist Stance

The family–counselor relationship depends on the therapists' provision of a good psychological space and a holding environment in which families can display their repeating defensive patterns and eventually face their underlying anxieties. We describe the way the family requires us to relate to them in order to fend off some less desirable way of being which, at the next level, defends against an even greater calamitous relationship. We call this type of interpretation the "because clause" (Ezriel, 1952).

The family reacts to us in our role as providers of a service, analogous to the mother's role in providing arms-around holding for her infant (Scharff & Scharff, 1987a). We create a space where the family can be together naturally and where they can do their family tasks. Based on previous experience with families of origin, the family brings to treatment an expectation of how (or whether) therapy will provide help. We call this "contextual transference." Contextual transference generates contextual countertransference. If this is negative, the therapist feels helpless or useless. If it is positive the therapist feels appreciated and confident. Monitoring these reactions leads to awareness of contextual transference, which can then be made conscious to clarify what is needed to support the therapy. In being available for direct relating, analogous to the role of the object mother, therapists stimulate focused transference from an individual family member who is speaking on behalf of the group. This is detected in the focused countertransference. Interpretation based on this focused experience opens the family unconscious to the need for reworking issues of intimacy.

The counselor monitors her own reactions to the flow of the session. First of all, she tells herself not to try and do too much in order to make herself feel effective. She tells herself to relax and let the session happen without directing it. She asks herself to remember what just happened and how it connects to what is happening now. She tries to figure out how an individual is speaking for the family group. She lets her mind wander so that her associations can be triggered by the family's material. She connects with how she is feeling, notices any fantasies that cross her mind, observes any lapses in concentration, moments of anxiety, and experiences of physical discomfort, and then she thinks about them and links them to the unconscious theme. Casement (1991) has called this process "internal supervision."

Specific Interventions

In object relations therapy, technique consists mainly in tuning the unconscious to receive unconscious communication from the family. That is why we do not try to get things done, create exercises, give instructions, or ask many questions. The main technique is a matter of maintaining a respectful, engaged, following attitude. We wait, watch, and wonder, the same as the infant psychiatrist advises the mother to do. We trust that, if we free the unconscious process, the wisdom of the group will emerge to guide the family through to its next developmental stage. We depend on analyzing our countertransference to arrive at a dependable understanding of the family, but that requires self-knowledge acquired from therapy, supervision, and clinical experience that has been fine-tuned in constant self-analysis.

Working with families, we listen to and respond to individuals but we link our individual comments to the group process. We work with an individual's dream and the family members' associations to it, so that a dream becomes a group puzzle to solve. We talk and we play with art media and toys appropriate to the developmental stage of the family and let the unconscious theme emerge from the play (J. Scharff, 1989b). We deal with loss and mourning. We rework early trauma, including trauma in the previous generation. We work toward an ideal of tact and timing in giving our interpretations so the family can listen and use them. Without revealing our own feelings, we nevertheless base our comments on our own experience in contact with the core of the family. Meaning then emerges from shared experience rather than being imposed in an intellectual or oracular way.

Clinical Example of Therapist Stance, Style, and Technique

To illustrate the clinical perspective and the therapist's stance, style, and technique, we refer to the video of the family session with Adrian, Judy, and Pam. As

Jill Scharff

volunteers in the videotape series, *Family Therapy with the Experts* (J. Carlson & D. Kjos, 1997), Adrian, Judy, and Pam have already seen one of the therapists in the series, and have returned for their next therapy session, this one with David and Jill Scharff, who will use object relations therapy. A complete, accurate view of the interview is given in the transcript that accompanies the videotape. But the transcript can show only the final result, not the internal working in the therapist's mind, so Jill Scharff summarizes the process of the session, as she remembers it from discussion afterwards with her cotherapist, to show the therapists' processing of the dynamics of the interview in which they work with the family's unresolved grief and delayed development.

David Scharff

The Family and the Complaint

Adrian and Judy, parents in their fifties, came with their thirty-two-year-old daughter Pam, who lives at home and works part-time as a grocery store stock clerk. The parents are chronically upset by their daughter's behavior. Pam is uncooperative, does nothing to help, and wastes time. Adrian and Judy are hoping that therapy will help Pam to change.

The Session

Initial Impressions.   As David Scharff and I (J. S. Scharff) waited for the cameras to roll, Adrian referred to getting some useful ideas from the last session with the first therapist in the series. Adrian went on to ask Pam why she was sitting in the same seat as last time and he tried to get her to move out of the seat next to him and let her mother sit there, but she refused. Her seat was in the middle between her parents, and the family threesome was between the two therapists. Pam said she liked the seat she had, and she stayed in it. We thought that he was trying to free the seat next to him so he could sit with his wife, perhaps in response to the previous therapist's work with them. But later, when we referred back to this moment before the interview had begun, his behavior refuted our idea that he was usefully trying to sit next to his wife.

Adrian was a large, overweight, outgoing, apparently jovial man. The tattoo on his biceps had a few women's names scored out until the final one was Rita. I wondered who she was, but I didn't ask, and I didn't find out. Like Adrian, Judy was overweight, but she was short, and much quieter than Adrian. Between them sat Pam, a slim young woman with a shaggy haircut who looked like a boyish pre-teen girl. Her speech was impulsive and not well articulated and her gestures were awkward. Her facial expression and her eyes were hard to see under her hair, but it looked as if her eyes did not quite match. Was there a drooping lid or a squint? It was hard to tell. She seemed unlike her parents in physical type and less endowed with intelligence.

Stating the Complaint

The cameraman indicated that it was time to start. Adrian took charge of the session. "We had our first interview with the other therapist," he began. "The wife and I done our airing on all that Pam done wrong. It was 99 percent us talking. Today it is time for Pam to do her airing on what we done wrong."

Pam explained, "They're mad, because I don't do housework. I just sit in front of my computer. Don't do anything. Just sit. My attitude is on the rocks. It's icky."

They all laughed at her choice of word.

"That is slightly understated," Adrian commented sarcastically.

Then Judy took over. "What we came for was for Pam to build her self-esteem," she volunteered. "When we talk to her she doesn't give you an answer. Like, she went out with a friend and I asked her, 'What did you

eat?' No answer. I asked again. 'So what did you eat' All I got was
'Breakfast.' "

Adrian and Judy laughed. Pam looked extremely upset.

"When you talk about how difficult Pam is, you join in laughter, but Pam's
eyes fill with tears," I noted.

"We're laughing because it's been going on for so many years," Adrian
explained. "We don't do this at home. We don't laugh there. I'm trying to
keep my temper down here."

I suggested to Adrian and Judy, "You're laughing to release the tension of
holding in your anger."

In response to my comment, the parents started to vent their anger at Pam, and
Judy repeated the story of her not telling them what she is doing, with many elaborations, leading to the final point.

"I say, 'What did you eat?' and there's no answer," she concluded.

Adrian introduced a new example. "Like, for coming to this interview, I tell
her to take a shower. It's 4:00 P.M., but she puts it off, and puts it off. She
doesn't get into the shower until 5:00 P.M., so she's not out of there until
5:40, and it puts me behind. So I get angry. I yell and throw a fit. I don't hit
her anymore. Well, maybe I'll hit the wall, bang the table, and leave. I'd hit
her when she was younger to get her attention. It didn't work then, either."

"It used to hurt me when he hit me," Pam said. "Now he jumps at me with
anger."

Anger as a Defense

"She's referring to when I really yell at her to get going," Adrian explained.

"You're a big person with a strong voice," I said to Adrian. "You could seem
powerful and pretty scary. Yet, at the beginning you told Pam loud and
clear that you didn't want her to sit in the middle, but she's still doing it.
What do you feel about that?"

Adrian told me what he wanted, not what he he felt. He said, "I wanted her
to sit nearer to the therapist." He pointed to where Judy was sitting next
to me. So he meant for her to sit close to the female member of the co-therapy team, and she had not wanted to.

"Did you want to stay away from me, Pam?" I asked.

"No," she said. "I want to sit in the middle."

The Underlying Wish

"You want to be in the middle between your two parents," David emphasized. "Do you feel good there?" David asked Pam.

"Hmmmm," she considered. "Not at the dinner table," she said. "But it's
alright here." She looked to either side of her. "Father's there, Mom's
there," she said looking small and snug between the two large bodies of
her parents on either side of her.

"That makes you really happy," David noted.

"Even though they're mad," I added.

"Yes, they are," Pam agreed.

"Or because they're mad," I continued. "It doesn't make sense, but that's where you are. Perhaps it's better to be in the middle for some reason."

"What do you think?" David asked.

"Don't know," Pam replied. "I like the middle. Don't know why."

Working toward the Basic Anxiety

Thinking of Pam as filling the empty space, David wondered aloud, "Are there other kids?"

"Pam's it!" the parents said.

I asked, "Had you decided on one child by choice, or were there other reasons to limit your family?"

"She's adopted," Judy answered. She shot a glance at Adrian that signaled trouble of some sort.

Adrian drew himself up as if about to make a resolution, and in a few short bursts he got it out. "All right I'll say it. We had a son. He committed suicide ten years ago. She takes it hard, but not as hard as I do."

Adrian and Judy seemed to be gulping back their feelings, and Pam's eyes filled with tears again.

Following the Affect

We felt shocked and sad for them. It was emotionally wrenching for them. David encouraged them to go on nevertheless. "Can you say more about him?"

"I can't," said Judy, obviously controlling her emotions.

"He blew his brains out," Adrian said flatly. "What else is there to say? No rhyme, no reason, no note, no nothing. I said to the coroner, 'Tell me he was on dope. Please. What dope was he on?' You'll wonder why a parent would want that."

"It's obvious," David said. "You wanted a reason." Judy nodded. She looked deeply pained.

"I can't visit his grave," Adrian added.

"You're tortured because you don't know why he killed himself," I said. "And you're angry at him for leaving you this way."

"We're angry that things are going wrong with Pam, since then. We think it's because she's hurt that she doesn't have her brother with her. He was four years younger than her and she looked out for him, did lots of things with him."

Facing the Loss

"Were you that close to your brother?" David asked Pam. "What was his name?"

Pam whispered the name so quietly that neither of us could catch it.

"Peter?" I guessed.

"No, Victor," Pam corrected me. "I liked having him to talk to."

Adrian interrupted to say, "You can always talk to us."

Pam ignored his offer, and continued in a sad tone full of longing. "We would do so much together, so many things. That's why I sit in the room with the computer."

"That's where you and he would talk together," Judy said compassionately.

"The room was a favorite place then," David realized. "And it still is, but now it has a new meaning."

"Pam's room is where Victor is for you," I said, following David's point.

"Yes," Adrian acknowledged. "I think she goes to sit in the room, because that's where he did it. She'd always be sitting there. At first, she'd be on the bed playing with her little toys. As she got older it was the hand games. She'd spend hours on his bed."

"I still do," said Pam. "Now I just sit there. Don't think anything." As an afterthought, she added, "Now we have a dog," as if that was some kind of explanation. Perhaps she meant that the dog was a companion for her in Victor's absence.

"We always had a dog," Adrian corrected her, as if to disprove the point.

"I get to play with her. Sleeps in my room," Pam continued, uninterrupted.

"I didn't really want to bring it up," Adrian apologized. "You have to understand that Pam will tell you what you want to hear. She's very smart. She'll listen, and tell you what you want to hear to satisfy you. Like telling you about her dog. I told her to get rid of it. She still hasn't gotten rid of it."

What was he trying to say? It didn't make sense. He seemed to want to discredit her.

"What are you thinking she'd tell us?" David asked.

"Not that she doesn't miss Vic," Adrian replied. "But that she's not thinking about him as much as she says she is. Her mind is somewhere else."

Helping the Mourning Process

"It's hard to talk about Victor," Judy said. "You only remember the good times. It's hard to bring up the other times."

Taking up the challenge, Adrian began to talk about their son. "You always have a kid who is mischievous. He wasn't a bad kid. He was a typical boy. There was nothing wrong about him."

Once Adrian had started, Judy was able to fill in the picture. "He was always helpful," she said. "He'd clean up the house. I was working and he knew that the housework had to be done and the dinner had to be ready when I came home from work. He'd get on Pam to help. Now she doesn't have him to yell at her." Looking at Adrian, she concluded, "So she gets you to yell at her."

Recognizing that Adrian was filling in for the lost Victor, I asked him, "Were you and Victor close?"

"Fairly close," said Adrian.

"Pretty darn close," said Pam.

"Very close," said Judy, approvingly.

"Were you close to Victor?" David asked Judy.

"Oh yeah, he was Mom's old boy," she said with satisfaction.

"Was he adopted, too?" David asked.

"Yes, at one week old, same as her," Judy told us.

"Had you been wanting a child for long before you found Pam and Victor?" I asked.

"We had been hoping for a child," Judy said, mainly to me, woman to woman. "We'd been trying for eight years, but it just wasn't happening. We'd been under strain about not having kids. Then we got Pam. She was our Christmas baby, December 18. And Victor came around then, too, four years later."

"So Pam was a wonderful gift, and Victor, too, four years later," I said, reflecting their joy, and thinking sadly of how it had been replaced by grief and frustration. "How did Pam take to the newcomer?" I asked.

"She was real pleased with him," Judy maintained. "She helped with him. She was like a little mother."

"Were you also upset with him? An only child can feel that way when a baby comes along," I said, intending to give her permission to express her feelings directly instead of in behaviors that were annoying to her parents.

"I didn't get angry, I was excited," Pam agreed enthusiastically, and then sighed. Her sigh seemed to express unspoken, conflictual feelings about Victor, in addition to loss and longing.

Judy didn't want to hear about it. "Oh, it's easier left alone," she said.

"Oh, right," said Adrian sarcastically. Nodding in Judy's direction, he said to David, man to man, "She goes to the grave a minimum of once a week. I tried on my own. I can't do it. My sister passed away a few months ago."

"Uh-uh," Judy objected. "One year ago."

"Really? Time flies. She was being lain out in the same cemetery he was. I went to her grave okay. He was right next to her, but I couldn't go near." Adrian looked very upset, and paused. Responding to a sympathetic, encouraging look from David, he went on, speaking mostly to David, "I lost my best buddy. I'd get angry, and holler at him, and threaten like most fathers. And I hit him—only correctional spanking. I'd hit him across his backside and raise him up off the ground. Nothing to injure him."

Adrian seemed to be confessing and at the same time justifying his physical violence as loving limit-setting. I noted that he was talking to David, buddy to buddy, perhaps as a way of recalling his relationship with Victor. Similarly, I had noted how Judy talked mainly to me.

Interpreting, Linking the Symptom to the Loss

I said, "You each talk a little to us about Victor but it's hard to talk together about it, just like you don't go together to the grave to help each other with your grief. The loss of Victor is a deeply felt, shared pain, following a great gift. I think that that is why Pam is sitting between you today to prevent you coming together to deal with that loss. And at home she lives between you filling his spot, behaving partly like Victor in being your buddy, and partly opposite to him in not being helpful."

"She mows the grass. She tries to fill in for him," Adrian confirmed.

"Are you trying to be your Father's buddy, Pam?" David inquired.

It was Judy who answered, "Yes, she likes to go with him a lot. She doesn't care to go with me."

Continuing the Mourning Process

Adrian was still thinking about Victor, and was finding the substitution of Pam for Victor unsatisfactory. "Victor and I would go fishing and hunting. Vic and I, male bonding type thing. Call it selfish, if you like. Or maybe it's me that's going goofy, but the way I see it is, I lost and I'll never be able to have what I did have. Pam tries to be my buddy. She used to go fishing with me, and all of a sudden she stopped. I haven't gone fishing in a long time either," he concluded sorrowfully.

"Did she go with you after Vic died?" David asked.

"Couple of times," Adrian said.

"Didn't catch anything, though, darn it!" Pam joked.

"I don't care about catching things," Adrian said. "I like the old fiberglass pole, set out there by the water. Let the sun catch you."

"He likes sitting there doing nothing," Judy explained. "After an hour of catching nothing, I'm ready to go home, but that's a good day for him."

Revisiting the Traumatic Memory

"Judy, when you go to the grave, alone, what do you do?" David asked.

"Talk to him. Tell him I miss him. Tell him how much I loved him." Judy bit her lip. "That's all. It's hard going there."

"Does he hear you or give you any comfort?" I asked, hoping to help her keep expressing her pain.

"I hope he hears me," she said uncertainly. "It's hard out there. I haven't gone as much. I was out there last week. I guess I went for Easter. I didn't make it for his birthday, or for Christmas this year." Judy wiped her eyes.

"Too hard," I murmured.

"I just didn't get the time to get out there. Things are not getting done at home. It's not getting easier to go out there. I think I should've been there. Take a fresh flower. I felt guilty this year. I didn't do it."

We were all finding this painful. David sighed, and then pushed himself to speak.

"This is a hard one," he began. "Was there anything that you feel guilty about before he died?"

But Adrian and Judy welcomed the question.

"Maybe I didn't tell him how I'd loved him," Judy said. "That night, I'd asked him to cook dinner. Then I was going to take him out to buy him a sports jacket, and while we were out we could look at pool tables for him.

Dad had said 'no' to the pool table he wanted, but I thought we'd look for a smaller one and maybe we'd change Dad's mind."

"Are you angry at Dad as well?" David asked.

"No, it's just the combination," she replied. "One night he looked up at me and I thought, 'Gee, you're so handsome and you're such a good kid.' But I didn't say it to him. He was going on seventeen. He knew I loved him, but I didn't say so."

Adrian joined in to say, "That night Vic said to me, 'G'night Dad, I love you,' and I said, 'I love you, too.' He never said that to me, and it struck me as real funny. Next day I got home from work before her. She said he'd have the dinner on, but there was no dinner ready. So I went up to look for him, but his door was locked. I went in his room, and there he was. So I called the paramedics. I told my father—he was eighty-six and living with us at the time—to sit in a chair and not move. Then I called her to grab her purse and come home immediately, and she did. I didn't tell her on the phone why. I told her boss. Minutes later she came home."

"Where was Pam?" I wondered.

"I was at school," she said. "I was in a work-study program at the community college. I was on my way home. When I got there, I thought, 'What's an ambulance doing in front of my house?' My mother stopped me before I went in the house. I look across the street and I see my buddy Mark. All of a sudden, I see them pulling Victor out." Pam started to cry.

"So you saw him before you'd been told," I said, feeling the horror of it.

"Ohhh," she groaned.

Judy told a comforting little story. "We have a little light in the bedroom that goes on by itself. We said it was his way of coming back."

"Every night at the same time," Pam added.

"He hasn't done it lately, though," Judy said sadly.

"It's not been as easy to find Vic lately," David said. "It's been hard for you to hold on to the memory."

Judy corrected him, "No. He'll always be there."

Adrian was still in the moment of his loss. He continued, "I looked at that ambulance and cried like a baby."

Still correcting David and avoiding her husband's pain, Judy said, "We can talk about it at family reunions or something."

Linking the Symptom and the Loss at a Deeper Level

Undeterred, David returned to his point. He said, "I was thinking that the three of you are doing something to keep Victor with you by having Pam stay home, be in the middle, fill the spot."

"And be in the bedroom where he often was," I added. "As though you have to stay stuck because you feel that you would lose him completely if you changed anything."

Agreeing that things have to change, Adrian said, "I don't feel we would lose him if we changed anything. If you live in a house, you have to clean and cook. You have to do it every day. Things have to be done. If I don't get on her, nothing happens."

I returned to my earlier theme about how Pam filled in for Victor both willingly and reluctantly. I said, "Cooking and cleaning—those are things that Victor did. Pam's staying in his room to be like Victor, and not doing cooking and cleaning to not be like him, to be separate from him, to be her own person. Pam, you must be in a struggle against your wish to join Victor and your need to be different, because if you stay too much like him you could lose your life, like he did."

"That's why I wanna change," she said. "I'm trying to give more cooperation. I'm trying."

Adrian persisted with his complaint. He said, "She's usually very negative."

"I wanna change," Pam insisted.

"You want to be yourself," I said.

"I wanna do what he did," she said, meaning to be helpful, but suggesting the unconscious meaning of wanting to replace him in her parents' affections and also to kill herself and get out of the painful family situation.

To clarify her ambivalence, I said, "You wanna do what he did and kill yourself?"

"I said I *won't* do what he did," Pam corrected me.

"She *won't* do what he did," Adrian repeated.

"She won't be helpful like him—and then she won't kill herself either," I said.

David joined in. He said, "Being between your parents keeps the love alive. Perhaps you think that you can't afford to leave because then the love wouldn't be there."

"No!" Pam objected angrily.

Moving from Self-Destructive Behavior to Angry Words

"Pam, what are you so mad about?" David asked.

"I go to work and come home," she said. Pointing at Adrian, she said, "Then I'm supposed to cook and clean. He's in front of the TV. I like a break from playing house. Why can't Dad help just one day?"

"She'd like you to join her like Victor did," David suggested.

Ignoring him, Adrian said, "I usually clean house. On Wednesday, she's off. So I ask her to vacuum the house and clean the floors. She doesn't get up until 10:30 or 11:00."

"No, 9:45," she corrected him.

"Well, okay," he conceded. "That's just 45 minutes difference," he added testily.

"I think you're about to get mad at her," David observed.

"Yes, I can always get mad," Adrian agreed.

Interpreting Anger as a Defense against Grief

"You are getting mad because you are in very sore territory," David said.

"You mean I'm mad because of Victor," Adrian said roughly. "No, I don't think so. This is not about Victor."

"Let me say it, please?" David asked.

"Okay, go on say it," Adrian answered.

"It's so painful to think about Victor and how to go on living," David said. "It's easier to get in a scrap than stay with the pain of loss. Pam is trying to move beyond the stuck place."

Interpreting How Loss Prevents Oedipal Resolution

"Pam wants to change," I said. "But if you do change, Pam, then then the next thing you know, you'll be in a group home, living independently. Then Adrian and Judy lose a child and Pam will have no parents to help her feel safe. If you manage that loss, then Pam might meet someone and have a child and a home of her own without parents. Perhaps you are all afraid of that."

"No, I won't live in a group home," Pam asserted. "I have a home." Then she added assertively, "I will have a child eventually."

"You don't have much more time, Pamela," Adrian said menacingly.

"You can't have a life of your own, and a sexual life, with the computer," David pointed out. "Perhaps you feel that they need you more than you need a life."

"Why do I need you when I got your Mom?" Adrian demanded.

"Oh, you need me too," Pam responded coquettishly.

"He's teasing you," Judy said.

"He needs me," Pam repeated. "He needs someone to pick on."

"I won't be able to say, 'Pam bring me a can of pop,' " Adrian joked. "And what if she goes out every other night looking for who knows who? I'll be putting a stop to that, because the work's not getting done." He was laughing and smiling as he said this in a mock threatening tone.

David saw what he was doing. He said, "Adrian, you got past pain with hopeful ideas about grandchildren, and you started to joke. What Pam said, that she knows you need her and that she'll be there, relieved your anxiety. Knowing she'll stay and be your child relaxes the pain."

I added, "If Pam began to do things, move on, and have a life of her own, she'd leave you, and you'd be back to where you were before you got Victor and Pam. You'd like her to stay on and be the child in the family."

"I'd rather her be the child to go out and get me grandchildren," said Adrian.

"Yes, a large part of you wants that, but it's such a relief to think she'll stay as a child," David said.

"I keep saying 'goodbye,' " Adrian asserted. "If she thinks of leaving, I'll say 'Look out—the door'll hit you.' "

"And she keeps saying 'hello!' " David joked. "As long as it looks like Pam can't manage on her own, she won't be able to go. But if she's able to leave, you'll start to feel lonely. Do you know what it's like to feel lonely, Pam?"

"I do and I don't," she answered.

"Because you have Dad cooking breakfast for you every morning," Judy reminded her. To me she said, "He gets her lunch and shoves her out the door."

David responded, "That's all very caring and devoted. But the problem is that Pam isn't growing up and having a life of her own. To let her do that, you'd have to take the loss of Pam as a person who's been two people— herself and the lost Victor."

Hope of Change

To our surprise and relief, Judy reported, "She can do it when we go to our place in Michigan. She may take all day to get it done, but she manages."

"So when you're not there, Pam's fine," I said, grateful to Judy for sharing this more positive outlook on Pam's capabilities. "I'm so glad to hear of another side to Pam. She wants to change, and this lets me know that she can, if she wants to."

"Victor's loss was such a great loss," David said. "For all of you to get over it and get on with your lives, you'd have to be able to talk together like this, cry, and visit the grave together. Not this week, but sometime soon. That's what you'd have to be aiming at. Do you think you could work toward that?"

"Oh, maybe in ten years' time!" Adrian joked.

David replied in a tone equally joking yet utterly serious, "Well, you said Pam doesn't have that much time!"

Illustration of Principles of Object Relations Therapy

Before the session begins, the therapists are interacting in a friendly but subdued way. We are observing the way that the family members relate to each other and to us. In object relations therapy, we pay particular attention to how we are feeling in response to the family. We immediately feel surprise at the daughter's insistence on being between her parents like a younger child. We feel she doesn't belong there and yet, for some reason, she needs to fill that space. Our discomfort and curiosity lead us to realize that she fills a space between them and brings them together to complain about her instead of the loss that she fails to replace.

I focus on Adrian's "Rita" tattoo and it leaves me feeling that there may be things right in front of me that I can't ask about. This is a countertransference response that alerts me to a theme of attachment being scored out and denied. Again, when I feel myself resisting being pulled into the joke about not letting Pam grow up or shoving her out the door, I am alerted to themes of ambivalence about separation and individuation. My reaction to Adrian's wince when I asked about other children and his quick glance at Judy is to feel anxious and so to sense that again there is something about which it is dangerous to speak. The feelings engendered in me are clues to underlying points of anxiety and they connect me to the family members at an affective level. Then, when I subject my experience to cognitive review and tell them what I am thinking, they will feel connected to my insights. These moments are turning points for change. I sense that I will have to work with these family members to create an atmosphere of safety in which they can admit to their affections and their past experience. I will have to respect their denial and yet not go along with it so as not to inhibit our understanding.

We follow their lead, listening carefully to the words that they say, but we are equally interested in what is not said, but only indicated—by a pause, a catch in the breath, a glance, or a shift in posture. Attending to the nonverbal communication, we follow the affect and encourage its expression in words. We point out repeating patterns of interaction—in this case angry arguments—and we try to figure out why they happen. As we work, we try to understand the symptom of an individual's behavior as a repeating familywide pattern that operates as a defense against something much worse that the family cannot deal with. This attitude creates a nonjudgmental psychological space in which the family can join us to express previously unmanageable feelings and then to think about their situation. By containing anxiety and metabolizing it, we give back to the family their unthinkable anxiety and pain in a form that they can tolerate as a group so that it does not have to be expressed in crippling symptomatology affecting one of their members.

The object relations approach works toward emotional expression and understanding through interpretation arrived at through a shared experience of their repeating interactions and their underlying pain. The therapists monitor the effect of the family on their feelings and behavior—their countertransference response—and use this to detect feelings that the family cannot communicate except in distorted ways. The goal is understanding through interpretation leading to insight, then change, and growth.

The Task in a Subsequent Session.   In a subsequent session, we would not be surprised to find some retreat from the intensity of this session. We might see some lateness, confusion about the time of the meeting, or just a general opaqueness. We would need to interpret the family's reluctance to reenter the emotional field and continue with their grief work and restructuring.

Because I was the one drawn to notice the "Rita" tattoo, I would like to learn what that represents. Is it a memento of a previous relationship with a woman, and if so what did she mean to Adrian, and how does this reminder of Adrian's previous loves affect Judy and Pam? David would want to renew his suggestion that the family make a visit to the grave and would help them toward that goal. If they had already done so, he would want to review their experience thoroughly. We would also ask whether any of them had had a dream, because working on a family's associations to an individual's dream gives us another way of reaching a deeper level of understanding.

We would ask for more history of Adrian and Judy's families of origin, but not in a systematic inquiry. We tend to wait for a moment when it comes close to consciousness in association with an interaction that is occurring with feeling in the here-and-now. That way, the relevance of the family history to the emotional experience is clear, as the old experience penetrates the current relationship. We call this a "core-affective experience," when events from the there-and-then of their life in the past come alive in the here-and-now.

The main goal in work with this family is to help them resolve their highly ambivalent adherence to an oedipal triangle as a defense against differentiation, which has become associated with loneliness, loss, and danger. To help Pam become more separate, we need to ask more about her as a single woman. How does she get along at work and in her social life? Can Adrian, Judy, and Pam imagine a future? We would also need to attend to Adrian and Judy's couple relationship by asking them about their shared activities. After some work in the family setting, we would hope to arrange a couple session without Pam present so that Adrian and Judy could focus on their intimate life, but we would not expect them to be comfortable with this suggestion yet.

Finally, we need to continue talking about Victor. What was he like at different ages? What kind of friends did he have? We bring to the family our capacity for tolerating pain and this is what helps them to face their experience and recall their lost child. Our aim would be to retrieve old memories of Victor in childhood as well as at the time of his suicide until Adrian, Judy, and Pam become less traumatized by their memories of shocking loss, more accustomed to the impact of those memories, and even comforted, rather than anguished, by good memories. Detoxifying this experience should free them to discover a new reality and move them as a group to a new developmental stage with differentiated roles appropriate to their family as it exists in its current membership and at the present ages of the individual members.

But our main goal at this opening stage of treatment is to secure the next session, and to make sure that Adrian, Judy, and Pam will have a place to bring the pain of loss and find a therapeutic relationship in which they can trust. Adrian, Judy, and Pam need to have therapy until their mourning no longer interferes with their satisfactory progression through the life cycle.

Summary

The strength of object relations therapy lies in its capacity to work in depth with family issues. It is of no use, however, if the family remains uninterested in understanding after interpretation of their resistance. Some families simply want a symptom removed, or a child removed, and they will not attend for this kind of personal therapy. It is based in theory that applies equally well to other modalities and so there is no conflict when concurrent individual, couple, and family treatments are needed. We need further research into fundamental concepts such as Drew Westen's work on clinically relevant, empirically sound assessment procedures for personality assessment, and his findings on affect regulation, motivation, object relations, and unconscious process (Westen, 1990; Westen & Shedler, 1999; Westen, in press). We need more access to questionnaires like the PREOQ (People Relating to Each Other Questionnaire) that the clinician can use to evaluate object relations before and after therapy (Birtchnell, 1993). We need research to show the effectiveness of object relations family therapy.

Specialized Training and Certification

The International Institute of Object Relations Therapy offers a two-year training program leading to a certificate in couple, child, and family therapy. Any qualified mental health professional may apply for this as part of their continuing education. The program consists of two week-long summer institutes offered only in Washington, DC, and eighteen four-hour monthly seminars or forty-eight one and a half-hour weekly seminars offered in Charlottesville, Chevy Chase, Long Island, Manhattan, San Diego, Panama City, Republic of Panama, and elsewhere by videoconferencing. Those interested in the application of object relations to all modalities can enroll in the two-year program in Object Relations Theory and Practice (only in Washington, DC), which consists of two week-long summer institutes and eight weekend conferences featuring distinguished guest instructors who are leading object relations theorists. The teaching and learning is organized by faculty using multiformat learning in which lecture, video, large group discussion, and small group discussion are combined. Mental health professionals who have completed the two-year program can proceed to the advanced certificate in Clinical Application, which takes approximately another two years of individual and group supervision and personal therapy.

Suggested Readings

Box, S., Copley, B., Magagna, J., & Moustaki, E. (1981). *Crisis at adolescence*. Northvale, NJ: Jason Aronson.

Scharff, D. E. (1982). *The sexual relationship: An object relations view of sex and the family*. London: Routledge and Kegan Paul. Reprinted 1997, Northvale, NJ: Jason Aronson.

Scharff, D. E. (Ed.). (1995). *Object relations theory and practice*. Northvale, NJ: Jason Aronson.

Scharff, J. S., & Scharff, D. E. (1992). *A primer of object relations therapy* (formerly known as *Scharff Notes*). Northvale, NJ: Jason Aronson.

REFERENCES

Bion, W. (1959). *Experiences in groups*. New York: Basic Books.

Bion, W. (1962). *Learning from experience*. New York: Basic Books.

Bion, W. (1967). *Second thoughts*. London: Heinemann.

Birtchnell, J. (1993). *How humans relate*. Westport, CT and London: Praeger.

Carlson, J., & Kjos, D. (1997). *Family therapy with the experts*. Boston: Allyn & Bacon.

Casement, P. (1991). *On learning from the patient*. New York: Guilford.

Dicks, H. V. (1967). *Marital tensions: Clinical studies towards a psychoanalytic theory of interaction*. London: Routledge and Kegan Paul.

Ezriel, H. (1952). Notes on psychoanalytic group therapy II: Interpretation and research. *Psychiatry, 15*, 119–126.

Fairbairn, W. R. D. (1952). *Psychoanalytic studies of the personality*. London: Routledge and Kegan Paul.

Klein, M. (1946). Notes on some schizoid mechanisms. *International Journal of Psycho-Analysis, 27*, 99–110.

Klein, M. (1975). *Envy and gratitude and other works 1946–1963*. London: Hogarth Press and the Institute of Psycho-Analysis.

Ravenscroft, K. (1988). Psychoanalytic family therapy approaches to the adolescent bulaemic. In H. Schwartz (Ed.), *Psychoanalytic Treatment and Theory* (pp. 443–488). Madison, CT: International Universities Press.

Scharff, D. E. (1989a). An object relations approach to sexuality in family life. In J. Scharff (Ed.), *Foundations of object relations family therapy* (pp. 399–417). Northvale, NJ: Jason Aronson.

Scharff, D. E. (1989b). Transference, countertransference and technique in object relations family therapy. In J. Scharff (Ed.), *Foundations of object relations family therapy* (pp. 421–445). Northvale, NJ: Jason Aronson.

Scharff, D. E., & Scharff, J. S. (Eds.). (1987a). *Object relations family therapy*. Northvale, NJ: Jason Aronson.

Scharff, D. E., & Scharff, J. S. (1987b). Couples and couple therapy. In D. E. Scharff & J. S. Scharff (Eds.), *Object relations family therapy* (pp. 227–254). Northvale, NJ: Jason Aronson.

Scharff, D. E., & Scharff, J. S. (1991). *Object relations couple therapy*. Northvale, NJ: Jason Aronson.

Scharff, J. S. (1989a). *Foundations of object relations family therapy*. Northvale, NJ: Jason Aronson.

Scharff, J. S. (1989b). Play: an extension of the therapist's holding capacity. In J. S. Scharff (Ed.), *Foundations of object relations family therapy* (pp. 447–461). Northvale, NJ: Jason Aronson.

Scharff, J. S. (1998). Discussion of Arietta Slade's paper, "Attachment theory and research: Implications for the theory and practice of individual psychotherapy." Conference on the Clinical Implications of Attachment Theory and Research sponsored by The Center of Adult Development and the International Institute of Object Relations Therapy, Saturday May 2, 1998, Bethesda, MD.

Scharff, J. S., & Scharff, D. E. (1994). *Object relations therapy of physical and sexual trauma*. Northvale, NJ: Jason Aronson.

Scharff, J. S., & Scharff, D. E. (1998). *Object relations individual therapy*. Northvale, NJ: Jason Aronson.

Shapiro, R. (1979). Family dynamics and object relations theory: An analytic group interpretive approach to family therapy. In J. S. Scharff (Ed.), *Foundations of object relations family therapy*, (pp. 225–258). Northvale, NJ: Jason Aronson.

Slade, A. (1996). Attachment theory and research: Implications for the theory and practice of individual psychotherapy. Unpublished manuscript. In preparation for J. Cassidy and P. R. Shaver (Eds.), *Handbook of attachment theory and research*. New York: Guilford.

Slipp, S. (1984). *A dynamic bridge between individual and family treatment*. New York: Jason Aronson.

Stadter, M. (1996). *Object relations brief therapy: The therapeutic relationship in short-term work*. Northvale, NJ: Jason Aronson.

Westen, D. W. (1990). Towards a revised theory of borderline object relations: Contributions of empirical research. *International Journal of Psycho-Analysis, 71*, 661–693.

Winnicott, D. (1958). *Collected papers: Through Pediatrics to psycho-analysis*. London: Hogarth.

Winnicott, D. (1965). *The maturational processes and the facilitating environment*. London: Hogarth.

Winnicott, D. (1971). *Playing and reality*. London: Tavistock.

Zinner, J., & Shapiro, R. (1972). Projective identification as a mode of perception and behavior in the families of borderline adolescents. *International Journal of Psycho-Analysis, 53,* 523–530. Also in J. S. Scharff (1989). (Ed.), *Foundations of object relations family therapy* (pp. 109–126). Northvale, NJ: Jason Aronson,

12 Internal Family Systems Therapy

RICHARD SCHWARTZ AND MICHI ROSE

Richard Schwartz

Overview of Internal Family Systems

Internal family systems therapy uniquely applies systemic principles and processes to the individual, family, and sociocultural levels of human organization. The basic orientation of internal family systems (IFS) therapy is that people have healing resources within them, but their access to these resources is blocked by constraints. The IFS healing cycle involves releasing these constraints and reconnecting people with their inner resources. The IFS approach for doing this combines multiplicity of mind with systems thinking.

The internal family systems model is based on the concept of the multiplicity of mind. The mind is composed of different parts or subpersonalities, which take on different roles such as anger, fear, doubt, skepticism, and so on. These intrapsychic parts, or subpersonalities, carry "burdens" or beliefs and feelings that have been absorbed from the outside environment. These "burdens" of extreme beliefs or feelings are like scripts that set the parts' agendas and force them into their extreme roles. Many of these burdens are "legacy burdens" that people have absorbed from members of their family of origin or the culture. The IFS therapeutic process offers a systematic approach to release these burdens, which, in turn, releases the parts from their extreme roles.

In addition to parts, internal family systems therapy has a unique concept of Self, which distinguishes it from many other therapeutic models. The IFS concept of Self is akin to the soul. In IFS therapy, the Self is the key resource for healing. When people are in Self-leadership, they are compassionate and calm, confident yet curious, capable of both agency and communion. IFS therapy focuses on bringing people into the energy of Self, so the Self can take the lead in healing the client's own inner system and relationships with others. IFS has developed special ways to release a person's Self.

IFS applies systems thinking to this internal multiplicity of parts and Self. There is a network of relations within the inner ecology of mind. The parts or subpersonalities often distrust each other, and even distrust the Self of the person in which they reside. Within an individual's psyche, there is a system of relationships among the parts or subpersonalities (coalitions, polarizations, scapegoating, isolating, etc.) that is similar to the dynamics of families, hence, the name internal family systems therapy. These inner parts function together as a system. Their interactions with each other can be tracked, similar to tracking sequences of interactions externally among family members. IFS therapy involves establishing relationships of trust among the parts, between the parts and the Self, and among the Selves of different people.

An individual is "nested" within the larger social system of his or her family and the culture. These internal and external levels are intricately interwoven. This allows IFS therapists to use the same principles and processes with families (externally) as with individuals (internally) and vice versa.

The basic goal in work with couples and families is to bring people into Self-to-Self relationship with each other. In a Self-to-Self relationship, the Self of one person relates directly to the Self of another, rather than the parts of one person relating directly to the parts of the other. Parts of one person often become "polarized" with the parts of another person, constraining or occluding the Self of each, and creating chronic conflicts between them.

The overall objective of internal family systems therapy is to bring balance, harmony, and Self-leadership to both the intrapersonal system (parts and Self within a person) and to the interpersonal system (parts and Self between people). Although beyond the scope of this paper, IFS further extends its objective to also include the unfolding of balance, harmony, and Self-leadership in the greater sociocultural realm of the nested systems. IFS does not work with one level of the nested system to the exclusion of the others. The IFS framework encompasses individuals, families, and sociocultural levels, and applies the same theoretical model, principles, and methodology to all of them.

Development and Historical Background

Internal family systems therapy was developed in the mid 1980s by Richard Schwartz (Breunlin, Schwartz, & MacKune-Karrer 1992; Goulding & Schwartz, 1995; Schwartz, 1987, 1988, 1992, 1995). The framework for this model was "client-driven." It derived from the way clients talked about their feelings, beliefs, and behaviors. As Schwartz worked on an outcome study using a structural family therapy approach with bulimics, he listened to his clients talk about their relapses into binge eating. Clients talked about their parts, i.e., a part of them would binge, then a part would feel guilty, then a part of them would get retriggered and eat again, and so on. He noticed how these parts formed an internal system, a complex of parts in relationship to each other within the client that could be tracked as patterns.

While designing this model, Schwartz and his colleagues tried to presuppose as little as possible so as to build it in collaboration with clients and their subpersonalities. We tried to listen carefully to people's (and our own) parts and learn from them how to help them transform. With embarrassing frequency, the presuppositions they did have were destroyed in this process and replaced by the ideas and techniques described in this essay.

The IFS model represents a new synthesis of two already existing paradigms: systems thinking and the multiplicity of the mind. It brings concepts and methods from various schools of family therapy to the world of subpersonalities. This synthesis was the natural outcome when Schwartz, as a young, fervent family therapist, began hearing from clients about their inner lives. After he was able to set aside his preconceived notions about therapy and the mind, and began to really listen to what clients were saying, he heard over and over descriptions of what they often called their parts—the conflicted subpersonalities that resided within them. This was not a new discovery. Many other theorists have described a similar inner phenomenon, beginning with Freud's id, ego, and superego, Jung's archetypes and complexes, and, more recently, the object relations conceptions of internal objects. This idea is also at the core of less mainstream approaches like transactional analysis (ego states), psychosynthesis (subpersonalities), and is now also known in cognitive–behavioral approaches as *schemata*.

As he listened to clients, Schwartz's understanding of the nature of subpersonalities shifted from a unidimensional position akin to a schema—that is, that there was an angry part, a sad part, a self-critic, and so on—to the multidimensional view that each part has a full range of feelings and beliefs, but displays only a portion of those because of its role in the system.

This multidimensional view of subpersonalities situates the IFS model within the tradition of Jung (1962, 1969a, 1969b) and his younger contemporary,

Roberto Assagioli (1973, 1975; Ferrucci, 1982), who developed psychosynthesis. Since Jung and Assagioli, a number of theorists have recognized our natural multiplicity and, in exploring this territory, have made observations that are remarkably similar to one another. They share a belief that these internal entities are more than clusters of thought or feeling, more than mere states of mind. Instead, they are seen as distinct personalities, each with a full range of emotion and desire, and of different ages, temperaments, talents, and even genders. These inner personalities have a large degree of autonomy in the sense that they think, say and feel things independently of the person in whom they exist. Jung's later writing describes archetypes and complexes in ways that approach autonomous multiplicity, as does a Jungian derivative called "voice dialogue" (Stone & Stone, 1993; Stone & Winkelman, 1985). In addition, ego state therapy, developed by hypnotherapists John and Helen Watkins (Watkins, 1978; Watkins & Johnson, 1982; Watkins & Watkins, 1979) approaches, and Assagioli's psychosynthesis subscribes to, full-personality multiplicity (see Rowan, 1990; and Schwartz, 1995, for more on multiplicity).

A Systemic View

Most of these groundbreaking approaches focused on individual aspects of different subpersonalities, giving less attention to how these inner entities functioned together, as a system. Because Schwartz's training steeped him in systems thinking, it was second nature to begin tracking sequences of internal interaction in the same way he had tracked interactions among family members as a structural/strategic family therapist. As he did, he learned that, across people, parts take on common roles and common inner relationships. He also learned that these inner roles and relationships were not static and could be changed if one intervened carefully and respectfully. He began conceiving of the mind as an inner family and experimenting with techniques he had used as a family therapist.

Boundaries

For example, the structural family therapy techniques called "enactment" and "boundary-making" involve improving the boundaries around subsystems within a family (Minuchin, 1974; Minuchin & Fishman, 1981). When two polarized family members are discussing issues, the therapist prevents others from interrupting and keeps the two engaged until some new resolution is achieved. In working with internal families, it quickly became clear that parts were as highly polarized as the external families in which they developed. Many parts had never related directly to one another and maintained extreme views of what the others were like. They formed alliances and coalitions and would interrupt one another with impunity. As Schwartz began trying to improve inner boundaries by asking parts to step back and not interfere when other parts were interacting, he found that, as was true in external families, long-standing polarizations often melted once two parts communicated directly and without the influence of other parts. It also became clear that parts had boundaries, in the sense that they could separate their idiosyncratic emotions and beliefs from one another. Helping them do that not only allowed them to resolve their conflicts more easily but also helped them each identify what their feelings and beliefs really were, separate from the role they are forced into or from the general inner tumult.

Characteristics of Internal Family Systems

Internal family systems brings together a number of aspects, which, when combined, encompass a unique approach to therapy. These aspects include: the parts, the Self, the nature of the problem, the nature of the therapy, the role of the therapist, and a nested systems framework.

The Parts

Intrapersonally, an objective of IFS therapy is to bring multiplicity of mind, the inner ecosystem of parts, into balance and harmony under leadership of the Self. IFS does this by using a systems approach that respects all the parts.

Imagine a person's psyche as an orchestra. In this analogy, the instruments are the parts or subpersonalities and the conductor is the Self. For instance, the trumpet may play fear and the drum play anger. The trumpet can blast out its voice of fear without regard to the other instruments, without regard to the music played, and without regard to the conductor or Self. The trumpet and drum can get into a fight and blast each other, creating chaos. They may even kick the conductor off the podium and take over control, overwhelming the leadership of the conductor. The parts can control and overwhelm the Self.

The IFS therapeutic process of "unblending" parts to establish Self-leadership is analogous to getting the trumpet and drum to leave the podium, to go back to their seats in the orchestra, and to trust the leadership of the conductor. IFS has systemic ways to "unblend" parts to reestablish Self-leadership.

IFS is based on a systems approach. Just as each member of the orchestra is honored for the voice it contributes to the whole, IFS honors each part. In an orchestra, some instruments may have broken strings, or be out of tune, or even be locked up in the basement cellar. IFS involves the repair of wounded parts through the release of their "burdens," the compassionate witnessing of the parts' stories, the retrieval of parts that have been exiled from the system, and the restoration of parts to their true voices and new roles. IFS treats each part respectfully, honoring each part's role, as it works systemically with the whole to bring balance and harmony to the internal system, just as the members of an orchestra come to play together well, as a whole, under the leadership of a conductor.

The parts within a person are able to function relatively autonomously, expressing their own thoughts, feelings, and beliefs with a substantial degree of independence from the person in whom they exist. Each part has a much fuller range of beliefs and feelings than a single instrument, but is constrained from expressing this range because of its role in the system. Parts have full personalities, but because of the "burdens" that they carry, their full personalities are restricted to more limited roles such as anger, depression, sadness, fear, self-doubt, perfectionism, and so on.

IFS recognizes three categories of roles of parts in this internal system: the "managers," "exiles," and "firefighters." The three groups of parts are distinguished by the different roles they take in the internal system. The "managers" are the parts that function to maintain control of both the person's internal and external environment. Manager parts are in responsible, protective roles. They work to keep the system stable, safe, and under control. They function to keep painful, hurt, frightened, shamed, and worthless feelings from consciousness, i.e., to keep the parts that carry those feelings in exile. Managers feel responsible for keeping the vulnerable parts from being triggered; they want to keep those parts repressed, locked up, or deeply buried. This is also to protect the vulnerable parts. Examples of parts in manager roles are client resistance, critical parts, pleasing parts, performing parts, and perfectionist parts.

"Exiles" are the parts that carry the pain, hurt, wounds, and suffering in the internal system. Humiliation, shame, vulnerability, and worthlessness are carried by these parts. These parts are exiled and isolated in the internal system. Exiled parts are often young, needy, and scared. A wounded inner child is an example of an exile part. The internal system views exiles as dangerous because, not only do they bring out painful feelings, but they also look for ways to relieve their pain that can be destructive. For example, an inner child part that carries the pain from early child abuse may seek a partner who is similar to the initial abuser, in the hope that this person will be the redeemer to remove its burden of pain from the past. Ironically, in attempting to unload their problems, these parts can recreate the very problems they are trying to fix, so manager parts try to keep them exiled.

When the exiles surface, then "firefighter" parts are triggered. The firefighter parts function is to put out the fire of the pain carried by the exiles, as if they were firefighters putting out a fire. They attempt to douse the pain or distract from the pain. Examples of firefighter activities are alcoholism, overeating, sexual addiction, overwork, rage, sleeping, cutting, and suicide. Firefighter behavior is actually well intentioned, i.e., the intention is to protect the internal system from experiencing the pain or hurt. However, firefighters do not solve the problem because they do not heal the exiles. The ways in which firefighters douse the pain can, itself, create other problems.

Internal family systems therapy views this multiplicity of mind—the manager parts, exile parts, firefighter parts, as well as the Self—as a dynamic network of interactive energies. It is an internal ecosystem of relationships. There are internal coalitions, alliances, polarizations, conflicts, and trusting and non-trusting relationships that affect the nature of external relationships. The relationships within a person play out in the relationships outside the person and vice versa.

The Self

The concept of Self sets the foundation of internal family systems therapy. The goal of IFS is to establish the state of Self-energy. When the Self is differentiated, then its resources are released. The Self is a loving, healing force. From the state of Self-leadership people can balance, harmonize, and heal their own internal ecosystem of parts and release parts from their extreme roles. People in Self-leadership can make clear choices from Self rather than be compulsively driven into choices by their parts' agendas for them.

The internal family systems concept of Self is different from other psychological orientations. The IFS concept of Self is closer to that of the Soul. The Self is the core, the essence of a person. The IFS model holds that everyone has a complete Self. The IFS perspective is that people are born with the Self fully intact. This differs from other psychological developmental models in which the self needs the proper environment (good parenting) in order to develop. Many schools of therapy view clients as lacking this healthy inner state, and work to develop ego strength where they presume none resides. IFS recognizes a fully intact Self at everyone's core, which can be accessed by releasing constraints.

The experience of Self is the experience of an internal energy state: the flow of chi, ki, prana, or life force. Many people experience the state of Self as similar to certain states of mindful meditation. Many martial arts cultivate this sense of Self or inner balance. The Self is not an abstraction; its presence can be fully sensed in the body. Mental clarity, focus, and awareness are heightened in the state of Self.

When people are Self-led they are in a state of energy that buffers or protects them from environmental stress. They can be in traumatic situations without being traumatized. The state of Self can protect parts from absorbing the "burdens" of extreme beliefs and feelings from the outer environment.

People in Self-leadership are characterized by their qualities of calm and compassion. When people are in Self, they are confident and curious. There is a quality of equanimity about them. They are distinguished by a centered, spacious, open quality. They act from a sense of inner balance and harmony. When Self-led, there is ease in a person's eyes, voice, body language, and energy that people experience as "real," substantial, genuine and authentic.

The Self is capable of holding dualities without contradiction. Like a photon, the Self acts both like a wave and a particle. The Self is both yin and yang, passive and active. The IFS concept of Self differs from many Eastern religions' concepts of a compassionate, passive witness. In the IFS model, the Self simultaneously holds the duality of agency and communion. People speak and act from Self. In IFS, the Self is an agent of action that acts in the world; on the other hand, it is also a receptive seer, a silent observer, and a compassionate witness. The Self is not only warm and receptive, but can also be forceful and assertive.

The Self can express the thoughts and feelings of the parts. The Self can speak for the parts, voicing their thoughts and feelings so they are acknowledged, without the parts taking over control. For instance, anger can be expressed either directly by an angry part or indirectly through the Self expressing for the angry part. Anger can be voiced through the Self. On the other hand, when the angry part overwhelms the Self, the expression of the anger comes directly from the angry part. This is a very important distinction. Recipients of the anger can easily sense this difference. The choice of words, the intensity of the verbal behaviors, music of the nonverbal behaviors, the very nature of the communication differs depending on whether the anger is coming directly from the angry part or being expressed through a fully present Self. Anger experienced directly from a part is more likely to trigger the receiver's parts (retaliatory anger, fear, withdrawal, etc.) than if the anger of that part were expressed through the person's Self. For this reason, much of the work with couples or families involves getting people to speak for, rather than from, their parts.

The amount of Self presence is variable. If parts occlude the Self, then only a little Self will be available to the client. Parts can overwhelm the Self to varying degrees. In people who have been highly traumatized, the parts can fully occlude the Self's functioning as if the Self had become frozen, been shut away, or had left the body. In such situations, manager parts attempt to function in place of the Self. A critical mass of Self needs to be present for it to be an active resource for healing.

When couples are in conflict, the ideal is a Self-to-Self relationship, i.e., the Self of one person interacts with the Self of the other to the greatest degree possible. In couples with relationship problems, the parts of one person typically become polarized with the parts of the other. This interpersonal part-to-part polarization not only creates problems, but also is a manifestation of the lack of Self-leadership within each individual. The IFS methods are designed to establish Self-connections within individuals and between them.

Many clients report that being in Self also brings them into a greater experience of spirituality, an expanded experience of connection to Source, God, Spirit, Higher Self, Intuition, or whatever they regard as a greater energizing force. Maintaining Self-leadership can be, like holding the state of mindfulness, a spiritual practice.

The spiritual aspect of being in Self or Soul distinguishes IFS from many other forms of therapy (Rose, 1996a). "Self-to-Self" relationships are similar in nature to the "I–Thou" relationships described by Martin Buber (1937); they share the same qualities of deep universal connection and respect. The IFS approach to bringing harmony into the multiplicity of mind and increasing Self-leadership becomes an operational way to bring the spiritual qualities of "I–Thou" relationships into family therapy.

Nature of the Problem

The internal family systems model views problems as manifestations of lack of balance, harmony, and Self-leadership at internal or external levels. The problem can be identified at all the different levels of the nested system: the individual, family, and sociocultural levels. Internal family systems therapy works with problems at all three levels.

Intrapersonally, IFS frames the therapeutic problem as discovering how to release the client's inner resources to reestablish balance, harmony, and Self-leadership in the system. The imbalances, disharmony, and lack of Self-leadership in the individual's internal system are due to the parts or subpersonalities being forced into extreme roles. These parts are in their extreme roles because of the "burdens" that they carry. IFS defines "burdens" as extreme beliefs, emotions, feelings, and energies that are absorbed from the outside environment. Through the IFS process of in-sight imagery, clients can actually identify these burdens on the parts. For instance, a scared child part will identify the burden of worthlessness as a dark rock in her heart. These "burdens" set the agendas for the parts, affecting their attitudes and behavior. The burdens that the parts carry put them into extreme roles that occlude the Self and create systemic imbalances. Ironically, the parts themselves do not want to be in these extreme roles, but often feel that they need to be for the sake of the system.

These burdens are often "legacy burdens." Legacy burdens are the extreme beliefs and/or emotions that are passed down through generations from grandparent to parent to child. In these cases, the individual's parts have become intergenerational players in a greater family-of-origin problem. This is a unique way of framing family-of-origin problems because it views the legacy burden as the problem, not the parts or the people. Legacy burdens are beliefs or feelings such as, "You're not good enough," "You are stupid," "You are worthless."

Burdens force parts into their extreme roles, which cause problematic relationships with other parts and with the Self. The primary relationship problem is that the parts do not trust the Self. This lack of Self-trust, which occurs in internal relationships, is played out interpersonally. Interpersonal balance and harmony is a function of intrapersonal balance and harmony and vice versa. The leverage point for working with a couple is getting each person's parts to trust that person's own Self, rather than looking primarily to their partner for healing.

The initial steps of such an intervention are illustrated in the IFS videotape session that accompanies this book. The videotape session shows how the wife's fearful part comes into a more trusting relationship with her own Self, which decreases her vulnerability to her spouse.

The videotape session shows that a loss of Self-leadership can come about when parts overwhelm the Self; IFS calls this "blending" because the parts blend with the Self and occlude it. In the orchestra analogy, this occurs when instruments come up to the podium, kick the conductor off, and take control. For instance, a fearful part can overwhelm the person's Self with its feelings. The loss of Self-leadership can also come about when extreme parts polarize with each other. In the orchestra analogy, if the trumpet and drum blare out at each other in a fight, they can disrupt the orchestra music and overwhelm the conductor.

There are many different types of "polarizations" between parts. Polarizations can occur between all three categories of parts: managers, firefighters, and exiles. A critical manager can be polarized with the firefighter part that wants to drink alcohol. A manager who wants to get things done can be polarized with another manager who demands perfection. Client resistance is sometimes a manager polarized with an exile in order to prevent the pain carried by the exile from surfacing. In the tape, Lauren's "wandering" part (a firefighter) is polarized with other parts that don't want Kathy to be mad at him (managers) and criticize him for doing it. Kathy's caretaking manager is polarized with the exiled scared part that wanted her to think of herself first.

Polarization between parts can be interpersonal, as well as intrapersonal. The scared part of a wife can be polarized with the rageful part of her spouse. Or a wife's critical manager can be polarized with her husband's critical manager. Parts in extreme roles can become polarized and create imbalance and disharmony in any system. In the tape, for example, Lauren's manager, which pretends there are no problems, is polarized with Kathy's angry part, which wants to talk about issues.

Just as in families, parts not only polarize but they also protect one another. Lauren's wandering part tries to find someone who will take care of the hurt little boy inside him. Kathy's angry firefighter protects her scared little girl. The important thing to remember is that any extreme part is likely polarized with another part within or outside the person and also may be protecting another part. As long as the polarization or the protection exists, the part cannot change. So, rather than pushing a part to give up its role, therapists need to help explore the constraints it faces in giving it up: what parts might take over (polarization) or might get hurt (protection) if it stopped doing what it is doing.

The therapeutic problem is essentially the same at all levels of the nested system; it is to establish Self-leadership within the individual's parts, Self-leadership within the individual, and Self-leadership in each member of the family, Self-leadership in groups and in society. The therapeutic problem is to have people's parts trust their Self and relate from Self to Self. Self-leadership brings about the restoration of balance and harmony in the nested systems.

Nature of the Therapy

The IFS therapeutic process involves reestablishing the leadership of Self within an individual and reestablishing Self-to-Self relationships between individuals. It achieves this through a systems approach to working with the multiplicity of mind within and between people.

Internal family systems is a transformational therapy. It involves transforming: the parts, the relationships among parts, the relationships between parts and the Self, and the relationships between people. The nature of these transformations involves releasing the constraints on the system. The IFS therapist works to release both the internal and external constraints that keep parts in their extreme roles.

The IFS model takes the position that the resources for healing are within the clients themselves. The nature of the therapy is to help clients to release the constraints that block them from connecting with their own inner healing resources. The IFS therapeutic process involves unblocking the constraints to Self-leadership. The state of Self-leadership is itself the most primary and important internal resource for the client's own healing.

When a client is Self-led, then the Self of the client and Self of the therapist can form a healthy collaborative partnership. In many regards, the Self of the client becomes the client's therapist, which decreases the risk of client dependency on the therapist. When the client is in Self, it allows the therapeutic process to organically unfold, following a principle of Self-organization, in which the deep wisdom of the inner system inherently knows how to guide the healing process. It is critical for the IFS therapist to discern when clients are, and are not, in Self in order to help them into Self-leadership. IFS therapists are trained in parts' detection.

The IFS uses a modality referred to as "in-sight" that is similar to the Jungian active imagination. In-sight is used to identify the parts and work with them. In-sight is an active process that includes sound, kinesthetic, felt-senses, and energy, in addition to vision. Clients sense their parts as images (tree, animal, light, rock, etc.), sound (tone, words, etc.), body sensations (heat, tightness, heaviness, etc.), felt-senses and energy. As the parts themselves transform, often their images transform. As examples, the image of a rock may transform into a light cloud, a part initially seen as a young child may grow older, or a felt heaviness may lift. Through the in-sight process, clients are able to communicate with the parts of themselves that are subconscious and elude direct awareness. Through in-sight, parts can give messages, tell or show their stories, share their feelings, and become understood and release their burdens. The modality of in-sight imagery helps clients work by intuition rather than intellect, through direct experience in the body rather than analytic thinking, and at a deeper level of consciousness than surface awareness.

Internal family systems therapy has therapeutic guidelines for systems intervention. One guideline is to work with the managers and firefighters prior to working with the exiles. IFS therapists are trained to get the permission of the managers and firefighters before they use interventions with exiled parts. Managers and firefighter parts are asked about their fears and those fears are reassured before proceeding. This respectfully honors the protective role of these parts and respects the safeguards already in place in the client's internal system. It also elicits the cooperation of the parts in the manager and firefighter roles as allies in the therapy. Some other therapies make the mistake of trying to bypass this step of joining with the managers and firefighters and getting their permission before entering into vulnerable psychological territory. Without their cooperation, the manager and firefighter parts, in doing their job to protect the system, can sabotage the therapeutic outcome. Unfortunately, the videotape that accompanies this text is not a good example of observing this guideline. Because he sensed that a lot of her Self was present, Schwartz didn't check with Kathy's managers initially to get permission to work with her exile. He did check periodically to get permission to proceed, however.

Rather than further polarizing parts, the therapist respectfully explores the inner relationships that keep parts in their roles and then has ways to release these constraints. Parts often wish to change roles, but feel that they cannot until the parts that they protect, or are polarized with, have also changed. Thus, the system, itself, constrains change. The nature of internal family systems therapy involves releasing the constraints on the system. IFS has developed ways to identify and release the constraints that keep parts in their extreme roles. When the client is in Self-leadership, then the client's own system will move toward healing.

From the IFS systemic perspective, healing the internal system as a whole ultimately requires healing the exiles. Even if the firefighter parts responsible for behaviors such as rage, alcoholism, overeating, affairs, and so forth are transformed, when the exiled parts carrying the pain remain and continue to be triggered, then the internal system will come up with new firefighters or bring in other ways to cope with the pain. The IFS therapeutic cycle involves releasing the constraints and inviting in strengths; the more strengths or inner resources available, the easier it is to release the constraints, and the more constraints released, the easier it is to bring in more strengths.

With couples or families, the therapist works in distinct stages, as the videotape illustrates. First, Schwartz introduced the parts language as he listened to them describe sequences of interaction around their problems. Next he helped both Kathy and Lauren identify the parts of themselves that they wanted to change to improve the relationship, and got permission from them to stop their interactions when those parts emerged. He asked them to talk to each other about an issue and tried to ensure that they communicate through their Selves. As it became clear that their system was constrained by Loren's wandering firefighter and Kathy's fear of it, Schwartz worked with Kathy's fear to help her feel more empowered. In general, when a system is constrained by any one part, IFS therapists work first with the parts that fear it. After that, the oppressive part loses power and is usually more accessible and easier to transform.

In working with Kathy's scared little girl, Schwartz had to ask managers to step back at times to keep her Self present with the girl, to hold her in a state of compassion and curiosity relative to the part. He kept her there until the girl finally could trust that she had "come home." This is just the beginning of a healing sequence with a part that would have included the following steps that Schwartz would have led her through if there had been more time. After the little girl really trusted that Kathy cared about her, Kathy would ask the girl to show what she wanted Kathy to know about the past and Kathy would have begun witnessing scenes from her life in which she learned not to trust. After the part felt that Kathy now understood how she had taken on these burdens of distrust and fear, Kathy would ask her where she carried those burdens in the girl's body. The girl might have found a dark spot in her heart, for example, and Kathy would ask her to take the spot out. This process is called "unburdening."

With the removal of their burdens, the parts themselves often change in nature. The little girl feels lighter, more playful, when the the dark spot has been released. The "burdens" can be transformed into different, more useful forms of energy. The burden had determined the part's agenda or role. The release of the "burdens" allows parts to take on new roles and develop new role relationships with other parts and the Self. After the burdensome feelings and beliefs are released, a newly cleared space exists that the burdens had previously occupied. These and other techniques are described more fully elsewhere (Goulding & Schwartz, 1995; Schwartz, 1995).

Role of the Therapist

The IFS therapist forms a partnership with the Self of the client in such a way that the client's Self takes the lead in the person's own healing. The therapist's job shifts from working directly with clients, interpreting and reshaping or providing reparenting experience, to helping clients stay in Self-leadership so they can heal themselves. This is difficult for many therapists because it means that they need to trust the inherent healing wisdom of the client's Self, regardless of symptoms and inappropriate behaviors.

A prerequisite for being an effective IFS therapist is for the therapist, him- or herself, to stay in Self-leadership. When therapists are worried, analytic, distracted, caretaking, bored, irritated, or impatient, then they are blended with parts and not in Self-leadership. IFS therapists pull out their "parts detectors" to monitor themselves or consult with other therapists to help identify interfering parts. An IFS therapist's job is to unblend his or her own parts so as to be fully present in his or her Self. A therapist's ability to effectively facilitate IFS therapy is directly proportional to his or her ability to stay in Self-leadership.

The therapist staying in Self-leadership is more than a prerequisite; it is the essence of being an IFS therapist. As an analogy, when a tuning fork is struck it induces another tuning fork to resonate with it. Similarly, when the therapist is in Self-leadership, a relational resonance is set up between therapist and client that brings the client into Self-leadership. A therapist can know all the IFS techniques, but if he or she is not in Self-leadership, they will be ineffective. On the other hand, a therapist who does not know the IFS techniques, but is in Self-leadership, can be highly effective. The more a therapist can stay in Self and trust the client's Self, the more therapy becomes effortless and invigorating rather than draining. The more the therapist helps the client's Self do the healing, the less likely the client is to become dependent on the therapist.

The hallmark of IFS therapists is that they are very respectful. The essence of the therapist–client relationship is one of collaboration. The therapist and client join in a partnership to facilitate the process of clients uncovering their own inner resources and allowing the wisdom of the clients' internal system to bring about its own healing. Heider (1985) reflects the spirit of the IFS process and the role of therapist:

> Remember that you are facilitating another person's process. It is not your process. Do not intrude. Do not control. Do not force your own needs and insights into the foreground. If you do not trust a person's process, that person will not trust you.
>
> Imagine that you are a midwife; you are assisting at someone else's birth. Do good without show or fuss. Facilitate what is happening rather than what you think ought to be happening. If you must take the lead, lead so that the mother is helped, yet still free and in charge. When the baby is born, the mother will rightly say: 'We did it ourselves!'

Nested Systems Framework

The concept of multiple levels of Self, within nested systems, distinguishes the IFS view of Self from other models of psychotherapy. Every person has a fully intact Self from birth. Within each person there are parts (subpersonalities). Each part also has a Self. Because every part has a Self, an aim of IFS is to restore each part to its own Self-leadership and its own true nature.

Arthur Koestler (1976) developed the concept of holons, which allow us to treat any phenomenon as being both a part and a whole. A person, for example, is a holon, a discrete entity, yet he or she is also part of a family. A family is also a holon: an independent system at one level, but also embedded in a community, which is part of a country, and so on. Within a person's systems are parts, and those are also holons because they have a Self, and yet they are nested within the person. All of this forms a holarchy: different levels of holons that are nested within one another. That is, a part is a holon within a person, who is a holon within a family, which is a holon in a community, and so on.

The IFS model is intended to increase the amount of Self available at all levels of the nested holarchy. To do this, the model helps a client connect his or her Self with the Self of his or her parts. It also tries to connect the Self of one client with the Self of his or her spouse, parents or children, or others. In addition, the model often helps people connect to their own spirituality, improving the connection between their Self and what one might call the "Big Self". The goal, then, is to connect Selves both horizontally (people to people), and vertically (person to parts and to spirituality). This understanding of multiple levels of nested systems, from the intrapsychic to the sociocultural to the spiritual, allows IFS to apply the same principles and methods to all levels.

How IFS Is Like Other Theories

Because it's derived from family therapy, IFS has elements in common with several different schools of family therapy. Because of space limitations, we can only mention these many similarities.

Much of the way IFS understands and intervenes with internal systems comes from structural family therapy. The concept of boundaries and boundary-making is as applicable to internal families as it is to external. Some parts are enmeshed with us and others are disengaged. When a client interacts with a part, the therapist watches for boundary violations—the interference of other parts— just as structural family therapists do.

IFS uses the concept of positive feedback loops from strategic family therapy to understand how parts polarize with each other in ways that resemble the vicious circles of external families. Bowen theory stresses the concept of differentiation of self and, through getting parts to separate, IFS is also differentiating or releasing a client's Self. Bowen also coached clients in family-of-origin voyages during which they tried to stay differentiated in the face of their family members' provocations. In IFS we do something similar.

Virginia Satir's emphasis on creating an empathic, open-hearted connection with clients is reflected in IFS, as are her attempts to get clients to listen inside themselves and communicate directly what they find there. She actually thought of people in terms of parts and held what she called "parts parties." Narrative therapy's concern with issues of social justice is also a theme in IFS, as is the use of questions rather than directives.

IFS also has much in common with a variety of models of individual therapy. It shares a similar understanding of parts with psychosynthesis, Gestalt therapy, transactional analysis, and some versions of object relations and Jungian analysis. Like cognitive–behavioral therapy, IFS encourages inner dialogues and exploration. IFS shares a profound respect for the impact of the past on the present with most psychodynamic and trauma-based approaches. In its basic trust in the human organism's ability to heal itself, IFS is compatible with EMDR (Eye Movement Desensitization and Reprocessing), and thought-field therapy. That assumption has made for a wonderful collaboration with Hakomi, a body-centered psychotherapy, which has influenced IFS toward an increased body focus. When IFS therapists take people inside, they are entering a world familiar to hypnotherapists and shamanic practitioners. Other models also have a concept of Self or center that has some things in common with IFS. Jung, for example, wrote about such a Self.

Put more generally, IFS has many commonalities with approaches that believe people have an innate capacity for healing themselves and their relationships. It has less in common with pathology-based models that are predicated on giving something to clients that they don't have.

View of Human Functioning

The IFS is quite optimistic about human functioning. Because people are born with a fully intact Self, they have within them an inherent propensity for healing themselves emotionally, much as our bodies know how to heal themselves physically. When the Self is released from internal and external constraints, this Self-healing occurs naturally. Releasing the constraints to Self-leadership is the main goal.

Parts are also inherently positive, but may not seem so because of being forced into extreme roles by the burdens they carry. Burdens of worthlessness, shame, and fear make parts behave in ways they would prefer not to and they will gladly change once the burdens are released.

From this perspective then, seemingly pathological thinking, emotions, and behavior are the output of only small parts of people. In addition, those parts aren't defective; they have just been forced into bad roles, and they want to change into useful roles. These ideas help couples see themselves and each other differently. Rather than blaming each other for being the problem, they can see that they and their partner carry burdens from the past that are making parts on each side interfere in their Self-to-Self connection. This view increases their ability to respect and support one another rather than having their parts fight to change each other.

Range of Application

While IFS has been applied to a wide range of difficult-to-treat problems (most notably: eating disorders, depression, the traumas of child sexual abuse, PTSD (Post-Traumatic Stress Disorder), DID (Dissociative Identity Disorder), there is only one outcome study so far. It found IFS to be very effective with emotionally disturbed adolescents (Selmistraitiene, 1999).

Its application is limited not so much by diagnosis, but by the degree to which the therapist can maintain Self-leadership with a client and the degree of danger to the client in the external environment. That is, if a therapist is triggered by certain kinds of problems or people, then he or she shouldn't use IFS. Also, if a client's family, work, or community environments would react severely to their being vulnerable, then the therapist might reconsider its use. Also, there are many levels at which to use IFS, from just introducing the language to taking people on extended internal journeys. The language, by itself, is a powerful and safe tool. When therapists are uncertain about proceeding further, they can remain at that level and still help people change.

In addition, the model has been adapted for use with groups and has been combined with other techniques (dance/movement therapy, EMDR, play therapy, meditation, etc.). It helps people in all kinds of diverse or alternative families understand and change the impact of their differentness on their self-concepts. It has also been used extensively with children down to age four and with people of all levels of socioeconomic status and education.

Because of the nested systems orientation, IFS also offers a unique way of looking at larger systems and is being used by organizational consultants and by people exploring social issues like racism.

The Videotape Session

This tape is a good demonstration of the early steps of IFS couple therapy. It illustrates how an IFS therapist tracks sequences of behavior and emotion between a couple, introduces the language of parts, identifies parts of each connected to the problem, gets permission to help them try to talk Self-to-Self about an issue, helps one partner do inner work while the other witnesses, and consolidates the change that occurs. While this demonstrates only a few of the many basic IFS techniques, it shows how quickly the process can begin releasing constraints.

Tracking Sequences and Introducing the Language

As the therapist asks about the way the couple fights, he assesses which parts go to war with each other. He does this by asking how each person feels or thinks at different points in their sequence, and then reflecting back their response with the phrase, "So a part of you _____ (gets afraid/wanders/gets angry/says mean things, etc.), is that right?"

Identifying Key Parts

There are often certain parts in a couple system that are particularly polarized and constraining. In exploring their sequences, it became clear that his wandering part frightens her fearful part enough to keep her from being "real" with him.

> TH: "Difficult to trust and let your guard down."
>
> KATHY: "Not safe."
>
> TH: "What are you afraid would happen if you were more real? What kind of danger?"
>
> KATHY: "He would be unhappy."
>
> TH: "And what would be bad about that?"
>
> KATHY: "He may wander."
>
> TH: "Okay, so this wandering part of Lauren is feeling like a big heavy weight that keeps you in fear."
>
> KATHY: "Yeah, it's very real."

Asking Permission

With every step, the therapist asks permission to help in different ways. This helps reassure the protective, manager parts of each partner that they are still in control of what happens in the therapy. For example, once the key parts have been identified, the therapist asks permission to play referee as they talk to each other, and to stop the action when he notices parts taking over. That is a common role for an IFS therapist when doing couples therapy, having the couple talk to each other while trying to keep their protective parts from doing the talking and encouraging their Selves to speak. When couples achieve Self-to-Self communication, it is common that problems that seemed so large quickly evaporate. The primary job of the therapist is to help the couple remain connected that way. With Kathy and Lauren, it soon became clear that Self-to-Self communication was not possible while his wandering part had so much power to intimidate her. To reduce the power of parts like that, IFS therapists often begin working with the parts that are afraid of them.

Working with One Partner with the Other Witnesses

The therapist has Kathy find the fear in her body and then checks how much Self-leadership is available by asking her how she feels toward the part. Both the tone and content of her answer to that question contain clues for the therapist about whether she is blended with another part or not. When she says, "Almost like a fight," the therapist knows that a part that does not like the fearful one is blended with her Self. By definition, her Self would have compassion for the fear, so, if she's fighting it, her Self is not fully differentiated. So the therapist asks the one fighting with the fear to "step back," that is, to separate or unblend from her Self. When that part steps back, she immediately shifts and says the fight is less and the fear seems to be okay. It now sounds as if there is enough of Kathy's Self present to begin to help the fearful part.

The therapist then begins to help her form a trusting relationship between her Self and the fearful part, which behaves like a little girl. It is important to notice that, as Kathy's Self increasingly emerges, she knows just what to do to help the little girl and the therapist's job is mainly to keep other parts from jumping in. An example of the therapist functioning as referree occurs when Kathy said the little girl went away, and the therapist asked the part that worries about appearances to let her come back.

The little girl is an exile and the parts that fight her or worry about appearances are managers. The little girl carries the burdens of fear and mistrust that Kathy likely picked up in her family of origin. Lauren's wandering part crushes this little girl who reexperiences the earlier betrayal, and so Kathy's managers go to work to distance from him and protect that exile. Her cold and angry protectors trigger his exiles, who then trigger his wanderer, and so on. The only way out of these kinds of vicious circles is for both partners to get their exiles to trust their Selves and to unload the burdens those exiles carry.

To really take care of the little girl so that it will trust her and not depend so much on Lauren, Kathy will have to work with another part.

> TH: "Maybe you could ask [the little girl] what would make her feel safer right now. What would help?"
>
> TH: "You getting anything? What did she say?"
>
> KATHY (CRYING):   "She said, 'Stop trying to please everybody else and just take care of me.' "

Kathy has been dominated by managers that try to please and care for everyone else. Before the little girl can trust her, she will have to release the grip of those

Schwartz w/ clients

parts. If she does this and the little girl begins to trust, there are subsequent steps in IFS that lead to a full unburdening of the little girl (Schwartz, 1995). If that happens, there will be a shift in her relationship with Lauren, a shift that was foreshadowed by how she spoke to him at the end of the session. She seemed firm and strong in the message that he needed to do his work before she could let him get close to that girl again, but she was not judging him. This is how people speak when they have more Self-leadership.

As Lauren witnessed the work she did, he was able to see more clearly the damage his wandering part does to her. It is common for couples not to know how they hurt each other because, like Kathy, they usually only show their protective parts to each other. The IFS process lets people see behind the scenes and recognize the true consequences of their actions. Lauren had a moment in which he spoke from his Self, but his protectors quickly jumped back in. Despite the return of his protectors, it is likely that he will be more motivated to work on his wandering part and the exiles it protects now that he has witnessed its effects. This is a much more effective strategy for motivating people to stop hurting each other than any moralizing the therapist might be tempted to do. In subsequent sessions, the therapist would want to do that work with Lauren while Kathy witnessed. It is important to note, however, that some couples are so polarized that it is not safe to have them watch each other doing the internal work. Therapists should carefully monitor how safe it is for each partner before allowing the other to witness.

This is the way that IFS gradually allows couples to achieve Self-to-Self relationships. When each partner contains exiled parts that are stuck in the past, extremely vulnerable, and desperately needy, they will also have highly protective parts. As a result, most couples cycle around phases during which they try to get close followed by hurtful distancing and resentment. Until their exiles are unburdened and learn to trust their Selves, allowing their protectors to relax, there is little they can do to achieve lasting connections.

Summary

As is illustrated in the video, IFS offers a way for therapists to help clients find and release the constraints (both internal and external) that keep them from being the way they would like to be. It is a healing process that accesses inherent client resources to unload the pain, fear, and shame they've accumulated in their lives. This allows for Self-to-Self connections between and within people that promotes harmony and balance. It also releases the therapist from the position of the expert who gives clients something they lack (ego strength, interpretations, information, medication, corrective experiences) and, instead, enables the therapist to guide them on an inward journey to find their own truth. IFS therapists can keep their hearts open and be present for clients because they don't have to come up with the right intervention for them.

Because the goal is to bring Self-leadership to all levels of nested human systems, therapists can shift their focus fluidly from the intrapsychic to the family to any other level and maintain the same approach. For this reason, the IFS perspective also lends itself well to understanding larger social problems.

Training Opportunities

There are two-year training programs in IFS therapy running in many different sites in the United States and in Germany. In addition, there is an annual IFS conference each year in the Chicago area. Information on training opportunities as well as how to obtain other videotapes can be found through the IFS Web page at http://www.selfleadership.org or by contacting Peggy Dickson, IFSCSL@aol.com, phone: 773-463-6634. Allyn and Bacon is publishing another tape series in which Richard Schwartz works with a couple over six sessions. [It should be available by fall of 2002].

REFERENCES

Assagioli, R. (1973). *The Act of will.* New York: Penguin.

Assagioli, R. (1975). *Psychosynthesis: A manual of principles and techniques.* London: Turnstone.

Breunlin, D., Schwartz, R., & Mac Kune-Karrer, B. (1992). *Metaframeworks.* San Francisco: Jossey-Bass.

Buber, M. (1937). *I and thou.* Edinborough: T. & T. Clark.

Ferrucci, P. (1982). *What we may be.* Los Angeles: J. P. Tarcher.

Freud, S. (1923/1961). The ego and the id. In J. Strachey (Ed.), *The standard edition of the complete psychological works of Sigmund Freud (Vol. 21,)* pp. XX–XX London: Hogarth.

Goulding, R., & Schwartz, R. (1995). *Mosaic mind: Empowering the tormented selves of childhood sexual abuse survivors.* New York: Norton.

Heider, J. (1985). *The tao of leadership*. Atlanta: Humanics New Age.

Jung, C. G. (1956). *Two essays on analytical psychology*. Cleveland, OH: Meridian.

Jung, C. G. (1962). *Memories, dreams, Reflections*. New York: Pantheon.

Jung, C. G. (1969a). *The collected works of C. G. Jung: The structure and dynamics of the psyche (2nd ed., Vol. 8)*. Princeton, NJ: Princeton University Press.

Jung, C. G. (1969b) *The collected works of C. G. Jung: The archetypes and the collective unconscious (2nd ed., Vol. 9)*. Princeton, NJ: Princeton University Press.

Koestler, A. (1976). *The ghost in the machine*. New York: Random House.

Minuchin, S. (1974). *Families and family therapy*. Cambridge, MA: Harvard University Press.

Minuchin, S., & Fishman, H. C. (1981). *Techniques of family therapy*. Cambridge, MA: Harvard University Press.

Rose, M. (1996a). Internal family systems therapy: Managing personal anger. *Proceedings of the 40th annual conference of the International Society of the Systems Sciences*, Budapest, Hungary.

Rose, M. (1996b). Systemic spiritual psychology. *Proceedings of the 40th annual conference of the International Society of the Systems Sciences*, Budapest, Hungary.

Rowan, J. (1990). *Subpersonalities: The people inside us*. London: Routledge.

Schwartz, R. (1987). Our multiple selves. *Family Therapy Networker, 11*, 25–31, 80–83.

Schwartz, R. (1988). Know thy selves. *Family Therapy Networker, 12*, 21–29.

Schwartz, R. (1992). Rescuing the exiles. *Family Therapy Networker, 16*, 33–37, 75.

Schwartz, R. (1995). *Internal family systems therapy*. New York: Guilford.

Selmistraitiene, D. (1999). *The effects of internal family systems therapy on psychological maturation of adolescents with emotional and behavioral problems*. Unpublished doctoral dissertation, Vilnius University, Lithuania. (Copies can be obtained through Tom Holmes, Department of Social Work, Western Michigan University).

Stone, H., & Stone, S. (1993). *Embracing your inner critic*. San Francisco: HarperCollins.

Stone, H., & Winkelman, S. (1985). *Embracing ourselves*. Marina del Rey, CA: Devross.

Watkins, J. (1978). *The therapeutic self*. New York: Human Sciences.

Watkins, J., & Johnson, R. J. (1982). *We, the divided self*. New York: Irvington.

Watkins, J., & Watkins, H. (1979). Ego states and hidden observers. *Journal of Altered States of Consciousness, 5*, 3–18.

13 Experiential Family Therapy

KIM SNOW

Gus Napier

Evolution of the Theory

Experiential family therapy was born in the 1960s when humanistic theories of psychology were in their prime and family therapy was in its infancy. The creative, spontaneous, and innovative movements of the sixties were ripe for this new facet of psychotherapy. Following the development of such popular theories as existential, humanistic, phenomenological, and Gestalt therapy, this intuitive theory combines the *here and now* emotional experience of encounter groups with such expressive techniques as *sculpting, paradoxical intention*, and *role playing*. Experiential (or symbolic therapy, as it is sometimes called) focuses on the immediate emotional experience that occurs for all members involved in the therapy (including the therapists). Everything that occurs in the session between the therapist and the family members is said to have intense meaning for all the participants.

Developed by Carl Whitaker and his colleagues at the Atlanta Psychiatric Clinic, experiential therapy was initially created as an individual approach to psychotherapy. It was based on the premise that insight alone is not enough. The client must have an emotionally meaningful *experience* in therapy, one that touches the deepest level of his or her person, in order to really grow and change (Napier & Whitaker, 1978). Whitaker then expanded this approach and adapted it to fit the family.

Experiential family therapy can be described as a growth-oriented and expressive interpersonal encounter in which both the therapist and the client(s) strive to be real and authentic. Rather than offering insight or interpretation, the therapist provides an experience, an opportunity for family members to open themselves to spontaneity, freedom of expression, and personal growth. The interpersonal experience is, in itself, the primary stimulus to growth in this approach to psychotherapy (Goldenberg & Goldenberg, 2000). Experiential therapy is known for the emphasis that is placed on the realness of the therapist and the relationship between the therapist and the family members. It provides a more *intra*personal perspective from which to view the family. Unlike other forms of family therapy, the focus is on the individuals within the family rather than the family system.

Historical Background and Leading Figures

Carl Whitaker is credited with being the founder of experiential therapy. He is also one of the first therapists to work with families. Carl Whitaker's interesting and diversified background is the source of many of the attributes that are synonymous with experiential therapy. After growing up on a dairy farm in Raymondville, New York, Whitaker received his formal training as an obstetrician and gynecologist. After World War II, he was granted board credit in psychiatry although he had no formal experience or education in this domain. While working for two years as a resident psychiatric administrator in a small diagnostic area, Carl became involved in working with schizophrenic patients and other psychiatric patients where he developed most of his hypotheses. Whitaker then went on to receive training in child therapy, was based on the Rankin tradition, in which symbolism and nonverbal communication are important. Carl then worked with an adolescent and adult population. He was forced to adapt his clinical child therapy to working with neurotic adolescents and adult psychosomatic patients. At this time, he also began teaching psychotherapy to medical students, although he had no formal training in this area.

As noted by Carl Whitaker (1981), his inexperience as a psychotherapist and the psychological stress of the work setting led him to use and rely on co-therapy with fellow colleagues. Dr. John Warkentin and Whitaker began to see patients together so that they could talk to each other and learn from the other's different background. Whitaker attributes most of his experience to co-therapy, consultation, and learning from his patients.

The next several years were filled with trying out various innovative techniques, at University of Louisville ranging from bottle-feeding and nursing psychotic patients, to arm wrestling patients, to pykenolepsy (Carl would fall asleep in the middle of a session and then relate his dreams to the patient).

In the late 1940s, Dr. Thomas Malone joined the Department of Psychiatry at Emory University and a new union was formed. In 1953, Whitaker and Malone cowrote *The Roots of Psychotherapy*, and established their own theory of psychotherapy, experiential therapy. Dr. Whitaker's involvement with treating schizophrenics also peaked at this time. Using co-therapy, Whitaker created an aggressive form of play therapy in which the co-therapists acted as symbolic parents and created an atmosphere where the schizophrenic patients could regress to an infantile state and experience their needs being met by the symbolic "co-parents." Whitaker then adapted this treatment one step further to incorporate treating the whole family with the schizophrenic patient rather than isolating and focusing on just the "identified patient." This new form of treatment was called "non-rational therapy," and was based on the notion of getting to a more primary level of emotional sharing and connectedness. Therapy was viewed as reparenting the family. Experiential therapy was based on the assumption that many families have not been provided with emotional resources by their parents. The focus is on getting to the deeper level of emotional hunger within the family and symbolically reparenting the family so that it can function and grow independently, while allowing the individuation of all of the family members.

Whitaker's colorful background and his iconoclastic, innovative personality was the ideal combination for the creation of a radical and intuitive form of psychotherapy, experiential/symbolic family therapy. Whitaker's wisdom and provocative, challenging style influenced several of his associates and co-therapists, who then took experiential therapy to another level. Among his associates were August Napier and David Keith.

Dr. August Y. Napier received a Ph.D. in clinical psychology from the University of North Carolina. While interning at University of Wisconsin-Madison, Napier had the privilege of working and performing co-therapy with his mentor, Carl Whitaker. This experience led to the writing of *The Family Crucible* (1978), which is based on their working relationship and their encounters with families. Napier credits his interest and passion in experiential therapy to the "attraction and power of the style, and the person of Carl Whitaker" (Carlson & Kjos, 1999). Though Napier was trained and worked as a co-therapist with Whitaker, he had his own interpretation of the theory, which he describes as more structured than that of Whitaker. Napier views his approach as a combination of structural family therapy and the intuitive, provocative approach of

Whitaker. Napier is a faculty member at the University of Wisconsin, and has directed the Family Workshop, a family training institute in Atlanta, Georgia. He currently resides in North Carolina.

David Keith, another colleague and co-therapist, met Carl Whitaker in 1971 when he left the Air Force and came to the University of Wisconsin to begin his psychiatry residency. Their relationship developed around several shared interests: psychotherapy for families with schizophrenia and psychosomatic illness, psychotherapy for problems related to children, and marriage therapy that emphasized the role of marriage in personal growth and in marriage. Keith maintained a close working and personal relationship with Carl Whitaker until Whitaker's death in 1995. Keith currently is professor of Psychiatry, Family Medicine, and Pediatrics at SUNY Upstate Medical University in Syracuse, New York.

Keith has written a variety of articles and book chapters from the perspective of Symbolic Experiential family therapy, many with Dr. Whitaker. One of the most important papers from the early years was their chapter in the first edition of *The Handbook of Family Therapy* (Gurman & Kniskern, 1981); another was "Play Therapy as a Paradigm for Family Therapy"(1980). With Gary and Linda Connell, he wrote *Defiance in the Family: Finding Hope in Therapy* (2001).

Although David Keith is a psychiatrist, his clinical orientation is psychotherapy with families. He characterizes himself as a "pharmacological minimalist." The profound effect that Whitaker's approach to family therapy had on David Keith was synthesized with Keith's medical and psychiatric background. These diverse ideas were integrated into a pattern of work with families in a variety of clinical settings: inpatient units, medical consultation, and mental health centers.

Keith believes that experiential family therapy is an alternative, countercultural way to deal with psychiatric problems, and works in a way that depathologizes the human experience. He views play as a crucial component of experiential family therapy. The opposite of play is being purposeful and when therapists are purposeful they lose sight of the family's initiative and are likely to introduce their own agendas into the therapeutic setting. Psychoeducation is purposeful, and so does not fit his definition of psychotherapy. In Keith's view, all psychotherapy is play.

How This Theory Is Similar to Others

Though claiming to be *a*theoretical, experiential family therapy shares many of the core elements of humanistic, existential, phenomenological, and process encounter groups. Like these approaches, the experiential approach stresses the natural striving of all humans toward growth, actualization, freedom, choice, and self-determination. Experiential family therapy takes these fundamental premises a step further and synthesizes them in a creative, spontaneous, and artistic manner.

Like its existential counterparts, this approach also emphasizes the relationship between the therapist and the clients. Techniques and professional training are secondary to the therapist's ability to be authentic and self-aware and to apply the full use of the therapist's self when encountering a family. As with many individual approaches, such as person-centered therapy, Gestalt therapy, and existential therapy, experiential therapy also prioritizes the significance of the therapist as a person and regards the therapeutic alliance as the determining factor in affecting the process, the progress, and the outcome of therapy. All of these approaches stress the importance of empathy, interactions, joining, enactments, and experiments within the therapeutic setting.

What Makes This Theory Different or Unique

Experiential family therapy uses a perspective that differs radically from most current family systems-oriented approaches. Rather than focus on the communication and interaction between family members, experiential theory concentrates on expanding the experience and the awareness of individual members. The underlying assumption is that, if individuals are able to attain a new and deeper level of insight, personal awareness, and growth, the family members will naturally evolve to a deeper and more authentic way of relating and communicating. As the individuals become more aware of who they are, the increased awareness and feelings will promote new growth and insight within the family.

Most contemporary family approaches maintain more of an interpersonal family systems philosophy, believing that family growth rests on promoting communication and interaction between family members. Everything is viewed from a family context and each member is seen within the framework of that larger context. These theories assume more of an outside-in approach, working with family interactions as a means to support the growth of its individual members. The experiential approaches assume more of an individualistic way of dealing with the family, focusing from the inside-out, working with individual members and increasing their awareness in order to help the family as a whole.

Most systemic family theories tend to view communication and interaction as the medium to promote change within the family. Experiential therapists believe that expanding the individual experiences of all family members will shatter the defenses that the family typically uses, and bring members to a new, deeper, and more genuine level of awareness. This enhanced awareness increases the communication and the level of connection between family members and growth within the family.

Research Related to the Theory

There is not a lot of research on this approach. The personal and intuitive nature of the therapy, the critical components of the therapeutic relationship, and the personal experiences of each member cannot be clearly defined, which limits the possibility of good research. Experiential therapy is based on the realness and the person of the therapist and on the change that occurs within the therapist and the families. These variables cannot be measured or duplicated and, thus, are challenging to study or research.

Experiential therapists do contend that the change and growth that they experience within the therapeutic process is evidence of success, but no clear correlation has been studied between the personal growth of the therapists and the changes that the family reports after treatment.

Clinical Perspective

View of Human Functioning

Experiential symbolic therapy subscribes to core existential and humanistic assumptions. There is an underlying assumption that all people have a natural tendency toward growth and self-actualization (Rogers, 1951). Mental health is considered a continuous process of growth and change, not a homoeostatic or stagnant state (Nichols & Schwartz, 2001). Healthy families are able to grow and adapt to life's challenges, no matter how difficult they are. Furthermore, healthy families deal with stressful situations by coming together as a family unit and pooling their resources, coping skills, and support to work through the difficulties as a team rather than placing the blame or focus on one individual (Whitaker & Keith, 1981). Experiential therapists view healthy families as nurturing entities in which the family and the individuals within the family have a sense of identity, support, and growth. Healthy families foster a delicate balance in which the family can support, problem-solve, and develop together, and there is an environment of encouragement and acceptance that enables individual members to individuate and grow in their own ways while still maintaining a connection to the family.

Healthy families are seen as places for sharing experience and nurturing one another. Problems arise when families get caught up in dysfunctional patterns that resist the awareness of family members, suppress feelings, blunt responsiveness, and are restrictive and toxic for the growth of the family and for the individual within the family.

How the Theory Sees Mental Illness

According to experiential theory, it is assumed that dysfunction is related to an identity and power struggle as the newly formed family struggles with integrating the interactional patterns and learned behaviors of two very diverse families of origin into the present family (Whitaker & Keith, 1981). Dysfunctional families operate out of a system of rigidity and fear rather than awareness, choice, and support. Whitaker describes people as being trained by their families of origin. Some families have deep emotional voids because they never received the emotional resources from their own parents or families of origin. Lack of emotional connection and destructive patterns of communication, criticism, and blame in families of origin are often recreated within newly created family systems. These family members do not have the resources to change. It is assumed that families come to therapy because they do not feel close and are unable to individuate. Mental illness can be described as emotional sterility: lack of any feeling at all. It occurs when families deny their impulses and suppress their feelings.

This concept is illustrated by Bill, the male client, in the accompanying videotape. Bill emotionally shuts down and won't allow himself to feel any negative emotions. This dysfunctional pattern of interaction is attributed to Bill's experience within his family of origin and keeps getting played out in his current relationships. He continues to keep all of the negativity bottled up inside and the result, as we see, is the recipe for a heart attack. Gus Napier focuses on Bill's pattern of interaction and Bill's experiences. Gus then confronts and shares his concern (as a symbolic parent) for Bill.

GUS: " . . . this style of dealing with your feelings is killing you."

BILL: "I realize that."

GUS: "Well, I think that's what it is. It's not just your heredity. You grew up in a family where you had so little support that it felt like the only way to deal with life is to shut your mouth and be good. It doesn't leave any room for your feelings. So, of course, it's going to be hard to hear hers [Pat's] because there's no room for yours. What I'm wondering, see, you can't reparent each other, but you could use psychotherapy together as a way to try and figure out how you could help and support each other and where the limits are of what you can and can't do for each other. Like you can't cure him [Bill] of not having had a mother back then . . . " (Carlson & Kjos, 1999, p. 32 [in study guide]).

Oftentimes, stresses and developmental changes in everyday life (marriage, pregnancy, childbirth, new job, job loss, etc.) may act as catalysts for families to become stuck in a negative and defensive way of being. This concept is also illustrated in the videotape. Pat had quit her job two weeks before Bill had a heart attack. She was then out of work for eight months. Though their interactional pattern of communication was still dysfunctional, the added stressors placed on them by the job loss and medical concerns strained the relationship to the point that it became toxic for both of them.

Assessing Families

Experiential family therapists use a very informal and comprehensive evaluation when diagnosing families. This assessment occurs during the first interview. Experiential therapists tend to shy away from using any formal assessment instruments, using only themselves as the tool. The person of the therapist assesses the family while in session. Though experiential therapists generally go into the session with an open mind, they are constantly evaluating the interactional patterns and the intimacy demonstrated between family members.

Experiential therapists do an elaborate assessment of the whole family system, the subsystems of each generation, the triadic patterns, the dyadic collusions and teaming, and the individual dynamics. This is done by noting where family members sit, who dominates the conversation, who avoids the conversation, who is the subject of the conversation, and so on. Everything, nonverbal, verbal, and behavioral communication, is analyzed.

Though experiential therapists focus on the *here and now,* they do believe that many of the problems the families experience are due to the synthesizing of family-of-origin issues within the newly formed family. Thus, therapists do delve into the cultural and historical backgrounds of the families of origin to look for dynamics that could be causing present problems with the family. Examples of family-of-origin issues can be ethnic or religious differences, ghost members, and cultural residuals (Whitaker & Keith, 1981).

Experiential therapists also try to get a sense of the situational stress present in families (divorce, death of a family member, illness, relocation, job change, or other changes within the family). Due to the intensive observations that occur within the initial session, experiential therapists tend to have a pretty good feel for what is going on within the presenting family.

Goals of Therapy

The goals of experiential family therapy are to establish the family members' sense of belonging within the family while, at the same time, providing family members with the personal freedom to individuate. Growth, deep emotional connectedness, and expanded awareness are seen as the mediums to reach these goals. Experiential therapists achieve these goals through a delicate balance of promoting individual growth in family members while constructing a strengthened family unit. This interplay of heightened individual awareness and deeper familial connectedness is the true vision of experiential family therapy.

Experiential proponents stress families' learning to work out their own problems. Though therapists strive for this goal, they do not follow a set pattern or structure. It is accomplished through spontaneity and intuitive prompting and provocation by the therapist. Experiential therapy involves the clients working on two different levels: the rational and nonrational. The rational focuses on family members becoming more aware and gaining a deeper level of understanding. The nonrational includes the use of creativity, spontaneity, and a degree of "craziness." Whitaker was a strong proponent of "craziness," nonrational, creative experiencing and functioning as a means to family health. He contended that, if families allowed themselves to let down their guards and become a little "crazy," they would also be able achieve deeper levels of zest, spontaneity, and emotionality (Nichols & Schwartz, 2001).

Stages of Experiential Therapy Process

The process of experiential family therapy occurs in three stages: the engagement phase, involvement phase, and disentanglement phase. The role of the therapist adapts to the changes that occur in the various phases.

The Engagement Phase.   This is the initial phase of therapy, which typically starts with a member of the family calling for help. Experiential family therapists like to work with the whole family and generally insist that all members be present for the sessions. This invitation may also be offered to members of the extended family. During this early stage, the therapists assume an all-powerful role, that of an astute observer and interviewer. By engaging with all members of the family, the therapists are able to get a feel for what is going on within the family, how each member sees the problem, how members of the family relate to each other, and who plays what role within the family dynamics. Each member of the family can provide valuable information about how the family operates. Having all family members present is such a rigid condition of experiential therapy that therapists have been known not to start therapy until the whole family is present. As astute observers and models of how to be genuine and real, experiential therapists share out loud exactly how they are feeling and what they are perceiving, even to the point of seeming rude and being confrontational. The focus is on the here and now: what is happening at that moment within the session with all of the members of the family and with the therapists.

During this initial stage of therapy, the therapists need to be kind yet firm, assuming the role of symbolic parents. Families often tend to test the limits and boundaries of therapy. Therefore, it is important for the therapists to lay down the rules of therapy and make it clear that they, the therapists, are in charge during the session. The ability of the therapists to be both firm yet kind and personal sets the tone and helps to establish the rules of therapy. In addition to establishing the rules, this is also the time that the therapists will discuss the importance of having a co-therapist or consultants, define the therapeutic process, decide who will be present, schedule the time, and assume the role of rule makers. (Whitaker & Keith, 1981). In essence, the therapists take on a symbolic, parental role that provides the family with the knowledge that the therapists can, indeed, handle the family's problems. This process is often called the battle for structure because families often feel the need to resist or sabotage the therapy to see just how powerful and sincere the therapists really are. Though families enter therapy wanting help, they tend to be comfortable with the status quo and their ineffective interactional patterns. Families tend to resist any change. Experiential therapists increase the anxiety by disturbing or frustrating family process. This heightened anxiety challenges family members to recognize interactional patterns and to then adopt new ways of working as a family. Once the ground rules have been established, and the family has experienced change, the therapists then take on their role as coaches. This phase is sometimes called the "battle for initiative," because this is when the therapists usually give the power back to the family. Because experiential therapy is based on growth, it is assumed that only the family can truly define its goals and control its growth. The initiative for growth and change is returned to the family, and the therapists provide guidelines, support, and model genuineness and growth.

Involvement Phase.   The midphase occurs after trust and a level of comfort have been established between the family and the therapists and the true work really begins. The involvement phase of therapy is usually characterized by a therapeutic dance in which the therapists join with the family, yet are free enough to confront the family. The therapists can weave in and out of the family dynamics, intervening when the family is engaged in negative patterns, and supporting and nurturing the family as it becomes more aware of its patterns and growth potential.

While engaged in this symbolic dance of joining with the family, yet pulling back and playing the observers, it is paramount that the therapists maintain their own sense of self and do not become overly involved within the family and its power or pull back so far that they lose sight of what is going on. The benefits of co-therapy also come into play at this point, because each therapist can check on the other, and one can assume more of a supportive role while the other is more actively engaging or confronting. The ability of the therapeutic team to *be with* the family, yet still be able to individuate, provides the family with a model enabling the individual members to become a collective unit while still maintaining their separate sense of themselves. The central goal of experiential family therapy is to facilitate the individual autonomy of all members of the family *and* a sense of belonging in the family (Corey, 2001).

Many techniques may also be employed during this second phase that are very helpful in getting the family to become more authentic: redefining symptoms as efforts for growth (a reframing technique), modeling fantasy alternatives to real-life stress (turning an attempted suicide into murderous rage and playing with the possibilities), separating interpersonal stress from intrapersonal fantasy (a suicidal client being encouraged to talk about how the family would function if she did die, who would attend the funeral, how long family members would mourn, etc.), augmenting the despair of a family member so that the family unites around him or her, and highlighting the family revolution (Whitaker & Keith, 1981). The late phase of involvement becomes apparent as the family becomes more comfortable with the changes that it has endured and has emerged with a sense of family unity while having the flexibility to allow the growth of individual members. The family appears to operate without much guidance from the therapists and seems to have redefined itself and its subgroups in a more flexible and holistic manner that has accommodated the changes that have occurred. During this phase, the therapists assume more of a passive, coaching role and appear more personable. The family can basically operate, function, and deal with its own issues without much insight or assistance from the therapeutic team.

The Detanglement Stage. The final stage of therapy, when the family or the therapists acknowledge that the treatment has come to an end, is called the "detanglement stage." There are as many endings to therapy as there are families that seek therapy. As therapy is ending, the therapists can ease the separation anxiety and the family's need to individuate by addressing their own grieving and thoughts about termination. This allows the family to then process their own feelings and behaviors.

Effectiveness of Experiential Family Therapy

Whitaker and Keith (1981) cite little empirical evidence for the success of this model of family therapy, but proclaim that the goodwill of the community, referrals from previous patients, and successful reports and reviews of families after treatment are clinical evidence of success. The personal and intuitive strengths of the approach cannot be clearly defined, and such characteristics are not amenable to empirical research. Experiential therapy is based on the realness and the person of the therapist and on the change that occurs within the therapist and the families. Such variables cannot be measured or duplicated and, thus, are challenging to study or research.

Experiential therapists do contend that the change and growth that they experience within the therapeutic process is evidence of success, but no clear correlation between the personal growth of the therapists and the changes that the family reports after treatment has been studied. Other areas of study that could substantiate the validity of this approach would include the benefits of co-therapy, more outcome studies with follow-up, and studies of the therapy process (Whitaker & Keith, 1981).

Treatment Applicability

Experiential therapists advocate exploring the uniqueness of each family, listening carefully to each family without stereotyping or judging, and then adapting the therapy to each individual family. Though the therapy is tailored to each family, it does have some limitations. Experiential family therapy was developed out of Whitaker's work with biologically intact families, and is not a "one-size-fits-all" approach. This therapy generally is best suited for nuclear families, families in which three generations are available, and families that are open to challenges and motivated to change. Experiential family therapy has been found to be effective with extended families, divorcing couples with a history of infidelity, divorced couples with a child in crisis, lesbian and homosexual couples, multiracial and multiethnic families, blended families (if the other parents will get involved), families in crisis, families with a serious scapegoat (for example, a schizophrenic in the family), families with young children, families with multilevel problems, high-powered or VIP families, and disorganized families that are affected by an overattached outsider (i.e., a family that has a social worker, probation officer, or alcoholic counselor who has become too attached to them).

Experiential therapy has not been found to be effective with people who do not believe in the family, families that are resistant to change, families who need to blame, couples that are going through a divorce but have wounds too deep and tender for reexploration, families who have had too much therapy (professional patients), families with a manic psychotic member, and those families in which the scapegoat is an adopted child (Whitaker & Keith, 1981). Experiential therapists also view couples work as limiting and prefer to work with three generations of the family so that they can get a fuller and clearer picture of the family. No research was found that examined the efficacy of working with single-parent families.

Relationship to the Past

Experiential family therapy focuses on the "here and now" experience rather than looking at past experiences and patterns of behavior. What is important is what is currently going on in a therapy session (everything that is occurring with the individual family members, the therapists, and the therapeutic interaction among all involved). Because of the focus on what the family is experiencing in the session and how those experiences shape the family's behaviors, little focus is given to past experiences and behaviors. Therapists will listen to stories of past interactions and experiences to get a sense of why the family is having problems in the present, but the focus is on understanding the symbolism behind what is experienced in the session and the change that must occur. This is illustrated in the accompanying video when Gus Napier listens to the health problems and interactional history of the couple. This information helps Gus to determine what the couple's interactional pattern is. The focus is then on what occurs in the session. Pat, the woman, tends to operate in a motherly, overfunctioning, adult role, which casts Bill in the role of an underfunctioning, helpless child. He, in turn, resists her behavior by shutting down, even to the point of sabotaging his own health. Their past experiences help the therapist to understand *why* they are stuck in a dysfunctional pattern and the symbolic meaning of their experiences, but the emphasis is on changing those behaviors and the clients' present experience (Carlson & Kjos, 1999).

The Role of the Therapist in Symbolic Experiential Therapy

The role of the therapist is critical in symbolic experiential therapy. Though professional skills and training are considered important, they are secondary to the therapist's personality and ability to be genuine within the therapeutic process. It is the person, the authentic and human side of the therapist that can reach the family and allow its members to risk letting down their safeguards and to be "themselves."

By having direct encounters with the clients, the therapists attempt to expand their own experiences, often having to deal with their own vulnerabilities in the process. Their therapeutic responses are likely to be spontaneous, challenging, and often idiosyncratic as they attempt to help clients gain self-awareness, self-responsibility, and personal growth (Goldberg & Goldberg, 1996).

The therapist plays an active, directive, and symbolic part in the therapy process. Indeed, the therapist's use of self frees the family to be real, more honest, and more caring. This use of self and the personal investment of the therapist is critical to this approach. Oftentimes, this requires the therapist to "become one" with the family. Gus Napier describes this process in the accompanying videotape (Carlson & Kjos, 1999):

> The therapist is really the key component. The therapist has to join with the family and yet has to be free enough to confront the family. The word *symbolic* also applies to the therapist in that he tries to supply something that's missing within the family that is in itself symbolic. It's a little piece of something that the family has missed in life. It could be a little bit of parenting, friendly support, confrontation, sometimes. The therapist supplies a deep slice but an important part of what's missing in their experience. The therapist is therefore a symbolic figure. What's important is what happens in the room between the therapist and the family.

Because the therapist becomes so involved in the therapeutic process, it is important to be aware of countertransferance and the vulnerable personal experiences from his or her own family that may be triggered by the ongoing family sessions. Gus Napier discusses this possibility in *The Family Crucible* (1978): "However caught up in the family the therapist feels, he should always be less involved in the therapeutic process than is the family."(p. 189). The primary safeguards that are implemented and recommended by experiential therapists include the use of co-therapists, trainees working together in small process groups, and personal therapy experience.

Co-therapy is strongly endorsed by experiential family therapists because it allows the two therapists to work in an intuitive rhythm and dance in which one can take a more aggressive, confrontive stance, while the other observes the various dynamics taking place within the family. Co-therapy allows for a lot of freedom and innovation within the therapeutic team. One therapist can follow his intuition and be playful, while the other can join with the family. Therapeutic teamwork also allows for therapists to openly discuss their thoughts with each other during the session, to disagree with one another, to embellish on each other's interventions, to use self-disclosure, and to model creative and productive interaction based on mutual respect and emotional expressiveness (Goldberg & Goldberg, 1996). Co-therapy also safeguards against either of the co-therapists becoming overly involved or affected by countertransference with the families that they are working with.

Not only are the therapists' personalities and experience key in what they bring to the session, but what is also important is the personal experience they gained in their own families of origin. Because experiential therapists bring so much of themselves to the therapy, it is strongly recommended that all therapists have their own therapy. This may include personal, marital, and family counseling. This personal counseling experience not only enhances the therapists' personal growth and creativity, but also allows them to have a better understanding of their own family of origin and prevents countertransference between the therapists and the families that they are working with.

Interventions

Experiential therapists tend to use creative and spontaneous interventions. This is one of the ways that therapists let their intuition and personality guide them through the process of therapy. One of the key interventions that experiential therapists use is the interactional "dance" of joining and distancing from the family. The process of becoming deeply involved with the family and then pulling back models the fundamental process of family growth, which is being a part of the family and then individuating. This is the goal of family therapy, for members to be able to have a sense of belonging to the family while still maintaining a separate sense of self. The therapists model this interactive process through their dance of joining and distancing from the family.

Some of the interventions that therapists use to join the family include beginning the initial session by talking to the person who is the most psychologically distant in the family (usually the father) and playing with the children. Joining can also occur by bilateral transference (Whitaker & Keith, 1981): The therapist adopts the posture, mannerisms, and language of someone within the family. The mother is usually the last family member that the therapist talks to because she is typically the emotional cornerstone of the family.

Techniques Used in Experiential Family Therapy

As mentioned earlier, techniques are secondary to the significance of the therapist as a person and the importance of the therapeutic relationship. Though techniques do take a lesser role within experiential therapy, they do, nevertheless, play a role. One of the techniques that has become associated with

Whitaker's style is his use of *paradoxical intention.* This is a technique whereby the therapist confronts the family in order to break the impasse within the family, heighten the anxiety, and promote change and growth. For example, if a wife complains that she is not happy with her husband, the therapist would suggest that she have an affair or find a more interesting partner. The therapist's unconventional response places the wife in a double bind so that, either way, she must change her behavior; she cannot continue to just complain.

Some other techniques that are employed in experiential therapy include "redefining problematic symptoms as efforts for growth." Therapists use this method to depathologize the symptom and reframe how family members perceive each other. A schizophrenic child who is seen as the family scapegoat will be defined as a savior because his behavior brought the family to treatment. He is seen as sacrificing himself for the sake of the family.

"Modeling fantasy alternatives to real-life family stress" is another innovative technique. A suicidal client may be asked to share with the family and therapist how she would direct her anger outward toward another target. For example, if a suicidal wife is angry with her husband, she will be asked how she would murder her husband in a fantasy role play instead of directing the anger inward on herself.

Silence may also be used as a way to increase the family's anxiety and to change the tone of therapy. When the family comes in, if the therapist just sits there and says nothing, the family isn't sure quite what to do. Some families may remain silent, whereas others will ask a lot of questions trying to evoke some sort of direction from the therapist. Regardless of the family's response, silence does change the emotional tone of the session.

One of the most used techniques involves confrontation and provocation. This is used to heighten the emotional anxiety within the client and to lead to a deeper level of awareness. This intervention is illustrated in the video when Gus Napier confronts Bill, the quiet male, about why he doesn't fight for himself or stand up for himself.

GUS: "So why don't you fight for yourself better?"

BILL: "I don't think it's a matter of fighting for myself. I think it's trying to avoid an argument or try to, rather than saying the wrong things."

GUS: "Well, how far are you willing to go to avoid an argument? Heart Attack? Stroke?"

BILL: "No, I don't think we need that."

GUS: "No? Oh, come on! That's the way you're headed" (Carlson & Kjos, 1999, p. 34 [in study guide]).

Experiential therapists do not believe in giving the families homework assignments to be completed between sessions. If anything, the therapists tell families not to discuss the interviews between sessions.

Napier w/ clients

As mentioned earlier, techniques and interventions are not seen as significant in experiential therapy. There is also no format or structure as to when they are used. The decision to use a particular intervention or technique is a personal choice based on the therapist's style, clinical experience, and intuition.

Case Example

Gus Napier met with a middle-aged, unmarried couple, Pat and Bill, who have been living together for the past three years. As Gus becomes more familiar with the couple, he learns that there are some major health concerns and stresses within the relationship. Bill, age forty-seven, had had a heart attack a year earlier, and both Pat and Bill are fearful of a recurrence. Gus was able to connect with the couple's fear and be fully present with a personal experience that involved a serious medical issue and recalling the fear and stress that it placed on his own family. (He shares this in the discussion that occurs after the session, saying that he felt connected and involved with the family pretty quickly.)

Pat then went on to talk about other stressors that have been affecting the relationship, financial concerns and job issues. Pat lost her job two weeks before Bill's heart attack, and then was unemployed for eight months. Bill was also out of work for three months while recovering from his heart attack. Both are currently working but still feel the financial pressures of the past year.

As Gus listens to their story, it is very evident that Pat talks for both of them, while Bill just sits and says or does nothing. Pat tends to assume the parental role and thinks that she knows what is best for Bill. Bill resists her controlling by shutting down emotionally and verbally. Gus points out the pattern of interaction to them.

GUS: "... Did you hear his remark about it feels like you're kind of motherly?"

GUS: "... see what I'm hearing is a parental tone. I wanted him to have. Can you hear that? It sounds like [you] kind of know what is right."

PAT: "Well, one of us has to take the leading role. One of us does."

GUS: "... Okay and he is resisting your leading role by shutting up."

By pointing out the dysfunctional interactional pattern and making the clients aware of how they interact, Gus can now confront them when he sees them continuing to interact in this way. He does this by laying down some ground rules, establishing his position of power. He does not want Pat to talk for Bill. Gus tells Bill to stand up for himself and tells Pat not to interject on Bill's behalf. She is just to listen.

"... Why do you let her dominate the conversation?"

"... What would happen, if when she, if when she tries to parent you, you said, please stop parenting me. I'm an adult for God's sake. Stop it!"

Such questions heighten the anxiety between the couple because it disrupts their natural process and interaction (battle for structure).

This heightened anxiety and the couple's feelings and experiences allow Gus to understand why Pat tends to overfunction and assume more of a parental role, and why Bill assumes a passive, childlike role. Gus then looks at the symbolism behind the couple's reactions and interactions. This does involve asking about their previous experiences (their past). Bill says that he grew up in many foster homes and lived with an abusive stepfather. It was never safe for him to "act out" or to be anything other than "quiet and nice." It was never safe for Bill to show strong emotions, such as anger, so he learned to keep everything in and bottle up his emotions. This, as Gus points out, is a recipe for a heart attack.

Pat also grew up in an abusive family in which her parents weren't around to protect her from an abusive and mentally disturbed older sister. Pat was also unable to help her sister. These experiences prompted her to overfunction in a parental and helping role. One of the underlying themes that Gus was able to uncover was anger. Pat tends to direct her anger outward in a rageful temper. Bill, on the other hand, is self-punitive, turning his anger inward on himself.

Once Gus and the couple have an understanding of their personal experiences and history, Gus then brings their experiences into the present and confronts them about their current behavior and ineffective coping styles. Gus directly asks Bill if he is willing to kill himself to avoid any confrontation. Gus also confronts Pat on her inability to let Bill talk for himself and be less involved.

At this point, Gus takes on more of a directive, coaching role, helping Bill to stand up for himself and encouraging Pat to sit back and assume a more passive role. He also points out the importance of both of the partners seeing how their styles of dealing with their feelings are toxic for each of them and for the relationship. Bill needs to learn how to express his own feelings and be in touch with them. This will prevent him from "killing himself"(bottling up his feelings to the point of inducing a heart attack), and being able to relate to other people's feelings. Gus, in the symbolic parental role, directs his guidance and encouragement toward Pat, asking her to try to look within herself rather than always focusing outside herself and on others. He also addresses her rage, and how important it is for her to deal with her past experiences and come to a full understanding of how her experiences continue to affect her present-day relationships.

Because of the life-and-death issues that are being played out within this relationship, Gus shares his concerns and urges both Pat and Bill to consider couple's counseling. Following Whitaker's stance, Gus also recommends that Pat discontinue individual counseling while working in couples counseling.

Gus says that, if he were to see this couple again, he would take a less directive role, giving them more initiative. This follows the general transition in roles that the experiential therapist must assume, from a directive and powerful parental figure to a more passive, encouraging coach.

Strengths and Limitations of Experiential Family Therapy

Experiential family therapy reached its height of popularity in the 1970s when family therapy was young and encounter and process groups flourished. The intensity and the captivation of this intuitive, provocative approach slowly waned as society emerged from the sixties and seventies and took a more conservative and empirical stance. At that time, family systems concepts and methods became more popular. Today's popular family theories are more congruent to the family's reality, focusing less on eliciting the emotional experiences of individuals within the family and placing more emphasis on the family system as an entity.

Though this approach is not as widely used today as it was in Whitaker's prime, experiential/symbolic family therapy did leave some lasting influences and positive effects on the therapeutic community. Of key importance was the promotion and expansion of intense experiences through the creative and intuitive use of techniques. This approach also placed value on the therapeutic experience. The relationship that is fostered between the therapist and family is a fundamental element that is necessary for building rapport and initiating change within the family structure. Experiential therapy also allowed the therapist to be human and promoted the use of self and honesty within the therapeutic alliance. This promotes a deeper level of connection and authenticity between the therapist and the client.

Another positive impact of experiential therapy is a new way of looking at families. By dealing with individuals and their emotional responses and feeling within the session, family therapists can assist family members to get past their defensiveness that alienates the various members and work toward a deeper, more genuine connection among them.

Experiential therapy continues to be limited by its lack of empirical research. Because experiential therapy is known for its atheoretical (even antitheoretical) stance, no major figure has given much credence to the necessity of measuring or duplicating the studies to check for its validity or success.

To Learn More about Experiential Therapy

Experiential symbolic therapy views people as being changed as a result of their experiences rather than through education. Experiential therapists see affective expression as a natural process that must evolve rather than be taught. This premise has led to experiential therapists placing more emphasis on counselors-in-training being encouraged to learn from experiencing co-therapy and directly working with families rather than just understanding the theory and going through an accredited university program.

Although therapists are required to go through an accredited program and to gain experience in couples, individual, and family therapy, experiential therapists emphasize the importance of learning through being part of a co-therapy team. Clinical experience is seen as the cornerstone to learning and understanding the experiential process. It is believed that, if students work with a supervisor as part of a co-therapy team, they will gain a lot more from the "hands-on" clinical experience of directly working with families than they would from just sticking to a regimented study program or studying specific theories.

Students interested in learning more about experiential therapy can begin by reading some of the suggested books and articles in the next section.

Suggested Readings

The Family Crucible (Napier, A. & Whitaker, C. 1978. New York: Bantam Books). This is a very readable and interesting narrative about working with a family using the experiential approach to family therapy. This book allows readers a glimpse into the world of experiential family therapy. It illustrates the significance of co-therapy when working with families and provides readers with insight into how a family progresses, and the importance of the therapeutic relationship. It is a "must read" for anyone interested in this approach.

Dancing with the Family: A Symbolic Experiential Approach (Carl Whitaker & William Bumberry, 1988. New York: Brunner/Mazel). This book allows the reader to share in the internal processes of Carl Whitaker as he works with a family. This book provides a vivid description of Whitaker's ideas, his treatment methods, and his warm, caring personality. Also included are lively verbatim transcripts, along with Dr. Whitaker's personal commentary on the thinking behind his interventions and the family's reactions and progress.

The Roots of Psychotherapy (Whitaker, C. A. & Malone, T. P. 1981. New York: Brunner/ Mazel). Since it was published in 1953, this influential volume has not only become the basis for a thriving school of experiential psychotherapy, but also has significantly influenced the growing fields of family therapy and humanistic psychology and psychiatry. This book traces the evolution of experiential psychotherapy and the authors share their thoughts about the divergent paths they have taken, as well as the new directions that they see for the future of this innovative and intuitive style of psychotherapy.

Other suggested resources include:

Experiential/Symbolic Family Therapy (Keith & Whitaker, 1991). In *Handbook of family therapy.* Gurman, A. S. & Kniskern, D. P. (Eds.), New York: Brunner/Mazel. (pp. 187–225).

Symbolic experiential family therapy. Keith, D. V. (2000). In A. M. Horne (Ed.), *Family counseling and therapy* (3rd ed., pp. 102–139). Istasca, IL: F. E. Peacock.

Reshaping Family Relationships: The Symbolic Therapy of Carl Whitaker (Connel, G., Bumberry, W. & Mitten, T., 1999). New York: Brunner-Routledge.

Midnight Musings of a Family Therapist. Whitaker, C., (1990). New York: Norton.

The Hindrance of Theory in Clinical Work. Whitaker, C. (1976). In P. J. Guerin, Jr. (Ed.), *Family Therapy: Theory and Practice.* (pp. 154–164). New York: Gardner Press.

REFERENCES

Carlson, J., & Kjos. D. (Producers & Moderators). (1999). *Experiential therapy with Dr. Augustus Napier (Family therapy with the experts: Instruction, demonstration, discussion)* [Videotape]. Boston, MA: Allyn & Bacon.

Corey, G. (2001). *Theory and practice of counseling and psychotherapy* (6th ed.). Pacific Grove, CA: Brooks/Cole.

Keith, D. (1980). *Play therapy as paradigm for family therapy.*

Keith, D., Connell, G., & Connell, L. (2001). *Defiance in the family: Finding hope in therapy.* Philadelphia: Brunner-Routledge.

Goldenberg, I. & Goldenberg, H. (2000). *Family Therapy: An Overview* (5th ed.). Pacific Grove: Brooks-Cole/Wadsworth.

Napier, A. Y., & Whitaker, C. A. (1978). *The family crucible.* New York: Harper & Row.

Nichols, M. P., & Schwartz, R. C. (2001). *Family therapy: Concepts and methods* (5th ed.). Boston, MA: Allyn & Bacon.

Rogers, C. R. (1951). *Client-centered therapy.* Boston, MA: Houghton Mifflin.

Whitaker, C. (1981). Process techniques of family therapy. In R. J. Green & J. L. Framo (Eds.), *Family therapy: Major contributions* (pp. 419–444). New York: International Universities Press.

Whitaker, C., & Keith, D. V. (1981). Symbolic-experiential family therapy. In A. S. Gurman and D. P. Kniskern (Eds.), *Handbook of family therapy* (pp. 187–225). New York: Brunner/Mazel.

Whitaker, C., & Malone, T. P. (1953). *The roots of psychotherapy.* New York: Blakiston.

14 Integrative Therapy for Couples

RICHARD B. STUART

Richard Stuart

The A-to-G of Integrative Therapy for Couples

Why Integrate?

Since their origin, mental health services have been dominated by schools of thought that have gained and lost favor in a series of predictable waves.[1] Derived from selected assumptions that are held dear but rarely tested, each school developed its own theory of human behavior and with its commitment to *the* way to promote change. Members of each group protected their beliefs by interacting only with like-minded souls, by shunning the other groups' litera-ture, and by limiting admission to their ranks to those who completed specified training and met stiff certification requirements. Organizations were formed, officers were elected, and members were offered prepackaged identities. Skirmishes were often intense but entertaining, because no group won, so no group lost. Why did the party end?

While the intertheory war waged, two developments gained the strength to radically change the field. Systems theory grew in favor, highlighting the fact that all dimensions of human behavior were interrelated, so no narrow formulation could suffice. At the same time, behaviorally oriented psychologists developed and popularized the use of operational definitions of terms and functional analysis of results. Together, systems notions and an operational language opened new doors for mental health practitioners.

Systems theory achieved power as a heuristic for learning about human behavior although some of its specific hypotheses (e.g., the role double-bind in the etiology of schizophrenia) were not supported by research, but its logic helped solve a major problem for behavior therapists. Behavioral interventions yielded exciting initial results, indeed, showing unprecedented levels of rapid change. But as results were followed up for increasing periods of time, the original dramatic changes began to weaken. For example, the frequently cited results of Stuart's (1967) protocol for the treatment of overeating reported very encouraging levels of weight loss after one year. But follow-up studies revealed that much of the weight was regained over time. That led to further studies (e.g., Stuart & Jacobson, 1987b) that showed that overeating was only one of the challenges. Identifying and counteracting the role of body image was another factor that requires attention, as do the possible roles of intimate partners in creating pressure to gain or lose weight. Scores of other findings also highlighted the need to take a broad, systemic approach to understanding and influencing human behavior.

In addition, more sophisticated research designs began to show that in accounting for the variance in treatment outcome, focal intervention methods were often far outweighed by the power of placebo (Brown, 1998; Shapiro & Shapiro, 1997) and the nonspecific factors common to all approaches (Frank, 1973; Karasu, 1986; Orlinsky & Howard, 1995; Wampold, Mondin, Moody, Stich, Benson, & Ahn, 1997). These findings weakened faith in the ideologies, as did two additional sets of evidence. It has been noted that much of what clinicians do when they see patients is, at best, distantly related to their avowed theoretical orientations (Smith, 1999). And, as has been recognized for many years, paraprofessionals who are untrained in the theoretical modalities were found to achieve results that compared quite favorably with the outcomes of therapy offered by highly trained professionals (Durlak, 1979, 1981).

One would have thought that the growing weight of this evidence would lead clinicians to give up monotheoretical, reductionist approaches. But, in point of fact, it took a push from an unexpected direction to move our field toward integration: Managed care wielded enormous financial power and fostered long overdue change. By raising questions about the utility of mental health services and by demanding replicated demonstrations of the costs and benefits of the various approaches, clinicians were forced to address issues that had rarely been raised before. No single approach could provide satisfactory answers, so it became incumbent on the adherents of various schools to collaborate with others. In this way, systems theory, research findings, and an external threat have all combined to provide the logic, technique, and economic incentive for integration.

Significant Characteristics of ICT

What Is Integration?

Integration is hardly new. Over half a century ago, Dollard and Miller (1950) applied learning principles to psychoanalytic practices. Since then, a number of scientists (e.g., Miller, 1991) have translated many of the ideas that Freud derived from neurology into modern-day hypotheses about the soma–psyche connection. To name but a few, other examples of integration are the constructivist reformulation of Jung's beliefs (Young-Eisendrath & Hall, 1991), attachment theory formulations of the tenets of object relations theory (Sperling & Berman, 1994), and the subsequent recasting of attachment theory in cultural (Harwood, Miller, & Irizarry, 1995) and neurological (Siegel, 1999) terms.

In a comprehensive review, Arkowitz (1997) identified three approaches to integration. Theoretical integration combines the resources of two or more theories. Common factors approaches build their perspectives from the empirically derived commonalities of a wide range of approaches. Technical eclecticism chooses a theoretical approach deemed best for each client. All three approaches have been fruitful and continue to evolve.

Lebow (1997) believes that integration has permeated the field of family therapy in which "the pure form of schools . . . has become a rarity" (p. 2), a change that he believes to be inevitable but one that became a reality much sooner than anyone anticipated. Nowhere is this more evident than in the definition of behavior therapy recently published by the Association for the Advancement of Behavior Therapy (2000):

> Behavior therapy is a particular kind of therapy that involves the application of findings from behavioral science research to help individuals change in the ways they would like to change. . . . Most behaviorally oriented therapists believe that the current environment is most important in affecting the person's present behavior. Early life experiences, long-time internal psychological or emotional conflicts, or the individual's personality structure are considered to be less important than what is happening in the person's life at the present time . . . (unnumbered).

Here, in a statement that would have been virtually unutterable thirty years ago, the role of the past is understood to be a qualifier of present behavior. The drawbridge has been lowered so many diverse points of view can now filter into the arena of behavioral theories about family life. However, merely being termed *integrative* does not merit the Good Housekeeping Seal of Approval. One might be considered "eclectic" but one does not integrate by adding a few disparate techniques to a unitary therapeutic approach (Norcross & Goldfried, 1992). Rather, effective integration must occur at the level of philosophy, theory, operational strategy, and intervention technique.

What Are the Core Components of This Approach to Integrative Theory for Couples?

Before describing my model, it is important to stress that there are as many unique blends of ideas under the rubric of integration as there are clinicians who are flexible enough to adopt them. *No* claim is made that this approach is better than any other: It is offered merely as one model of how the varied elements can be fit together into a rationale for intervention. Moreover, my model is more an epistemology than a static theory. Models identified as "territory-driven" are generally restricted to blending the ideological triumvirate of psychodynamic, humanistic, and behavioral notions. As such, they are culturally restrictive and lose much of the phenomenology of the thinking, behaving, and interpersonal self (Rigazio-Digilio, Goncalves, & Ivey, 1996). To facilitate the openness of this model, every individual is considered as a unique cultural being, and this uniqueness is reflected in every service offering, with each treatment individualized for the client served, so no two are ever exactly alike. And care is taken to adapt the elements of the model to fit the needs of clients. For example, a health crisis may need a much more present-oriented and practical focus than efforts to enrich a relationship that has lost its vigor and can be strengthened by a thoughtful effort to promote increased mutual understanding (see, for example, Grunebaum, 1988; Gurman, 1981).

My model of Integrative Theory of Couples is crafted from an understanding of Affective, Behavioral, Cognitive, Developmental, Environmental, Family-of-origin, and Genetic aspects of the partners' interaction. This is in keeping with well-established traditions that link physiological, psychological, and environmental correlates of behavior (e.g., Meyer, 1957; Montague, 1956). The notions of reciprocal determinism (Bandura, 1977), symbolic interactionism (Stryker, 1980), and field forces (Lewin, 1935) provide the logic for explaining the interaction among these behavior-controlling influences and the meanings they create. According to this logic, no one of the A-to-G factors is deemed to be more influential than any other in general, although for any given event some elements may explain more of the variance than others. As a result of their continuous interplay, the impact of the varied components is subject to ongoing change.

Two core assumptions are basic to the way in which knowledge about these diverse influences is integrated into this approach. The first, *operationalism,* provides the means for testing the assumptions of this model and for evaluating the results of the interventions through which it is applied. Houts and Krasner (1998) see approaches such as this as relying on

> quantitative as opposed to qualitative analyses; operational definition of terms; experimental and empirical methods of investigation; a more rational and empirical as opposed to intuitive epistemology; and endorsement of some version of the unity of science thesis where the social sciences are viewed as sharing common methods of investigation with the physical sciences if not reducibility from one to the other (p. 33).

Every testable hypothesis has the potential of being included in, and thereby expanding, the approach whenever it passes the tests of verification and relevance.

Stricker (1997) contrasted the basic science approach with what he termed the "local clinical scientist." In his view, basic scientists must take a skeptical approach to explorations of hypotheses that apply to general reality, the core logic being *dis*proof of beliefs. In contrast, local scientists test the relevance of these hypotheses in explaining and predicting the behavior of the clients they serve. Theoretical case conceptualization (Murdock, 1991) affords a means of combining these two approaches by using theory as a source of sensitizing hypotheses and explaining client behavior in terms of these assumptions. When client behavior does not conform to theory-driven predictions, different hypotheses are explored as sources of explanation of diagnostic findings and as bases for estimating the probable outcome of various intervention options.

The second major assumption is the role accorded to constructivism in creating the meaning of human experience. If not its founder, George Kelly (1955) certainly gave modern constructivism its major impetus. The fundamental postulate of his theory is the assumption that "a person's processes are psychologically channelized by the ways in which he anticipates events" (p. 46). In other words, one can only follow paths of thought or action that one can identify. Subsequently, Mahoney (1991) brilliantly elaborated Kelly's ideas with his belief that "the organism is an active participant in its own experience as well as in learning" (p. 100). He believes that we are all "co-constructors of personal realities to and from which we respond" (loq. cit.), and that "learning and knowing necessarily involve predominantly tacit (beyond awareness) processes that constrain (but do not specify) the contents of conscious experience" (p. 104). This suggests that what we identify as "facts" are, in most instances, assumptions to which we assign a high degree of probability, and that others exposed to the same phenomena may perceive a very different "fact pattern." This helps to explain the different assessments made by therapists with different orientations who discuss the same clients at case conferences. Differing perceptions also help to explain the common experience of clients' intense disagreements about what really happened during shared experiences. However disparate their accounts may be, both could very well be right. This goes far beyond recognition of the fact that partners react differently because they punctuate events differently (Watzlawick, Beavin, & Jackson, 1976); they don't just disagree about the sequence of events, but they often have very different constructions of what the events were. Therefore, accounts of the same encounters given independently by each participant may appear to be descriptions of entirely different events.

Underlying Philosophy

The underlying philosophy of my approach is *principled pragmatism* that draws from many sources (Stuart, 1980). Philosophical humanism (Lamont, 1949) provides a belief that humans have an inherent capacity for constructive change. The idealistic positivism developed by Vaihinger (1924) contributes the recognition of the role of the fictional belief in achieving more positive outcomes. That is, by adopting more positive behavior through acting "as if" the hoped-for reality is present, one may be able to create it. And acceptance of a midpoint between free will (the unrestrained power of choice) and determinism (which posits the absence of choice) supports the belief that many aspects of human behavior are shaped by the interaction among nature, nurture, and environmental opportunity (Jones, 1975). The pragmatic emphasis stems from Hume's (1896) stress on the need to verify all assumptions because we know that our senses are apt to offer incomplete or inaccurate information. Operational philosophy (Burtt, 1946) brings recognition of the need to objectively define all of the terms so assumptions can be tested and procedures evaluated. Finally, phenomenological psychology provides the core assumption that every aspect of psychology is subject to interpersonal influence, so nothing should be construed as entirely intrapersonal (Kruger, 1979).

Value Dimensions of This Approach

In addition to philosophy that contributes to their structure, all approaches have value bases that contribute to the direction in which they influence their clients. With regard to work with couples, a core value in my approach is respect for the decisions that partners make concerning the future of their relationships. Unlike some, I am *not* committed to the preservation of marriages. Instead, I view my mission as that of helping partners to decide whether to stay together and enhance their relationship or to separate as constructively as possible. Sometimes the partners are not the best possible match for each other and there is reason to believe that they might be able to be happier with others. But that choice is theirs to make, not mine. Unless there is uncontrolled abuse, unforgivable breaches of the marital contract, a major conflict in basic goals, or other compelling reasons to suggest separation, I try to help every couple improve their relationship to the greatest extent possible, and then to decide whether to recommit to a shared future. Conversely, if it is clear that prolonging the relationship is contrary to either partner's interest, my efforts are devoted to helping the partners disentangle their lives in the most constructive manner possible.

Theoretical Roots of ICT

By definition, ICT draws from many different traditions in psychology, with each clinician mixing the brew in an idiosyncratic fashion (e.g., Gurman, 1981; Jacobson & Christensen, 1996; Nichols, 1988; Sager, 1976; Stuart, 1980). Table 14.1 summarizes just some of the many sources that contribute to my brand of integration. As will be seen in the publication dates of these significant resources, notions of the role of family experiences in generating the structure of the unconscious developed early in the twentieth century; they were enhanced by the contributions of systems, social learning, and interpersonal theories after midcentury; and they now flourish as notions of attachment orientation that are quantified by research in neurobiology and cognitive psychology. In the same vein, the highly subjective intervention methods introduced by the psychoanalytic movement have been enhanced by the mid- and later-century introduction of a broad range of procedures that utilize operationalized variables. For example, clients' descriptions of their life histories, as well as inferences drawn from these accounts by therapists, are understood to be constructions rather than factual reckonings, drawing attention to the need to understand the cognitive and emotional biases that influence them. Finally, every aspect of intervention planning is construed as a testable hypothesis leading to the treatment that can be assessed through a range of individual and group experimental designs. As noted, the strength of each of these contributors is not static: It changes in response to emerging knowledge and the needs of the clients at hand.

Strategy of ICT

Strategy refers to the overarching intervention logic that applies to all clients, while *tactics* refer to the specific clusters of techniques designed to meet specific client needs.

For years, most models of therapy (e.g., Cashdan, 1973) described a four-stage process in service delivery that includes relationship formation, treatment analysis, planning, and implementation. Since managed-care organizations began to insist on accountability, outcome assessment is now commonly added as a fifth stage.

Case Structure. Therapists' first task is to answer the question: *Who is the client?* In my approach, whenever the issue concerns the partners' relationship, both are the clients. In addition, even if the presenting problem concerns only one individual, I try to see both partners if one is believed to play a role in maintaining the problem or might assist in overcoming it. I therefore invite both partners to attend most first sessions in order to be able to gather more comprehensive information about the presenting complaint and resources for change. If I define the problem as one that is best addressed through conjoint therapy, I have established rapport with both partners from the beginning. If I decide that the goals can be met through individual therapy, contact with the partner allows

TABLE 14.1   **Theories Contributing to Integrative Therapy for Couples**

Theory	Contribution	Sample References
Psychoanalytic theory	Basic awareness of the role of early life experiences in the family as a source of a host of subliminal patterns that profoundly influence subsequent psychological adjustment and maladjustment.	Flugel, J. C. (1929). *Psychoanalytic study of the family.* (3rd ed.). London: Hogarth. Ackerman, N. W. (1958). *The psychodynamnics of family life.* New York: Basic Books. Meissner, W. W. (1978). The conceptualization of marriage and family dynamics from a psychoanalytic perspective. In T. J. Paolino & B. S. McCrady (Eds.), *Marriage and marital therapy: Psychoanalytic, behavioral, systems perspectives* (pp. 25–88). New York: Brunner/Mazel.
Object relations theory	Specification of the interactive processes that produce enduring influences and the processes through which these processes influence adult relationships.	Cashdan, S. (1988). *Object relations therapy: Using the relationship.* New York: Norton. Horner, A. J. (1979). *Object relations and the developing ego in therapy.* NY: Aronson.
Attachment theory	A language for describing the social impact of internal working models formed early in life.	Bretherton, I., & Munhollan, K. A. (1999). Internal working models in attachment relationships. In J. Cassidy & P. R. Shaver (Eds.), *Handbook of attachment: Theory, research, and clinical applications* (pp. 89–111). New York: Guilford.
Neuropsychology	Explanation of the mechanisms and structures in the brain that are the sites of the emotional and cognitive components of attachment orientations and internal working models.	LeDoux, J. (1996). *The emotional brain: The mysterious underpinnings of emotional life.* New York: Simon & Schuster. Siegel, D. J. (1999). *The developing mind: Toward a neurobiology of interpersonal experience.* New York: Guilford.
Cognitive psychology	A language for describing the conscious aspects of internal working models, expectations that shape the creation and evaluation of relationships and facilitate planning for the development of new patterns.	Csikszentmihalyi, M. (1990). *Flow: The psychology of optimal experience.* New York: Harper. Mikulincer, M., & Arad, D. (1999). Attachment working models and cognitive openness in close relationships: A test of chronic and temporary accessibility effects. *Journal of Personality and Social Psychology, 77,* 710–725.

TABLE 14.1   Continued

Constructivism	An approach to understanding the meaning of behavior from the perspectives of both the actor and reactor, stressing the role of personal culture and respect for the uniqueness of every individual.	Mahoney, M. J. (1991). *Human change processes: The scientific foundations of psychotherapy.* New York: Basic Books.
Social exchange theory	A description of the process through which equity is sought, sustained, and lost in social interaction.	Burgess, R. L., & Huston, T. L. (Eds.). (1979). *Social exchange in developing relationships.* New York: Academic Press.
		Kelley, H. T. (1979). *Personal relationships: Their structures and processes.* Hillsdale, NJ: Earlbaum.
Interpersonal theory	Explanation of the overt and process meaning of social behavior.	Carson, R. C. (1969). *Interaction concepts of personality.* Chicago: Aldine.
		Watzlawick, P., Beavin, J. H., & Jackson, D. (1967). *Pragmatics of human communication.* New York: Norton.
Social-learning theory	The development of an operationally specific language for describing and enhancing social behavior.	Bandura, A. (1977). *Social learning theory.* Englewood Cliffs, NJ: Prentice-Hall.
Family studies	An evolving description of the processes through which potential partners meet, bond, and form families, and the internal and external forces that influence change in these core relationships over time.	Olson, D. H., & DeFrain, J. (2000). *Marriage and the family: Strengths and diversity.* Mountain View, CA: Mayfield.
		Also, journals such as *Journal of Marriage and the Family* and *Family Issues.*
Systems theory	Offers a logic for the structures and processes that organize stable and destabilized patterns of social and individual behavior.	Lazlo, E. (1972). The systems view of the world. New York: Braziller.
		van Gigch, J. P. (1974). *Applied general systems theory.* New York: Harper & Row.
Cognitive-behavior therapy	Provides a model for the delivery of services aimed at changing behavior in the context of its cognitive and affective dimensions.	D'Zurilla, T. J. (1986). *Problem-solving therapy: A social competence approach to clinical intervention.* New York: Springer.

me to enlist her or his support in our efforts to help the person who becomes the identified patient.

Sometimes it is useful to have individual sessions with partners when the basic approach is conjoint therapy. When I see partners separately, I do so with the understanding that I have the freedom to share any information gleaned during the separate contact. That's because trust in the therapist is severely compromised if one partner believes that the therapist has information that is not being shared and is, thereby, colluding with the other. With this caveat, I may see partners separately for any of three reasons: to experience a side of the individual that is not evident in interaction; to establish rapport when doing so has not been achieved during three-person sessions; or to help in the resolution of purely personal issues that are better addressed individually.

Therapeutic Relationship.   The basis of psychotherapy has been identified as "the communication of person-related understanding, respect, and a wish to be of help" (Reisman, 1971, p. 123), implying that the creation of an effective therapeutic alliance is the *sine qua non* of therapy. My brand of ICT calls for creating a collaborative, nonhierarchical relationship with clients, the therapist being neither an inspired guru nor an obedient servant who follows clients' leads. The collaboration I seek is one in which *clients are the acknowledged authorities on their goals* and the *therapist is acknowledged as the authority on the means to achieve* them. The relationship is cemented through negotiation of a therapeutic contract that uses methods suggested by the therapist to achieve goals chosen by the clients, evaluating the process using criteria that are contributed by both.

Critical to the establishment of rapport is the need for the therapist to allow each person to feel heard and understood. Accomplishing this task in a three-person discussion is sometimes a challenge, one that requires use of tactics that are quite different from those used in individual therapy. For example, if the presenting concern is a secret affair by one of the partners, the therapist must understand this liaison from the perspective of the partner who had it. But the offended partner is apt to want the therapist to condemn the unfaithfulness, not try to verify that it really happened or try to understand it; doing either is likely to be construed as implicit justification. But condemning the affair creates four other problems. It puts the therapist in the role of moral authority, undermining the collaborative relationship that is sought. Major resistance may be created in the "offender." The aggrieved partner is likely to feel absolved of contributory responsibility, and the therapist will lose access to information that may be critical to resolution of the problem. Therefore, assessing affairs or any other issue that evokes strong anger or defensiveness requires careful planning and great tact. The unavoidable stress that most couples' therapist's experience stems from the fact that all words, gestures, and even silences convey messages to everyone exposed to them. Therefore, therapists are called upon to use a "leading consciousness" that sensitizes them to the partners' potential reactions in every aspect of their intervention.

Assessment Methods.   In order to meet the demands of the evidence-based approach that is currently in fashion (Gambrill, 1999), therapists face new challenges in pinpointing and evaluating the accuracy of their assessments and evaluating the effectiveness of their intervention efforts. If current research findings are correct, clinicians tend to bias their assessments by discarding data that are inconsistent with their orientations and to forget salient information when it is too complex (Garb, 1989). Moreover, their impressionistic evaluations of treatment outcome often bear little resemblance to outcomes as determined by the use of standardized measures (Bickman, 1999). Accordingly, it is helpful to standardize assessment and treatment evaluation methods, and to limit both to the smallest amount of data sufficient to complete both tasks reliably and validly.

I rely on multidimensional, multimethod assessments for planning and evaluating treatment. In order to avoid bias in my judgment, I try to avoid assessing the partners as individuals unless personal issues clearly contribute to, or result from, the partners' interaction. But I always take into consideration the partners' affective state at the time of my evaluation because the quality of their accounts are very likely to be colored by their moods at the time (Davis & Oathout, 1987). However my major focus is *assessment of the interaction, not the partners, because the relationship is the client, not the individuals.* This is often easier said than done because, like most clinicians, I am better trained in the assessment of individuals and thus have a much broader vocabulary for describing them. Lacking a reliable and valid language for categorizing couples, I rely more heavily on description of partners' strengths and concerns than on categorizing them.

It is useful to begin by making note of the history of the relationship. How old were the partners when they met? Had they become the people they were destined to be at the time or did they change in important ways after they met? How well did they know each other at the time that they made the commitment to spend their lives together? What attracted them to each other? For example, did they choose to commit because they really wanted to be together, or in order to solve a personal problem such as the wish to appease parents or to have a child? And did they articulate what they expected from their relationship before making a commitment?

Three primary instruments provide my core data. The Couple's Precounseling Inventory (CPI, Stuart & Jacobson, 1987a; Stuart, in press) provides primary data about the relationship. This sixteen-page form addresses many of the critical areas of partner's interaction that have been shown to relate to relationship satisfaction and stability. These areas include, among others, emotional and physical intimacy, support, communication, negotiation, division of family responsibilities, conflict management, parenting style, personal style, and goals for counseling. In addition, the form can be scored to quantify the partners' relative power, commitment to their relationship, and sense of equity. In every instance, data are collected about the partners' strengths as well as the dimensions on which they seek improvement. Partners are asked to present their own evaluations and, in many instances, predict each other's responses. These data can then be used to measure the extent to which they agree, understand each other's perceptions, and feel understood by the other (i.e., meta-understanding).

CPI data are most useful when obtained prior to the first session, with subsections readministered as needed during treatment. By completing the form prior to the first session, clients are cued to attend to the strengths in their relationship as well as their concerns. They are also guided through a comprehensive view rather than focusing on single problems, and they are prompted to decenter their evaluations by appraising their relationship from the other's perspective. In this way, clients are socialized into the roles that will facilitate successful therapy. The CPI can later be used in whole or in part to assess treatment outcome and, over time, the maintenance of treatment results.

In addition, the Family of Origin Inventory (FOO; Stuart, in press) is frequently used to learn about the developmental experiences that contribute to each partner's internal working models. This sixteen-page form solicits data about family history and other influential relationships in childhood. In addition, a version of the REP Grid (Kelly, 1955) affords an overview of the criteria that each partner uses for assessment of self and significant others in the past and present. The FOO can be administered either before the first session or early in therapy. The REP Grid is occasionally readministered during or after therapy.

As a means of systematizing therapists' ongoing judgments, the Goal Attainment Scale (GAS; Figure 14.1) can be used to rate couple's functioning after the first session, and given at regular intervals during therapy and follow-up sessions. The GAS presented here reflects the variables that I find it useful to assess as treatment progresses, while others may prefer to develop scales that better fit their intervention models. In addition, measures addressed to specific concerns, such as mood states, mental status, and drug and alcohol use, can be administered as needed.

Finally, after meeting with the couple, as a means of integrating diverse information, I find it helpful to write a paragraph or two about each partner's philosophy and goals, the strengths in their relationship, the challenges they face, and the changes they will each have to make to achieve their stated goals.

Tactics of ICT

I was the first to offer what I called an "operant–interpersonal" approach to couples therapy (Stuart, 1969). That early approach relied on social–psychological explanations of relationship development and recommended a token economy technique to structure partners' exchanges of desired behaviors. This method was subsequently expanded to a five-step approach (Stuart, 1976). Caring days (LeCroy, Carrol, Nelson-Becker, & Sturlaugson, 1989; Stuart, 1980; in press) replaced the token exchanges as a means of beginning therapy by increasing the rate of their small affectionate expressions. Time-outs were recommended as a response to conflicts early in therapy, until partners could develop the skills to deal with crises more effectively. The first of these skills, improved communication, facilitates the enhancement of intimacy through mutual understanding. It also aids the expression of requests for changes in larger behaviors, setting the stage for two-winner negotiation as a means of structuring larger exchanges. Next, couples were helped to equitably distribute the authority to make

FIGURE 14.1   Couple Therapy Goal Attainment Scale*

Name: _____ Partner's Name: _____ Date: _____ Interviewer: _____

A. Expression of Rejection vs. Affection
1. Generally very distant and rejecting
2. Distant although not rejecting
3. Neither distant nor tender: generally affectively neutral
4. Expresses tenderness verbally or nonverbally, not both
5. Expresses tenderness verbally and nonverbally

B. Mind Reading vs. True Understanding of Other
1. Tells partner what he/she thinks, ignoring corrective feedback
2. Tells partner what he/she thinks, reluctantly accepts feedback
3. Tells partner what he/she thinks, then asks for feedback
4. Asks other's thoughts, but ignores answers
5. Asks other's thoughts and accepts the answers

C. Discounting vs. Respect for Others
1. Attempts to exercise invasive control of partner's thoughts
2. Attempts to exercise invasive control of partner's actions
3. Tries to negotiate for control of partner's actions
4. Negotiates appropriate boundaries of behavioral influence
5. Negotiates appropriate boundaries of information flow

D. Sees Self as Victim vs. Accepting Responsibility for Own Role
1. Views all unwanted events as result of other's hostility
2. Views unwanted events as result of other's indifference
3. Views unwanted events as unintended slights by other
4. Sees own role in negative events, but thinks other must change
5. Accepts own role in co-creating and changing negative events

E. One- vs. Two-Winner Orientation To Problem Solving
1. Insists on having everything as he/she wants it to be
2. After own demands are met, willing to make small concessions
3. Accepts idea of two-winner outcome, but still seeks to win
4. Willing to accept two-winner outcome when issues become clear
5. Begins negotiation by looking for two-winner outcome

F. Coercive vs. Problem-Solving Approach To Conflict
1. Relies on physical abuse or intimidation in conflict
2. Escalates conflict to threats of violence, divorce, etc.
3. Withdraws from conflict with little discussion
4. Willing to listen to other's concerns as conflict is processed
5. Tries to understand other's hurt and goals during conflict

G. Inconsistency vs. Consistency in Honoring Commitments
1. Denies or forgets ever making commitments
2. Admits commitments but very rarely follows through
3. Admits commitments, tries, but irregularly follows through

*Copyright © 2000, Richard Stuart. Reprinted with permission by the author.

(continued)

FIGURE 14.1 Continued

4. Honors commitments with reasonable consistency
5. Honors commitments with great consistency

H. Rigidity–Flexibility in Beliefs
1. Does not listen to any alternatives
2. Listens impatiently but will not consider alternatives
3. Listens attentively but still strongly holds to own beliefs
4. Listens attentively and is willing to consider alternatives
5. Elicits and seriously considers alternatives

I. Constructive vs. Punitive Use of Themes
1. Disparages implications of other's themes
2. Ignores other's themes
3. Listens to other's themes but draws own conclusions
4. Understands other's themes but is not moved to take them into account
5. Understands other's themes and negotiates respectful way to accommodate them

A___+B___+C___+D___+E___+F___+G___+H___+I___=TOTAL:___

decisions and allocate resources within the family through the use of the "power-gram" technique. With the intensity of conflict reduced to manageable proportions, couples could then develop techniques that would help them contain it and agree on changes that would prevent its recurrence. This approach was taken a step further by Stuart (1980) with the addition of techniques for addressing partners' sexual interaction and helping them prepare for the inevitable testing of positive change. Meanwhile, others (e.g., Harrell & Guerney, 1976; Jacobson & Margolin, 1979; O'Leary & Turkewitz, 1978; Weiss, 1978) developed alternate protocols that expanded the model in a variety of different ways (Cassidy & Shaver, 1999).

The next twenty years saw an elaboration of the core behavior-change techniques (e.g., Stuart & Jacobson, 1987a) as well as the addition of techniques for changing cognition (Fincham, Bradbury, & Scott, 1990) and affect (e.g., Greenberg & Johnson, 1988). Most recently, improved tools for measuring various conceptualizations of internal working models provided the next vital step toward the evolution of a truly integrative approach to conjoint therapy.

Empirical Support for ICT

No definitive test of the effectiveness of ICT is possible because every clinician develops a unique, personalized approach. Research that evaluates marital and family therapy generally has recently been reviewed elsewhere (Baucom, Shoham, Mueser, Daiuto, & Stickle, 1998) with essentially positive results that must be accepted cautiously in light of the limitations of the studies. With regard to behaviorally oriented couples' therapy, these authors found the evidence "sparse and equivocal, yet highly encouraging" (p. 76). We can use their conclusion to encourage therapists to evaluate the results that they achieve using ICT, to pool their findings with those of others, and to disseminate their results in an effort to more precisely define the potential for this highly general approach to conjoint therapy.

But, despite the present emphasis on the need to operationalize and validate, a word of caution about the research literature is in order here. Scientific studies generally publish nomothetic or group results with an estimate of the probability that these results could have occurred by chance, but clinicians must make idiographic decisions and cannot be certain that the group results reported by researchers apply to the client in their office. Moreover, many research findings reach statistical significance but the differences obtained are not clinically significant. When studies do show strong associations between variables or positive treatment results, the associations and outcomes are far from absolute and, therefore, only explain a portion of the variance or offer an estimate of possible outcome. Sample sizes are often too small and nonrepresentative to warrant projection to general client populations. Manualized methods often bear little resemblance to the methods used in clinicians' offices. These and other flaws in the research designs are reviewed elsewhere (Metzoff, 1998). While the research literature does and should play an important role in every clinician's thinking, the research must be approached with a cautious, critical eye. One does well to be particularly leery about accepting any claim that an approach is uniquely "scientifically based." There is some science in all approaches, and in none is everything empirically validated.

Summary

Our field has reached the point at which virtually every theory is integrative whether this fact is or is not recognized by its proponents. Basic components of theories are no longer pure: Emotions are recognized as having definitive cognitive and somatic properties (Greenberg & Safran, 1987; Ortony, Clore, & Collins, 1988), while the role of interpersonal experience and internal working models is reflected in cognitive theories (e.g., Alford & Beck, 1997). This precludes the possibility of developing a robust unifactorial theory. Moreover, the apparent fact that most treatment approaches share many service-delivery characteristics and overlapping techniques pushes theoretical purity further out of reach. We are, therefore, left with a situation in which clinicians either acknowledge the integrative nature of their practices, or they allow most of what they do with clients to escape their theoretical understanding.

I do not strive to have a complete theory of human behavior. Instead, my goal is the development of a theory sufficient to guide my clinical practice. I consider every hypothesis and observation to be potentially relevant to my model. I will incorporate it if: (1) its terms are objectifiable; (2) its assumptions testable; (3) its content consistent with the philosophy and values I embrace; (4) it is relevant to the types of problems with which I work; and (5) it expands the explanatory power of my theory and/or the potential scope of its applications. I will retain it in my system unless data suggest that it must be either modified or deleted, and I will seek sources of verification for any assumptions for which I lack suitable evidence.

Comparison with Other Approaches

Similarities with Other Approaches

I believe all people are unique cultural beings, with deeply held, often preconscious expectations for their own behavior and that of everyone who plays an important role in their lives. Because they are unique, the cultures that two people bring to a new relationship will inevitably have points of conflict. Should change in behavior be required every time one of these differences surfaces? With Jacobson and his colleagues (Christensen & Jacobson, 1999; Hayes, Jacobson, Follett, & Dougher, 1994; Jacobson & Christensen, 1996), I believe that change is sometimes in order, but acceptance of the difference is more often the proper choice. Because no one delivers perfect behavior, no one can reasonably expect to receive perfection. To spare oneself the need to change every minor detail at the other's behest, acceptance is necessary to preserve equity. I believe that, to be acceptable, behaviors must not be harmful to either partner, nor should they significantly interfere with agreements that are core to the relationship. To achieve acceptance, each partner must be helped to understand the *psycho-logic* of the other's behavior. That accomplished, they can then be helped to agree on an equitable level of reciprocal acceptance.

This emphasis on learning the psychological origins of one's own behavior and understanding the roots of the other's reactions is the core of Hendrix's (1988) method of bringing into consciousness the unconscious aspects of behavior so that they can be controlled. I share that goal with Hendrix as well as the methods of enhancing communication to facilitate the processes of self-disclosure to achieve comprehension of the other's meaning.

Differences from Other Approaches

My conception of ICT differs from many other approaches in four major respects. First, it is my belief that every therapist operates from a blend of intuitive reactions based on life experience and a personalized blend of assumptions derived from theory and research. Therefore, the therapy of two people who have similar training and beliefs will always show some important differences, so my approach cannot be identical to any other. The brand of ICT I have adopted differs from others in several other respects.

My preference for objectively measurable terms in every phase of my thinking differentiates my approach from many others. That means adoption of a verifiable theory of human behavior through use of assessment terms with the lowest possible level of inference, planning treatment through a series of testable assumptions, and use of objective criteria for evaluating treatment outcome. When the terms I use are not directly measurable, they are at least verifiable in principle (MacCorquodale & Meehl, 1953). This sensitivity to data allows me to have an open-ended theory. For example, I have long been identified as a "pro-maritalist," implying that I generally prefer to see couples stay together. But I am strongly persuaded by research showing that children suffer when exposed to prolonged or intense parental conflict (Krishnakumar & Buehler, 2000), so I am careful to factor into my treatment planning the potential impact on the children if partners remain in contentious relationships. In the same vein, research on the role of internal working models in interpersonal behavior led me to add attention to personal history to what began as an essentially social-skills training approach. In this way, research findings strongly influence the goals that I pursue in therapy as well as the strategies and techniques that I use to pursue them

Another difference lies in my preference for objective assessment measures. While many other approaches focus on identifying covert and manifest pathology, I stress the importance of finding clients' strengths as the keys to helping them achieve their goals. In that regard, I view pathology as the best solution clients can find to the adjustment problems they face. Years of clinical experience have taught me that, in most instances, even the most heinous behavior is aimed at meeting one of a small number of universal goals. The domestically abusive partner may seek security while the philanderer often seeks validation or sexual satisfaction, and those who act out in other ways do so to get attention. Security, validation, sexual satisfaction, and attention are all perfectly acceptable ends, but these means of pursuing them are clearly unacceptable. I view my role as helping clients find better means of achieving their goals by mobilizing and building on their existing strengths.

I also try to establish a type of therapeutic relationship with my clients that is different than that sought by a number of other approaches. To level the playing field, I use my first name, reveal aspects of my values and life experience, and explain the logic of my approach. Use of first names removes an artificial barrier to nonhierarchical collaboration. Sharing values reduces the likelihood of clients being unsuspectingly manipulated by my personal preferences. Sharing life experience helps clients feel less exposed and is a useful means of offering models of ways to conceptualize and master common life challenges. Self-disclosures can be useful if they are brief and targeted, helping to build rapport while offering mnemonic triggers to aid recall of the essential principles being offered. But care must be taken with self-disclosure because it can also be distracting if prolonged or, if it is carelessly offered, it can incidentally illustrate actions that are not congruent with the therapeutic goals. Because I offer principle-driven therapy, I explain the logic of intervention techniques to clients in a straightforward manner. When clients understand the logic, they can engage their higher-order cognitive processes in shaping the development of new and better strategies. Also, because they are active in the planning, they are more likely to be able to follow through on instigations and to apply what they have learned to future challenges. Finally, engaging their creative thought processes enables me to help them strive toward the conscious marriage described by Hendrix (1988). In short, my goal is to empower couples to be their own therapists when treatment ends.

The focus on positives supports the creation of a collaborative therapeutic relationship. Because I acknowledge and support clients' goals, they feel understood and are open to change. Conversely, when assessment focuses on pathology, therapists are judging clients' behavior in an inherently hierarchical relationship. This often results in attempts by therapists to manipulate changes that the clients instinctively resist making. Paradoxical instigation is an attempt to sabotage resistance by what is often called "reverse psychology." I believe that paradox brings out the worst in a clinician–client encounter and is the antithesis of my model. It assumes that the therapist knows best in a profoundly hierarchical mode. It models manipulation and indirectness, precisely the kind of interaction problems that my therapy attempts to counteract. While it may produce some degree of immediate change, clients learn nothing about how to promote similar changes on their own. They must depend on the therapist's magic to produce change, and, if the therapist misconstrues the couple's underlying dynamics, as everyone is at risk of doing, the instigation can misfire with iatrogenic effects.

While many other approaches view personality in trait terms, I assume that a major share of human behavior is state- rather than trait-driven. I accept the notion that infants are born with varied temperaments (Chess & Thomas, 1986) that endure throughout their lives (Rothbart, Ahadi, & Evans, 2000). I also accept the research showing that parenting strategies can strongly influence the way in which children's temperaments develop (Eisenberg & Mussen, 1989), while children, in turn, influence the parenting styles their caregivers adopt (Bell & Harper, 1977). As a result of these interactions, children develop internal working models (Bretherton & Munholland, 1999) that become the templates for their future relationships. Yet, while both temperament and these internal working models may significantly influence children's developing brains (Siegel, 1999), they do not determine their future behavior. Neurophysiological and developmental factors influence individuals' predispositions but they are not response mandates. Those who don't like the results of acting on these predispositions can learn new ways to conceptualize their options and to control their emotions in order to follow the new paths. Bowby (1988) believed that every infant has "an array of pathways potentially open to him [and the] . . . particular pathway that he proceeds on is determined by the environment he meets with" (p. 136). In the same vein, I believe that a nurturing therapeutic relationship can provide the environment in which clients can learn to identify internal working models and learn to control their influence so that even the worst childhood experiences are viewed as challenges, not life sentences.

Nature of Intimate Relationships

Intimate relationships evolve through a similar natural history, whether they involve partners of the same or opposite sex, and whether couples marry or cohabitate. When individuals are ready to seek intimacy, they screen potential partners with varying degrees of care. Some use an unconsciously selected set of criteria, evaluate these and ignore many others, and commit too strongly, too soon. These may be the couples in which Zielinski (1999) believes that "partners are chosen based on their incompatibility during a phase of romantic love that blinds each partner to this incompatibility" (p. 91). But others are far more deliberate and thoughtful in making what may the most far-reaching choice in their lives. They use a progressively finer set of filters that often operate outside their awareness. First, they screen out those who do not have targeted demographic (e.g., gender, race, religion, socioeconomic status, etc.) and somatic (e.g., height, weight, build, etc.) characteristics or sexual orientations. Then they look for shared interests and values. Those still in the running are then screened for similarity in goals, for example, to have or not have a family, to pursue or turn away from a spiritual life, to travel widely or use the resources to feather a nest, and so forth. As relationships develop with the few who meet all the requirements, evaluation of social and physical intimacy begins. If their interaction meets both partners' standards, and the time is right for both, they will commit to a shared future. But, even the most careful may be unhappily surprised if they succumb to what Stuart and Jacobson (1985) have termed the "secret contract of courtship." They may fail to ask some of the most important questions, may misinterpret some of the answers they receive, and may be misled by some of what they accurately apprehend.

Courtship is the time of maximal human deceptiveness: We are selling ourselves, and we will go to great lengths to present ourselves in a positive light. This is usually not deliberate deception, but it has the impact that would have resulted from planned deceit: Partners enter into agreements without knowing what they have implicitly promised to deliver, and often without even being aware of what they expect to receive. Even the most well-matched partners can run into difficulty when their unstated expectations are thwarted, either because of misunderstanding or because subsequent events necessitate changes. Putting these unspoken compacts into words and negotiating agreements that work well for both can provide the foundation for stabilizing intimacy after the commitment is made, and deepening it as the partners cope with the radical changes that will shape their lives like parenthood, illness, job and economic change, and aging. Access to the right cognitive skills, the ability to manage affect, and a repertoire of effective social skills, all influence the likelihood that the partners' connection will be warm and long-lasting.

Marital Cognition

The way partners feel and think about each other is due, in part, to deeply held beliefs of which they may or may not be aware (Baucom & Epstein, 1990; Bradbury & Fincham, 1992; Fincham & Bradbury, 1989). Some of the most significant findings regarding marital cognition concern causal attributions. In marriage, these are people's beliefs about why they and their partners behave the way they do. Studies comparing the attributional styles of distressed couples with those of nondistressed couples have resulted in some interesting findings. Passer, Kelley, and Michela (1978) found that, in distressed marriages, partners tend to be overly evaluative and assign more negative than positive motives to each other's behavior. Additionally, distressed spouses more often view their partners as the source of their relationship problems, due, in large measure, to their belief that their spouses view them negatively (Fincham, 1985).

Distressed couples generally attribute their partners' negative behaviors to permanent personality traits while attributing their own negative behavior to temporary circumstantial (i.e., state) variables (Fincham, Baucom, & Beach, 1987; Bradbury & Fincham, 1992). Similarly, distressed couples typically attribute their partners' positive behaviors to temporary circumstances and their own positive behavior to enduring personality characteristics. In contrast, nondistressed couples enhance their relationships by carrying certain positive beliefs about their partners, some of which are illusory (Fowers, Lyons, & Montel, 1996). Among distressed couples, the pattern of negative expectation and attribution ends up perpetuating negative behavioral reciprocity. This contributes significantly to the entrenched downward spiral of relationship problems experienced by so many distressed couples.

How can we account for this finding? It may be that the problems in distressed relationships are so persistent that the partners have learned from experience that change is unlikely. But a more interesting explanation was recently offered by Milkulincer and Arad (1999). They found that individuals with secure attachment orientations tolerate unpredictability and ambiguity well due in part to the flexibility of their cognitive processes. In contrast, those with anxious orientations have been shown to block the input of new information in an effort to keep from being overwhelmed by it, while avoidant persons are immune to new input to avoid hurt and to maintain self-control. Given my clinical observations that truly negative behaviors occur infrequently, and that most conflicts are triggered by very trivial events, much of the unhappiness in distressed marriages seems to be better explained by cognitive biases resulting from internal working models than by real issues in the interaction.

It is from this perspective that I regard attachment orientation an important influence on marital cognition. There has been increasing interest in attachment theory over the last decade among personality and social psychologists, particularly as it pertains to adult romantic relationships (Cassidy & Shaver, 1999). Attachment has been conceived as a process that forms in infancy and is continually reinforced over the entire life span (Bowlby, 1988). It functions through the internal working models that are created through experiences with caregivers in infancy. Attachment orientation becomes the template—one might say wish-fulfilling prophesy—of later life. Those fortunate enough to enjoy secure early relationships come to feel safe with others, while those whose early relationships were less stable bring a blend of anxiety and hostility to subsequent interactions. Internal working models thus function as internal templates of expectations, and, by acting as if we were in safe or threatening situations, we end up creating these very conditions. Acting as if others were trustworthy increases the probability that they will earn this trust, while acting as if they are rejecting or exploitive is likely to induce these behaviors even in those who are not naturally inclined to act in these ways. Internal working models function as affective predispositions, but the resulting experiences are encoded in words, and the constructs that result provide the conscious logic of interpersonal behavior.

Marital Affect

As an interventionist, I approach emotions from a cognitive perspective. In this view, emotions are understood to be physiological responses to the way in which events are construed, a position introduced by Schacter and Singer (1962) and developed by Lazarus and Lazarus (1994). External events don't trigger emotions; rather, the triggers are the way the events are labeled. This labeling is often neither conscious nor literal. Instead, minimal cues are instantly interpreted as signs that certain biologically mediated approach or avoidance strategies are needed. Once the cue occurs, our brains make a host of instantaneous inferences through a process of associative reasoning that is guided by emotion. Emotions are the repositories of responses needed for survival that have been developed throughout our collective human (Tooby & Cosmides, 1990) and individual (LeDoux, 1996) evolution. As such, they facilitate survival because they allow for immediate action, but sometimes they elicit actions that can make matters worse. This is seen when, for example, one partner interprets the other's facial expression while pondering options as though it were a direct statement of profound disapproval and, through an emotionally self-fueling process, construes it as a sign of intent to end the relationship. Because both partners are apt to respond in the same way, albeit to different cues, both are "at once the creators of the relationship dance and the victims of it" (Greenberg & Johnson, 1988, p. 60).

Because the appraisals that elicit emotions occur outside of conscious awareness, therapy can help both partners delay responding to negative emotions long enough to translate their feelings into words. This is accomplished therapeutically by helping them develop their metacognitive abilities (Nelson, 1992; Nelson, Stuart, Howard, & Crowley, 1999). Therapists can then develop their clients' mindfulness (Langer, 1989) through which they can form new categories, be open to new information, and adopt alternative perspectives. The relabeling that results can go a long way toward damping the intensity of conflicts between partners, allowing them to achieve greater intimacy.

Marital Behavior

I believe that it takes three things for relationships to succeed. Partners must share the values that are basic to either of them such as spirituality, the desire to procreate, or the wish to have a sexually exclusive relationship. They should have enough style symmetry to have a reasonable level of comfort, but enough complementarity to allow them to compensate for each other's deficits. And both should have the skills and motivation to use two-winner negotiation as the best alternative to conflict or acquiescence, both of which debilitate relationships. Accordingly, a major interim goal is to help clients enhance their skills in communication and bargaining to build confidence in the likelihood that their exchanges will be equitable.

Conceptualization of Adaptive and Maladaptive Functioning

I regard all human behavior as an attempt to achieve a sense of personal well-being. These efforts have one of three possible outcomes: They may benefit self only, others, or both. Sometimes behavior that was intended to have beneficial consequences produces destructive outcomes. If the behavior is patently antisocial, as is the case for coercion and abuse, it may very well be pathological because of its impact on all who are affected by it. But, more often, the problems that couples bring to therapists are not pathological but are problems caused by otherwise innocuous actions that would not have caused difficulties under other circumstances. If they occur once, they are a learning opportunity; but if they recur often they become maladaptive patterns. Therefore, I rarely see partners as pathological, but often consider their repetition of patterns that cause unhappiness as maladaptive and suitable targets of change. Actions, not personalities, are targeted for change or acceptance.

How Change Occurs

Among the distinguishing features of intervention theories are their prescriptions of how to initiate change. Because it is assumed that "A-to-G" factors interact reciprocally, change in any one is expected to influence all the others. Therefore, therapy can be initiated at any of these points. The choice will depend on the clients' resources and the therapist's inclinations. London (1986) differentiated between two types of therapy. Insight-oriented approaches like the psychoanalytic model used by Paolino (1981) are "based on the fundamental principle that combined verbal and emotional expression of thoughts and feelings is more clinically effective than the influence of overt behavior" (p. 54). They place great emphasis on painstakingly building clients' self-understanding, and trust that this knowledge will be leveraged into future behavioral changes. My approach, which London would classify as "action-oriented," starts with an effort to understand clients' outlooks just well enough to promote early changes in their behavior. Reactions to these changes then become the building blocks of new repertoires that hopefully help them feel better and have a much more positive appraisal of their circumstances. We all want to help our clients reach their goals, but our efforts to do so begin from very different starting points. Thus, one major group of therapists starts with insight and hopes to promote changes in behavior, while the group with which I identify starts with behavior change as a route to promoting insight.

Generally, I believe it is best to begin by framing goals in the language of thoughts, feelings, or actions that comes most naturally for the clients, using their metaphors, and then to instigate change in one of the other areas. For example, if clients complain that they don't feel enough intimacy, it is wise to focus on encouraging intimacy-building behaviors. If clients complain about each other's actions, the most helpful first step is to promote understanding of the meaning of these behaviors to both parties. Couples can learn to understand the emotional logic of their own behavior, and each partner can decode the other's seemingly irrational reactions when he or she learns to see events as the other perceives them. When each realizes that the other lives in an internal world very different from his or her own, the frustrated confusion that permeates distressed relationships diminishes. While research in this area is still sparse, it has been shown that, when partners accurately understand each other, their satisfaction increases (Kobak & Hazan, 1991). Once they develop enough insight into their own underlying motivations to be able to express them, and when these expressions have been understood, partners can then negotiate compassionate ways to satisfy each other's deepest desires.

Finally, positive-change-oriented techniques are the basic tools of this approach. This emphasis follows from observations by Bandura (1969) and others in the behavioral tradition (see Spiegler & Guevremont, 1993, Chapter 6) that it is futile to attempt to suppress unwanted behaviors without first strengthening desirable alternatives. If it is correct that partners' problematic behaviors are efforts to achieve important common human goals, they will not cease these efforts until they learn better strategies. Therapy can abbreviate the trial-and-error approach that most people follow by suggesting new routes to achieve the desired ends.

Application to Diverse Family Forms

Sensitivity to multiculturalism is one of the principal assets of this model of ICT. Because of the central role of constructivism, I am always careful to elicit clients' perceptions of their present realities and goals and resources for change.

Because I do not restrict myself to the narrow range of concepts that limit the scope of many theory-driven approaches, the clients' perspectives dominate my epistemology-driven approach. The limitations to the application of this approach lie in the therapist, not the method or the clients. First, I may not always succeed in truly understanding the client because I may not be able to "enter the client's system." Also, because I can't avoid working within the framework of my own values, I can't always accept my clients' goals. For example, if an abused wife asks me to help her accept the realities of her relationship, instead of doing so, I would have to offer to help her assess the chances of changing his behavior or leaving the relationship if those efforts fail. In general, however, my intervention can only work when I come close to seeing the world through my clients' eyes, allow this percept to prevail over my own values and beliefs, and effectively communicate this understanding.

Intervention Strategies Associated with the Theory

As noted, I ask couples to complete at least the CPI, and sometimes the FOO, prior to the first session. To motivate them to do so, I generally speak with them directly rather than arranging the appointment through a receptionist. This contact provides an opportunity to screen out clients whom I may not be qualified to help. It allows me to begin to establish rapport and hope. This often takes the edge off some of the conflicts and it is not uncommon for clients to tell me that just making the appointment seems to have made a difference. The call also allows me to clarify fees, insurance, schedules, and other practical details. It is my chance to explain the logic of the inventories and motivate clients to complete them. Finally, the call gives me a chance to help the clients decide how to present their concerns even before we've met.

When they request help, the partners' complaints are often scattered throughout several different dimensions of the relationship and expressed in negative terms. In response to the stress that motivated them to invite a stranger into their lives, they almost always lose sight of the strengths of their relationship. Each portrays the other as the culprit and him- or herself as the hapless victim, generally in the global, rigid language of traits, e.g., "he's inconsiderate" or "she's passive aggressive." Their accusations are usually quite general, even when they pinpoint one or two particulars for illustration (Fincham, 1985). This is often frustrating and confusing to the couple. They know they are unhappy but they cannot always pinpoint exactly why, and are frustrated by the fact that they have exhausted all of their own ideas about how to improve matters. The initial phone conversation, rarely lasting longer than ten minutes, can help crystallize their thinking and make it more constructive.

When and How Interventions Are Best Applied

When clients first contact therapists to request service, the therapist must decide whether to see the clients or refer them elsewhere. Ethical principles demand

Stuart w/ clients

that therapists practice within their competence, so clinicians must determine whether they have the training and experience required for adequately serving the client. Most therapists have been trained for work with individuals. Work with couples requires many skills beyond those needed for individual therapy. Those who have not been trained in couples' therapy techniques should not use them until their training is completed. And, occasionally, the problems presented by the clients may require specialized skills that the therapist lacks, such as those needed to manage abuse, excessive drug and alcohol use, or primary sexual dysfunction.

Clinical Illustration Tied to the Video

Preparation for First Session

Because couples come for counseling at times of stress, it stands to reason that they are not functioning at their best when they meet the therapist for the first time. Each normally comes in search of an ally who will collude in an effort to change the other. Therefore, if the clients are in control of the initial encounter, the sessions are apt to draw out behavior that reinforces negative scripts, embarrasses or insults either or both, and tarnishes therapy with an aura of hostility. Accordingly, it is more important for the therapist to be in control of the proceedings during the first session than at any subsequent time. All of the information gleaned from the CPI and FOO usually enables me to assume and maintain the necessary control. The inventories also help the clients arrive with more balanced perspectives on their relationship, a better understanding of their own goals, and a belief that the therapist has a head start on understanding them. Confidence that they are understood lends credibility to the instigations given in the first meeting and helps to get therapy off to a positive, quick start.

Assessment

Wesley and Adele completed both forms in time for me to review their responses before our first meeting. Both were in their late fifties and had full-time, blue-collar jobs. Adele's elderly, ill mother had recently moved in with them. Their CPI scores showed that, while both identified aspects of their relationship that were satisfying (e.g., free time together, trust, division of chores, etc.), neither was very pleased with the level of affectionate expression or the quality of communication in their interaction. Wesley felt that Adele put work and her mother ahead of him, and he had brought up the subject of divorce several times. Adele complained that Wesley had withdrawn from sex entirely and demonstrated a marked lack of support for her career and spirituality. In addition, the CPI revealed that Wesley had one fifteen-years-long happy marriage that produced five children and ended with his wife's death due to cancer. Neither of his two very brief subsequent marriages was satisfying in the least. Adele also had two prior marriages, one lasting eighteen years and producing two children, and one a good deal shorter, neither having been happy experiences.

Wesley's FOO revealed that his father was seriously injured and was unable to manage the family farm while Wesley was in grade school. But he, his mother, and his two brothers pulled together and maintained a happy home life, albeit on the edge of poverty. Adele's childhood experiences were very different. Her father was extremely demanding and could not be satisfied, and her mother often agreed with his criticisms. She alluded to experiences of abuse and described the pain of being a "fat" child who was shunned by peers. She established independence as early as she could and married as quickly as possible to escape the burden of her home life.

Wesley learned that work was essential, but, throughout his childhood, family came first. Adele also learned that work was essential, but for her it came first because it was what her father demanded and it served as her primary source of security. In effect, Wesley worked to live and Adele lived to work so she could feel safe in her treasured independence. They were, thus, in a sad pas de deux: Wesley construed Adele's working as rejection while she felt that his approval was as remote as her father's had been. Although the difficulties were clear, it seemed as though this couple had the resources for a better relationship because the roots of their major difficulties could be fairly easily traced to differences in their internal working models and to misunderstandings at the time that they married. Both of these could, in principle, be corrected by cultivating insight, understanding, and negotiation skills.

Intervention Themes

I believe that successful intervention depends on being able to keep therapy focused on the themes that are most useful to the clients. While the menu of themes is fairly general, the blending of options is unique to each client. For this couple, five themes seemed important:

1. It was clear that their families of origin and subsequent life experiences played an important role in magnifying the stress that Wesley and Adele have been experiencing. A major theme was to be the promotion of insight and understanding of their respective internal working models.

2. It appears that Wesley and Adele married without discussing the implications of their important values. Wesley probably expected Adele to put him and homemaking first as his first wife had done. Adele probably expected Wesley to support her in her career because he appeared to be so pleased by her work ethic when they first met. Their secret courtship contract was, thus, a design for trouble and it would have to be identified and reformulated.

3. Given my assumption that Wesley and Adele essentially liked many things about each other, had many shared values and interests, and seemed to enjoy each other when their relationship was not complicated by the intrusion of problematic themes, I considered them to be well matched. Because they had lost confidence in their marriage, another key goal was to restore their faith in what they might achieve as a couple.

4. Their CPI responses indicated that, while both partners were essentially aware of the other's concerns, they seemed immobilized when it came time to address them. Providing the skills to forge and deepen their connection was therefore essential to their long-term survival as a couple.

5. Finally, success in the first three areas would create an opportunity to help each one develop a more constructive attributional style so both could feel less overwhelmed when the inevitable difficulties arise in the future.

Nature of the Therapeutic Relationship and Techniques for Establishing Rapport

I generally begin first sessions by suggesting that we all address each other by our first names. I then normally acknowledge the clients' efforts in completing the inventories and ask them to recount their personal histories. I already know most of what they will say by having studied their written material, but it is important for them to bring these defining memories into the therapeutic arena. Whenever possible, I try to punctuate their accounts with comments or questions that convey sympathy and understanding. When possible, I try to enhance this through the use of shared metaphors that serve as a covert, connective code, for example, references to details of Wesley's family farm, Adele's weight concerns, their interest in classic cars, and Lancaster bombers, which related to Wesley's interests.

Initial Impressions

During the first few minutes of the session, I found it much easier to relate to Wesley. He was open and really tried to be good-natured about a very awkward situation. Adele, while not at all unfriendly, seemed a bit more difficult to reach. Both were sane, expressive, and respectfully responsive to the other's comments, so I anticipated a productive session.

Early in the session, I searched for an answer to the question of whether I should orient the session toward enhancing this marriage or facilitate their bringing it to a compassionate end. The answer soon became clear. Their moods improved greatly when they described the things they had liked about each other at first, many of which have continued to be true despite their present relative disengagement. As I stated often during the session, while Wesley verbally expressed some ambivalence, he looked at Adele very tenderly and was clearly deeply connected to her. I soon warmed to the task because it was clear that it would not be enough to save this marriage; this was a relationship that had the potential to be very good indeed.

I also pondered an apparent paradox in Wesley, one that I was not able to resolve during this session. While he describes his family of origin in very positive terms, and seems to have left his family's bosom with a secure attachment orientation, he is, nevertheless, ridden with a sense of insecurity that he expressed through avoidance. It led me to wonder if he idealized his memories of the past or if subsequent experiences, such as the death of his first wife, had severely affected him. For now, I operated as if he had a secure attachment orientation. With Adele having an anxious attachment style, as evidenced by her drive to please her mother, with whom she was still reenacting childhood dramas, the pattern that they presented was typical of mildly to moderately distressed couples.

Establishing a Treatment Contract

Before I could establish a treatment contract, it was necessary to verify my understanding of the ways in which the couple's developmental themes influenced their relationship. At about 2.13 on the videotape, I inquired about the meaning of work to Adele. Wesley referred to it as a "compulsion," a global, rigid attribution, while Adele characterized it as her way of gaining acceptance. Further discussion led to Wesley's acknowledgment that she was setting some limits at work despite being under unreasonable pressure on the job. Yet, despite this understanding, he still felt she put him second.

Unable to soften Wesley's attributions, I took a different tack by asking them about their goals for counseling. When they said they wanted to re-experience some of the joys of their courtship, I reinforced the idea with a self-revelation about my faith in the importance of acting as they did on their second date in order to feel what they did at the time. When they each offered descriptions of things that pleased them, we contracted, in effect, to make those wishes a reality.

Caring Days: Specific Interventions
Related to Theory

Therapists often elicit resistance when they confront clients with the need for change. Instead, at about 2.21 on the tape, I began to record their requests (e.g., notes, small gifts, etc.) on the Caring Days form (Stuart, in press) without explaining what I was doing.Reflecting on his desires reminded Wesley of his deep sense of rejection when Adele was slow to visit him in the hospital following two emergency admissions, and when she chose to spend many Thanksgiving and Christmas holidays with her mother in a nearby town. I attempted to help him understand the meaning of these choices for Adele, given her history, and she later helped by expressing her fear of having bad things happen to the people she loves.

In conjunction with discussing affectionate exchanges, Wesley acknowledged having withdrawn from Adele sexually. Clearly, he was under the influence of his global attributional style that led him to emotional extremes. I tried to help him take a proactive approach to rebuilding his own sexual interest and, at about 2.32, used another self-revelation in which I described household chores as foreplay. When he reiterated his fear of rejection, I repeated the principle of acting "as if," using a World War II story to which I was certain he could relate. To buffer his willingness to experiment, I offered my "guarantee" that they could achieve much greater intimacy if both would act as if it were within reach.

While listing other Caring Days items like hugs and kisses, they expressed their wish to discuss retirement. I stressed the importance of this as a shared goal and added my profound conviction that they had great potential, with Wesley wanting much greater contact and Adele having achieved considerable insight into her motivation for doing things that competed with creating this intimacy through individual therapy. I was prepared to help them negotiate a future contract to replace the unstated courtship expectations, but Wesley's palpable mood shift prevented my doing so. He became remorseful about his recent disappointments and seemed to despair of the potential to avoid further hurt. I attempted to help him manage these feelings, first by reinforcing the importance of commitment by relating my own joy when my wife recommitted to our marriage. Then, at about 2.41, I indirectly gave information to Wesley about the survival meaning of work to Adele by asking her questions. This appeared to help him overcome his sorrow and to reconnect with Adele emotionally. It was at that point that I explained the logic of Caring Days and reiterated the instigation to act "as if."

At about 2.45, I asked what problems they foresaw in using the Caring Days list. Wesley again cited Adele's work (rigid attributions die hard!) and concern about her mother, but he was able to acknowledge progress on both. He went further to assert his deep sense of responsibility for his mother-in-law, a clear derivative of his own experience with his father's injury. Adele helped by citing her guilt about work, which she related to her experience of abuse as a child, saying that she would continue to try to master it.

Running out of resistance, at this point Wesley told Adele that he really wanted to count on her being there when he was in crisis. She explained that her failure to do so was not a lack of caring, but just the opposite, a dread of having bad things happen to the people she loves. Building on the emotional connection that had been achieved, at about 2.49 I asked them to take each other's hand and recommit to their marriage. I repeated my confidence in their success if they balanced insight, understanding, and action as well they could. When asked if they were more optimistic, Wesley could muster no more than a "somewhat," so more work clearly remains to be done.

Evaluating the Results of the First Meeting

This session is representative of what I hope to see happen in first sessions: Rapport was established, a contract negotiated, the change process was initiated, and a commitment for follow-through was obtained. It was necessary to draw on multiple theoretical perspectives to achieve these results.

- Attachment and family-of-origin theories guided the articulation of the clients' internal working models.
- Constructivism guided an appreciation of the meaning of these themes in their current lives.
- Cognitive–emotion theory was used to help the clients examine the ways they labeled events, the emotional impact of these labels, and the power of relabeling in changing the way they feel.
- Attribution theory was invaluable in pinpointing the way in which Wesley's style of thought painted him into a corner and then kept him there.
- Acceptance theory afforded the logic for deciding between areas needing change and those to which compassionate accommodation was the best response.
- Social exchange theory helped to pinpoint the fact that the clients' current relationship compared favorably to their most recent relationships, and was probably a good deal better than potential alternatives.
- Social learning theory was a resource for techniques needed to increase their intimacy and to set the stage for the two-winner negotiation that would enable them to build on this improvement.
- Cognitive–behavior therapy suggested the structure for promoting these changes, beginning with the negotiation of the Caring Days lists.

A reasonable level of success was achieved in addressing the first three themes of the intervention. This success created the opportunity for the brief recommitment ceremony that ended the session. I can do this in about half of my first sessions with couples for whom staying together is a mutual desire. It is important, both because it reinforces the idea that the therapist's office is a place in which the common good will transcend individual hurts and because it reinforces the partners' motivation to adhere to the changes instigated by the therapist.

Next Steps, Including Specific Instructions for Two-Winner Negotiation

Several subsequent sessions would be needed to help Wesley and Adele improve their two-winner negotiation skills. They would have to learn the difference between good faith holistic contracts and partitive contracts that are built of quid-pro-quo exchanges (Stuart, 1980; Stuart & Jacobson, 1985). Holistic contracts are crucial because there are times when other concerns interfere with compliance with specific contract provisions; partitive contracts break down at such times. They would also have to learn the value of 90/90 agreements in which they take turns being in control as opposed to 50/50 contracts in which competing desires are balanced on every occasion. Most people think of negotiation as a process in which they bargain over one issue at a time and each must settle for half of what was desired. It is much more realistic to bargain over several issues at once in order to reach an outcome in which each person can have most of what she or he wants in particular areas, at specified times.

Wesley's cognitive style would also have to be a major focus. If left unchanged, he could undo major progress by using overly negative, global, and rigid constructs while construing his disappointments. He needs help learning to identify the dysfunctional patterns and using metacognitive processing to reformulate them. I would ease him into this process by relying on metaphor and analogy, for example, the way he monitors his truck's performance and takes corrective action when he detects signs of trouble. It would also be extremely helpful to help him overcome a tendency to feel victimized, replacing it with the readiness to redefine his disappointments as problems to be solved.

It would also be necessary to help Adele and Wesley prepare for, and cope with, the testing that inevitably follows major positive relationship changes (Stuart, 1980). Prior to the first session, both had signed off on their relationship to some extent, each ascribing the fault to the other's traits. Trait notions, as forms of attribution, are difficult to overcome. Moreover, each person knows that the changes made in therapy were influenced by a desire to create a good impression on the therapist, and, therefore, is apprehensive about the stability of the change. When this apprehension arises, each is apt to fall back under the influence of internal working models that trigger emotion-driven defensive reactions, Wesley by withdrawing emotionally and Adele by increasing the time she spends at work. They unconsciously expect to be disappointed by each other, but hope that therapy will have motivated the other to show the love and commitment that they both crave. To prepare for this testing, it is useful to promote some discussion of the way each would like the other to respond when the early signs of defensiveness are noted. My experience has shown that all major changes are tested twice, and passing these tests goes far toward making therapeutically mediated changes permanent. With proper planning, testing can actually strengthen rather than weaken their relationship.

Summary

Strengths and Limitations of the Theory

This is a very exciting time to be a couples' therapist: Our knowledge about the dynamics of intimacy is exploding and with it our ability to develop new and ever-more-effective intervention techniques. It is clear that we now have strategies and techniques that can make every relationship better, and some good to great. But we still don't have reliable means of helping some types of clients (e.g., those with Axis II disorders) meaningfully improve their relationships. Our methods can always benefit from techniques that improve efficiency and promote better maintenance of therapeutically mediated changes.

Questions to Consider

Integrative models face three never-ending uncertainties:

1. Do their assumptions account for enough of the variance in human relationships to support intervention methods that lead to lasting change? Should more variables be added to the mix because factors that can strongly influence treatment outcome have been ignored?
2. Conversely, have they included more than are necessary? The challenge inherent in this question is the need to have a parsimonious theory. Therapists can easily be overloaded, and it is important to limit their attention to those variables that have the greatest bearing on the success of their efforts.
3. Have the variables been weighted such that predictions have maximal accuracy? The problem with answering this question stems from the fact that research that supports inclusion of each element is based on group study results while the various elements play very different roles in predicting the outcome of each individual's behavior.

As should be clear for this discussion, those who seek simple answers will not be pleased with ICT: Few, if any, generalities apply across the board and the explanation and prediction of behavior is always more complicated than it appears. Conversely, complex thinkers who are intrigued by the complexity of human behavior will find ICT to be a never-ending source of increasing knowledge. ICT is a fine choice for the intellectually curious—for those who are at least as interested in the questions as the answers!

To Learn More

The bad news about ICT is that there is no one resource for developing or enhancing the skills needed for effective service delivery. The good news is that virtually all theories and research about the roots of interpersonal behavior and therapeutic efforts to change it are potentially useful. It is essential to read this literature critically because the mere fact that a study reports results to the third decimal place does not mean that its conclusions are either valid or reliable (Kazdin, 1999; Meltzoff, 1998). Each clinician's own practice is another invaluable source of information. By evaluating every therapeutic service rendered by using one of a host of single subject designs (Fonagy & Moran, 1993; Hayes, Barlow, & Nelson-Gray, 1999), therapists can learn from their own experience. Pooling these results with groups of peers can help to test the limits to which they can be generalized while also identifying new hypotheses to fill gaps in our constantly evolving understanding of the complexity and potential of human relationships.

ENDNOTE

1. I would like to gratefully acknowledge the invaluable contributions of my colleague, Rosemary Bannen Tyksinski. She is truly one of the most creative thinkers I have encountered, and interactions with her have greatly stimulated my thinking in many areas of this presentation. This paper could not have seen the light of day without the incomparable editorial assistance of my wife, Barbara Jacobson Stuart, Ph.D., who immeasurably helped to refine both the ideas and the way in which they are presented.

REFERENCES

Alford, B. A., & Beck, A. T. (1997). *The integrative power of cognitive therapy.* New York: Guilford.

Arkowitz, H. (1997). Integrative theories of therapy. In P. L. Wachtel & S. B. Messer (Eds.), *Theories of psychotherapy: Origins and evolution* (pp. 227–298). Washington, DC: American Psychological Association.

Association for the Advancement of Behavior Therapy. (2000). *Guidelines for choosing a behavior therapist.* New York: Author.

Bandura, A. (1969). *Principles of behavior modification.* New York: Holt Rinehart & Winston.

Bandura, A. (1977). *Social learning theory.* Englewood Cliffs, NJ: Prentice-Hall.

Baucom, D. H., & Epstein, N. (1990). *Cognitive behavioral therapy.* New York: Brunner/Mazel.

Baucom, D. H., Shoham, V., Mueser, K. T., Daiuto, A. D., & Stickle, T. R. (1998). Empirically supported couple and family interventions for marital distress and adult mental health problems. *Journal of Consulting and Clinical Psychology, 66,* 53–88.

Bell, R. Q., & Harper, L. V. (1977). *Child effects on adults.* Hillsdale, NJ: Lawrence Erlbaum.

Bickman, L. (1999). Practice makes perfect and other myths about mental health services. *American Psychologist, 54,* 965–978.

Bower, T. G. R. (1989). *The rational infant: Learning in infancy.* New York: W. H. Freeman.

Bowlby, J. (1988). *A secure base: Healthy human development.* New York: Basic Books.

Bradbury, T. N., & Fincham, F. D. (1992). Attributions and behavior in marital interaction. *Journal of Personality and Social Psychology, 63,* 513–628.

Bretherton, I., & Munhollan, K. A. (1999). Internal working models in attachment relationships. In J. Cassidy & P. R. Shaver (Eds.), *Handbook of attachment: Theory, research, and clinical applications* (pp. 89–111). New York: Guilford.

Brown, W. A. (1998). The placebo effect. *Scientific American, 288,* 90–98.

Burtt, E. A. (1946). *Right thinking: A study of its principles and methods.* New York: Harpers.

Cashdan, S. (1973). *Interactional psychotherapy: Stages and strategies in behavioral change.* New York: Grune & Stratton.

Cassidy, J., & Shaver, P. R. (1999). *Handbook of attachment: Theory, research, and clinical applications.* New York: Guilford.

Chess, S., & Thomas, A. (1986). *Temperament in clinical practice.* New York: Guilford.

Christensen, A., & Jacobson, N. S. (1999). *Reconcilable differences.* New York: Guilford.

Davis, M. H., & Oathout, H. A. (1987). Maintenance of satisfaction in romantic relationships: Empathy and relational competence. *Journal of Personality and Social Psychology, 53,* 397–410.

Dollard, J., & Miller, N. E. (1950). *Personality and psychotherapy: An analysis in terms of learning, thinking, and culture.* New York: McGraw-Hill.

Durlak, J. A. (1979). Comparative effectiveness of paraprofessional and professional helpers. *Psychological Bulletin, 89,* 80–92.

Durlak, J. A. (1981). Evaluating comparative studies of paraprofessional and professional helpers: A reply to Nietzel and Fisher. *Psychological Bulletin, 89,* 566–569.

Eisenberg, N., & Mussen, P. H. (1989). *The roots of prosocial behavior in children.* New York: Cambridge University Press.

Fincham, F. D. (1985). Attribution processes in distressed and nondistressed couples: 2.

Responsibility for marital problems. *Journal of Abnormal Psychology, 94,* 183–190.

Fincham, F. D., Baucom, D. H., & Beach, S. R. H. (1987). Attribution processes in distressed and nondistressed couples: 4. Self-partner attribution differences. *Journal of Personality and Social Psychology, 52,* 739–748.

Fincham, F. D., & Bradbury, T. N. (1989). The impact of attributions in marriage: An individual differences analysis. *Journal of Personal and Social Relationships, 6,* 69–85.

Fincham, F. D., Bradbury, T. N., & Scott, C. K. (1990). Cognition in marriage. In F. D. Finchman & T. N. Bradbury (Eds.), *The psychology of marriage: Basic issues and applications* (pp. 118–149). New York: Guilford.

Fonagy, P., & Moran, G. (1993). Selecting single case research designs for clinicians. In N. E. Miller, L. Luborsky, J. P. Barber, & J. P. Docherty (Eds.), *Psychodynamic treatment research: A handbook for clinical practice* (pp. 62–95). New York: Basic Books.

Fowers, B. J., Lyons, E. M., & Montel, K. H. (1996). Positive marital illusions, self-enhancement or relationship enhancement? *Journal of Family Psychology, 10,* 192–208.

Frank, J. D. (1973). *Persuasion and healing: A comparative study of psychotherapy.* Baltimore, MD: Johns Hopkins University Press.

Gambrill, E. (1999). Evidence-based clinical behavior analysis, evidence-based medicine, and the Cochrane collaboration. *Journal of Behavior Therapy and Experimental Psychiatry, 30,* 1–14.

Garb, H. N. (1989). Clinical judgement, clinical training, and professional experience. *Psychological Bulletin, 105,* 387–396.

Greenberg, L. S., & Johnson, S. M. (1988). *Emotionally focused therapy for couples.* New York: Guilford.

Greeenberg, L. S., & Safran, J. D. (1987). *Emotion in psychotherapy.* New York: Guilford.

Grunebaum, H. (1988). The relationship of family theory to family therapy. *Journal of Marital and Family Therapy, 14,* 1–14.

Gurman, A. S. (1981). Integrative marital therapy: Toward the development of an interpersonal approach. In S. Budman (Ed.), *Forms of brief therapy* (pp. 415–462). New York: Guilford.

Harrell, J., & Guerney, B. (1976). Training married couples in conflict negotiation skills. In D. H. L. Olson (Ed.), *Treating relationships* (pp. 151–165). Lake Mills, IA: Graphic.

Harwood, R. L., Miller, J. G., Irizarry, N. L. (1995). *Culture and attachment: Perceptions of the child in context.* New York: Guilford.

Hayes, S. C., Barlow, D. H., & Nelson-Gray, R. (1999). *The scientist practitioner: Research and accountability in the age of managed care.* Boston: Allyn & Bacon.

Hayes, S. C., Jacobson, N. S., Follette, V. M., & Dougher, M. J. (Eds.). (1994). *Acceptance and change: Context and content in psychotherapy.* Reno, NV: Context Press.

Hendrix, H. (1988). *Getting the love you want: A guide for couples.* New York: Henry Holt.

Houts, A. C., & Krasner, L. (1998). Philosophical and theoretical foundations of behavior therapy. In J. J. Plaud & G. H. Eifert (Eds.), *From behavior theory to behavior therapy* (pp. 15–37). Boston: Allyn & Bacon.

Hume, D. (1896). *A treatise of human nature.* Oxford, Great Britain: Clarendon.

Jacobson, N. S., & Christensen, A. (1996). *Integrative couple therapy: Promoting acceptance and change.* New York: Norton.

Jacobson, N. S., & Margolin, G. (1979). *Marital therapy: Strategies based on social learning and behavior exchange principles.* New York: Brunner/Mazel.

Jones, W. T. (1975). *The twentieth century to Wittgenstein and Sartre.* New York: Harcourt, Brace, & Jovanovich.

Karasu, T. B. (1986). The specificity versus non-specificity dilemma: Toward identifying therapeutic change agents. *American Journal of Psychiatry, 143,* 687–695.

Kazdin, A. E. (1999). The meanings and measurement of clinical significance. *Journal of Consulting and Clinical Psychology, 67,* 332–339.

Kelly, G. A. (1955). *The psychology of personal constructs* (Vol. 1–2). New York: Norton.

Kobak, R., & Hazen, C. (1991). Attachment in marriage: The effects of security and accuracy of working models. *Journal of Personality and Social Psychology, 60,* 861–869.

Kruger, D. (1979). *An introduction to phenomenological psychology.* Pittsburgh: Duquesne University Press.

Krishnakumar, A., & Buehler, C. (2000). Interpersonal conflict and parenting behaviors: A meta-analytic review. *Family Relations, 49,* 25–44.

Lamont, C. (1949). *Humanism as a philosophy.* New York: Philosophical Library.

Langer, E. J. (1989). *Mindfulness.* Reading, MA: Addison-Wesley.

Lazarus, R. S., & Lazarus, B. N. (1994). *Passion and reason: Making sense of our emotions.* New York: Oxford University Press.

LeBow, J. (1997). The integrative revolution in couple and family therapy. *Family Process, 36,* 1–17.

LeCroy, C. W., Carrol, P., Nelson-Becker, H., & Sturlaugson, P. (1989). The experimental evaluation of the caring days technique for marital enrichment. *Family Relations, 38,* 15–18.

LeDoux, J. (1996). *The emotional brain.* New York: Simon & Schuster.

Lewin, K. (1935). *A dynamic theory of personality: Selected papers* (Translated by D. K. Adams & K. E. Zener). New York: McGraw-Hill.

London, P. (1986). *Modes and morals of psychotherapy.* Washington, DC: Hemisphere.

MacCorquodale, K., & Meehl, P. E. (1953). Hypothetical constructs and intervening variables. In H. Feigl & M. Brodbeck (Eds.), *Readings in the philosophy of science* (pp. 596–611). New York: Appleton-Century-Crofts.

Mahoney, M. J. (1991). *Human change processes: The scientific foundations of psychotherapy.* New York: Basic Books.

Meltzoff, J. (1998). *Critical thinking about research: Psychology and related fields.* Washington, DC: American Psychological Association.

Meyer, A. (1957). *Psychobiology: A science of man.* Springfield, IL: Thomas.

Mikulincer, M., & Arad, D. (1999). Attachment working models and cognitive openness in close relationships: A test of chronic and temporary accessibility effects. *Journal of Personality and Social Psychology, 77,* 710–725.

Miller, L. (1991). *Freud's brain: Neuropsychodynamic foundations of psychoanalysis.* New York: Guilford.

Montague, A. (1956). *The biosocial nature of man.* New York: Grove Press.

Murdock, N. (1991). Case conceptualization: Applying theory to individuals. *Counselor Education and Supervision, 30,* 355–365.

Nelson, T. (Ed.). (1992). *Metacognition: Core readings.* Boston: Allyn & Bacon.

Nelson, T., Stuart, R. B., Howard, C., & Crowley, M. (1999). Metacognition and clinical psychology: A preliminary framework for research and practice. *Clinical Psychology and Psychotherapy, 6,* 73–79.

Nichols, W. C. (1988). *Marital therapy: An integrative approach.* New York: Guilford.

Norcross, J. C., & Goldfried, M. R. (1992). *Handbook of therapy integration.* New York: Basic Books.

O'Leary, K. D., & Turkewitz, H. (1978). Marital therapy from a behavioral perspective. In T. J. Paolino & B. S. McCrady (Eds.), *Marriage and family therapy: Psychoanalytic, behavioral and systems theory perspectives* (pp. 240–297). New York: Brunner/Mazel.

Orlinsky, D. E., & Howard, K. I. (1995). Unity and diversity among the psychotherapies: A comparative perspective. In B. Bonger & L. E. Beutler (Eds.), *Comprehensive textbook of psychotherapy: Theory and practice* (pp. 2–23). New York: Oxford University Press.

Ortony, A., Clore, G. L., & Collins, A. (1988). *The cognitive structure of emotions.* New York: Cambridge University Press.

Paolino, T. J. (1981). *Psychoanalytic therapy: Theory, technique, therapeutic relationship, and treatability.* New York: Brunner/Mazel.

Passer, M. W., Kelley, H. H., & Michela, J. L. (1978). Multidimensional scaling of the causes for negative interpersonal behavior. *Journal of Personality and Social Psychology, 36,* 951–962.

Reisman, J. M. (1971). *Toward the integration of psychotherapy.* New York: Wiley.

Rigazio-Digilio, S. A., Goncalves, O. F., & Ivey, A. E. (1966). From cultural diversity to existential diversity: The impossibility of psychotherapy integration within a traditional framework. *Applied and Preventive Psychology, 5,* 235–247.

Rothbart, M. K., Ahadi, S. A., & Evans, D. E. (2000). Temperament and personality: Origins and outcomes. *Journal of Personality and Social Psychology, 78,* 122–135.

Sager, C. (1976). *Marriage contracts and couples therapy.* New York: Brunner/Mazel.

Schacter, S., & Singer, J. E. (1962). Cognitive, social, and physiological determinants of emotional state. *Psychological Review, 69,* 379–399.

Shapiro, A. K., & Shapiro, E. (1997). *The powerful placebo.* Baltimore, MD: Johns Hopkins University Press.

Siegel, D. J. (1999). *The developing mind: Toward a neurobiology of interpersonal experience.* New York: Guilford.

Smith, D. A. (1999). The end of theoretical orientations? *Applied and Preventive Psychology, 8,* 269–280.

Sperling, M. B., & Berman, W. H. (Eds.). (1994). *Attachment in adults: Clinical and developmental perspectives.* New York: Guilford.

Spiegler, M. D., & Guevremont, D. C. (1993). *Contemporary behavior therapy.* Pacific Grove, CA: Brooks/Cole.

Stricker, G. (1977). Are science and practice commensurable? *American Psychologist, 52,* 442–448.

Stryker, S. (1980). *Symbolic interactionism.* Menlo Park, CA: Benjamin/Cummings.

Stuart, R. B. (1967). Behavioral control of overeating. *Behavior Research and Therapy, 5,* 356–365.

Stuart, R. B. (1969). Operant interpersonal treatment for marital discord. *Journal of Consulting and Clinical Psychology, 33,* 675–682.

Stuart, R. B. (1976). An operant interpersonal program for couples. In D. H. L. Olson (Ed.), *Treating relationships* (pp. 120–132). Lake Mills, IA: Graphic Co.

Stuart, R. B. (1980). *Helping couples change.* New York: Guilford.

Stuart, R. B. (in press). *Individual, couple, and family assessment forms.* New York: Guilford.

Stuart, R. B., & Jacobson, B. (1985). *Second marriage: Make it happy! Make it last!* New York: Norton.

Stuart, R. B., & Jacobson, B. (1987a). *Couple's Precounseling Inventory.* Champaign, IL: Research Press.

Stuart, R. B., & Jacobson, B. (1987b). *Weight, sex, and marriage: A delicate balance.* New York: Norton.

Tooby, J., & Cosmides, L. (1990). The past explains the present: Emotional adaptations and the structure of ancestral environment. *Ethology and Sociobiology, 11,* 375–424.

Vaihinger, H. (1924). *The philosophy of as if* (Translated by C. K. Ogden). New York: Scribners.

Wampold, B. E., Mondin, G. W., Moody, M., Stich, F., Benson, K., & Ahn, H. (1997). A meta-analysis of outcome studies comparing bona fide psychotherapies: Empirically 'All must have prizes'. *Psychological Bulletin, 122,* 203–215.

Watzlawick, P., Beavin, J. H., & Jackson, D. D. (1976). *Pragmatics of human communication: A study of interaction patterns, pathologies, and paradoxes.* New York: W. W. Norton.

Weiss, R. L. (1978). The conceptualization of marriage from a behavioral perspective. In T. J. Paolino & B. S. McCrady (Eds.), *Marriage and family therapy: Psychoanalytic, behavioral and systems theory perspectives* (pp. 165–249). New York: Brunner/Mazel.

Young-Eisendrath, P., & Hall, J. A. (1991). *Jung's self-psychology: A constructivist perspective.* New York: Guilford.

Zielinski, J. J. (1999). Discovering imago relationship therapy. *Psychotherapy, 36,* 91–101.

15 Narrative Family Therapy

JOHN D. WEST AND DONALD L. BUBENZER

Stephen Madigan

Considering the Narrative Perspective

The idea of life as a story has a long history manifested in many expressive venues. In his collection of short stories, *Winter Count*, Barry Lopez (1976) recalled that, among some tribes of Native Americans, the passage of time was recorded yearly by the noting of a single memorable event that was recorded as a picture on a buffalo robe or as a matter of spoken word, and each of these pictures or stories was called a "winter count." The sequence of such pictures or stories became a part of a larger story, each differing according to the point of reference of the record keepers. Thus, in any one tribe there might be several winter counts (narratives) in progress at any one time. Lopez drew attention to the time, action, and meaning dimensions of narratives.

At the close of his book, *Cities of the Plains* (1998), novelist Cormac McCarthy reveals a reflective dialogue about the constructed and constitutive nature of narrative between two characters:

> The narrator smiled wistfully, like a man remembering his childhood. These dreams reveal the world also, he said. We wake remembering the events of which they are composed while often the narrative is fugitive and difficult to recall. Yet it is the narrative that is the life of the dream while the events themselves are often interchangeable. The events of the waking world on the other hand are forced upon us and the narrative is the unguessed axis along which they must be strung. It falls to us to weigh and sort and order these events. It is we who assemble them into the story which is us (p. 283).

McCarthy introduced the idea that it is not the events of life that make the story. We can even change the events but still have the same story. It is the narrative (meaning making combined with the events) that makes the story. It is in the weighing and sorting that we construct, or author, the narrative and it is in having the opportunity to weigh and sort that the stories that constitute our lives can be re-authored. It is this re-authoring process that can offer hope. That is, the process of therapy assists families in re-authoring their stories in more useful ways. It does this by helping families to take steps toward different futures and by helping them discover meaningful and hopeful possibilities. As MaCarthy noted, through his character, it is the placement of events on an axis of meaning that constitutes the story that is us. Family therapy then helps people lay hold of sustaining narratives, an evolving set of actions and meanings that they find useful.

Finally, personal essayist and environmentalist William Kittredge (1999), in his book *Taking Care: Thoughts on Storytelling and Belief,* wrote to the issue of the evolving, alternative, or multistoried nature of our lives. Kittredge noted: "We all know a lot of stories and we're in trouble when we don't know which one is ours. Or when the one we inhabit doesn't work anymore, and we stick with it anyway." Kittredge also introduced the idea that stories exist outside of people, that they are cultural, a part of the cultural dialogue. We have cultural and community stories that "contain implicit instructions from a society to its members, telling them what is valuable and how to conduct themselves if they are to preserve the things they cherish" (p. 52). Further, Kittredge noted that both individuals and society may suffer from what is termed "narrative dysfunction." Such dysfunction comes from inhabiting stories with assumptions and plots that are no longer helpful. Finally, Kittredge wrote:

> Late in the night we listen to our own breathing in the dark, and rework our stories, and we do it again the next morning, and all day long, before the looking glass of ourselves, reinventing our purposes (p. 53).

Kittredge continued by developing further his thought on how stories function and the value of stories in our lives by noting:

> We figure and find stories, which can be thought of as maps or paradigms in which we see our purposes defined, then the world drifts and our maps don't work anymore, paradigms fail and we have to reinvent our understandings, and our reasons for continuing. Useful stories, I think, are radical in that they help us see freshly. That's what our stories are for, to help us see freshly. That's what stories are for, to help us see, and reinvent ourselves (p. 53).

Kittredge views our lives as ongoing projects; evolving stories that allow us to situate ourselves within a particular context.

In the development of their ideas on narrative therapy, Michael White and David Epston (1990) worked among many of the concepts, perspectives, and practices mentioned above. For example, their work has a literary perspective, that we are constituted by the stories of our lives. They also take the perspective that our stories are constructed in the discourses of society and that they have implicit and assumed dimensions. These stories have time dimensions, past, present, and future, and they have dimensions of both action and meaning. When we experience problems, our lived experience is in conflict with and invaded by problematic societal discourses. The hope of their work comes from the view that stories can be deconstructed and constructed, that we are multistoried and can pursue stories of possibility. Further, just as stories can be problem-saturated because of the particular discourses of our context, they can also have preferred outcomes as we situate our stories within communities of support.

We will spend the earlier part of the chapter discussing some of the theoretical underpinnings of narrative therapy and the latter part clarifying aspects of clinical practice, but first we will talk about some of the folks who have been most significant in the development of narrative therapy as both a perspective and a clinical practice: Michael White, David Epston, Stephen Madigan, Kenneth Gergen, Karl Tomm, Jeffrey Zimmerman and Victoria Dickerson, and Jill Freedman and Gene Combs.

Leading Figures

When one thinks of narrative therapy the names of Michael White and David Epston come immediately to mind. They are considered to be the codevelopers of the approach. Their pioneering work has grown to the point where the narrative approach has been described as now dominating the field of family therapy (Nichols & Schwartz, 2001). White serves as Codirector of the Dulwich Centre in Adelaide, South Australia and Epston as the Codirector of the Family Therapy Centre of Auckland, New Zealand. Their best-known book is *Narrative Means to Therapeutic Ends* (1990). The book explores both the theoretical underpinnings of the approach and describes and provides examples of the practices. Additional works (Epston, 1989; Epston & White, 1992; White, 1989a) further clarify both the theoretical perspectives and clinical practices of the approach. Both White and Epston are active travelers, presenting workshops throughout the world.

Basic to the approach are the ideas of life lived as multiple and alterable stories and that the realities that form the basis of our stories are formed in the perceptions of the social discourses of life. The problems of life can then be viewed as being housed in social discourse, external to the person experiencing the problem rather than internal to the person. It is this externalization of problems that Karl Tomm (Tomm, 1990b), considers to be the most important contribution of the narrative approach.

> In my opinion the single most important contribution domain that White has opened is that of "externalizing the problem." When the distinction of the problem can be clearly separated from the distinction of the person, it becomes possible to carefully examine the dynamics and directions of the interaction between persons and problems. One can then address a crucial question: Is the problem gaining more influence over the person or is the person gaining more influence over the problem? (pp. vii–viii).

As the reader continues in the chapter, more will be said regarding the theoretical and applied contributions of Michael White and David Epston to narrative therapy.

Stephen Madigan is among the most influential of North American narrativists and he is in private practice in Toronto, Canada. Much of his work (Madigan 1996, 1997) is focused on clarifying concepts and practices associated with community discourse and with the performance of knowledges that resist and transform discourses associated with the marginalization and oppression of human beings. He has been active in organizing communities of supportive subcultures battling similar problems. These groups provide support for members and also provide places for the exchange of ideas on how members have escaped from the problems of their lives. They also serve as communities of education and advocacy to challenge dominant societal assumptions.

Although most writers from the narrative perspective (Madigan, 1996; White & Epston, 1990) write of the constitutive quality of narrative, they also acknowledge that this constitutive power is lodged in the discourses of society. That is, knowledge and the accompanying power arise from socially developed constructs and performance of knowledge. A leading figure in the clarification and development of the social constructionist movement is Kenneth J. Gergen, Mustin Professor of Psychology at Swarthmore College in Pennsylvania. Of particular interest for narrative therapists are Gergen's views on the social construction of knowledges and the subjugating influences of these knowledges. His views offer special possibilities for the re-storying of lives, and the use of multiple stories that are available to individuals and families. His thought is most accessible in his recent work, *An Invitation to Social Construction* (1999), and through his widely read *The Saturated Self* (1991). An engaging interview with

Gergen can be found in Bubenzer and West's "Kenneth J. Gergen: Social Construction, Families, and Therapy" (1993).

One might imagine that all who write about family therapy entered the craft of writing to be student–practitioners. It is through their writing that they puzzle over the questions of their practice. Among those who write about family therapy, one of the star pupils is Karl Tomm. He is Director of the Family Therapy Program in the Department of Psychiatry at the University of Calgary, Calgary, Alberta, and he is a pilgrim in the learning process, visiting the shrines of learning and coming away with new ideas that improve the practice of therapy. For example, it was after spending time exploring the ideas on paradox of Selvini Palazolli, Boscolo, Cecchin, and Prata (1978) that he was able to offer the field his own ideas on asking reflexive questions (Tomm, 1987). After becoming familiar with Michael White's approach to externalizing problems, as well as developing an appreciation of social interaction as the source of meaning making (Maturana & Varela, 1987), Tomm developed his ideas and practices related to internalized other interviewing. In an interview (Bubenzer, West, Cryder, & Lucey, 1997), Tomm noted, "I began thinking of our minds as being made up of a community of the significant others we've related to, or that we've even heard about or read about, that have become a part of us. I began thinking of the relationships among these internalized others" (p. 92). As the narratives of the internalized others are brought forth a process of reconstructing their influences is begun.

Tomm, like White and Epston, has been deeply impacted by the social discourses that enroll sexism, classism, heterosexism, racism, and so forth in their service. He thinks that involvement in social justice issues is a way of addressing the subjugating aspects of these discourses, and wrote, "I feel compelled ethically to do something about altering our cultural drift as well as doing therapy" (1998, p. 181). Thus, it is as a reflective student of the history of therapy and of the theoretical and applied perspectives of others that Karl Tomm has been able to formulate his own writing and practice and offer his insights to us.

Two teams of writers, Jill Freedman and Gene Combs and Jeffrey Zimmerman and Victoria Dickerson, have made major contributions to the application of the narrative perspective in therapy. Freedman and Combs, Directors of the Evanston Family Therapy Center in Evanston, Illinois, in their primary work entitled *Narrative Therapy: The Social Construction of Preferred Realities* (1996), are well grounded in White's idea that narrative therapy is a perspective for viewing and practicing living; that is, the narrative approach becomes a way of living. Although they are immersed in therapeutic practice, their own lives as well as their work with colleagues and with the folks who come to consult with them are steeped in the practices of collaboration, multiple voices, intentionality, sensitivity to oppression, and preferred outcomes. They are cautious that their ideas on practice are not seen as disembodied techniques but as ways of working consistent with the narrative and social constructionist perspective.

Zimmerman and Dickerson, Codirectors of the Bay Area Family Therapy Training Associates in Cupertino, California, take a serious and playful approach to the discussion of narrative therapy in their book, *If Problems Talked: Narrative Therapy in Action* (1996). Through a dialogic presentation the reader is drawn into ideas of discourse and social construction. They illustrate clearly that problems have a life of their own with many and a varied set of invasive practices. Zimmerman and Dickerson's special strength lies in being able to raise and unmask the assumptions, training, and expectations that are a part of the cultural discourse in which clients swim. Yet, they keep a focus on clients and their experiences, rather than sacrificing them to cultural battles.

Theoretical Concepts

In the development of the narrative perspective, White and Epston (1990) were influenced by a number of ideas that brought greater intelligibility to their work. Gregory Bateson, Jerome Bruner, and Michel Foucault are among those noted as being especially influential (Epston & White, 1992; White 1989b; White & Epston, 1990). The work of the three authors helped them to clarify their therapeutic perspective. The word *perspective* is used to refer to narrative theory because it represents both a way of viewing and of giving meaning to life and a way of living (Bubenzer, West, & Boughner, 1994). The narrative perspective offers not only a view of where problems are located and approaches for assisting people to find more meaningful stories, but also invites the therapist to address problematic societal discourses. Of the three influential authors mentioned, Bateson (1972, 1979) provided ideas relative to the interpretive method, Bruner (1986) provided a voice to the temporal as well as meaning and action components of narrative, while Foucault (1979, 1980) influenced White's thought on power and knowledge and the externalization of problems.

White (White & Epston, 1990) credits Bateson (1972) for introducing him to the "interpretive method." This perspective acknowledges that we cannot know reality directly. Rather, our knowing requires an act of interpretation. Our knowledge of the world is present in the form of mental maps through which we filter the events of life. The interpretation of events over time provides us the stories that constitute our lives. Topistics sociologist E. V. Walter (1988) described a view of this process:

> Here I want to introduce the doctrine of selective support. We build a structure of consciousness by supporting the features of experience that we acknowledge. We make the obvious world by building it, and in constructing the world, we build ourselves, including our structure of consciousness. We build to support certain features of experience and to suppress others, and these decisions to acknowledge or deny them give form to the dominant structure of consciousness. The way in which people habitually and consciously combine or orchestrate three worlds of the mind—the domains of common sense, the intellect, and the imagination—gives form to their structure of consciousness (pp. 13–14).

Walter is using the word *consciousness* in a manner similar to that of Bruner (1986) and in a way that White sometimes refers to as the "structure of meaning." We support and structure various aspects of the context in which we live in a way that creates a story that is constitutive of us. Such a view allows for endless possibilities for interpreting life's events and, thus, we have the potential for holding more than one narrative or story as operational in our life at any time and for the changes in our narratives over time. That is, different maps or representations of the external reality are related to different meanings and actions.

This view becomes apparent when we enter into conversation with other readers of a novel. In that discussion, although we read the same words, we have different interpretations both of what happened and of the significance of what happened. The indeterminateness of the text (Bruner, 1986) allows for many stories or narratives to emerge. We each have our own map or story that, in dialogue with the author's story, creates a new story. Further, our discussion with our coreaders creates additional stories. Their view of the story and our view of the story come together to create new stories. Thus, it is through our social discourse that we coconstruct new interpretations (stories) that become constitutive of our lives. These stories are continually "in process" and have no final destination.

White's ideas of narrative were highly interactive with those of Jerome Bruner. Bruner (1986) had indicated that the narrative mode of thought lends itself to a connection of life events across time. This organization of experience and memories allows people to develop coherent accounts, stories, of themselves in the world around them. In particular, White had an appreciation for the possibilities inherent in a narrativistic versus scientific approach. The storied approach situates the person in time and does not make an effort at generalization. The storied approach also lends itself to multiple ideas and the generation of possibilities. The story's "soft data" encourages other ways of looking for new meanings and even new events that may lead to a change in the story. The storied approach allows "the parties to enter into a search for new meanings, new possibilities, which call into question the problem saturated description or dominant story" (White & Epston, 1990, p. 127).

White used Bruner's ideas about the time, action, and consciousness components of narrative as the scaffolding on which to build his views of the process of narrative construction. Bruner provided tools for thinking about life as a story and noted that life unfolds on the dual axes or landscapes of action and consciousness. The action axis, according to Freedman and Combs (1996), relates to what happened, who was involved, where the event took place, when it occurred, and how it happened. Plotting of a sequence of events in time acknowledges the temporal and fluid aspects of a story. But the events themselves have no meaning until they are imbued with motivations, beliefs, values, commitments, and so forth. It is the combining of action with meaning that creates the story.

Thus, a framework for the narrativist perspective was prepared from Bateson's (1972, 1979) ideas about the interpretive method and from Bruner's thoughts (1986) about the indeterminateness of stories and the temporal, action, and meaning components of stories. It was from the work of Michel Foucault (1965, 1979, 1980) that White gained clarity for his ideas about the nature of human problems.

Foucault was a French historian–philosopher of the twentieth century. His training in history led him to have the tools and interest to trace systems of thought over time. In doing so, he was able to provide an ontology of the present. For Foucault, reality and truth were expressions of the discourses of the time in which they occurred. *Discourse* refers to the way our language, both verbal and nonverbal, creates our world (Gergen, 1999). Gergen (1994) has also written, "to appraise existing forms of discourse is to evaluate patterns of cultural life" (p. 53). Foucault used the word *episteme* to describe the particular structure of thought that epitomizes the thinking in a particular moment in history. An episteme is inclusive of the underlying assumptions and thought processes, the frame of reference or "mindset" that limits the cultural thinking of an age. In much of his writing, Foucault (1965, 1973, 1979) traced particular epistemes or "mindsets" and the impact of those assumptions and practices over time. Thus, reality swims in the discourses particular to a context. Reality changes as discourses change and lies within the power of a particular discourse to prevail at a particular time. Such a dominant view is deemed to be knowledge. Foucault collated the terms *knowledge/power* because of the close connection between the two.

Foucault can be thought of as an archeologist in that his interest was in unearthing the assumptions and prejudgments (prejudices) behind what was considered to be knowledge in a particular period. By engaging in the archeology of knowledge, he saw that, just as knowledge shifted, there was a related shift in power, in how life was to be lived. Foucault traced changing discourses, *knowledge/power* bases over long periods of time. Yet, we can see his ideas of the connection between discourse and *knowledge/power* in our own lifetime. Many of us have been a part of and encouraged an evolving discourse in which homosexuality was seen first as a crime, then as an illness, and now is viewed by many as an "alternative" lifestyle. When the discourse involved seeing homosexual behavior as a crime, the response was punishment, and, when it was seen as an illness, the response was treatment. Now, when homosexuality is viewed by many as an alternative lifestyle, the response is neighborliness. We understand that there are significant vestiges of the two former discourses concerning homosexuality and that these vestiges have significant negative outcomes, but there is a changing discourse and that discourse has an impact and an outcome preferred by many.

White (White & Epston, 1990) drew on Foucault's (1979) discussion of Jeremy Bentham's architectural work related to the Panoptican to illustrate how our constructed ideas become considered to be truth. The truths we construct become considered as "normal" wherein these norms are the focus around which our lives are built. These norms provide the socially prescribed specifications for living.

Bentham's Panoptican was a circular structure with an open courtyard in the center, often used as a prison. The circular structure was divided into cells that were open to the courtyard but did not allow for communication between cells. In effect, the structure made the prisoners objects of study and control by the persons in the middle. Those in the middle, through their "gaze," could observe all that went on and, by keeping records over time, could develop norms for behavior. One of the authors had an experience with such a situation while visiting a monastery in about 1960. The structure was a multistoried Panoptican with a window in the cell of each door; the monks were to be in their cell by eight each evening. A monk was on duty in the middle of the structure to respond if there was a need. On our tour, the host monk, the sentry, explained who were the "abnormal" monks, that is, who left their lights on later than others, who arose earlier, and who was up and about during the night. Through this night-long vigil, his gaze and record keeping had created a story of normal and abnormal behavior. This "normalizing gaze" could easily become the discourse within the institution that both unintentionally and intentionally became a mechanism of control.

The normalizing gaze is a mechanism of control common to those of us who engage in therapy. Many of us were coopted into the view without much awareness. The normalizing gaze is practiced each time we use measures of central tendency. For example, *abnormal* is often defined as being those scores that fall more than two standard deviations from a mean score on any phenomenon that we assume we are measuring. Often, such a score triggers a "here is a problem" response. Efforts are then extended to edge the person to a normal view, even though our gaze, the measurement tools themselves, will always create the abnormal. Therefore, because the dominant discourse is contained within the conversation induced by the gaze, what is thought to be abnormal may be justifiably described as being created rather than found.

White (White & Epston, 1990) used the normalizing gaze concept and Foucault's idea that knowledge/power is contained in the dominant discourses of society to formulate the view that the problems people experience are external to them and their relationships. The problems themselves are located in the discourses in which the people experiencing them often unknowingly swim. For example, there is a conversation present in Western culture that thin is beautiful and being beautiful is critical to being of worth. Such a view is projected in most popular media. The normalizing gaze of much of our culture says, "Thin is beautiful, of worth, healthy, popular and even pleasing to the higher authorities." Therefore, anyone who is not thin stands outside of the normative discourse. For many people, particularly young women, the normative discourse of thinness invades their lives. The problematic external discourse about thinness cozies up to them and invites them, even tyrannizes them, into the pursuit of weight loss. We label these women as *bulimic* or *anorexic* and treat them as though they are the problem. White then took these perspectives of problems as existing in the dominant discourses of society and in the local cultures and incorporated them with his ideas on narrative. They provided him with a view for externalizing problems in ways that allowed his clients to develop narratives with preferred outcomes.

Research Perspectives

Those who take the narrative perspective recognize both conceptual and methodological issues when conducting and using research. From a conceptual perspective, they recognize that research is pursued within a particular, often unrecognized, or at least unacknowledged, narrative.

Often these narratives support what narrativist thinkers might view as dominant stories. For example, recently (July 7, 2000) there was an article by Jean Patteson in the Charleston, South Carolina, *Post and Courier* concerning a "backlash" by the clothing industry against the idea of "white-collar" workers dressing in business casual clothing on Fridays. The article reported that business suit sales had dropped by 31.2 percent between 1996 and 2000 and sport-coat sales were down by 25 percent during the same period. The clothing industry was concerned that Casual Fridays had permeated the whole week. The industry was funding a study they believed would show a relationship between casual dress habits and low productivity in the workplace. One spokesperson was quoted as saying, "There's evidence to suggest that casual dress can lead to casual attitude—to an increase in absenteeism, flirtation and a lack of office decorum."

Nowhere did the article state that the clothing industry is most interested in maintaining a narrative of profit margins and market share and, therefore, was going to pursue research questions the answers to which it hoped would cast doubt on the narrative of more casual dress in the workplace. They certainly were not going to ask questions about the possible benefits of casual dress, either from a social perspective or the financial perspective of the public. Assumptions about the meaning and value of certain kinds of productivity were not to be raised. Stories of economic gain and productivity, the dominant mythology, are often simply pursued.

Research conducted in the "therapeutic" professions can also be conducted in the pursuit of a specific narrative, or, at least, conducted in the service of a narrative with little thought given to the value of the narrative. For example, there has been considerable research conducted in the service of refining assessment instruments so that they may assist in making "accurate" mental health diagnoses. Such research is almost always conducted with the assumption that mental illness exists as a reality outside our description of it and that labeling it is somehow beneficial. At least some social constructionists and narrativists would question research practices with unexamined assumptions that result in labels that they think serve dominant mental health and societal practices. Psychiatrist Karl Tomm (1990a, 1998) has questioned whether such labeling practices as are promoted by the *Diagnostic and Statistical Manual of*

Mental Disorders (4th edition; DSM-IV) of the American Psychiatric Association are pathologizing. Thus, the narratives behind our research merit careful consideration.

Not only do the narratives of the content of our research studies merit our attention, so do the stories behind our methods. Much research is conducted using measurement and knowledge practices that employ measures of central tendency. Such research may promote generalization and marginalization. Such practices, although reflective of the dominant discourse in social science research, are not generally expressive of the values inherent in the narrative perspective. Narrativist research would value difference, thick description, metaphor, individual perception, and the voice of the participant over the voice of the expert researcher. Qualitative approaches tend to honor the assumptions of the narrative perspective, yet qualitative research does not seem to garner the headlines. It is doubtful that research conducted from a narrative perspective will ever address cure rates, or address the number or types of narratives present in a large population. Such "scientific" study is simply not what narrative is about. However, research/scholarship conducted from a narrative perspective and using qualitative tools will produce readers who say, "That sounds like me," "I've had a similar experience," or "That is different than anything I have been involved with, but it surely is interesting."

Research methods appropriate to narrative therapy are those that are capable of capturing a world of diversity and change. Kenneth Gergen (1999) indicated that what we need are research projects and methods that offer us a "sensitive and continuous social analysis" (p. 195), rather than extended data gathering methods that provide research "findings" that are continually outdated. Further Gergen stated:

> Required are the kinds of analysis that enable us to understand what is taking place from multiple standpoints, that will help us engage in dialogue with others from varied walks of life, and that will sensitize us to a range of possible futures. Most important social analysis should help us generate vocabularies of understanding that can help us create our future together. For the constructionist, the point of social analysis is not then to "get it right" about what is happening to us. Rather such analysis should enable us to reflect and create (p. 195).

Such a view of analysis is consistent with the narrative perspective. Narrativists are interested in looking at life from a variety of standpoints (narratives) in order to bring forth possibilities. The reflective exploration of possibilities is at the heart of the approach.

The thrust of the research endeavor for those involved with the narrative perspective is not focused on prediction or on tracing the etiology of problems, but rather on the stimulation of the subjective possibilities that people hold in their lives. From this perspective, research questions pursue hope, solutions, and preferred narratives. Questions of this nature might explore those practices within communities of concern that members find to be useful, or homework practices of parents that children find to be helpful, or views held by couples that are particularly satisfying. The goal would not be to find the best practices, because such a perspective leads to marginalization of alternative preferred practices; rather, the goal would be to lift up local knowledges that offer possibilities to some people both individually and as varied and diverse communities.

Considering the Clinical Perspective

Views of Human Functioning and Mental Illness

As has been suggested, the theory of narrative therapy views human behavior in terms of the narratives or stories with which human beings are involved, and the narratives or stories about oneself and relationships are a product of our interactions with others (Berger & Luckmann, 1966; Gergen, 1999). They are thought to help organize lives around specific meanings; that is, the story that is lived determines the meaning given to an experience (White & Epston, 1990). For example, a teenage daughter may have a story about herself as an Independent Young Woman, while a mother or father may have a story about being a Concerned Parent, and the teenager and her parent may have a story about their relationship that is described as one of Continual Conflict.

As noted earlier, Bruner (1986) mentioned that the dominant story that one lives is seen through a landscape of consciousness and action. Speaking of the landscape of action, Freedman and Combs (1996) noted, "This is similar to the 'who, what, when, where, and how' of journalism. In the landscape of action, we plot sequences of events through time" (p. 97). With regard to the landscape of consciousness, they mentioned that they are referring "to that imaginary territory where people plot the meanings, desires, intentions, beliefs, commitments, motivations, values, and the like that relate to their experience" (p. 98). For example, a couple may have developed a story about their relationship that signals how He's Always Right, so the actions taken by the couple may come from his dreams, values, and commitments.

It has been noted that some aspects of our lived experiences fall outside of a dominant story and so are eliminated from awareness; that is, they are events that do not fit within the evolving story of who we are. Thus, over time much of what one experiences falls outside of the dominant story and is not expressed; Consequently, the life that one lives has the potential to actually become multi-storied. White and Epston (1990) mentioned that, "Those aspects of lived experience that fall outside of the dominant story provide a rich and fertile source for the generation, or re-generation, of alternative stories" (p. 15). While a teenager and parent may entitle the story of their relationship as Continual Conflict, there are certainly times in their history when the conflict was less intense or hardly present. It is these experiences that fall outside of the dominant narrative that suggest the opportunity for an alternative story.

The dominant story is never complete and so it is continually evolving. As White (1993) noted, these stories help shape our lives, but they cannot, of course, handle all of the contingencies that come up in life; these stories or narratives contain "gaps and inconsistencies" and "run up against contradictions," and it is the resolution of these gaps and inconsistencies that requires people to consider additional meanings for their experiences and for their narratives and stories about themselves and their relationships (p. 38). So, when the couple who was living the story about how He's Always Right bumps up against a situation(s) in which he hasn't been "exposed to the correct answer or ultimate solution," and his partner may actually have the more helpful perspective, they are then faced with a gap or inconsistency in their narrative. This gap or inconsistency in the story may be handled by relegating the incident to a level of unimportance or the couple may take the opportunity to develop a new meaning and story for their relationship.

During an interview with Ken Stewart (1995), White noted that our large investment in the development of conversations about psychopathology has contributed to ways of interacting with people and these conversations about psychopathology tend to highlight a subject/object dualism; that is, mental health professionals have become able to "construct people as the objects of psychiatric knowledge" (p. 113). The metaphors used by mental health professionals have made possible the use of " 'expert' interpretation" of the experiences of peoples' lives (p. 114). Rather than thinking in terms of psychopathology and diagnosis, however, narrative therapy would prefer to view individuals and families as coming to therapy with stories about themselves and their relationships that are not seen as helpful and possibly not encapsulating of an individual's or family's lived experiences (White & Epston, 1990).

Chang and Phillips (1993) also suggested that Michael White, in his work with narrative therapy, has not focused on the causal explanations of problems. Rather, they proposed White to be suggesting that a problem develops when some difficulty in life becomes amplified and the original conditions associated with the problem are lost; with time, the problem then becomes more chronic in character. White and Epston (1990) have added that, "neither the person nor the relationship between persons is the problem. Rather, the problem becomes the problem, and then the person's relationship with the problem becomes the problem" (p. 40). For example, how often has it occurred that family members complain of an unending dispute even after the original context of the conflict has dissolved? Yet, the conflictual pattern has taken on a life of its own. Now, for these family members, the question becomes, "What can we do to stop this conflictual pattern from spoiling our relationship?"

Chang and Phillips (1993) proposed that, rather than searching for causal explanations of a problem, in White's work with narrative therapy the focus falls on that which "restrains people from taking alternative courses of action" (p. 102) and clients are considered to be "immersed in dominant 'problem-saturated' narratives" (p. 103). Freedman and Combs (1996) mentioned that, in

Michel Foucault's work, language is viewed as a vehicle of power, and they indicated how "the discourses of a society determine what knowledge is held to be true, right, or proper in that society, so those who control the discourse control knowledge" (p. 38). As a result, it is suggested that problem-saturated narratives often reflect discourses in society and those problem-saturated narratives can become subjugating of clients as they limit the clients' ability to appreciate aspects of their experience that fall outside the dominant story. An illustration of this point might be found in the relationship between a young person and her or his parents. For example, it may be that the parents and the teenager can both report some positive changes in their relationship, yet the parents may be hesitant to accept that the changes are "real" because "everyone knows that adolescence is a period captured by arguments."

How Change Occurs

From the above commentary, change in narrative therapy would seem to occur through an ongoing process of deconstructing problem-saturated narratives and the re-authoring of narratives that support preferred outcomes for clients. White (Bubenzer, West, & Boughner, 1994) noted that the process of change does not occur in a linear fashion in which the therapist and family move from deconstruction to re-authoring but, instead, they will find themselves moving back and forth between the deconstruction and the re-authoring of narratives.

Deconstruction.   Much of Michael White's work is premised on a constitutionalist perspective from which he noted "that persons' lives are shaped by the meaning that they ascribe to their experience, by their situation in social structures, and by the language practices and cultural practices of self and of relationship that these lives are recruited into" (White, 1993, p. 35). It has already been mentioned that these meanings are part of a story or narrative that is held about one's life and that it is the problem-saturated narratives that result in less than preferred outcomes for individuals and families. So, families in therapy may present with two or more members and offer a description of their relationship that is idiosyncratic, depending on who they are as members of the family (e.g., members of a parent–child relationship, a sibling relationship, or a grandparent–grandchild relationship). For illustrative purposes, one might be able to imagine familial relationships as being oppressed by problem-laden stories of Ongoing Conflict, Not Being Appreciated, or A Continual Lack Of Trust.

The deconstruction of these problem-saturated narratives is a way of questioning the worthiness of their character and White (1993) has commented that,

> deconstruction has to do with procedures that subvert taken-for-granted realities and practices: the so-called 'truths' that are split off from the conditions and the context of their production; those disembodied ways of speaking that hide their biases and prejudices; and those familiar practices of self and of relationship that are subjugating of persons' lives (p. 34).

The questioning of taken-for-granted realities may be facilitated by the therapist as she or he helps family members wonder how they have been recruited into a problem. White (1993) noted that therapists can help clients explore how they were recruited into various practices and attitudes according to gender, cultural, and familial contexts, e.g., "How were you first introduced to this way of responding?" "What thoughts have you used to sustain these ways of responding?" and "How have other people encouraged you to adopt these thoughts and live these patterns?"

In therapy the deconstruction of problem-saturated truths or stories includes objectification of problems for which a person is seeking therapy (White, 1993): "This objectification engages persons in externalizing conversations in relation to that which they find problematic, rather than internalizing conversations" (p. 39). It is these *externalizing conversations* that encourage "persons to provide an account of the effects of the problem on their lives. This can include its effects on their emotional states, familial and peer relationships, social and work spheres, etc." (p. 39). Examples include, "How has this problem made you feel about yourself as a parent?" "How has this problem with your parents influenced your life at school?" and "When would this problem say that you're most vulnerable to its influence and its ability to create bad feelings in your relationship?" Externalizing of the problem may help the clients become more familiar with the problem and the increased familiarity can lend itself to an understanding of the problem-saturated story, to the point where the family may be able to name the story or narrative. For example, the therapist may say to the family, "It sounds as though there's a story here about how you relate to each other. What would you call this story?" The naming of this family-related problem-saturated story, and the subsequent placing of it outside the familial relationships, may facilitate some distance from the problem and further facilitate the deconstruction process. One might ask, "What has this story—Lack of Respect in Our Family—required of you as a young adult?" "Has this story ever encouraged you to do things that you've later regretted?" "How has this story made you feel about yourselves?" and "What would this story require of you if it were to take further hold of your relationship?"

As people become involved with externalizing conversations, they "experience a separation from, and an alienation in relation to, these stories. In the space established by this separation, persons are free to explore alternative and preferred knowledges of who they might be" (White, 1993, p. 39). As individuals explore alternative knowledges about their family, they begin the process of re-authoring a story about preferred family relationships.

Re-authoring.   White (1993) suggested re-authoring to be a process of developing and/or retrieving alternative knowledge of the client and the client's relationships and noted, "As persons separate from the dominant or 'totalizing' stories that are constitutive of their lives, it becomes more possible for them to orient themselves to aspects of their experience that contradict these knowledges. Such contradictions are ever present" (pp. 39–40). He went on to mention that, "Previously, following Goffman, I have referred to these contradictions as 'unique outcomes' (White, 1993; White & Epston, 1990), and it is these that provide a gateway to . . . the alternative territories of a person's life" (p. 40). The *unique outcomes* reflect the landscape of action. For example, a therapist might ask, "When was a time that you made an effort to not let this story—Lack of Respect in Our Family—surface and create problems for you?" "Who else might have seen you making an effort to prevent this story from dominating your relationship and what might they have seen you doing?" and "What could you do to help prevent this story from surfacing and creating problems for you?" After identifying an event that could be considered to be a unique outcome, White (1993) noted that it is important for the client(s) to evaluate the event as to whether it is worthy of being considered a unique outcome, e.g., "Was this event preferable to times when the old story seemed to dominate your relationship?" If the event is judged to be preferable, then the client(s) can be encouraged to discuss what accounted for the unique outcome.

When events are thought to qualify as unique outcomes, "the therapist can facilitate the generation of and/or resurrection of alternative stories by orienting him/herself to these unique outcomes as one might orient oneself to a mystery" (White, 1993, p. 40). White (1993) suggested that only the client or family members can unpack the mystery and that this accounting occurs as they respond to the therapist's desire to know more about the unique outcomes. The therapist's curiosity can be framed within a series of *unique account* questions that explore the landscape of action and what it was that has accounted for the unique outcome (White, 1989). For example, a family member might be asked, "What do you think helped to prepare you for taking that initiative?" "What did you find yourself doing differently in each of these situations?" and "What was common to your response on those two occasions?" After exploring what family members see as accounting for the uncommon or unique experiences, the therapist and the family may hear and identify a theme that is somewhat different from the problem-saturated story. To help the family identify the theme the therapist might say, "Well, it sounds like there is more than one story about your family. What would you like to call or name this alternative story?" At times the therapist might mention what she or he hears as an alternative story and then inquire whether this description resonates with the family members, e.g., "From what you've said, I'm hearing an alternative story in your relationship; that is, one that talks to your investment in Listening with Interest. Does this story title have meaning for you or would you refer to it differently?" Identifying the alternative story by naming it helps affirm the idea that life is multistoried and that stories exist with preferred outcomes. White (1993) has referred to the alternative story as a "counterplot" and has enumerated the important aspects of a counterplot:

a. contributes very significantly to persons' sense of their life going forward in preferred ways;
b. makes possible the attribution of meaning to events or experiences that would otherwise be neglected or considered to be of little significance;

   c. facilitates the session-by-session sorting and linking of the events that have taken place between sessions; and

   d. provides for persons a sense of knowing what might be the next step in their preferred direction in life (p. 43).

This alternative story can be enriched by the therapist asking questions about the story's landscape of consciousness. White (1989) has referred to these as *unique redescription* questions and noted that, "Unique redescription questions invite family members to ascribe significance to the unique outcome and unique accounts through redescription of themselves, others, and their relationships" (p. 43). He also noted (1993) that landscape of consciousness questions might focus on issues like the client's beliefs, values, desires, and commitments, and the therapist may ask the client to wonder about an alternative story, e.g., "What does this new story—Being Proud of Our Family—have to say to you about how you might view yourselves?" "What does it suggest about commitment?" and "What would this story indicate might be valued in life?"

Likewise, the alternative story might be further developed as the therapist talks with the family members about what might be a next step in becoming more familiar with an alternative story. White (1989) noted that these conversations might be facilitated with the use of *unique possibility* questions. Such questions focus on the client's landscape of action as it is envisioned in the future, e.g., "What would this story—Being Proud of Our Family—suggest as a next step?" "If you were going to relive this last week what might this alternative story suggest could occur?" "If the old story—Lack of Respect in Our Family—started to make itself known again over the weekend, what would this alternative suggest might be done?"

White and Epston and others (Freedman & Combs, 1996; Morgan, 2000; White & Epston, 1990) have also discussed the use of *therapeutic letters* in order to help clients become curious about their alternative story and to possibly enrich their alternative story. Such letters introduce a discourse of support for desired outcomes by opening a possibility for a discussion of both action and meaning dimensions related to the alternative story, for example:

Dear Tom and John,

As I've mentioned to you, I often find myself thinking about the families I've seen after one of our appointments and so it was with our last session. That is, I found myself wondering about some of the things we discussed. At our last meeting you talked about a new story for your relationship—Being Proud of Our Family—and how this story was in contrast to a more dominant and problem laden story. You said this new story would be preferred in that it would suggest a number of ways that you might be more respectful of each other during the week. As a result, I've found myself wondering how you might become more familiar with this story in the days that lie ahead. I was wondering about what each of you would describe as an opportunity for living this new story. What would this story suggest as a way to interact with each other during the week?

Also, what might this new story say about who you are as a father and son; that is, what might it say to you about what you value in your relationship? I'll be interested in discussing these questions with you at our next meeting.

Because these letters are received by the clients at a time when they are outside of a therapy session, we hope that they provide space for the clients to reflect on their relationships. Morgan (2000) noted that people have told her that receiving a letter can be helpful: "They have found the written word . . . reminds them of the conversation shared. Letters that summarize a conversation and contain some further questions also assist people to stay connected to the emerging alternative story that is co-authored in narrative meetings" (p. 104). She went on to say that, as people continue to live the preferred story, they are more likely to gain some freedom from the presenting problem.

Madigan and Epston (1995) talked of how *communities of concern* can be used to distribute the knowledge of clients to each other and how these communities can also use their voices to oppose cultural practices that are supportive of problem-saturated stories. Madigan (Madigan & Epston, 1995) noted that David Epston had "collected his client wisdom in what he called an archive . . . an assort-ment of audiotapes, letter writings, and artwork that represented a rich supply of solutions to an assortment of long-standing problems such as temper taming, night fears, school refusing, asthma, and, of course, anorexia and bulimia" (p. 261). Madigan noted that Epston referred to "clients' knowledge as expert knowledge" (p. 261) and that he pulled together a group of clients that were referred to as a league for "the purpose of consultation, information, and mutual support" (p. 261). Madigan and Epston described these communities of concern as working from the assumption that the problem is the problem. For example, they may form an antianorexia/antibulimia league or antidepression and antianxiety leagues to honor the experiences of clients and to circulate client knowledge on how to defeat problems. They noted that letter-writing campaigns may be another way to develop a community of concern, that letters from friends and family members may re-count memories when the client was not as overwhelmed by the problem. Madigan (Carlson & Kjos, 1999) seemed to be suggesting this when he asked a young man if he could write a letter to his principal indicating Madigan's support for the young man's "good boy" reputation. Madigan (Carlson & Kjos, 1999) also pointed out that problems clients experience may isolate them from other individ-uals and that the communities of concern are attempting to move clients back into groups where concern and caring are demonstrated and where clients might have an opportunity to rewrite their stories.

Even before the appearance of comments made by Madigan and Epston (1995), White and Epston (1990) noted that, "The scope of these alternative sto-ries can be further extended through the introduction of questions that invite persons to identify and recruit an audience to the performance of new meanings in their life" (p. 41). Freedman and Combs (1996) talked of recruiting an audi-ence and developing a team, from either the people the family knows or people the family has not met or may never meet, to help enrich an alternative story. In establishing a team they mentioned asking questions like,

That makes me wonder if messages and comments from others would feed the taking-your-life-back lifestyle. Who would be on the team that supports the taking-your-life-back lifestyle? They could be from your present, your past . . . or someone who doesn't personally know you but would support what you're beginning to accomplish here (p. 247).

The therapist could continue to wonder about who else might be on the team until perhaps three to a dozen members have been identified. With team members who know the family a therapist could ask, "What might they [the team] have seen you doing that's supportive of this new story?" "What might they suggest that you consider doing in order to become more familiar with this new story?" and "What might they indicate that this new story says about what you value as a family?" As an alternative to structuring communities of concern from people the family has known, communities can be made up from individuals the family may never meet. For team members that clients have not known the therapist might ask, "What would 'Tiger' suggest as a next step if you were to more fully join with this new story?" "What would Harriet Tubman indicate that the new story—Being Proud of Our Family—says about your commitments?" or "If the old story starts to create a problem in your relationship, what would Harry Potter suggest as a way to get back in touch with the new story?" Of course, in developing an audience or team to support a new story, the therapist wants to have the clients identify individuals who they believe will be supportive of enriching a new and preferred story.

Range of Application

It has been noted that, "The realities that each of us take for granted are the realities that our societies have surrounded us with since birth" (Freedman & Combs, 1996, p. 16). Narrative therapy values the local culture of the family, and Freedman and Combs went on to observe that, "In any culture, certain narratives will come to be dominant over other narratives. These dominant narratives will specify the preferred and customary ways of believing and behaving within the particular culture" (p. 32). In turn, these dominant cultures may support beliefs that attempt to capture the totality of individuals and families according to some predefined system of classification, by the privileging of certain voices over others in society, and by controlling behavior with a normalizing gaze.

Freedman and Combs (1996) noted that human beings construct personal narratives that are in relation to cultural narratives: "We want to develop an understanding of the influence on particular people of the dominant stories of their culture while cherishing the knowledge that each person's stories are different from anyone else's" (p. 33):

> We believe it is our responsibility as therapists to cultivate a growing awareness of the dominant (and potentially dominating) stories in our society and to develop ways of collaboratively examining the effects of these stories when we sense them at work in the lives and relationships of the people who consult us (p. 58).

For example, stories that only value ideas of a particular gender or socioeconomic group or cultural group may be presented and described by clients as contributing to less than a preferred ending. Similarly, as Madigan (Carlson & Kjos, 1999) suggested, narrative therapy would not restrict itself to working with certain families or people but would, rather, shift its attention to the meaning of language that has become associated with the lives of the family members. The therapist would also ask whether or not these meanings or narratives are contributing to preferred outcomes for family members (Hoyt & Combs, 1996; Wood, 1995). As a result, narrative therapy has a definite sense of responsibility for helping families to identify stories from various perspectives (e.g., stories associated with gender perspectives, cultural groups, various healthcare professions, or, perhaps, particular religious affiliations). This sense of responsibility also encourages the therapist and family to question whether the stories are limiting of potential or helpful in constructing opportunities.

White, in an interview with Lesley Allen (1995), spoke of the phenomenon whereby an individual's ways of talking about him- or herself and family (i.e., the stories they hold) become the totality of who they are, and noted that these "ways of thinking and speaking about oneself and others, and the practices of relating to oneself and others—those that are associated with internalized discourses—are all very much about the objectification or the 'thingification' of persons" (p. 43). These ways of thinking and talking can remove the context and can support the marginalization of people that occurs through the assignment of an identity. Here, marginalization refers to placing people on the margins of society or of the local culture and this can occur through the assignment of an identity or labeling; labels associated with particular disorders of psychopathology, gender or cultural groups, or age categories. It occurs as a result of believing that a particular story about individuals or families captures their reality, e.g., healthy families are characterized by two parents in a heterosexual relationship, young girls will automatically be closer to their mothers whereas young boys will have more in common with their fathers, separating from an extended family will help to increase the family's development, Eurocentric ways of life are preferred, and increased age or episodes of depression or anxiety or academic difficulty suggest little need for considering an individual's perspective.

In the interview with Lesley Allen (1995), White also said that we can assist people in challenging the dominant stories that they have been subjected to and that may have resulted in less than preferred outcomes. He noted that externalizing conversations can help to explore the dominant stories:

> One of the outcomes of these conversations is a renaming of the dominant plot— away from personal culpability and towards 'domination', 'exploitation', 'servitude', 'erasure', and 'torture'. In exploring the processes by which persons were recruited into these very negative private stories of their lives, and the associated practices of self-abuse, they find themselves describing various of the tactics of power (pp. 48–49).

In line with White's interest in exploring how people are recruited into problem-laden stories, Morgan (2000) noted that, during the course of therapy, the "therapists can consider the context in which the problem story exists, the ideas and beliefs that are sustaining the problem and the history of the ideas" (p. 46). For example, a therapist might ask:

- "What beliefs do you hold about parents/teenagers that might support this story of Lack of Respect in Our Family?"
- "Who in your recent or distant past would also support this belief about not being able to trust teenagers (or that parents can't understand what it's like to be a teenager)?" "What would they have said that would have supported this belief?"
- "Where has our society (in magazines, newspapers, movies, music, books, or television) supported this belief?" "What else might society be saying that is supportive of this story about a Lack of Respect in Our Family?" "How have these statements influenced this story and your relationship?"
- "Has this story and the beliefs that support it pushed you away from noticing or remembering moments when your relationship was enjoyable?" "Has there been a time when you've doubted the common belief about not being able to trust teenagers (or that parents can't understand what it's like to be a teenager)?" "If a father and son wanted to publicly announce their support for the new story—Being Proud of Our Family—what might they do?"

As a result, narrative therapy is interested in identifying the stories that families live and it is interested in considering how the dominant culture (e.g., the white male culture, the Christian culture, the dominant health care culture) supports these stories. Furthermore, narrative therapy asks the family members whether the dominant stories are leading to preferred endings. Because the focus of narrative therapy is on how problems are maintained rather than on labeling clients, it is difficult to imagine a circumstance in life that could not be addressed through this approach.

The Therapist's Position

With narrative therapy, the therapist is not seen as doing something to the clients but, rather, clients are seen as active and important agents in the process of therapy (Winslade, Crocket, & Monk, 1997). Facilitating a sense of client agency means that family members will take on a sense of their own active involvement and importance in therapy and gain a view of the influence they can have in their own lives. Winslade et al. noted that the social constructionist position supports a co-authoring of narratives and the honoring of clients' voices, and the co-authoring of alternative stories is, indeed, congruent with narrative therapy. They also mentioned that co-authoring challenges the notion of the therapist holding the only set of answers to questions about preferred relationships and the idea that the therapist is without an awareness about pre-ferred relationships.

Winslade et al. (1997) observed that, "If we want people to know that we support them in taking up opportunities for agency in their own lives, we need to offer them genuine agency in the relationship they have with us" (p. 56). These same authors suggested that we avoid using unilateral phrases like "An 'eval.' needs to be completed on the clients," "We must generate an intervention for the family," and "We need to assess the family's progress." They went on to note that, "if we hold that relations are constructed in the language patterns we employ, then it follows that the language we habitually use to speak of our clients and of our work will exert an effect on our thinking" (p. 57).

With regard to supporting clients in their efforts to pursue opportunities for agency in their own lives, White (Wood, 1995) mentioned that he will invite clients to interview him about therapy.

> I will ask if any of my comments or questions seemed unclear, or if any of these led to any uncertainty or confusion about my purposes, and so on. I then encour-age persons to ask me questions about all of this so that I might render my par-ticipation more transparent (pp. 68–69).

White went on to say that, "I also routinely encourage persons to evaluate the interview to determine what parts of it were relevant to them, which parts were not so, and what they found helpful and what they didn't" (p. 69).

Parry and Doan (1994) suggested that therapists also have stories that con-tribute to how clinicians define themselves and their work as practitioners. Some of the stories may facilitate more agency for clients while others may sup-port less agency. Parry and Doan observed that, "Difficult cases present thera-pists with very strong invitations to 'know about the clients,' as well as to begin to doubt their own effectiveness" and they suggested a number of questions that might be important for therapists to ask themselves in order to invite a more helpful story, for example:

- If I were more sensitive to the situation that my clients are in, and less tightly bound to a model of therapy, what might I notice that has gone unseen before?
- How am I making sense of my client's life that is different from how he or she sees it? What factors and influences might have led to his or her view that I need to understand?
- Is the gender of the client, or my gender, coloring my story about her or him in a significant way?
- What sort of story does the diagnostic label that has been applied to this case by others invite the client and me to participate in? Is the label doing most of the authoring? What evidence do I have that supports alternative descriptions of the client? (p. 190).

Freedman and Combs (1996) also noted a number of questions that they occasionally ask themselves when working with clients that assist them in being aware of their position relative to the client, for example, "Am I asking for descriptions of more than one reality?" and "Am I evaluating this person, or am I inviting her or him to evaluate a wide range of things (e.g., how therapy is going, preferred directions in life)?" (pp. 40–41).

During an interview with Michael Hoyt and Gene Combs (Hoyt & Combs, 1996), White was asked how therapists assist clients in making decisions on which options or ways of being in the world they might follow and he responded by saying, "This is to be in ongoing consultation with people about the real effects of specific ways of being in their relationships with others and on the shape of their lives generally" (p. 37). He went on to say that narrative therapy is about engaging "with people in a choice making, about these options, that is based on expressions of their lived experience and on expressions of alternative knowledge of life" (p. 38).

While the stance of narrative therapy honors client agency, it does not deny the influence of the therapist in the therapeutic relationship.

> The role of the counselor itself gives a person an advantage in the decision about what is to be the legitimate focus of my conversation. We therefore believe that counselors should adopt a deliberate ethical stance in this relation that yields significant authority to the client without giving away potency (Winslade et al., 1997, pp. 59–60).

Winslade et al. went on to note that, "we do endeavor to use our authority in ways that put our weight behind the client's preferences for agency in his own life. The narrative alignment we seek is *against* problems, against isolating, deficit-inducing discourses, and *for* people" (p. 63). Similarly, White (Hoyt & Combs, 1996) has commented:

> Of course we are influential, and of course there is a power differential. And it has often been claimed that because of this there can be no way of differentiating between different therapeutic practices on the basis of subjugation; that because of this fact of influence and because of this fact of power, one therapeutic practice cannot be distinguished from another. . . . But this blurring of important distinctions around forms and degrees of influence within the therapeutic context is unfortunate . . . there is a very significant difference between on the one hand, delivering interventions that are based on some external formal analysis of a problem . . . and, on the other hand, encouraging people to attend to some events of their lives that just might be of a more sparkling nature—events that just might happen to contradict those plots of their lives that they find so unrewarding . . . and to ask them to reflect on what these events might say about other ways of living that might suit them . . . (pp. 38–39).

In an interview with Andrew Wood (Wood, 1995), White spoke to the distinction between client agency and the realization that therapists are influential in therapy.

Madigan w/clients

He noted that therapists do develop and use skills to help families re-author their lives and he agreed with Wood that, in narrative therapy, the therapist is not perceiving him- or herself "as knowing the truth about how people should be" (p. 73). For example, White mentioned that the therapist cannot judge whether unique outcomes represent preferred outcomes for the family nor can the therapist unpack what may have accounted for the unique outcomes: "This is only something that family members can do from their lived experience and their imagination as they respond to the therapist's curiosity" (p. 73). Thus, narrative therapists privilege the expertise and goals of the family while recognizing their own influence in the therapeutic process.

Case Example

Stephen Madigan met with an African American family, including the mother and her son (Ollie), to help develop an instructional videotape of narrative therapy (Carlson & Kjos, 1999). The court system had referred this family for therapy and Steve opened the session by extending an opportunity for the family to share their story: "What I'm most interested in tonight is why it is that you come to see someone like me in counseling." The mother mentioned that her son had some trouble in school, and Steve responded with an effort to respect the importance of language and the clients' story: "And did you say it was something to do, in your opinion, something to do with anger? Was that your word or the court's word?" Steve further explored the mother's story after hearing that she does not think counseling is needed by asking, "What is it that you think the court might not have seen in Ollie that maybe you see in Ollie and that what they would call anger you would call something else? What would you call it?" Steve also asked Ollie about his story on how it was that the family had come to counseling: "What do you think about this? Would you agree with your mom . . . ?"

Later in the interview, Steve noticed that two stories were being cocreated with Ollie: "Yeah, so do [you] think that people aggravating you will eventually get you to be, get you to have a troubled reputation? Do you think that that's possible and then you'd have to give up your good boy reputation?" Steve later followed up with a preference question: "Which would you prefer to have? A troubled boy reputation or a good boy reputation?" When Ollie noted preferring a good boy reputation, Steve asked him a justification question, "How come?" and later he asked some questions directed at externalizing the problem and wondered what the problem could do to "continue to push Ollie around."

After the mother described their experience in court, that is, Ollie being placed on probation, being assigned to community service, and being presented with a fine to pay, Steve asked, "Do [you] have any idea as to why it is that you might have been treated this way?" The mother indicated that, in another school district, she had not experienced this type of problem and noted, "I was told that they hadn't got used to the, ah black kids goin' to his school." Steve asked the mother how it feels to have her son in a system that might treat him differently because of the color of his skin. The mother answered that she did not like it, and Steve asked her, "Do you think that the principal would respect your opinion of what went on?" and the mother said that he would have to because she was telling the truth.

Steve also asked Ollie if he felt that he belonged in the school, and Ollie responded, "Well, not really cause they moved us from one school to, ah . . . that was close to our house," and "I prefer the one, the one near where we live because it's, like it's close to our house." The mother then said that, when she walks in the school, they ignore her and, in response to Steve's question, she replied that white mothers would be treated differently than black mothers. Steve then asked a question and, at the same time, worked to externalize the problem-laden story, "What do you think is most upsetting for your mom about, you know, this reputation that has been placed on you?" and followed up with, "I see, [your] mom has a hunch that if it was two white boys that this had happened to maybe it wouldn't have gone to court. Would you agree or disagree with that?" Ollie agreed, and later Steve asked, "How do you continue to see yourself? As a troubled person or a good boy person?" and Ollie indicated that he continues to see himself as a good boy person.

Steve then attempted to construct an audience for Ollie's story about being a good boy, "Like, do you think if I interviewed some of your pals or your brothers or your mom, what do you think they'd tell me about who you are as a good boy?" With Steve's help, Ollie began to list some things that others might say that would describe him as a good boy (unique outcomes) and so a preferred story about Ollie began to be thickened. Then Steve asked the mother, "Okay, okay, are there things that you would tell me about Ollie that would lead me to believe that he is a really good boy and that he has a good reputation?" and followed up by asking Ollie, "Did you know that your mom was proud of you and who you were as her son and who you were as a growing man? Yeah? What's it like to hear that she believes that you're a good boy and do your homework, and you don't talk back, don't use bad words, and that you don't run away and that she recognizes that as qualities in you?"

Steve continued to work at creating an audience for the alternative story about being a good boy by asking, "Can you think of ways that you might be able to let people know that you're not a troubled person, that you're really a good boy person and have a good boy reputation?" He continued by asking Ollie if the people that are close to him might be able to "circulate these rumors" about Ollie being a good person. Steve asked if he might be allowed to search his archives for similar situations and write Ollie from Canada, and suggested what sounds like the possible use of a league, "And, maybe if there's other kids that I'm working with maybe I can send you stories about them. You know, what they've found, whether it would be troubled reputations or racism."

So the videotape of Ollie and his mother working with Steve is a nice illustration of an effort to identify a problem-laden story as well as an alternative story and how the alternative might become enriched. We were also taken by Steve's efforts, the efforts of a white male counselor, to provide a safe and respectful environment for an African American mother and her son. Furthermore, we were touched by the courage of Ollie and his mother in addressing narratives in their lives.

Summary

Narrative therapy originally arose from the work of Michael White and David Epston and has, more recently, been influenced by the writings of people like Gene Combs, Victoria Dickerson, Jill Freedman, Kenneth Gergen, Stephen Madigan, Karl Tomm, and Jeffrey Zimmerman. In part, their work seems to consider the social construction of narratives that are pictured in the evolving meanings families give to their relationships. The narrative therapist's interests reside in helping families to reflect on stories that have become problem-laden and, in turn, to consider the lives that these stories live. The therapeutic process then becomes one of helping families to realize that their lives are actually multistoried, with some stories being associated with more preferred endings. In considering stories that are alternatives to ones that are more problem-laden, the therapist tries to lift up the family's sense that they are active agents in changing their own lives. That is, therapy is a process that occurs *with* the family rather than something that is being done *to* the family.

Just as we can only talk to our understandings of narrative therapy, those reading this chapter will leave with their own views about narrative therapy. These views may be influenced by the reading of this chapter as well as by previous exposures to family therapy. Our own stories suggest the pleasure, stimulation, and benefit of becoming involved in the ongoing conversations about families and the therapeutic process. These conversations may occur with colleagues and students and may occur with oneself when reflecting on one's work with a particular family, after attending a particularly stimulating workshop, or after reading a meaningful article or book. Indeed, we are students of family therapy and it is with some sense of comfort and anticipation that we remain connected with our stories about learning.

Learning More about Narrative Therapy

There are many avenues available to the reader who wishes to learn more about the narrative perspective and narrative therapy. We have referred in the text to many of the writings central to the approach. There are many workshops and training opportunities available for those who desire to step more fully into the worlds of social construction and narrative.

The web site, www.narrativeapproaches.com is a rich resource that includes narrative papers and information, a narrative therapy bookshop, an index of the Archives of Resistance, a report of the Peace Family Project, and a narrative workshop schedule for the leading figures in the field. The following list of addresses is provided for those who might wish a more intensive and extensive exposure.

David Epston
The Family Therapy Centre
6 Goring Road
Sandringham, Auckland 4
New Zealand

Michael White
Dulwich Centre
345 Carrington Street
Adelaide, South Australia 5000

Bay Area Family Therapy Training Associates
21760 Stevens Creek Blvd., Suite 102
Cupertino, CA 95015

Evanston Family Therapy Center
636 Church St., Suite 901
Evanston, IL 60201

Counsellor Education Programme
The University of Waikato
Private Bag 3105
Hamilton, New Zealand
http://www.soe.waikato.ac.nz/counselling

REFERENCES

Allen, L. (1995). The politics of therapy. In M. White (Ed.), *Re-authoring lives: Interviews & essays* (pp. 41–59). Adelaide, South Australia: Dulwich Centre.

Bateson, G. (1972). *Steps to an ecology of mind.* New York: Ballentine Books.

Bateson, G. (1979). *Mind and nature: A necessary unity.* New York: Dutton.

Berger, P. L., & Luckmann, T. (1966). *The social construction of reality: A treatise in the sociology of knowledge.* New York: Doubleday.

Bruner, J. (1986). *Actual minds, possible worlds.* Cambridge, MA: Harvard University Press.

Bubenzer, D. L., & West, J. D. (1993). Kenneth J. Gergen: Social construction, families, and therapy. *The Family Journal: Counseling and Therapy for Couples and Families, 1*(2), 177–187.

Bubenzer, D. L., West, J. D., & Boughner, S. R. (1994). Michael White and the narrative perspective in therapy. *The Family Journal: Counseling and Therapy for Couples and Families, 2*(1), 71–83.

Bubenzer, D. L., West J. D., Cryder, A. P., & Lucey, C. F. (1997). Karl Tomm: Threads to his work. *The Family Journal: Counseling and Therapy for Couples and Families, 5*(1), 84–97.

Carlson, J., & Kjos, D. (Producers & Moderators). (1999). *Narrative therapy with Dr. Steve Madigan (Family therapy with the experts: Instruction, demonstration, discussion)* [videotape]. Boston, MA: Allyn & Bacon.

Chang, J., & Phillips, M. C. (1993). Michael White and Steve de Shazer: New directions in family therapy. In S. Gilligan & R. Price (Eds.), *Therapeutic conversations* (pp. 95–111). New York: W. W. Norton.

Epston, D. (1989) *Collected papers.* Adelaide, South Australia: Dulwich Centre.

Epston, D., & White, M. (1992). *Experience, contradiction, narrative & imagination: Selected papers of David Epston & Michael White 1989–1991.* Adelaide, South Australia: Dulwich Centre.

Foucault, M. (1965). *Madness and civilization: A history of insanity in the age of reason.* New York: Random House.

Foucault, M. (1973). *The birth of the clinic: An archeology of medical perception.* London: Tavistock.

Foucault, M. (1979). *Discipline and punishment: The birth of the prison.* Middlesex, England: Peregrine Books.

Foucault, M. (1980). *Power/knowledge: Selected interviews and other writings.* New York: Pantheon Books.

Freedman, J., & Combs, G. (1996). *Narrative therapy: The social construction of preferred realities.* New York: Norton.

Gergen, K. J. (1991). *The saturated self: Dilemmas of identity in contemporary life.* New York: Basic Books.

Gergen, K. J. (1994). *Realities and relationships: Soundings in social construction.* Cambridge, MA: Harvard University Press.

Gergen, K. J. (1999). *An invitation to social construction.* London: Sage.

Hoyt, M. F., & Combs, G. (1996). On ethics and the spiritualities of the surface: A conversation with Michael White. In M. F. Hoyt (Ed.), *Constructive therapies* (pp. 33–59). New York: Guilford.

Kittredge, W. (1999). *Taking care: Thoughts on storytelling and belief.* Minneapolis, MN: Milkweed Editions.

Lopez, B. (1976). *Winter count.* New York: Avon Books.

Madigan, S. P. (1992). The application of Michel Foucalt's philosophy in the problem externalizing discourse of Michael White. *Journal of Family Therapy, 14,* 265–279.

Madigan, S. (1996). The politics of identity: Considering community discourse in the externalizing of internalized problem conversations. *Journal of Systemic Therapies, 14*(1), 47–62.

Madigan, S. (1997). Reconsidering memory: Remembering lost identities back toward remembered selves. In C. Smith & D. Nyland (Eds.), *Narrative therapies with children and adolescents* (pp. 338–355). New York: Guilford.

Madigan, S., & Epston, D. (1995). From "spy-chiatric gaze" to communities of concern: From professional monologue to dialogue. In S. Friedman (Ed.), *The reflecting team in action: Collaborative practice in family therapy* (pp. 257–276). New York: Guilford.

Maturana, H. R., & Varela, F. (1987). *The tree of knowledge: The biological roots of human understanding.* Boston: Shambhala.

McCarthy, C. (1998). *Cities of the plains*. New York: Vintage Books.

Morgan, A. (2000). *What is narrative therapy? An easy-to-read introduction*. Adelaide, South Australia: Dulwich Centre.

Nichols, M. P., & Schwartz, R. C. (2001). *Family therapy: Concepts and methods* (5th ed.). Boston: Allyn & Bacon.

Selvini Palazzoli, M., Boscolo, L., Vecchin, G., & Prata, G. (1978). *Pardox and counterparadox: A new model in the therapy of the family in schizophrenic transition*. New York: Jason Aronson.

Parry, A., & Doan, R. E. (1994). *Story re-visions: Narrative therapy in the postmodern world*. New York: Guilford.

Patteson, J. (2000, July 7). Backlash begins to grow against business-casual, *Charleston South Carolina Post and Courier*, p. D2.

Stewart, K. (1995). Psychotic experience and discourse. In M. White (Ed.), *Re-authoring lives: Interviews & essays* (pp. 112–154). New York: Norton.

Tomm, K. (1987). Interventive interviewing: Part II. reflexive questioning as a means to enable self healing. *Family Process, 26*, 153–185.

Tomm, K. (1990a). A critique of the DSM. *Dulwich Centre Newsletter, 3*, 5–8.

Tomm, K. (1990b). Foreword. In M. White and D. Epston (Eds.), *Narrative means to therapeutic ends* (pp. vii–xi). New York: Norton.

Tomm, K. (1998). Epilogue: Social constructionism in the evolution of family therapy. In J. West, D. Bubenzer, & J. Bitter (Eds.), *Social construction in couple and family therapy* (pp. 173–185). Alexandria, VA: American Counseling Association.

Walter, E. V. (1988). *Placeways: A theory of the human environment*. Chapel Hill, NC: University of North Carolina Press.

White, M. (1989a). *Selected papers*. Adelaide, South Australia: Dulwich Centre.

White, M. (1989b). The process of questioning: A therapy of literary merit? In M. White (Ed.), *Selected papers* (pp. 37–46). Adelaide, South Australia: Dulwich Centre.

White, M. (1993). Deconstruction and therapy. In S. Gilligan & R. Price (Eds.), *Therapeutic conversations* (pp. 22–61). New York: Norton. (Original work published in the *Dulwich centre newsletter*, 1991, No. 3, 1–21. Also printed in D. Epston & M. White, *Experience, contradiction, narrative and imagination* [pp. 109–152]. Adelaide, South Australia: Dulwich Centre, 1992.)

White, M., & Epston, D. (1990). *Narrative means to therapeutic ends*. New York: Norton.

Winslade, J., Crocket, K., & Monk, G. (1997). The therapeutic relationship. In G. Monk, J. Winslade, K. Crocket, & D. Epston (Eds.), *Narrative therapy in practice: The archaeology of hope* (pp. 53–81). San Francisco: Jossey-Bass.

Wood, A. (1995). Outside expert knowledge: An interview with Michael White. In M. White (Ed.), *Re-authoring lives: Interviews and essays* (pp. 60–81). Adelaide, South Australia: Dulwich Centre. Also printed in *Australian and New Zealand Journal of Family Therapy, 12*(4), 207–214.

Zimmerman, J. L., & Dickerson, V. C. (1996). *If problems talked: Narrative therapy in action*. New York: Guilford.

NAME INDEX

SUBJECT INDEX